PENGUIN BOOKS

THE STRUGGLE WITHIN ISLAM

Rafiq Zakaria was born in Bombay and graduated with distinction from Bombay University. He received a Ph.D. from the University of London and qualified for the Bar from Lincoln's Inn. While in England, he worked for the *News Chronicle* and the *Observer*. Dr Zakaria worked for a decade as a lawyer (during which time he was appointed Special Public Prosecutor at the Bombay High Court) and then gave up law for a career in politics that has lasted thirty years. He entered the State Legislature in 1960 and for the next seventeen years held various portfolios in the Maharashtra Cabinet. He became a Member of Parliament in 1978 and was elected Deputy Leader of the Congress (I) under Indira Gandhi. He was deputy leader of the Indian delegation to the United Nations in 1965, leader of the Indian delegation to the USSR in 1984 and a Special Envoy to various Muslim countries during 1983 to 1984.

Dr Zakaria has also been involved in the field of education. He has established ten colleges and a high school and has been the Chancellor of Urdu University, Aligarh, for the last fifteen years. He has edited *A Study of Nehru* and has written several books on different facets of Islam, as well as two novels. He lives in Bombay with his wife Fatma.

THE STRUGGLE WITHIN ISLAM

The Conflict Between Religion and Politics

RAFIQ ZAKARIA

PENGUIN BOOKS

PENGUIN BOOKS

Published by the Penguin Group
27 Wrights Lane, London W8 5TZ, England
Viking Penguin Inc., 40 West 23rd Street, New York, New York 10010, USA
Penguin Books Australia Ltd, Ringwood, Victoria, Australia
Penguin Books Canada Ltd, 2801 John Street, Markham, Ontario, Canada L3R 1B4
Penguin Books (NZ) Ltd, 182–190 Wairau Road, Auckland 10, New Zealand

Penguin Books Ltd, Registered Offices: Harmondsworth, Middlesex, England

First published in India by Viking 1988
Published in Penguin Books 1989
1 3 5 7 9 10 8 6 4 2

Printed and bound in Great Britain by
Cox & Wyman Ltd, Reading
Filmset in Times Roman

To the memory of Ibn Khaldun,
one of the greatest historians of all time,
who in his Muqaddimah *observes:*

History is a science of fine principles, manifold uses and noble purpose.
It informs us about the people of the past—the characters of nations,
the lives of prophets, the kingdoms and policies of kings—thus
usefully providing examples for the emulation of those who desire it in
religious and worldly affairs.The writer of history requires keen
judgement and careful scrutiny to lead him to the truth and away from
lapses and errors.If reliance is placed on simple narrative and
transmitted, without studying the roots of custom, the foundations of
politics, the nature of civilization, and the circumstances of human
society, and without comparing far with near and past with present—
then there will often be danger of slipping and stumbling and straying
from the right road.

Contents

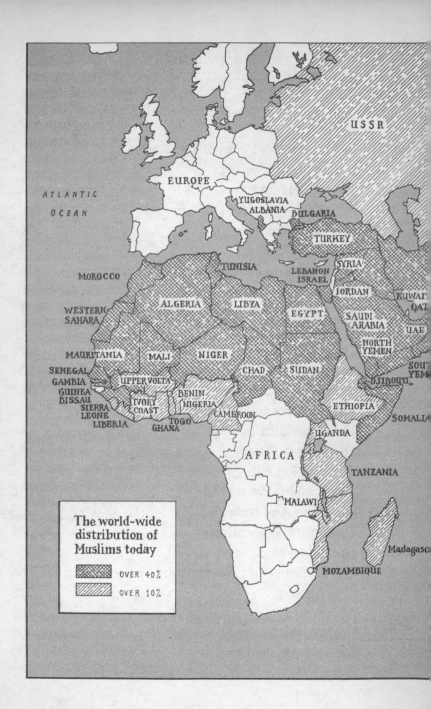

ATLANTIC OCEAN

USSR

EUROPE

YUGOSLAVIA
ALBANIA   BULGARIA

TURKEY

TUNISIA   SYRIA
MOROCCO   LEBANON
                     ISRAEL   JORDAN   KUWAIT
WESTERN   ALGERIA   LIBYA   QAT
SAHARA   EGYPT   SAUDI
                                             ARABIA   UAE
MAURITANIA   MALI   NIGER   NORTH
                                               YEMEN
SENEGAL   CHAD   SUDAN   SOUT
GAMBIA   YEM
GUINEA   UPPER VOLTA   DJIBOUTI
BISSAU
SIERRA   IVORY   BENIN   ETHIOPIA
LEONE   COAST   NIGERIA   SOMALIA
LIBERIA   TOGO   CAMEROON
            GHANA   UGANDA

                        AFRICA
                                                        TANZANIA

                              MALAWI

                                                        Madagasca

The world-wide
distribution of
Muslims today

OVER 40%

OVER 10%

MOZAMBIQUE

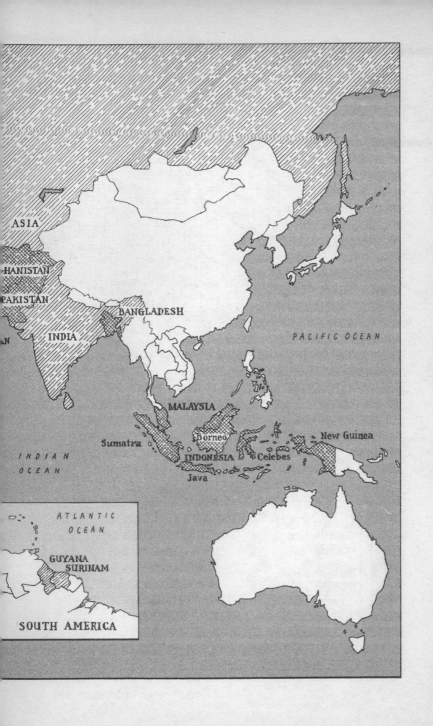

ASIA

HANISTAN

PAKISTAN

BANGLADESH

INDIA

PACIFIC OCEAN

MALAYSIA

Sumatra

Borneo

New Guinea

INDONESIA

Celebes

INDIAN
OCEAN

Java

ATLANTIC
OCEAN

GUYANA
SURINAM

SOUTH AMERICA

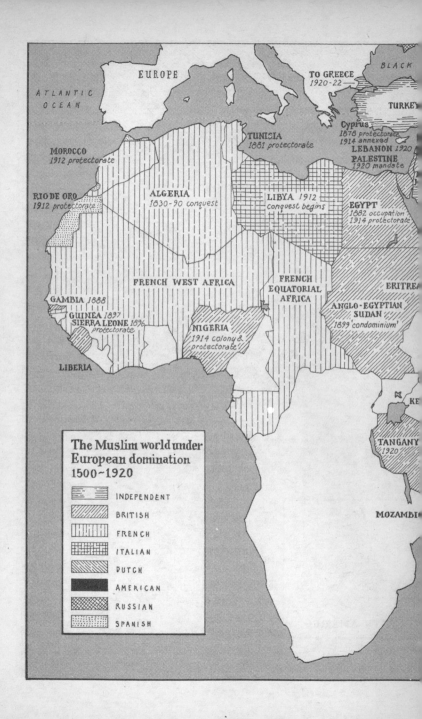

The Muslim world under European domination 1500~1920

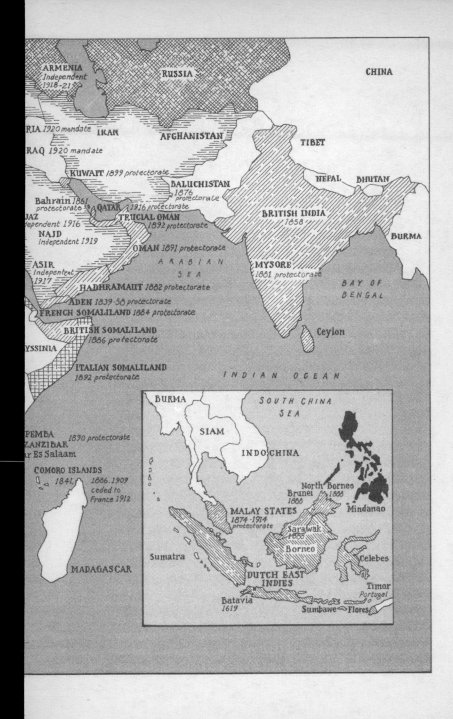

ARMENIA
Independent
1918-21

RUSSIA

CHINA

RIA *1920 mandate*   IRAN

AFGHANISTAN

TIBET

RAQ *1920 mandate*

KUWAIT *1899 protectorate*

NEPAL   BHUTAN

BALUCHISTAN
1876
protectorate

Bahrain *1861*
protectorate   QATAR *1916 protectorate*

AZ
dependent 1916   TRUCIAL OMAN
1892 protectorate

NAJD
Independent 1919

OMAN *1891 protectorate*

BRITISH INDIA
1858

BURMA

A R A B I A N
S E A

ASIR
Indepentent
1917

MYSORE
1881 protectorate

BAY OF
BENGAL

HADHRAMAUT *1882 protectorate*

ADEN *1839-58 protectorate*

FRENCH SOMALILAND *1884 protectorate*

Ceylon

BRITISH SOMALILAND
1886 protectorate

YSSINIA

I N D I A N   O C E A N

ITALIAN SOMALILAND
1892 protectorate

PEMBA   *1890 protectorate*
ZANZIBAR
r Es Salaam

COMORO ISLANDS
1841,   *1886, 1909*
ceded to
France 1912

MADAGASCAR

BURMA

SOUTH CHINA
SEA

SIAM

INDO-CHINA

North Borneo
Brunei   *1888*
1888

Mindanao

MALAY STATES
1874-1914
protectorate

Sarawak
1888

Sumatra

Borneo

Celebes

DUTCH EAST
INDIES

Timor
Portugal

Batavia
1619

Sumbawe   Flores

Preface

This is not a book of history; it does not claim to cover every aspect of Islam and does not even deal with the various phases of its historical growth and development. It confines itself to the struggle within Islam in respect of the conflict of ideas and movements between faith and power. In describing this aspect the historical part naturally cannot be ignored, though I have used history selectively to buttress my arguments. This, of course, is as it should be. For if this book dealt with history alone some very important aspects of Islam—theology and jurisprudence, for instance—would have been left out, but in this they find a prominent place.

There is no dearth of literature on all these matters, but what I have tried to do is focus on the continuous fight between the holders of power and theologians of all shades of opinion. The conclusions I have arrived at clarify many questions and, I hope, correct a number of misconceptions about Islam and its followers.

I had to draw on a large volume of material in the form of research dissertations and published works; to their authors I am indebted. I am also thankful to Khushwant Singh, who revised my first draft and made some valuable suggestions. His obsession with the English language, which he can manage with distinction, has greatly benefited me; his insistence on the use of correct idiom and on precision in expression has helped me be brief without being inaccurate. I am grateful to Prof. Shakil Hurzuk of Maharashtra College, Bombay, who assisted me with the historical part. I would also like to thank Mr Albert Pascal Lobo for his help in preparing the manuscript. My son, Fareed, a fellow at

Harvard, went through some of the chapters and gave me the benefit of his critical assistance. David Davidar of Penguin took a keen interest in the publication of the book and my wife, Fatma, was, as always, a constant source of encouragement.

I have worked on this book for many years; it is the result of my deep involvement with Islam as well the problems I faced in my public life in India. I hope its study will be worthwhile for all those who are interested in getting at the root of the controversy about fundamentalism versus secularism in Islam; its approach is not strictly scholarly as I believe that the subject is not only of academic interest but also of universal concern.

Bombay   *Rafiq Zakaria*
2 November 1988

Introduction: A Personal Statement

'I don't believe it. It cannot be true', I said to David Astor, then Foreign Editor of the *Observer*, London, which his family owned. That was my response to a despatch from his correspondent in India to the effect that the Indian National Congress had agreed to the partition of India into two separate dominions as demanded by the All-India Muslim League. The *Observer* correspondent had scooped what came to be known as the Mountbatten Plan almost ten days ahead of its official announcement on 3 June 1947. As I was the only Indian on the staff of the *Observer*, Astor thought he should consult me before clearing the despatch for publication. I argued vigorously that the report could not possibly be true; nevertheless, the correspondent had specifically mentioned in his note that he had obtained it from the 'horse's mouth'. Astor decided to put it on the front page. It created a sensation in India.

I was shocked. I was an Indian. I was also a Muslim. Besides, as a native of Bombay (which, though largely Hindu, had a sizeable Muslim population), I had grown up a nationalist believing in the freedom and integrity of my country. Since my days in Bombay University, I had cast my lot with the Congress because I accepted its ideology of composite nationalism which made no distinction on grounds of caste, creed or race.

I met Mahatma Gandhi once at Poona railway station in 1934; I was in my early teens. I asked the Mahatma what he proposed to do to foster Hindu–Muslim unity. He looked at me intently and replied that he was willing to lay down his life for it. I believed every word he said; he inspired faith. That short meeting had a profound impact on me. I resolved to follow in the Mahatma's footsteps and make Hindu-Muslim unity my life's mission.

Within three years of my all too brief encounter with Gandhi, the communal atmosphere in India deteriorated rapidly. The gulf between Hindus and Muslims widened. Mohamed Ali Jinnah, who was later to become the founder of Pakistan, returned from his self-imposed exile in London and began to organize the Muslims, not so much against the British as against the Congress. He demanded a settlement between Gandhi's Congress and his Muslim League before he would agree to the transfer of power to Indians by the British. He maintained that Hindus and Muslims were separate and must have their separate homelands. Although it was more a bargaining counter in a free united India than a serious proposition, Gandhi and the Congress party failed to see it for what it was. The outbreak of World War II in 1939 further complicated the issue; the Congress leaders increasingly came off second best in every encounter with Jinnah and it was soon apparent that there could be no rapprochement.

I need not go into the history of the Congress–League negotiations or the failure of the Gandhi–Jinnah talks; suffice it to say that the Congress and the League drifted more and more apart with the result that the country was finally divided.

In 1944 I went to London and enrolled myself in Lincoln's Inn to qualify for the Bar. I also started working on my doctoral thesis on Indian Muslims at London University. Those were exciting times; the war was about to end and with the Allied victory in Europe, Winston Churchill was thrown out of power. The Labour party won a landslide majority (1945). Its leader, Clement Atlee, formed the new government. He had always been sympathetic to Indian aspirations for independence and one of his first acts was to announce his government's decision to send a Cabinet Mission to India. This was to be the final effort by Britain to keep India united. As president of the London Majlis, an organization of Indian students studying in the British capital, I hosted a reception for members of the Mission on the eve of their departure and expressed the fervent hope that they would succeed. V.K. Krishna Menon, who later became independent India's first high commissioner in London, was then head of the India League in the United Kingdom, propagating the Congress cause; this League had strong links with the British Labour party. I collaborated with Menon, which angered the

Muslim students. They denounced me as a traitor to Islam. Even my relatives back home considered me a renegade. As negotiations between the Congress and the League failed, the British came out with the Mountbatten Plan to divide the country. I wrote a short article in the *Observer*, giving vent to my feelings against it. I also wrote a much larger piece for a socialist weekly, *Tribune*, showing the utter futility of partition.

What pained me the most was the attitude of the Congress; it seemed more eager to divide India than even the League. I had talked at length with Jawaharlal Nehru when he came to London with Jinnah and with the viceroy, Lord Wavell, to sort out points of disagreement over the Cabinet Mission's plan. It was their last desperate move to bring the warring factions together. Nehru had assured me then that under no circumstances would the Congress compromise with the League on the question of unity. Naturally, I was taken aback when I heard that Nehru was the first to agree to the division; even Gandhi succumbed, though till the last he prayed that God would save the unity and integrity of the land. I felt badly let down, as did my many Hindu friends in London who had worked tirelessly to keep India undivided.

Partition brought unimaginable misery to millions of people on both sides of the border. It worsened relations between Hindus and Muslims in the sub-continent. Muslims left behind in India, like Hindus in Pakistan, felt orphaned. They became unwanted strangers in their own land. Millions of Hindus and Sikhs were uprooted from Pakistan and came to India as refugees. Their plight made the position of Indian Muslims more vulnerable and desperate. Hindu–Muslim riots in Hyderabad and Junagadh drove the two communities further apart. Gandhi tried desperately to extinguish the hatred and ultimately paid for it with his own life. His martyrdom served to bring about a degree of sanity among a frenzied people. However, even two years after partition, when I returned to India, I found relations between Hindus and Muslims still very tense. War between India and Pakistan over the accession of Jammu and Kashmir had further strained relations that had been far from cordial.

No sooner did I return to Bombay than I went into active politics, though I had to initially concentrate on my legal profession. In both fields I came into close contact with Hindus and Muslims. The more I worked with them the more disillusioned I became. The barriers between Hindus and Muslims, which history had erected, showed no sign of disappearing; these were getting stronger, despite our protestations to the contrary. If this was what religion did to a people, then what good was it, I wondered.

Meanwhile the Congress leadership entrusted me with several positions of responsibility which gave me the opportunity to see for myself the price the Muslims who remained in India had to pay for their past. As a cabinet minister in the state of Maharashtra for almost two decades, I witnessed the suffering caused by partition, especially where my co-religionists were concerned. During my tenure in New York as India's representative to the General Assembly of the United Nations in 1965, I was repeatedly questioned by leaders of delegations from Muslim countries about the ill-treatment of Muslims in India. Even some of the non-Muslim delegates expressed their concern about the rapid deterioration in their condition since partition. Later, when I went to New Delhi as a member of the Rajya Sabha and deputy leader of the Congress (I) parliamentary party I was closely associated with discussions both in the government and the Congress party on measures to improve the lot of Indian Muslims. Also as member secretary of the high power panel for minorities appointed by the government of India (1980-84) I came across innumerable instances of discrimination against Indian Muslims. They felt helpless, deprived and rejected. At times, in sheer desperation, they exploded into angry invective. Though they had lost much of their old fanatical zeal, they were finding it difficult to adjust to the changed circumstances. Hindus, being the dominant majority, did little to assuage their anguish. At best they tolerated Muslims. It was hardly the kind of secular State that men like Gandhi and Nehru had dreamt of. In this environment, while one section of the Indian Muslims strove to reconcile Islam with the realities of the Indian situation, another fought tenaciously to retain their distinct identity and prevent it being submerged in the ocean of Hinduism surrounding them.

The more I wrestled with the problem, the more I realized that within our existing framework there was no solution to the ancient conflict between Hindus and Muslims. The Hindus were using secularism to encourage the resurgence of Hindu communal consciousness—or as Syed Shahabuddin, the irrepressible Muslim MP from Bihar calls it, 'Hindu chauvinism'—while the Muslims continued to be torn between secularism and fundamentalism. Who is to be blamed for this pathetic state of affairs? That is a question to which there are no clear answers.

The notion that Muslims are a nation apart from Hindus has come to the fore, intermittently, since the advent of the British. Sir Syed Ahmad Khan (1817–98), the foremost Muslim leader in the late nineteenth century, raised the question for the first time primarily as a reaction to the rise of the Congress, which he regarded as Hindu to the core. The formation of the All-India Muslim League twenty years later gave political shape to the deep-rooted antagonism of the Muslims towards the Hindus. The Khilafat agitation of the early twenties led by the Ali brothers, Mohammed and Shaukat, provided the only silver lining; it was helped actively by Gandhi, with the result that the Hindus and Muslims presented a united front against the British. This unity did not last long and was constantly threatened by the recurrence of communal riots in different parts of the country.

The movement for Muslim separateness changed the character of Indian politics. I had analysed it in my doctoral thesis for London University. I was therefore in a good position to see its practical implications. I recall an interesting controversy that took place between the leading Muslim divine of those days, Shaik-ul-Hind Maulānā Husayn Ahmad Madani (1879–1957) of Deoband and the poet-philosopher, Sir Muhammad Iqbal (1877–1938). They disagreed on what constituted a nation in Islam. According to the maulānā, religion was not an essential element in the formation of a nation. Iqbal disagreed. In a short Persian poem, he condemned the maulānā's attitude as bu-Lahabi (heretical). This was a grave charge against a theologian highly respected all over the Muslim world. The maulānā was deeply hurt, especially since he not only admired Iqbal as a poet, but also respected him as a man of faith. However, Madani accepted the challenge, quoted chapter and verse from the Qur'ān and the hadith or the traditions of the Prophet, to prove how, from its very inception, Islam had accepted the existence of nations comprising Muslims as well as non-Muslims. He pointed out that there was nothing un-Islamic about it as was exemplified by the Prophet entering into an agreement with the Jews, Christians and even pagans at Madina. Basing his views on this agreement, which is known as the 'Constitution of Madina', the maulānā asserted that Muslims and non-Muslims could adhere to their respective religions and yet be one nation.[1]

Iqbal stuck to his view that politics separated from religion became a devil's workshop. He accused Madani, without justification, of having fallen prey to Western materialism. In turn, Madani charged Iqbal with ignoring the practical compulsions in a believer's life. Shortly before his death, Iqbal wrote to a friend that the controversy was needless because what he objected to was the non-ethical approach of the West to the problem of nationalism and not the concept of a composite nation as elucidated by Madani. As he had explained elsewhere,

> Europe uncritically accepted the duality of spirit and matter probably from Manichaen thought. Her best thinkers are realizing this initial mistake today but her statesmen are indirectly forcing the world to accept it as an unquestionable dogma. It is, then, this mistaken separation of the spiritual and the temporal which has largely influenced European religious and political thought and has resulted practically in the total exclusion of Christianity from the life of European states. The result is a set of mutually ill-adjusted states dominated by interests not human but national.[2]

Gandhi's concept of Ram Rajya was more or less on Iqbal's lines and stressed the need for religion, in a broad sense, in a nation's life. Likewise, Madani's support for an undivided Indian nation was in consonance with Iqbal's concept of broad humanism.

Theoretically, there is no dichotomy between religion and the State in Islam; their indivisibility has been its essential feature from the very inception, as I shall explain later. This presented no problem during the lifetime of the Prophet because his supremacy was unquestioned. But after he died his followers began to argue whether or not religion could be separated from politics. They could not agree on either mixing the two or keeping them apart.

In a sense, most of the turmoil in the world of Islam emanates from this original tension. The conflicts took different forms at different times, but basically they revolved around spiritualism and materialism, or in modern terms, between fundamentalism and secularism. True, fundamentalism, as understood in the West, is different from the connotation given to it in Islam. In the West the word means both the second coming of Christ as well as the verbal inspiration of the Bible. Interestingly, this definition has never found much support among the clergy. It is wrong, therefore, to apply it universally. In fact, there is no such word as fundamentalism in any of the Islamic languages—Arabic, Persian, Turki or Urdu. Every Muslim is a fundamentalist in the sense that he accepts the Qur'ān as the word of God and its tenets and injunctions as binding, but the dichards among them insist that everything that happened during the lifetime of the Prophet is and must be followed as precedent unreservedly. They are construed in common parlance as fundamentalists (though they are also of many hues), as against the non-fundamentalists, who are, by and large, secular-minded.

The trouble began when different groups of Muslims gave different interpretations not only to the hadith but also to the Qur'ān. This has happened from the earliest times and continues to happen even now. In fact, there is a group which has always repudiated the hadith. Some well-known jurists and theologians in the past refused to accord any sanctity to them because of the long lapse in their narration and the manner and method in which they were reported.[3] It must be said though that they are a small minority; the mass of Muslims, including present-day secularists, accept their validity.

The secularists try to interpret the Qur'ānic texts and the hadith liberally but the fundamentalists oppose this on the ground that it amounts to bidat or innovation, which is as bad as heresy. Nevertheless, both swear by Islam.

In the course of my public life, I have come across both types of Muslims. The fundamentalists I have met are as scrupulous in the performance of prayers and rites as they are in the observance of taboos. Their lives are dedicated to restoring to Islam its pristine purity; but they are a small group. Because of their piety and dedication, they inspire respect and awe among the masses but have never been able to gain much electoral support in a contest in any Muslim country. Their devotion to Islam is admired by the people but rarely imitated. Recently, as reported by *Ittefaq*, the leading Bengali daily of Bangladesh, a fundamentalist, Gulam Mustafa, approached a group of Muslims in a tea shop in Chittagong and asked them to stop smoking as it was Ramadān, the month of fasting; instead of listening to him, the smokers emptied a can of kerosene over him and ignited it with a cigarette. Mustafa later died in a hospital. There was no public protest.[4]

The secularists (who are also variously called liberals, reformists, or modernists), claim to be as faithful to the spirit of Islam as the fundamentalists, but want to bring about reforms to make the religion more materialistic and worldly. They are able to manage the electoral process and the governmental machine better than the fundamentalists. They have, in many cases, exploited Islam for political gain. The outstanding example of this school is the founder of Pakistan, Jinnah, a Shï'ite, who never followed the rites of Islam, but whipped up a religious frenzy among Indian Muslims for a separate homeland of their own. They believed that it would give them an ideal Islamic state. For all their fervour Pakistan, even today, has failed to become one. In 1939, as general secretary of the Students' Union of a predominantly Muslim college in Bombay, I invited Jinnah to address the students. He declared he was proud to be a Muslim. 'I was born a Muslim, I am a Muslim and I will die a Muslim', he proclaimed passionately. He said that he was amused by Gandhi describing him as a brother. 'It suits him to say so', he told us, 'because while brother Gandhi has three votes, I have only one.' He warned the Hindus to keep their hands off Muslims and demanded the sharing of power between Hindus and Muslims on equal terms. After his speech, I accompanied him to his residence which was over an hour's drive from the college. I asked him why he was so bitter about Gandhi and other Hindu leaders. He replied that he did not trust them. I asked him if it was necessary to raise religious slogans to oppose the Congress. He was candid in his reply: 'How else will I mobilize the Muslims?' Later he ridiculed Gandhi's opposition to Pakistan. He told a Muslim audience, 'Gandhi has called Pakistan a sin. It is more than a crime in his eyes. He has damned you in this world as well as the next.' He successfully played with words to achieve his objective.

After the creation of Pakistan, which Jinnah had never quite believed would come about, he changed his tone. As governor-general, he told the Pakistan Constituent Assembly that the new state would be secular and would not make any distinction between followers of different religions. Such was the hypnotic influence he wielded that his words were acclaimed by an assembly whose members had fought for exactly the opposite objective. The ulamā were naturally unhappy. Some of those who agreed with the ulāma met Jinnah subsequently and pleaded that he should replace Anglo-Saxon jurisprudence with the sharï'ah. He retorted:

Whose shari'ah? Hanafi's? Hanbali's? Shafaie's? Maliki's? Jafferi's? I do not want to get involved. The moment I enter this field the ulama will take over, for they claim to be experts and I certainly don't prefer to hand over the field to them. I am aware of their criticism but I don't propose to fall into their trap.[5]

A contemporary of Jinnah was Abu'l Ala al-Maududi (1903–79), founder of the Jama'at-i-Islami, the foremost fundamentalist organization in South Asia. He was an erudite Islamic scholar who became a leading theologian. He had a mind as incisive as Jinnah's. Maududi began his career by editing a journal from Hyderabad (India) in which he carried his commentaries on the Qur'an. They were original, perceptive and forcefully written. One of his earliest admirers was Iqbal. Maududi opposed the demand for Pakistan on theological grounds. He had little faith in Jinnah's commitment to an Islamic state. He continued his opposition to it even after partition. He feared that Pakistan (which means 'Land of the Pure') would become na-Pakistan ('Land of the Impure') in the hands of Muslims of doubtful faith. After its formation, he strove to convert Pakistan into an ideal Islamic state. For this he was constantly harassed by the police and spent long periods in jail; finally he was charged with treason and sentenced to death (the sentence was later commuted). Undeterred, Maududi propagated his fundamentalist ideas to the last and created quite a stir not only in Pakistan but also in the rest of the Muslim world, particularly in the Arab countries. But politically he was never much of a force until the time when the free-living, modern-thinking Zulfikar Ali Bhutto was ousted from power by General Ziaul Haq. He was basically a military dictator, not answerable to the people; his support of the Jama'at, therefore, had no popular approval. He was not a fundamentalist, but in order to give legitimacy to his seizure of power, he made use of the Jama'at. Then he cooled considerably towards it, especially when he found it had no real power (even in the restricted 1985 elections the Jama'at's candidates were thoroughly trounced). The mass reception that Benazir Bhutto has been receiving throughout Pakistan in recent times shows that she has far more support among the people than the fundamentalists who had denounced her as a renegade. A more telling indictment of the fundamentalists' lack of real power would be hard to find.

Turkey provides another classic example of the conflict between religion and modernity; once the citadel of Islam, it has practised secularism for more than fifty years. In his impatience to modernize the country, Kemál Ataturk (1881–1938) abolished Islam from the country's public life; he ridiculed its practices and glorified the Western style of living. Instead of being cited as an example to emulate, Turkey became an outcaste in the Muslim world; as a result secularism came to be regarded as an enemy by other Muslim countries.

In 1984 I was sent by the then prime minister of India, the late Mrs Indira Gandhi, as her special envoy to some of the major Muslim countries; Turkey was one of them; the others were Egypt, Saudi Arabia, Iran and Tunisia. I found in the capital of Turkey, Ankara, and in the historic city of Istanbul, that most Turks were proud of their Islamic identity, but were equally averse to fundamentalism as Kemalism had taken deep roots in the soil. The president, the military junta, as well as the prime minister all believed in a secular State. The Turkish political leaders of various groups I met were quite keen to build bridges with the Arab world, but they were unwilling to make any compromises with secularism, which they regarded as the core of Kemalism. They talked nostalgically about their Islamic past but saw no reason to turn their country once again into an Islamic state.

In Iran the situation was exactly the opposite; after the Khomeini revolution fundamentalism ruled the roost. Some of the misguided but over-enthusiastic followers of the Ayatollah did not mind hijacking planes, taking over embassies and handing out instant justice according to their lights. They saw themselves as a breed apart—the self-appointed pasbans (guardians of the faith)—and strutted about the streets of Tehran with revolvers in their hip pockets; supervised by turban-wearing, bearded mullás; at their beck and call were teenagers sporting beards that had hardly sprouted. One evening my wife and I were being entertained at an Indian restaurant, when there was a sudden commotion. The manager rushed to my wife and asked her to cover her head and her bare arms. The pasbans were around, he warned, and said that women were required to be 'decently dressed'. The young guardians of the faith ensured conformity to their standards by being offensive, abusive and even violent. I spoke about this to the foreign minister, Dr Ali Akbar Vilayati; he dismissed it as the exuberance of newly liberated youth who wanted to make sure that Iran did not again sink into the pit of immorality into which the Shah had dumped it. Today there is much less approval of these attitudes by ordinary Iranians than before; a short while ago, in a television interview, even the venerable Imam Khomeini said he was opposed to such coercion. He explained that morality could not be imposed by force.

In Egypt we found the atmosphere different; there were of course young people in the mould of the pasbans, mujāhidūn or mujāhideen, or fighters for the faith, roaming the bylanes of Cairo in long robes, but their number was limited and their movements restricted. Loyalty to Islam was mouthed by everyone; at the al-Azhar, the renowned centre of Islamic theology founded more than a thousand years ago by the Fatimids, we were told that every Egyptian was a devout Muslim; the next day, at an official reception in our honour, we found most of the Egyptians present enjoying their scotch whiskey; their wives were attired in the latest Paris fashions.

It is because of such distortions of the faith by the secularists in the Islamic world that the fundamentalists are opposed to secularism; they are prepared to compromise with colonialism but not with secularism. According to the fundamentalists a truly Islamic State is the antithesis of a secular State. They believe that a secular State is a by-product of Christian 'heresy' or of Hindu 'hypocrisy'. They argue that secularism, whatever its form, is basically materialistic and a negation of spiritualism. Their case has been picturesquely presented by Altaf Gauhar, a disciple of Maulānā Maududi. Gauhar, former editor of the daily *Dawn*, published from Karachi, was hounded out of Pakistan by Bhutto, who despite his loud protestations of love of Islam, was as secular as his mentor, Jinnah. Gauhar now lives in London, from where he edits the weekly magazine *South* funded by the Third World Foundation. I discussed the Islamic question with him at some length when I was in London for the Festival of Islam in 1976. He was convinced that there was no place for secularism in Islam. An old friend, Sharifuddin Peerzada, once the foreign minister and attorney-general of Pakistan, and later the secretary-general of the Organization of Islamic Conference, who participated in our discussion, was also of the same view, but he was not as dogmatic as Gauhar. 'In a secular society, a man loses his soul', Gauhar maintained. He has put his case graphically:

The fundamental assumption of secularism is that material well-being does not remain only the means to an end but becomes an end in itself. This is the major dilemma of a secular culture. As secular society progresses from lower levels of material well-being to higher levels, efficiency becomes its sole preoccupation. Production and prosperity are the twin gods of secularism. Inflation, like Satan, becomes its mortal enemy. Hell is a place with high prices, recession and unemployment. Its concept of paradise is affluence with full employment and lots of leisure. Since there are no limits to man's desires, his life becomes a baseless quest in pursuit of pleasure.[6]

This, in essence, is the case which the spiritualists advance against the materialists, or the fundamentalists against the secularists. The fundamentalists' arguments need to be properly understood. They stand for purity in public life and believe that present-day Muslim secular leaders are nothing but opportunists. They are particularly bitter about the 'officers' corps' who have taken over many Muslim countries and condemn them, to use the words of Saeed Hawwa, a Syrian ideologue of the Muslim Brotherhood founded by Hasan al-Banna in Egypt in 1928, as 'the most depraved social group. . . .This is particularly true of the upper echelons, who are full of traitors, drunkards, and fornicators.'[7] It may be worth bearing in mind that the Brotherhood is the most powerful centre of Islamic fundamentalism in the Arab world.

The fundamentalists are not restricted to groups such as the Muslim Brotherhood and the Jamā'āt-i-Islāmī. They are to be found in many other organizations. They are active in Jakarta, Kuala Lumpur, Dhaka, New Delhi, Islamabad, Cairo, Tehran, Riyadh, Algiers, Istanbul and everywhere else that Muslims are found. They relentlessly pursue their efforts to 'Islamize' Muslims, and, in countries where Muslims form the majority, insist on the application of the sharī'ah in its entirety to citizens in every walk of life.

Apart from the practical difficulties that such an Islamization process creates for Muslims in the modern technocratic age, there is another difficulty that considerably bothers the secularists who are usually in charge of affairs of state. This is the issue of non-Muslims, who could become second-class citizens if the fundamentalist viewpoint is to prevail. Maududi unequivocally declared that both categories of minorities—non-Muslims in Islamic states and Muslims in non-Islamic states—should ungrudgingly suffer the consequences of belonging to a minority faith. While appearing before a commission of enquiry headed by Muhammad Munir, then chief justice of Pakistan, Maududi was asked what his reaction would be to India's becoming a Hindu state as a countermeasure to Pakistan becoming the Islamic state he advocated. Maududi's reply was unequivocal: 'I will have no objection if the Muslims in India are treated like sudras and mlechchas and Manu's laws are applied to them depriving them of all share in government and rights as a citizens.'[8] Sudras are the lowest of the four castes of Hindus whose very touch pollutes; mlechchas (unclean) are lower than the untouchables and beyond the pale of caste.

As in the past, the secularists, despite the challenge from the fundamentalists, have managed to consolidate political power either by force or through democratic processes. That is why the fundamentalists rarely succeed in taking over the administration for which they have neither the aptitude nor the skill. They continue to be in a minority and function as the opposition; they denounce the secularists as anti-Islamic and are forever plotting to eliminate them. As Abd al-Salam K. Faraj, an accomplice in the murder, by fundamentalists, of Anwar as-Sadat, the late president of Egypt, put it:

> Governments in the Islamic world today are in a state of apostasy—of Islam they preserve nothing but its name although they pray, fast and pretend to be Muslims. Our sunna has determined that the apostate must be killed even if he is in no position to fight while an infidel does not merit death in such a case.[9]

And in this sort of offensive, the fundamentalists have quite often succeeded. Nasser barely escaped assassination, Sadat was not so lucky. Jinnah's successor and chief lieutenant, Liyāquat Ali Khan, then premier of Pakistan, fell to an assassin's bullets in 1951; Sukarno of Indonesia was kept in solitary confinement until his death for involvement in an alleged conspiracy with the communists to defeat the fundamentalists; and of course the Shah of Iran was most ingloriously ousted from power. The fundamentalists, too, have had their problems—Hasan al-Banna, the founder of the Muslim Brotherhood was assassinated; its chief ideologue Sayyid Qutb was executed; Maulānā Maududi spent many years in jail and was almost hanged.

And so the battle goes on. Apart from the religious, there are social and economic factors which have also contributed to this conflict. The poor and the downtrodden, frustrated by the self-seeking politics of the ruling classes, have often sought refuge in the arms of the fundamentalists who assure them a better life, if not in this world, then in the next. This has been as much a cause of the rise of Khomeini in Iran today as that of Afghani in the early years of this century. The militancy of the Shi'as in the Lebanon has also much to do with their economic backwardness. On the other hand, the consolidation of secularism in Kemalist Turkey was largely due to the social and economic betterment that was brought about by Ataturk. The same factors worked in suppressing the fundamentalists in Soviet Russia and communist China, where the Muslims were economically uplifted.

The battle between the fundamentalists and the secularists can perhaps be more accurately described as a struggle between forces who resist change in Islam and those who wish to accelerate it. As we shall see, this is not a new phenomenon. Indeed, the growth and development of this struggle is, in many respects, the story of political Islam.

1

Nature of the Conflict

On the death of Prophet Muhammad in 632 the question of succession
assumed paramount importance; it threatened to be as much religious as
political. The successor had to be both a temporal and a spiritual leader,
a combination which the Prophet had embodied. But who, among his
companions, could come up to this ideal? A consensus among the
faithful was difficult to arrive at; but eventually, because of the trauma
of the Prophet's death, the problem was resolved without any serious
dispute. The first two successors of the Prophet, known as caliphs,
proved remarkably resourceful; they united the faithful under one banner
to spread the faith. But after them there was trouble: rival groups took
to arms, caliphs were murdered and their murders plunged the Caliphate
into a succession of civil wars. Since then the Muslims have never
been a united community. As the wars of the Caliphate dragged on,
temporal and religious factions drifted apart and each faction broke into
sub-factions; all of them swore by the shariah—the canonical law of
Islam—but each faction interpreted it differently and went about it in its
own way. Those who operated in the temporal domain used Islam for
their own ends while the theologians busied themselves with the coin-
ing of new theories and the charting out of fresh paths for the faithful.
The vast majority remained silent spectators to this frenetic activity;
they were content with their routine and the simple rituals they practised. Islam was simple enough for them to follow without external
guidance.

For more than two hundred years this state of affairs continued, leading to a plethora of contradictory doctrines, which finally divided the

Muslims into two broad groups—one lot owing allegiance to their temporal rulers, the other opposed to them. The ruling group was not much concerned with the dictates of religion. To it, power mattered more than faith. The other group was against the rulers' 'heathen' activities; it aimed at purifying Islam. But the conflict did not much perturb the common people; they kept out of it. Their attitude, all through the various phases of Islam, was much more practical; their conscience seemed to have been satisfied so long as the rulers and their cohorts did not interfere with time-honoured institutions and formally accorded sanction to the sharī'ah.[1] The temporal authorities were only too happy to do so. But the theologians insisted on much more; unless they were allowed to oversee the implementation of the laws and regulations as decreed by them, they did not feel secure.

This conflict between religion and politics extends far into the past; it did not begin with Islam or Christianity but existed much earlier. As R.M. Maclever, a professor of political philosophy at Columbia University has put it:

> There was religion long before there was the Church, long before there was the State. It was at first, as it were, a mental atmosphere, which enveloped each society, clinging most densely, like mist on the hills, to the salient features and occasions of its life, to sex and birth, to spring and harvest, to death and pestilence, to the darkness and to the light that pursues it, to the sudden revelations of natural power, to the kin-custom, and to the authority of the chief. It was a diffused feeling of sanctity and dread, of ecstasy and horror, expressing itself in worship and dance and ritual, sacrifice and taboo, as the groping mind of man reached everywhere the perilous verge of the unknown beyond the narrow limits of its power.[2]

As man and society evolved, someone took over duties which would ordinarily be performed in later ages by a priest and also in course of time acquired the authority of a tribal chieftain. The combination was short-lived and rarely proved satisfactory. The religious head and the temporal chief soon became distinct entities with occasional conflicts erupting between the two. For restoring peace one had to accept the supremacy of the other. In Greece the temporal head had the upper hand; in Egypt, the religious. In India the king was supreme; but it was the brahmin priest whose blessings and advice the king sought. Gautama, the Buddha, was neither attracted by the lure of temporal power nor promises of life hereafter. He renounced the State and refused to found a religion. But after his death his followers became involved in both and soon there was as acute a conflict in Buddhism between its kings and monks as in other religions. The Jews were able to avoid this until the formation of Israel; since then the conflict between the two forces among them has been no less intense. Earlier they accepted the civil law of the country in which they lived as binding in terms of religion as well and thereby avoided a clash with the State; now they are as assertive about their personal laws as the Muslims.

All through history mankind has been faced with this dilemma; only its manifestations have varied from religion to religion and country to country. The conflict between the State and the Church came to the fore when the persecuted Christians in the fourth century became the ruling class of the Roman empire, when Emperor Constantine converted to Christianity. Suddenly, from a persecuted institution, the Church became the dominant force. Constantine clothed it with sanctity, as did some of his immediate successors. Priests became advisers whose opinions, even in temporal affairs, were unchallenged. Drunk with power, they began to harass and persecute other religious groups. They used the machinery of the State to close down non-Christian places of worship and even imposed the death penalty on non-Christians. This situation did not last long. Increasingly occupied with affairs of state, the temporal authorities had no time for the repressive acts of the Church. They started to clip the wings of the popes and their cohorts. The popes fought back. Hostilities broke out in the open between the Church and the State.

The issue could not remain unresolved and soon enough Pope Gelecious I came forward with his famous 'doctrine of the two swords'. In a letter to Emperor Anastasius I'in 494 he wrote: 'There are, indeed, most august Emperor, two powers by which this world is chiefly ruled; the sacred authority of the popes and the royal power. Of these the priestly power is much more important because it has to render account for the kings of men themselves at the divine tribunal.'[3] Later the Church further asserted its superiority by claiming that all powers, spiritual as well as temporal, belonged to God and hence the pope, as God's representative on earth, was supreme. It was on this basis that

Charlemagne was crowned the first head of the holy Roman empire in 800 by the pope. In course of time, Charlemagne became too powerful a ruler to accept the pope's authority. The conflict continued.

In 1302 Pope Boniface VII delivered his historic bill *Unam Sanctam*, which said in effect that Christ's investing of St Peter with temporal supremacy gave his successors equal authority. But Philip the Fair, king of France, refused to honour the pope's edict and instead imposed taxes on the clergy to prove his overlordship.

And thus the conflict went on. Some popes even excommunicated the kings they clashed with and declared them unfit to wear the crown. The clash between Pope George VII and Emperor Henry IV of England is a case in point. The pope excommunicated the emperor but in three years King Henry marched on Rome and deposed the pope. His successors compromised and the quarrel between the two was amicably resolved.

With the passage of time temporal power acquired greater authority. The popes could not prevent the rulers of the various kingdoms which arose on the ruins of the holy Roman empire, from meddling in the affairs of various bishoprics. Henry VIII of England defied the pope on the question of his marrying Anne Boleyn and proclaimed himself *Fider Defensor*, or Supreme Defender of the Faith. Gradually the supremacy of the secular authority in affairs of state came to be consolidated. There was near universal acceptance of the doctrine that temporal power had to be exercised independently of the Church. But it could not be put into practice fully. Even Luther, who had advocated freedom of conscience in the sixteenth century, agreed that 'heresy', which was to be adjudged by the Church, had to be punished by the State. He accepted the formula *Cujus regio ejus religio*, 'the religion of the ruler is the religion of the State'. Hence followers of not only other religions, such as the Jews, but even those belonging to other denominations among the Christians, continued to suffer various hardships, legal disadvantages and personal humiliations.

In England, for instance, the Act of Toleration of 1689 gave no protection to the Catholics; they had to wait until 1829 for the removal of the iniquities practised against them. The English philosopher John Locke, was one of the earliest to demand the complete separation of the Church and the State, with the State alone being responsible for an individual's life, liberty and property.[4] Some French philosophers, aghast at the aftermath of the Restoration in 1815, also supported separation on the ground that 'religion has need of only one thing, liberty. Its strength is in the conscience of people, and not in the support of government. It fears from the side of the latter only their dangerous protection, for the arm which is extended to defend it, is employed almost always to enslave it.'[5]

As science advanced, religious intolerance declined and the concept of a secular State gained further ground everywhere in the Christian world. The American Revolution had admittedly prepared the environment for the establishment of a secular order; unfortunately, it was dissipated by the subsequent union between the Church and the State following the Restoration, which resulted in excessive religious persecutions. Soon after, Karl Marx (1818–83) propounded the view that religion had been used as an instrument of oppression of the common people and gave a new interpretation to human development with his theory of historical materialism.

In his perception of the role of religion Marx was much influenced by the philosophy of Hegel, who had denounced religion as 'the harshest bondage'. The Bolshevik Revolution of 1917 struck a severe blow to the hold of religion on the people; it denounced it as an 'opiate' of the masses and banned its practice in Russia. The Bolsheviks encouraged atheism and turned places of worship into museums for inquisitive sightseers. Stressing its aim as the material uplift of the poor and the downtrodden the Revolution was not bothered about their spiritual welfare. The result was that the Russians achieved a total separation of the Church and the State, though this was done by eliminating the Church altogether.

This, in short, is the story of the emergence of the secular State in the Christian world. In Islam, according to the fundamentalists, there is no place for such a State. Many Muslims consider secularism 'a sub-facet of specifically Christian heresy';[6] or an aid to the establishment of a godless society, with its emphasis on materialism. They condemn it as anti-spiritual. Islam treats man as a slave of God though God in His munificence has placed him as His vice-regent on earth. He has created the various religions as ways to reach Him, and not to divide mankind. Even in regard to conversion from one religion to another the Qur'ân warns against compulsion and ridicules the concept of a chosen people.

There is no instance of an Islamic state having instituted an inquisition or organized pogroms or concentration camps for non-Muslims.

Those Muslims who oppose secularism rely on the dictionary meanings of 'secular' and 'secularism', which are invariably defined as 'opposed to religion', or as a 'spirit or tendency, especially a system of political or social philosophy, that rejects all forms of religious faith.'[7] According to these definitions only communist states qualify as truly secular. Surprisingly, none of the standard dictionaries have taken note of the changes in the concept of secularism since it was first conceived. The non-communist states are far from being anti-religious; on the contrary most of them, including India, afford equal status and opportunities to the followers of different faiths, notwithstanding the fact that the predominant religion, by force of circumstance, acquires a special status. One of the best definitions of a secular state has been given by the American scholar, Donald Eugene Smith: 'The secular State is a state which guarantees individual and corporate freedom of religion, deals with the individual as a citizen, irrespective of his religion, is not constitutionally connected to a particular religion nor does it seem either to promote or interfere with religion.'[8] By this interpretation, the United States of America, France, Switzerland, India, Indonesia and several other modern states qualify as secular. But there are some, seemingly secular, which are not. Not even the United Kingdom, because it requires its monarch to be the defender of the Protestant faith; there are also some other European countries, which though secular in practice, have not formalized the separation between the State and the Church.

The concept of secularism is not more than two hundred years old. According to the Oxford English Dictionary, the word itself came into usage in 1846, and represents the doctrine that morality should be based solely in regard to the well-being of mankind in the present life, to the exclusion of all considerations drawn from belief in God or in the future state.[9]

History shows that among the Muslims, although there has always been a tendency to oppose the separation of politics and religion in practice, they have invariably reconciled themselves to the opposite. This is as much true of the pious among them as the sinful; the fundamentalist has been in many respects no less compromising than the secularist. The fundamentalist has protested against adjustment but ultimately connived at it, especially when faced with the pressure of the immediate; and the secularist has been equally willing to dilute secularism to be acceptable to the umma (community). Seemingly contradictory but in reality complementary, the two approaches have often caused confusion among the faithful, but Islam has been able to live with both all through the ages and there are good reasons for it.

First, unlike Christianity, Islam mixes the temporal and the spiritual; second, it has no organized priesthood; and, third, unlike Christ, Muhammad was not only the spiritual but also the temporal leader of his followers. Despite these differences, there has been, from the earliest beginnings, as we have seen, a struggle within Islam between religion and politics. As pointed out earlier, this was inevitable because no successor of the Prophet could fulfil both roles. The conflict began when Uthmān, the third caliph (644–56), was opposed by a combination of forces, who denounced him as a usurper and a heretic. He was asked at swordpoint to give up office. He refused to comply. His supporters pleaded for tolerance and understanding and urged his enemies not to disrupt the unity of Islam. They propounded the pragmatic theory that no Muslim had the right to question the faith or behaviour of another Muslim. Once a person declared that he was a Muslim, it was enough; his conduct was for Allah to judge on the day of judgement. Until then the matter was to be deferred; hence they came to be known as 'murja' or Murji'ites, meaning those who defer.

On the other hand, the Shi'ites—supporters of Ali—argued that anyone who committed a wrong and whose faith was in question and behaviour sinful, should be disowned in the quickest time possible. According to them, Uthmān could not be a legitimate successor to the Prophet because of his close links with the family of Abū Sufyan, who was an implacable enemy of the Prophet until the fall of Mecca, when he converted to Islam. Uthmān's appointment was therefore wrong and had to be undone, if need be, by armed rebellion. In the process he took over the Caliphate. Mu'āwiya, governor of Syria and a descendant of Abū Sufyan, charged Ali with being an instigator of Uthmān's murder and refused to accept him as the caliph. Ali and his supporters marched against the rebel governor. A fierce battle was fought at Siffin in Syria in 657. As Ali's side was poised for victory, Mu'āwiya and his men sued for peace and asked for the dispute to be arbitrated on the basis of the Qur'ān. Ali and a majority of his supporters agreed; but a group within his fold rebelled and accused the caliph of betraying their cause. They used the same argument against the Shi¨ites as the latter had used against the Murji'ites; a wrong is a wrong and cannot be undone by arbitration. Ali was in the right and Mu'āwiya in the wrong. Hence there was no reason for arbitration. Ali pleaded with them in vain. This group then withdrew from his fold and were called the Kharijites, from the word khawārij (those who withdrew).

Fanatical to the core, the Kharijites contended that Ali had sinned grievously and assassinated him as soon as they could. Thereafter they plotted to kill Mu'āwiya who had usurped the Caliphate. He escaped with minor injuries and founded the Umayyad dynasty, changing its republican character, and turning it into a monarchy. His family ruled the world of Islam from Damascus, the new capital, from 661 to 750. The Umayyad caliphs who succeeded him were condemned by their detractors as godless. Nevertheless, the Murji'ites rose to their support and went to the extent of asserting that even if the Umayyads did not adhere to all the religious precepts and practices, they had to be obeyed. They were persons in authority, and obedience, as enjoined by the Qur'ān, was due to them.[10] In their support, the Murji'ites relied on a saying of the Prophet: 'He who obeys me obeys God. Likewise he who disobeys me disobeys God. Further, he who disobeys an amir disobeys me. Verily an amir is a shield behind which one fights and is protected. If he gives orders in the fear of God and with justice, he will have his reward; if contrary thereto he will suffer for it.'[11] The punishment in this respect lay with God; therefore, no revolt against the ruler was permissible. Of course, there are many hadith to the contrary, but since the Murji'ites were principally concerned with upholding the temporal power of the Umayyads against attacks by the orthodox and the puritans they concocted several hadith to buttress their arguments. Another group, the Mu'tazillites, meaning the separatists, by adopting a neutral stance between the Umayyads and their detractors, tried to underplay the conflict. They argued that man was a free agent and there was no eternal law governing human actions. Hence divine ordinances had to be interpreted in the context of changed circumstances and tested by reason; whatever was reasonable was good for Islam. In a sense they were the first free thinkers of Islam. They achieved a certain eminence under the Abbasids (750–1258) whom they defended against attacks by the orthodox. In doing so they went to the other extreme of denouncing the orthodox and even having some of them beheaded. Although their influence was shortlived, their intellectual contribution was of a pioneering nature. They laid the foundation for liberty of thought and action in Islam.

From the beginning of the Umayyad rule the Companions of the Prophet disapproved of the former's activities, particularly the way in which they had turned the Caliphate into a mulk or kingdom. Mu'āwiya was aware of the adverse effect of such an attitude.Why then did he decide to opt for the kingship? His explanation was that he feared that tribal jealousies, rampant among the Arabs of the time, would plunge the Caliphate into fratricidal wars and weaken the structure of administration in an empire which now extended from West Asia and North Africa to Central Asia and parts of India. From the city-state that it had been in the days of the Prophet, its powers had increased enormously. These could not be left to the whims and caprices of tribal leaders, or the theological disputations of the Companions. Mu'āwiya was convinced that only a monarchical pattern of administration could assure continuity of rule. He was aware that it would lead to despotism but felt it was better than chaos. The hereditary ruler symbolized the majesty of power, giving him an aura of sanctity to exercise unchallenged control over the affairs of state. He could afford to be neutral in any internecine dispute and still assert his authority whenever he chose to do so. Hence the best bet, or so Mu'āwiya argued, was to go in for a hereditary kingdom as the king had always been traditionally accepted as the final arbiter of their destinies by the people; this was so not only among the Arabs but also the Syrians, Iraqis, Egyptians, Berbers, Persians, Central Asians, Indians and the Chinese who were more inclined towards kingship than any form of republican headship. In course of time the Umayyad pattern was found to be so successful that it was followed not only by the Abbasids but also by all subsequent Muslim rulers everywhere. As a result, temporal power gained ascendancy over religious leadership. Theologians receded to the background with marginal impact on the administration of the state. Perhaps the most important reason for this state of affairs was that the Muslims were unlike the Christians, as we have seen earlier. The Muslims had no pontiff or central figure to unite and mobilize them against the caliph. The theologians were confined to their madrasas or maktabs. And gradually the faithful were led to believe by most theologians that godless tyranny was better than civil anarchy. Once the theologians chose the path of least interference with the State, they stayed away from the corridors of power, avoided temporal connections and instead endeavoured to spread the faith through piety and learning, thus guiding their followers along the right path. Some of them concentrated on codifying the traditions of the Prophet by weeding out the spurious from the genuine; others systematized his precepts and practices in order to provide the faithful with a comprehensive code of conduct and spelt out their rights and obligations in this world as well as their rewards and punishments in the next. This course of action had a profound effect on the faithful; the piety and simplicity of the theologians turned them into objects of veneration. Even caliphs and their advisers bowed before them. Collectively their works helped to consolidate the faith, without making it a rival to temporal power. However, this sort of attitude was restricted to the Sunni theologians.

The Shi'ites continued to be rebellious: the more radical among them organized revolts against the caliphs. Their imams or leaders condemned not only the Ummayads but also the Abbasids as traitors to the cause and advocated the establishment of a theocratic State which alone they believed could safeguard Islam. Hasan-i-Sabbāh, known as the Old Man of the Mountain, was one of them. He carried on a guerrilla war against the Abbasid rulers. His followers, known as the Assassins (hashish addicts) drugged themselves before undertaking suicide missions and were responsible for the assassination of many persons in power, whom they regarded as enemies of Islam.

None of these uprisings succeeded in achieving their main objective. All they gained was to further weaken a Caliphate already plagued by internal jealousies and court intrigues and reduce it to helplessness against the onslaught of the Mongols (1258). As the Caliphate collapsed, many independent Muslim kingdoms arose, all claiming to be the guardians of Islam. The caliph was reduced to a mere figurehead.

Almost all the theologians were caught unawares by these developments. So far they had dealt with a central power; its dispersal in varied forms of kingdoms posed new problems. Most of them found some excuse or the other to justify monarchies on the theory that order was better than chaos. Even Ghazāli (1058–1111), the greatest of the Islamic jurists, regarded as hujjat al-Islām, or proof of Islam, legitimized the actions of the military usurpers on the ground that misrule was better than no rule.

After the downfall of the Abbasid Caliphate and the rise of independent kingdoms, there was a miraculous Islamic resurgence. Three powerful Muslim empires emerged, whose sway extended over large parts of Asia and Africa and even to provinces of Europe. These were the Sunni Ottomans in Turkey, the Mughals in India and the Shi'a Safavids in Iran. The three together constituted the biggest territorial extension of Islam. Not one of the three was a theocracy but each one of them exploited Islam to suit its temporal requirements. The orthodox reconciled themselves to this state of affairs. They seemed content, nay happy, with the glory that the Muslim rulers brought to Islam; the latter's nominal allegiance to the shari'ah was enough for legitimizing them. In subsequent chapters I shall explain how this transformation took place and what effect it had both on the polity and the faith.

However, many centuries later, even these magnificent empires crumbled as European powers extended their domain over large parts of Africa and Asia. The occupation of the heartlands of Islam by Christian colonizers created an entirely new situation, which in its turn changed the character of the conflict between the temporal and religious forces in Islam. Instead of opposing their own brethren-in-Islam, the faithful had now to contend with alien powers who introduced their own systems and laws, replacing the shari'ah, in their newly acquired territories. Not only were criminal, commercial and civil codes changed, but inroads were even made into Muslim Personal Law. There was occasional resistance by the faithful, but on the whole the changes were willy-nilly accepted by the Muslims. Religion had to give in to the State.

The picture changed dramatically after World War II (1939–45), when most Muslim countries regained their independence. The long rule of the Europeans and their continued impact on the subjugated people had created a class among them which was enamoured of secularism. Having been trained in Western institutions it readily accepted Western notions about the nature of the State. The orthodox resisted it, but they were unable to stem the tide, which transformed not only the political structure but also social behaviour. I will take a closer look at all these developments in subsequent chapters and explain more fully the conflicts that arose in their wake, but broadly speaking, the conflicts were confined to two opposing forces: temporal versus religious. The former were more pragmatic; the later more rigid.

The world of Islam today faces the same challenge it has in the past. Only it is more intense. As the noted Orientalist, Prof. Bernard Lewis, observes:

> If the metal is harder, so too is the hammer—for the challenge of today is incomparably more radical, more aggressive, more persuasive—and it comes not from a conquered but a conquering world. The impact of the West, with its railways and printing presses, aeroplanes and cinemas, factories and universities, oil-prospectors and archaeologists, machine guns and ideas, has shattered beyond repair the traditional structure of economic life. . . .[12]

It has affected every Muslim in every land. The future of Islam depends on how its followers respond to this challenge. The fundamentalists have one solution, the secularists another. The question is: are their differences irreconcilable? In the past the fight of the fundamentalists was with the rulers who readily made compromises with doctrinal obligations to achieve their own ends; today their dispute is with the modern secularists over norms of social behaviour and systems of government. The struggle within Islam for the soul of Islam continues. Will the struggle be resolved in the present and the foreseeable future, as it was in the past? Or will it make life more difficult for the faithful? This book attempts to find the answers.

2

The Model State

The conflict between the fundamentalists and the secularists centres around the form and substance which a state with a Muslim majority should take. There are more than forty such states throughout the world which cover almost two-thirds of the total Muslim population. In other countries, where Muslims are in a minority, there is, of course, no question about the Islamic character. Towards the Muslims in these states the attitude of the fundamentalists is quite clear; they should learn to live as second class citizens and avoid participation in politics or administration.[1]

Even in states where Muslims are in a majority, the situation is complicated. Modern compulsions drive such states towards secularism. The process has become accelerated because of the impact of science and technology on the one hand and a growing awareness of the concept of egalitarianism on the other. These have, inevitably, broken down historical barriers separating people of different faiths. Because of these factors, the hold of religion has considerably eased and made people more materialistic in their outlook, although there are still many countries where religion plays a dominant role and where secularism has yet to gain a foothold. The confrontation between religion and politics is a characteristic of most non-communist countries. It may not be as pronounced as before but it persists. As we have noticed earlier, Christianity has succeeded in resolving this conflict to a large extent, but Islam has still to come to terms with secularism. This is as much due to the basic structure of Islam as to its historical development. Consequently, the conflict between spiritual and temporal power has created innumerable problems for the Muslims. It has produced a number of theological compromises to suit varying situations. To understand them it is necessary first to look at the origin and characteristics of the state that the Prophet founded soon after his migration from Mecca to Madina in 622 and then to examine the changes through which it has passed in the course of history.

To start with it must be clearly understood that the Prophet had no intention of setting himself up as a ruler. His mission was to preach the message of the Qur'ān and to bring people to the right path. It was the vicious and violent opposition to his mission that forced him to resort to arms. He was compelled to organize his followers to protect their faith. The most practical way to do so was to establish a state and take upon himself the burdens of a ruler. It is this state that the Muslims cherish and the fundamentalists hold up as a model. One of the Prophet's earliest acts after bringing the migrants, Muhājirūn and the helpers, Anṣar, together in Madina was to forge an alliance between his followers and the Jews who formed an important segment of the population. This was achieved through a working arrangement for the conduct of day-to-day affairs. It was later put into writing and came to be known as the 'Constitution of Madina'.[2] Though some critics have doubted its authenticity, it is generally accepted as a genuine document and formed the basis of the first Islamic state. According to this constitution, the Jews and the Muslims were guaranteed equality of status and were clubbed together as one unma or nation. It is on this provision that the secularists rely and base their stand that Islam recognizes a composite state which does not discriminate between the followers of different faiths. Some of the provisions of this document give an insight into the workings of the Prophet's mind. It still has relevance today, especially in Islamic states where different religious groups live and work together.

The document declares at the outset that believers in Islam and all other individuals of whatever origin, who have made common cause with them, shall constitute one nation. It is this important declaration that eminent Muslim divines of undivided India, particularly those belonging to the Jam'iyyat al-ulamā-i-Hind (organization of Muslim theologians in India), relied upon while opposing the two-nation theory of Jinnah, the founder of Pakistan, who held that Hindus and Muslims constituted two distinct nations and, therefore, had to have separate states of their own. These savants supported Gandhi in his struggle for India's independence and argued that if the Prophet had conceded that the Jews, the Muslims and even the pagans of Madina could form one nation, it did not lie with anyone to pronounce that the Hindus and the Muslims of India could not become one nation and work in harmony with each other.[3] This was the argument which Madani used against Iqbal.

There are many other features of the document which support the contention that Islam accepts a composite state of Muslims and non-Muslims ensuring equality of status, treatment and opportunity to both groups. For instance, it states: 'The Jews who attached themselves to our commonwealth shall be protected from all insults and vexations. . . they shall have an equal right with our own people to our assistance and good offices.' Furthermore, it provided that 'the Jews shall practise their religion as freely as the Muslims; their clients and allies shall enjoy the same security and freedom; the guilty shall be pursued and punished; the Jews shall join the Muslims in defending Madina against all enemies; the interior of Madina shall be sacred to all those who accept this document; the clients and allies of both the Muslims and the Jews shall be as respected as their patrons.' There was a special warning for his followers: 'All true Muslims shall hold in abhorrence every man culpable though he were his nearest kin.' For the Jews also, it was specified that 'those of them who join us are entitled to our aid and support so long as they shall not have wronged us or lent assistance [to any enemies] against us.'

In regard to expenses incurred on behalf of the State, the document prescribed that 'the Jews shall contribute to expenses along with the believers as long as they fight side by side' with them. And finally, it emphasized that they (the Muslims and the Jews) shall help one another in the event of any attack on the people covered by this document. There shall be sincere friendship, exchange of good counsel, fair conduct and no treachery between them. Even the pagans of Madina were assured of the State's protection provided they did not give shelter to any person of the tribe of Quraish, either his goods or his person, or take his part against any believer.

In the document certain special obligations were cast on the Muslims. For instance, they were to help believers who were heavily indebted; and not to kill a believer because of his connection with non-believers. The believers were to help one another and 'even the humblest among them was to be given full protection, and even aid'. In the event of war, no Muslim was authorized to make peace individually. If any Muslim was killed by a non-Muslim, then all Muslims must make common cause against the murderer and those who helped him and either fight them or accept the blood price together. Evil-doers or violators of the common code were warned that they shall be given no aid or shelter. Every believer was required to maintain internal law and order and to help the State to punish the wrong-doers among them. 'In case of dispute arising among the people of this document, which it is feared will bring harm to them, they shall refer it to Allah and to Muhammad, for Allah is the most strict and faithful guarantor of the contents of this document.' Apart from the Jews, who were covered by the Constitution of Madina, a similar guarantee was given by the Prophet to the Christians of Najrā`n in a separate document. Its terms were:

> To [the Christians of] Najrā`n and the neighbouring territories, the security of God and the pledge of His Prophet are extended for their lives, their religion and their property to the present as well as the absent and others besides; there shall be no interference with [the practice of] their faith or their observations; nor any change in their rights or privileges; no bishop shall be removed from his bishopric, nor any monk from his monastery, nor any priest from his priesthood, and they shall continue to enjoy everything great and small, not oppress or be oppressed; they shall not practise the rights of blood-vengeance as in the days of ignorance or jāhiliyah; no tithes shall be levied from them nor shall they be required to furnish provisions for the troops.

According to a tradition, when Christian deputationists went to see the Prophet, he accommodated them in his own house and when the time for their prayer came, allowed them to perform it in his own mosque. Some of his Companions protested but he ignored their protest.[4]

These documents, which the Prophet gave to the Christians and the Jews immediately on assuming rulership of Madina, stand out for their enlightened attitude when compared to the state of affairs prevailing at that time in the two great empires of Rome and Persia. In Rome, despite the Corpus Juris Justinian had compiled, the worst kind of tyranny, corruption and religious persecution was rampant. In Persia, the empire that Khusraw Anushirwan had bequeathed to his successors in the name of Zarathushtra, the non-Zoroastrians, especially the Christians, were blinded, crucified, stoned and starved to death. As H.G. Wells has observed,

> Islam prevailed because it was the best social and political order the times could offer. It prevailed because everywhere it found politically apathetic peoples, robbed, oppressed, bullied, uneducated and unorganized and it found selfish and unsound governments out of touch with any people at all. It was the broadest, freshest and cleanest political idea that had yet come into actual activity in the world and it offered better terms than any other to the masses of mankind.[5]

Despite the strong moral base that the Prophet had given to his state, it could not meet all the requirements of the times. There was no organized secretariat, no regular police force, no established courts of justice. Also there was only a volunteer army. He repeatedly impressed upon the people—both the Muslims and the non-Muslims—that they were to maintain law and order by themselves and guard the security of the State. It was only the commanding presence of the Prophet and the devotion he inspired in his followers which enabled the government of the day to be run smoothly and effectively. His role was much more than that of an arbitrator of disputes. Being essentially a teacher, he tried to inculcate among the inhabitants of Madina a sense of confidence in themselves so that they could look after their own affairs. On every crucial occasion he consulted chiefs of different tribes and his own Companions. He took their counsel when slanderous gossip was circulated against his own wife A'isha as he did regarding the action to be taken against the Jewish tribe, Banu Qurayzah, for treason and the many battles he had to fight in defence of his faith. Could there have been a more democratic approach by a ruler in those medieval times?

Though the Prophet's main concerns were the propagation of Islam and the consolidation of his following, he did not neglect administration. He chose men of impeccable character, integrity and talent to perform the various governmental functions. He appointed a deputy to look after the affairs of state in his absence, deputed army commanders to lead expeditions, governors to administer different provinces, judges to dole out justice without fear or favour, supervisors to distribute the booty of war and look after prisoners, inspectors to oversee the collection of taxes such as zakāt or alms tax, assess and collect ush`r or the levy on the annual harvest. To quote Montgomery Watt, 'The general picture is thus one of Muhammad making use of capable men from the friendly tribemen, who already had a high standing in their tribes and in the case of other tribes appointing as his agents men of administrative ability from Mecca and Madīna.'[6] Maxime Rodinson puts it more picturesquely,

> In this Muhammad, inspired by Allah, was able to carry through measures to ensure internal peace, which were in the interest of all. But only the swearing of solemn oaths and the force of public opinion guaranteed that these rules would be observed. No police force existed, any more than the public funds to maintain one. It was to take all the wits and adroitness of Muhammad and his counsellors, further aided by circumstances and pressure of social forces of which they were unaware, to turn this morality into an effective, practical power.[7]

This was the state founded by him, which the Shi'as and the Sunnis, theologians and laymen, the orthodox and the pragmatists, the fundamentalists and the secularists present as the model. However ideally suited to its times, by its very nature it could not be expected to meet the demands of expanding empires and diverse situations. Hence, with every age new theories were formulated and new schools of thought sprang up. Qur'ānic directions and injunctions had to be viewed in the light of whichever situation was current. This led to the enunciation of new directives. Although the Qur'ān enshrines eternal truths and its laws are binding for all time to come, these have to be properly understood in their historical context. That is the only way it can be interpreted and used properly in every new age.

The first four caliphs, the Companions and early scholars exercised considerable freedom of interpretation and showed much ingenuity in arriving at their conclusions by applying both ijtihād (independent judgement) and qiyās (analogy) in interpreting the Qur'ânic texts and the hadith. The eminent Muslim jurist, al-Shatibi (d. 1388) has stated that eternal validity applied only to the general principles enunciated by the Qur'ân and not to the particulars in the scriptures. For this purpose reason had to be brought in as a partner.

The Qur'ân is replete with anecdotes drawing morals for the faithful: fully eighty per cent of the text is devoted to their narration. Out of 6,666 verses less than 300 are of a mandatory nature. The noted Egyptian scholar, Abd al-Wahhāb ibn Khallaf, has classified them under the following heads:

1. Sources of law: 50 verses
2. Constitutional provisions: 10 verses
3. International law: 25 verses
4. Jurisdiction and procedures: 13 verses
5. Penal law: 30 verses
6. Civil law: 70 verses
7. Family and personal law: 70 verses
8. Economic and financial directives: 20 verses.[8]

Most of the Qur'ân is allegorical in content. Hence, there is enough scope for varied interpretations. The Qur'ân itself has hinted at this. Despite the best efforts of some of the most outstanding exegists, much confusion prevails as many of them, down the ages, have taken contradictory positions on important issues. For instance, there is no mention in the Qur'ân about how an imam or leader is to be selected, nor what his qualifications should be for the post. There are two verses on consultation, or consensus. Theologians of all hues have maintained that these should be the basis for the selection of the chief executive and for the conduct of the affairs of the state. The content of these two verses are as follows.

That which you have been given is but the fleeting comfort of this life. Better and more enduring is that which Allah has for those who believe and put their trust in Him; who avoid gross sins and indecencies, and are willing to forgive, who obey their Lord, attend to their prayers, and conduct their affairs by mutual consent; who bestow in alms a part of that which we have given them and, when oppressed, seek to redress their wrongs. (42:36 to 40)

These verses have been relied upon not only by the religious but also the temporal authorities to justify whichever approach most suits them—election, selection or nomination. The scope has been deliberately widened for conflicting interpretations. For instance, kings resorted to bai'ah or consent by getting their hands kissed by their subjects in the main mosque of the capital as a gesture of acceptance. Local chieftains asked congregations assembled in the main mosques of their domains to voice their consent to their rule. In recent times, the last Ottoman caliph, while opening the new session of Parliament, established under pressure from the secularists, declared in his speech on 1 November 1909 that as the parliamentary system was sanctioned by the Qur'ān, it was sacrosanct. Monarchists, feudal satraps, military dictators, democratically elected presidents and prime ministers have quoted these verses in their favour; so have theologians, religious scholars and ulamā of different schools to lend support to their stand.

As we analyse the varied development of Islamic polity, we see how some of the most celebrated jurists accorded their approval to autocratic regimes that came into existence in their times—the Caliphate, sultanates, satrapies, protectorates, even those propagating secularism—by giving their own interpretations to these verses. Then there is the other text, which every one of them has used to silence the opposition: 'O you who believe, obey God, and obey the Prophet and obey those who are in power amongst you.' (4:59) To equate obedience to God and the Prophet with obedience to the ruler was ingenious, but surprisingly it worked (and still works) to pacify the faithful.

Whatever the means by which a ruler acquired power he found an appropriate chapter and verse from the Qur'ān to impress upon his subjects the fact that rebellion was not permitted in Islam; in this, he was supported by the theologians he patronized. There were, of course, others who did not fail to voice their dissent. But, by and large, dissent was silenced by authority. As a result, the concept of constitutional opposition to the government could not be developed in Islam. The Prophet's injunctions regarding non-Muslims are clear but there has always been some controversy over their treatment in an Islamic state. Verses are quoted in support of the view that the Qur'ān calls upon

Muslims to continue fighting non-believers till they are destroyed or accept conversion to Islam. Those who quote these verses do not take into account their historical background. The Prophet was surrounded by detractors who were forever plotting to kill him and liquidate his followers. Conspiracies were hatched and wars were launched by his enemies to defeat his mission. Even after he emigrated to Madina, neither he nor his followers were left in peace. The Jews did not reciprocate the confidence he reposed in them; the Christians also distrusted him. The pagans, who were his inveterate enemies, were determined to crush him. Under these circumstances, the Prophet had to protect himself and defend his followers. The Qur'ānic verses that came to him on these occasions were more in the nature of military commands than directive principles of state policy; they were necessarily of a temporary nature, meant to deal with the prevailing situation. The general attitude towards non-Muslims is contained in verses which are unencumbered by any such context. There is, for instance, the oft-repeated dictum: 'There is no compulsion in religion' (2:256), which has been elaborated in many other verses in the Qur'ān and forms the basis of secularism in Islam.

The manner in which the provision for the jaziya was used by various Muslim rulers and interpreted by theologians will be discussed by me at appropriate places. For the present it is enough to note that its origin lay in the needs of the time and the wars in which the Prophet was involved. It was never meant to humiliate non-Muslims conquered in war. One of the greatest biographers of the Prophet, Allama Shibli Noamani, has opined that the jaziya, by its very nature, was a temporary measure. Prof. Bernard Lewis concedes that the Qur'ānic verse did not connote humiliation, but observes: 'What concerns us is not the original meaning of the verse but the way in which it was interpreted in historic Islam.'[9] No interpretation, however learned, can expand the text or distort its meaning.

Another injunction has to do with a believer's marriage to a non-believer. The prohibition in this regard is clear; Muslims are not to marry 'unbelieving women', nor give their women in marriage to 'unbelieving men'. (2:221) The point to be noted is that this revelation came at a time when pagans and other non-believers were making 'a laughing stock and jest' of the Prophet and his religion and trying to weaken the faith of his followers. Hence, any kind of close alliance with them was bound to prove harmful to the cause, especially in the prosecution of war. It was not so much discriminatory against non-Muslims as protective of newly converted Muslims. It is a moot point whether the prohibition was temporary or meant to be of a permanent nature. In regard to Jews and Christians, the prohibition was partially modified. Muslim males were permitted to marry Jewish and Christian women without obliging them to change their religion; this applied to all those who fell into the category of 'People of the Book'. The pagans were excluded because they had no book; but again this was confined to the idol worshippers of Mecca.

The resources at the disposal of the Prophet to administer the state were extremely limited. The Qur'ān mentions five: (1) The zakāt or tax on assets; (2) the ush`r or levy on harvest; (3) the khums or one-fifth of the spoils of war; (4) the jaziya or poll tax, levied on non-Muslims; and (5) the fay' or property captured without fighting a war. All the monies, chattels or properties collected under these heads had to be deposited in the Bait al-Māl, or the 'House of Property' to be used for the good of the public. The rate of taxation and the mode of collection were determined by the Prophet.

The zakāt literally means 'increase or augment' but refers to alms; it is of a compulsory nature. It is to be distinguished from sadaquat, which is alms given voluntarily. In both cases the objective is to ensure due reward from Allah. There are more than eighty references to the zakāt in the Qur'ān; they are mostly bracketed with ṣlāt or prayer. The emphasis is as much on being steadfast in prayer as on giving alms. Alms so collated are only for the poor and the needy, those who work for them and those whose hearts are reconciled, for ransoming captives, for paying the debts of debtors who cannot pay them, for the advancement of God's religion and for the wayfarer. The well-to-do are required to pay the zakāt in order to purify themselves thereby. The rich are asked to give it out of the good things that they have earned and 'what we have brought forth for you out of the earth', namely, the harvest. (2:26)

The Prophet made sure that the officers appointed to collect the zakāt were honest and god fearing. The zakāt was disbursed by him for the welfare of the poor, the construction of mosques and for providing maintenance to families which had suffered in wars. It was collected once a year and the rate was fixed at two and-a-half per cent of assets in hand. Hence, though the zakāt is euphemistically called alms, it was a well-regulated tax.

Ush`r or levy on the harvest is also a form of zakāt. There is a specific reference to it in the Qur'ān: 'And render the dues that are proper on the day that the harvest is gathered.' (6:141) It was levied at the rate of ten per cent of the agricultural produce on crops fed by rain and twenty per cent on crops raised by irrigation. Kharāj is a levy on the produce of agricultural lands belonging to non-Muslims.

There are many references in the Qur'ān to the khums, which means one-fifth of the spoils of war. Its distribution is provided for by the Qur'ān: 'When you have taken any booty, a fifth of it belongs to God and His Apostle, and to kindred and orphans, and to the poor and the wayfarer.' The Qur'ān also cautions that it should not be given to those 'among you who are rich'. (59:8)

As regards the jaziya the Prophet, it must be noted, did not obtain much, as his mission was to convert non-believers and not to penalize them; it was invariably levied as a last resort and as a measure to make non-believers taxable, as they were exempt from the taxes levied on believers.

The fay' deals with property and assets captured from enemies without fighting a war against them. It also receives its sanction from the Qur'ān.

The Prophet's administration of justice came under three heads: (1) Crimes, (2) Civil wrongs or dealings, and (3) Personal and family disputes. The majority of the cases were disposed of by the Prophet personally. He also appointed judges, whose character and integrity were irreproachable, and whose piety and intellectual honesty were unimpeachable. His son-in-law, Ali, who became the fourth caliph, was appointed the judge at Yemen. Ali was specifically told by the Prophet that when two persons came to him for judgement he should not decide the case in favour of the first one unless he heard the other.

Among crimes, murder is mentioned in several Qur'ānic verses. There is also reference to retaliation: 'The free for the free, the slave for the slave, the female for the female.' (2:173) Also the admonition: 'Nor take life—which God has made sacred—except for a just cause.' (17:35). No specific punishment for murder is prescribed, but a general rule is stated: 'A life for a life, an eye for an eye and a nose for a nose, and a ear for a ear, and a tooth for a tooth.' (5:49). The punishment could be waived by payment of money to the next of kin; it is in fact recommended: 'But whoso remitteth it as alms, shall have therein the expiation of his sin.' (5:49) This measure was resorted to by the Prophet in order to curb the spirit of vengefulness among the Arabs, who took pride in taking revenge against those guilty of homicide. Unintentional murder was more leniently dealt with. The Qur'ān prescribes: 'And whoever kills a believer by mistake should free a believing slave and pay compensation to the family of the deceased unless they remit it freely.' (4:94) All Islamic theologians are agreed that the Prophet never inflicted the death penalty on anyone accused of causing accidental death; this sort of crime was dealt with by the payment of blood money to the family of the deceased.

There is only one verse in the Qur'ān about theft: 'As to the thief, male or female, cut off his or her hands. A punishment by way of example from God for their crime.' (5:41) There is immediately there- after a proviso for pardon: 'But if the thief repents after his crime, and amends his conduct, God turneth to him in forgiveness for God is oft-forgiving, most merciful.' (5:42) According to some traditions, the Prophet was harsh towards thieves and cut off their hands; some cases of pardon are also cited. We should look at the harsh justice meted out to thieves from a historical standpoint. As E.H. Palmer, in the intro-duction to his English translation of the Qur'ān points out: 'An Arab looked on work or agriculture as beneath his dignity and thought that he had a prescriptive right to the property of those who condescended to such mean offices. Muhammad had to curb this tendency ruthlessly, hence the Qur'ānic prescription.'

Allied with theft is the crime of al-Hiraba or armed robbery. It also includes treason. The verse relevant to it is broad-based: 'The punish-ment of those who wage war against Allah and His Apostle and strive with might and main to spread mischief through the land is: execution or crucifixion or the cutting off of the hands and feet from opposite sides or exile from the land.' (5:37) According to a tradition, the verse was revealed to the Prophet when he was faced with the question of punishing some persons belonging to Ukul, a neighbouring tribe, who came to Madina pretending to want to become Muslims. When they complained of being in poor health, the Prophet sent them to a health-ier spot to recuperate but there they killed the keeper and ran away with his cattle. They were caught and brought before the Prophet. He punished them by cutting off their hands and feet, exactly as the tribe of Ukul had done to the keeper. Likewise, the Prophet executed eight persons for treason on the ground of fasad fil Ardh, meaning mischief in the land.

In regard to adultery, the admonition is:

> The woman and the man
> Guilty of adultery or fornication,
> Flog each of them
> With a hundred stripes:
> Let not compassion move you
> In their case, in a matter
> Prescribed by God, if ye believe
> In God and the Last Day:
> And let a party
> of the Believers
> Witness their punishment. (24:2)

There is no mention of stoning people to death. On the contrary, it is implicit that punishment must not result in death because the verse that follows immediately, the one in which the punishment for adulterous behaviour is prescribed, is clear about it.

> Let no man guilty of
> Adultery or fornication marry
> Any, but a woman
> Similarly guilty, or an Unbeliever:
> Nor let any but such a man
> Or an Unbeliever
> Marry such a woman:
> To the Believers such a thing
> Is forbidden. (24:3)

However, according to Caliph Umar, there was a Qur'ānic verse which prescribed stoning to death which was later abrogated. Despite the abrogation, Umar insisted that the Prophet had ordered adulterers to be stoned to death. Hence, though not prescribed by the Qur'ān, a majority of purists uphold it as sunna or practice of the Prophet. This punishment can only be inflicted if four witnesses testify to the act, a proviso most unlikely to be met. The idea appears to be that the death penalty is to be awarded only if adultery is shamelessly committed in public. The interpretation of adultery by Saudi Arabian theologians to European jurists attending a conference in Jiddah on Muslim Doctrines and Human Rights in Islam is worth quoting: 'The primary condition, required by the verse, is the presence at the moment of the act of four witnesses, who can be trusted and have never been indicted.' They went on to add that this was because 'public order [had] been seriously offended'. Even in the present, if such an act was publicly performed, the theologians pointed out that 'passersby would take it upon themselves to lynch the performers'. They argued that there was not one case of adultery which had been brought by witnesses before the Prophet. He had, however, dealt with a case where the culprit, out of a spontaneous urge to confess and purify himself, came to him of his own accord and confessed to his crime. The Prophet turned away even after his confession, not once but thrice; however, the adulterer persisted and demanded to be punished. It was then that the Prophet ordered him to be stoned to death. The Saudi theologians declared, 'Fourteen centuries have elapsed since that most severe penalty was inflicted and we can strongly affirm that fourteen cases of stoning could hardly be numbered in all that time.'[10]

People making charges of adultery were to be punished if they could not substantiate their accusations. The relevant verse is explicit:

> And those who launch
> A charge against chaste women,
> And produce not four witnesses
> (To support their allegations),
> Flog them with eighty stripes;
> And reject their evidence
> Ever after; for such men
> Are wicked transgressors. (24:4)

For an apostate or murtadd, 'one who turns back', there is no punishment in the Qur'ân. According to one verse: 'O true believers, whoever of you apostatizeth from his religion, God will certainly bring other people to supply his place, whom He will love and who will love

Him, who shall be humble towards the believers, but severe to the unbelievers, they shall fight for the religion of God and shall not fear the obloquy of the detractor.' There are no recorded cases of the Prophet punishing those Muslims who reneged upon their faith. They were only warned that the wrath of Allah would fall upon them unless they had done so 'under compulsion' (16:106). Subsequent laws, which jurists formulated and some rulers applied, are not in consonance with Qur'ān or the sunna; they are a part of classical jurisprudence.

There are verses dealing with usury. First, we have to be clear what usury is. On this subject there is considerable difference of opinion. According to the Arab historian, Ibu Kathir, Caliph Umar was doubtful about the matter as the Prophet had not clarified the position. Allama Abdulla Yusuf Ali, the eminent exegesist, observes:

> Our ulamā, ancient and modern, have worked out a great body of literature on usury, based mainly on economic conditions as they existed at the rise of Islam. I agree with them on the main principles, but respectfully differ from them on the definition of usury. The definition I would accept would be: undue profit made, not in the way of legitimate trade, out of loans of gold and silver, and necessary articles of food, such as wheat, barley, dates and salt (according to the list mentioned by the Holy Apostle himself). My definition would include profiteering of all kinds, but exclude economic credit, the creature of modern banking and finance.[11]

There is also much debate about slavery, does Islam sanction its continuation? This issue has been explained by Prof. Fazlur Rahman:

> To insist on a literal implementation of the rules of the Qur'ān, shutting one's eyes to the social change that has occurred and that is so palpably occurring before our eyes, is tantamount to deliberately defeating its moral-social purposes and objectives. It is just as though, in view of the Qur'ānic emphasis on freeing slaves, one were to insist on preserving the institution of slavery so that one could earn merit in the sight of God by freeing slaves. Surely the whole tenor of the teaching of the Qur'ān is that there should be no slavery at all.[12]

These were the basic features of the model state which the Prophet established and which he administered according to injunctions and directives revealed to him by Allah from time to time.

Following from this it is obvious that the development of both religious and temporal authority within an Islamic state has to be viewed not only in the light of the primitive nature of Arab tribal society at the dawn of Islam but also in the unique character of the origin of the State as a handmaid of religion. Unlike Christianity and Judaism, which had suffered centuries of persecution before they acquired temporal power, Islam became, within less than a decade, the religion of the State. The mixing of religion and politics, therefore, was an accident of history in the case of Islam and influenced the course of its development; it was not a theological necessity as many ulamā have held.

3

Fitting into the Mould

The state founded by the Prophet was essentially a city-state; it had to work within its limitations. Nevertheless, it provided the basic structure on which his immediate successors—the first four 'rightly guided' caliphs, as they came to be known among the Muslims—built the Islamic empire, which in time embraced within its fold heterogeneous lands and varied races. The pattern of administration which emerged during the short period (632–661) immediately following the Prophet's death is accepted by the Sunnis, who form the overwhelming majority of Muslims, as a model, but the Shi'as, the main minority in Islam, not only have reservations about it but are extremely critical of the role of the first three successors and only acknowledge Ali as the true ruler. Obeying the injunctions of the Qur'ān and respecting the traditions laid down by the Prophet, each of these caliphs had to innovate a great deal in order to meet the changing demands and differing backgrounds of their subjects. In the process the shape of the State inevitably altered.

The Prophet's death temporarily paralysed his followers; even his closest Companions were not prepared for this eventuality and, having lost their mentor, did not know how to handle the new faith as well as the new state he had bequeathed them. Every group, and within every group its respective leaders, had their own views on every administrative aspect. It was not so much the religious but the political implications that bothered them. The struggle for power erupted even before the Prophet's body was laid to rest. Four groups came to the fore. First, the original inhabitants of Madina, known as Anṣar or helpers. They claimed pre-eminence on the ground that they had given refuge to the Prophet and helped him to complete his mission. Second, the Muhajirun, or immigrants from Mecca, and the first to accept Islam. Most of them belonged to Quraish, the Prophet's tribe, and included stalwarts like his two fathers-in-law, Abu Bakr and Umar. Third, the descendants of the Prophet's family, Banu Hashim, led by his son-in-law, Ali. Lastly, there were the not-so-conspicuous Umayyads, who represented the Meccan aristocracy headed by that inveterate enemy of the Prophet, Abu Sufyan, who was one of the last to convert to Islam. He was related to another son-in-law of the Prophet, Uthman, whose wife did not survive the Prophet. This group did not lay claim to succession but secretly played one group against the other with a view to safeguarding its own future.[1]

The Ansars took the initiative. Their leaders met in a hall known as Saqifa or Hall of Bani Saidah, to elect a successor. Abu Bakr and Umar rushed to the scene. A heated discussion ensued between the two groups. Finally, Umar, by force of his personality, managed to get Abu Bakr accepted by general consensus. Other contenders gave in because Abu Bakr was the seniormost of the Companions! He was also a Quraishi and had, during the Prophet's illness, deputized for him in leading the prayers. Ali and his supporters knew nothing about this meeting; no one bothered to let them know. When they came to know of the decision, Ali's wife, Fatima, the only surviving daughter of the Prophet, was very upset. She believed that the right to succeed the Prophet legitimately belonged to her husband; hence their group came to be known as Ashab al-nass Walkavn or the 'Legitimate'. It included the Prophet's uncle, Abbas, and some Companions. Their claim was based on several verses in the Qur'an, one in particular which referred to Ahl al-Bait, the family of the Prophet (33:33), as also on a passage in the Prophet's address to some of his followers at the wada' or the farewell pilgrimage undertaken a few months before his death. It read, 'He who loves me will choose Ali for a maula. May God be with them, who protects him and forsakes those who are his enemies.' The Sunnis and Shi'as differ on the meaning of the word maula. The Sunnis maintain that it means 'friend'; the Shi'as, that it means 'ruler'.

The struggle for power, initially political, took a religious turn with Banu Hashim supporting Ali on the ground that, being the nearest of the Prophet's kin, his succession had divine sanction as in the case of Moses or Aaron, or Abraham and his progeny. The Qur'an testifies to this (4:54). Abū Bakr and Umar contested this claim and relied on the tribal custom of choosing the chief by consensus. Ali's supporters were adamant. They refused to be reconciled to Abū Bakr's succession. As long as Fatima was alive, she organized secret meetings against the recognition of Abū Bakr. Umar grew so infuriated with her intriguing that he once went to Fātima, and said, 'O daughter of the Prophet, I swear by God, that we love you best of all, but if your house continues any longer to be a rendezvous for conspiring men, then I will set fire to it.'[2] Ali's supporters contended that it was nothing but an exhibition of conflict between power and faith, in which power had succeeded in usurping faith. To quote Allamah Sayyid Muhammad Husayn Tabatabbai, a leading Iranian scholar of Shī'ism:

> Ali, in order to safeguard the well-being of Islam and of the Muslims, and also because of lack of sufficient political and military power, did not endeavour to begin an uprising against the existing political order, which would have been of a bloody nature. Yet those who protested against the established Caliphate refused to surrender to the majority on certain questions of faith and continued to hold that the succession to the Prophet and religious authority belonged to Ali by right. They believed that all spiritual and religious matters should be reserved to him and invited people to become his followers.[3]

The majority—as we have seen—came to be known as the Sunnis and the minority, the Shi'as.

Abū Bakr's succession, though apparently by consensus, was by no means unanimous. There were two strong groups opposed to it, the Anṣars and the Alids. They contended that it did not follow any laid down principle; nor was it based on any recognized procedure. An attempt was made to arrive at a consensus at a meeting at the Saqifah, but it was a hurried affair and did not have the support of all sections. Apart from Ali, many other prominent Companions, such as Abbās, Zubayr, Salman, Abū Dharr, Miqdad and Ammar were kept in the dark about it and only came to hear about it much later. It was further alleged that even those present at the meeting were browbeaten by Umar to toe the line. Umar admitted as much in a subsequent address to the people. He said that his intervention had saved Islam from disintegration; in retrospect, it was probably essential for the preservation of the community.

It is not known who proposed the word khalifah (caliph) for the successor of the Prophet. According to one report it was Abū Bakr himself who assumed the title of Khalifat al-Rasul al-Allah, 'the Caliph of the Messenger of God'. Some theologians trace the use of the word khalifah to the Qur'ān. It occurs in several verses, including the one which refers to Adam as khalifah or vice-regent of God on earth (2:30). It had, however, no religious significance. It has been defined by the celebrated Arab scholar and historian, al-Ṭabari (839–923) as 'one who takes the place of another after him in some matters'.[4] The Qur'ānic sanction to the selection of Abū Bakr and the other three caliphs who succeeded him is sought on the ground that all the four khulafā al-rāshidūn ('rightly guided' caliphs), were appointed to this high office after 'consultation'. This is not quite correct. Any 'consultation' was limited to a few Companions; and the manner of consultation and the mode of appointment differed in each case.

Abū Bakr ruled for only two-and-a-half years. Most of his time was spent in military operations conducted against Arab tribes, Muslim and pagan, which rebelled against his authority, some by proclaiming their leaders as prophets and others by refusing to pay the zakāt. After restoring peace at home, Abū Bakr turned to waging wars beyond Arabia. He was a gifted military commander and was able to conquer several neighbouring territories and consolidate Islam. His Caliphate has received the highest praise from Orientalists. According to Sir William Muir, 'His regime was short but after Muhammad himself there is no one to whom the faith is more beholden.'[5] H.G. Wells' observation is more graphic: 'There can be little doubt that if Muhammad was the mind and imagination of primitive Islam, Abū Bakr was its conscience and its will. Throughout their life together it was Muhammad who said the thing but it was Abū Bakr who believed the thing.'[6]

What was Abū Bakr's contribution to Islamic polity? Foremost was his unflinching adherence to the concept of equality of all believers, irrespective of their tribe or standing. He did not allow any barriers to be created between the ruler and the ruled. The rule of law was applicable to all, he said, no one was above it, not even the caliph. He translated this into action by refusing to give more out of the Bait al-Māl to those who had been among the first converts to Islam and therefore claimed a special status. He favoured equality in the distribution of spoils of war and taxes and levies collected. He maintained that those who embraced Islam first would be rewarded by Allah on the Day of Judgement. But in this world their share was equal, he proclaimed. On assuming office he told the gathering:

> Behold me, charged with the cares of the government. I am not the best among you. I need all your advice and help. If I do well, support me; if I make a mistake, counsel me. To tell to a person commissioned to rule, is faithful allegiance; to conceal it, is treason. In my eyes, the powerful and the weak are alike; I wish to render justice to both. As long as I obey God and the Prophet, obey me; if I neglect the laws of God and the Prophet, I have no right to your obedience.[7]

Secondly, he made no compromise on the question of payment of the zakāt by the faithful. He maintained that a state could not function without taxation; to remit a tax under threat of force would paralyse the administration. Thirdly, he was scrupulous in the utilization of state revenues. They were meant for the welfare of the people and not for any particular group of individuals, however elevated. He denied himself any share of the Bait al-Māl for his own maintenance and continued to earn his living as a tradesman. It was only after Umar and the other Companions had convinced him that he should accept a certain sum from the public treasury for his own and his family's expenses, as he was devoting all his time to affairs of State, that he reluctantly agreed. Lastly, he emphasized the humanistic aspects of Islam. Even while fighting an enemy, these values were to be adhered to. He admonished Osama, the commander of the Arab forces, on the eve of his expedition to Syria: 'See that you avoid treachery. Depart not in any wise from the right. You shall mutilate none, neither will you kill child or aged man, nor any woman. Injure not the date-palm, neither burn it with fire, and cut not down any tree wherein is food for man or beast. Slay not the flocks or herds of camels, saving them for needful sustenance'. He also warned the commander that 'if the monks with shaven heads submit do not molest them.'[8]

On his death-bed, Abū Bakr nominated Umar as his successor. Some of the leading Companions whom he consulted accepted his choice, but others did not. Ṭalḥa opposed it bitterly, saying that Umar was ruthless 'and would rule with an iron hand. Abū Bakr ignored his plea. He had confidence in the correctness of his choice. Hence, while in the selection of the first caliph there was some kind of consultation, in that of the second it was an act of pure and simple nomination followed by popular acclaim. The supporters of Ali assailed it as usurpation on the ground that there had been no agreement about it among the Companions, and that popular acceptance had been stage-managed by Abū Bakr. Although Umar's selection was not based on any principle or rule, no one can now dispute the fact that his Caliphate was extremely beneficial for Islam.

Like Abū Bakr, Umar propagated Islam with great vigour. By the end of his nearly ten-year-long tenure as caliph, Islam's dominions were extended to Iraq, Syria, Egypt and Persia. The capture of Jerusalem was the high watermark of his achievements. The conquered people, being much more sophisticated and cultured than their Arab conquerors, created many problems of management. Although alien in every respect to the Arabs, their conversion to Islam made them one brotherhood. Never before had a nascent state been faced with such a complex situation where racial distinctions were sought to be suddenly eliminated and the subjugated treated not as aliens but as members of the ruling community. It was only the genius of Umar which enabled the dilemma to be resolved. The decisions he took in this regard had a far-reaching effect and totally transformed the character of the Islamic polity. Umar realized that he could not make the victorious Arab and the vanquished non-Arab equal immediately and so proceeded to demolish the barriers between the two gradually.

To strengthen his administration, he constituted the office of amir (governor) and chose able, energetic and good men to administer the provinces. He impressed upon them the need to continue the Byzantine and Sassanid systems and not to attempt any radical changes. Imitation was no vice if it better served the interests of the people, he told the amirs. To maintain links with the centre, he appointed an amil (agent) in each province to function as its watchdog and directly report to the caliph on the actions of the amirs. From Madina, he kept a vigilant eye on the Quraish, lest their ambitions tempt them to adventurism. He did not permit them to leave the city or engage in factionalism. Some of the leading Companions had restrictions placed on their movements lest they intrigued and conspired against the State. His hold on the people was so great that none dared oppose him. With a firm hand he introduced reforms to restructure the Caliphate and make it responsive to the needs of the times. Although he respected conventions and traditions, if these did not meet his requirements he had no compunction in replacing or modifying them. Some jurists have criticized his innovations as not being in consonance with the Qur'ān or the hadīth. But no one has questioned Umar's commitment to the ideals of Islam or his zeal in spreading the message of the Qur'ān farther and wider than any other Muslim ruler. Whatever privileges he conferred on the Arab Muslims were for their military services and administrative functions. Neo-Muslims were treated as mawali or clients of Arab officers and functionaries and given full protection. Umar allowed no discrimination against them; in fact, he was indulgent towards them. Arabs and neo-Muslims stood beside each other in public prayers, as indeed did masters and their slaves. This helped greatly to foster a sense of brotherhood among the faithful. Moreover, non-Arabs paid the same taxes as the Arabs. The Qur'ān preaches unity among Muslims and the Prophet devoted his life to putting it into practice. Umar refused, therefore, to give any preferential treatment to Arabs over non-Arabs; this was seen in his disbursement of pensions and grants from the Bait al-Māl.

After the conquests of Iraq, Syria and Egypt, Umar was faced with the problem of distributing the lands belonging to the conquered people. According to the Qur'ān, after the khums or one-fifth of the spoils of war was taken for the Bait al-Māl, the remaining land was to be distributed among Arab soldiers. But the Arabs were no cultivators and hence he did not encourage the grant of conquered lands to them, for fear of reduced yields. Umar decreed that these lands be retained by the owners and cultivators, provided they paid the kharāj or land tax. Conquered lands were regarded as public property which their former owners could cultivate but not sell. After the conquest of Iraq, when the commander, Sa'd, asked Umar whether he should distribute the appropriated land amongst his soldiers, Umar made it clear that 'lands and canals' were to be regarded as State property, because if they were distributed amongst non-cultivating soldiers nothing would be left 'for the coming generation'. [9] He said the same to Amr bin al-'As, his commander in Egypt, and refuted the charge that he was depriving the soldiers of rights granted to them by the Qur'ān. He explained that these lands had 'to be left with their tillers' for meeting the expenses of 'the army, children of Muslims, and the coming generations'. He added, 'You have seen big cities; to protect them a regularly paid army is necessary, and if I distribute the lands, how will they be paid?' [10] He was so strict in the enforcement of these rules that when a Companion bought some land on the banks of the Euphrates, Umar summoned him and asked, 'From whom did you buy it?' He replied, 'From the owners.' Pointing to the people who had gathered round him, Umar said, 'They are the owners. Did you buy from them?' The Companion was dumbfounded. Umar then ordered the transaction to be cancelled. He went so far as to take away the land which the Prophet had granted to the first muezzin (the negro, Bilāl), who called the faithful to prayers, on the ground that he did not cultivate it. Umar also encouraged hima or collective land ownership and instituted State ownership in order to boost production. Once he confiscated a long tract of hima land when he found that it had not been properly cultivated. Under his system, the small peasant proprietor was the most favoured; he jealously protected his interests.

The Arabs were largely tradesmen. Umar reorganized both domestic and external trade to bring prosperity to his people. The Bedouins, who had lived off their camels and goats, and had regarded wheat-flour, dates, olives and fruits as luxuries, now started dealing in textiles and precious metals from neighbouring Iraq, Syria and Egypt. Umar warned them that indulgence in luxuries would sap their vitality and erode the spartan life-style which was the strength of Islam. He wanted them to preserve their moral fibre and showed, by his own example, how piety, simple living and dedicated service to the cause of Islam were important. He kept a watchful eye on business transactions and severely punished those who resorted to unfair practices and immoral activities.

Umar classified taxes under two heads. The first included those which were levied on Muslims such as the zakāt and the ush`r. The second type was applicable to non-Muslims, and included taxes such as the jaziya and the kharāj. Apart from these taxes, State revenues consisted of the spoils of war, confiscated lands and properties, mines, treasure troves and the estates of people who had died intestate or without leaving heirs. Taxes were collected by officers in both cash and kind.

There are two opinions about the institution of the diwān or treasury started by Umar. One group of jurists felt that it stabilized the fiscal system and helped to maintain a proper account of the wealth of the people, including the sums paid from the public exchequer to different groups. Unlike Abū Bakr, Umar classified the recipients. He permitted larger payments to the relatives of the Prophet, the Companions, army commanders and officers. Those who were later converts to Islam or performed less responsible tasks were put on lower pay-scales. This classification, according to another group of jurists, made the Arab elite lazy and indolent, and also led to economic disparities among the faithful. Before starting the diwān, Umar consulted the leading Companions; most of them expressed approval. Hakim b. Hazm alone objected. He told Umar that the Quraish were tradesmen; if they were given allowances, they would abandon their respective trades and would not work for a living. This in fact happened. As the Arab biographer Haikal, in his *Al-Faruq Umar*, a biography of the second caliph, observes,

> When the period of victories was over and the non-Arabs entered the Muslim governments, i.e., when the capital of Islam was shifted from Madina to Damascus and then from Damascus to Baghdad, the allowances of the people of the Arabian peninsula were totally stopped. The nation brought up in a climate of laziness and gaiety could neither turn to trade nor bear hardships to earn its livelihood. The result was that the hijāz became sterile and has never been able to regain its lost vitality.[11]

Though the Prophet instituted the Bait al-Māl, it was Umar who regularized its functions. Never before were the collections so large as during his time; never before was the need for their safe-keeping so great. A few years after Umar became caliph, Abū Hurairah, the governor of Bahrain, came to Madina bringing with him 500,000 dirhams as the kharāj. Umar did not know what to do with such a big sum. He called a meeting of the leading Companions and asked for advice. Ali suggested its immediate distribution; Uthmān opposed it. Others recommended a via media. Finally, it was decided that the money be deposited in the Bait al-Māl for the use of the State. Umar worked out a proper scheme for its management. He built a house of the exchequer and appointed Abd Allâh b. Irqam, a Companion, as its first treasurer. It was later turned into the central treasury, with sub-treasuries in the capitals of every province. The treasurer was given independent status and put in charge of both income and expenditure. His functions were clearly defined and he acted independently of the executive. Likewise, the sub-treasurer. Thus, the finances of the Caliphate were freed of executive control, a measure which gave stability to the State and ensured incorruptibility, as well as justice and fair dealing.

Umar normally took a liberal view in interpreting Qur'ânic injunctions. There were some matters in which his decisions were of questionable wisdom: as, for instance, when he sanctioned the legality of a divorce pronounced by a husband three times in one breath.[12] To this day this form of dissolution of marriage is known as ṭalāq al-bid'a or innovative divorce. In other respects, Umar was far ahead of his time. He had the courage to take unorthodox and unpopular decisions. When, drought-hit, a large part of the Caliphate took to stealing food, he suspended the punishment for theft prescribed by the Qur'ân. He held that a man compelled by hunger to commit petty theft should not be deprived of his hands. Likewise, he was lenient towards dhimmis or non-Muslims like Jews, Christians, and Magians who came in large numbers under his jurisdiction after the conquest of neighbouring countries. He guaranteed them security of life and property and equal justice. The so-called 'Covenant of Umar' prescribing discrimination against the non-Muslims was a fabrication of later times; it has been proved to be a forgery.[13]

Though authoritarian by nature, Umar had the sagacity to consult leading Companions on key issues. He often called them either singly or collectively for advice. They met him in the Prophet's mosque and conferred with him for hours. These constituted the shūrā (council) with some permanent members like Ali, Uthmān and Abdur Rahmān bin Awf. Occasionally Umar also called a larger Council of Tribal Chiefs to discuss broader policy issues and programmes involving the tribes and their participation in wars. He met all the governors and army commanders when they came for hajj and took stock of the affairs of the provinces and apprised them of the state of the Caliphate. Once he convened an international conference of high functionaries at Jabiya near Damascus to discuss administrative reforms he was contemplating. He sought their cooperation to implement them. He encouraged a frank exchange of views and consulted with his subordinates before embarking on new schemes. He quartered the soldiers away from towns so that their discipline might not be adversely affected by too close a contact with the citizenry; these quarters were known as cantonments and were equipped with facilities for military training as well as religious instruction.

Umar had a quick temper and was easily roused to anger; however, when his mistakes were pointed out, he listened patiently and made amends. Despite some shortcomings, he was a born leader of men, with an innate ability to command obedience and inspire loyalty. In a decade, he achieved for Islam what lesser men would not have been able to accomplish in a century. The state which he created reflected his empirical approach to the use of power to enlarge Islam's horizons. His sincerity and earnestness of purpose put him beyond reproach. All in all it was his powerful personality that made the Caliphate a spectacular success; every bit of it bore his stamp. His dynamism, courage and resourcefulness were responsible for containing internal dissensions as well as external dangers.

When he died the stability of the Caliphate was put to the test; there were too many claimants to it and in an attempt to forestall the chaos that he knew would follow his death, Umar brought the six leading Companions together and asked them to choose one among them as his successor. He made them promise not to appoint his son and to reach a consensual decision which should be made within three days of his demise. The six were Ali, Uthmān, Abdur Rahmān bin Awf, Sa'd b. Abi Waqqās, Talha and Zubayr. Of them, Abdur Rahmān was the only one to withdraw his claim. Talha was not in Madina at the time. The other four staked their claim to the Caliphate. A deadlock ensued. Finally, Abdur Rahmān was agreed upon as the sole arbiter. His was no easy task, but he patiently listened to everyone and consulted every important person, tribal chief and religious divine. After three days and nights of endless discussion, he went into seclusion to decide the issue. The next morning, after the prayers, in the presence of the congregation in the Mosque of the Prophet (Masjid al-Nabawi) in Madina, he asked Ali whether, if he were made the caliph, he would abide by two conditions: first, whether he would rule according to the Qur'ān and the sunna (the way of the Prophet), and, second, whether he would follow the precedents of the first two caliphs. Ali replied 'yes' to the first question; and 'no' to the second, saying that he would follow his own judgement. Abdur Rahman then called Uthman and put the same two questions to him. He said 'yes' to both. Thereupon, Abdur Rahman took Uthman by the hand and proclaimed him the new caliph and the congregation took the oath of allegiance to Uthman.

This was the third time that Ali had been passed over for caliph. He was deeply hurt and disappointed. His followers strongly resented the arbitrator's award in favour of Uthman. Later, when Uthman proved inept in handling a crisis that came about due to mismanagement, Abdur Rahman admitted that he had made the wrong choice. If he had succeeded Umar, the history of Islam would, indeed, have been different.

Uthman was more than seventy years old when he took over as caliph. He was a scion of the House of Umayyah which represented the aristocracy of Mecca headed by Abu Sufyan. In a sense, it was the rival of the House of Hashim to which the Prophet and Ali belonged. Uthman was partial to the members of his family. He appointed some of them governors and put others in important jobs. He was a wealthy man, well disposed towards the rich. He had no qualms about dipping into the Bait al-Mal to favour friends and supporters. His decisions were often arbitrary and contrary to the Qur'an. His moves were dictated by expediency. He refused to execute Abd Allah, the son of Umar, who, without any just provocation had killed Hurmuzan, a Persian slave, on suspicion of having instigated the murder of his father. When there was an uproar over his decision, Uthman extricated himself by paying blood money out of the Bait al-Mal. This was patently illegal. Many Companions resented this flagrant violation of Qur'anic injunction. Later, when the ring which the Prophet and the first two caliphs had worn (it bore the Prophet's insignia) slipped off his fingers and fell into a well, the faithful were convinced that Uthman had forfeited divine grace.

Uthman has been castigated by Arab historians; al-Tabari records a long list of his shortcomings. The Shi'as portray him as a heretic because of his affiliation to the House of Umayyah. But in retrospect, he appears to have been more sinned against than sinning. His nepotism can be explained by his desire to curb the growing independence of the amirs who were challenging the caliph's authority. He believed that by appointing relatives and friends as governors and commanders, he could exercise better control. Moreover, as the frontiers of the empire extended and consequently the treasury became enriched, Uthmān felt they could be indulged. He permitted the use of State revenues for providing them with gifts. This resulted in the more deserving being deprived of their pensions; soldiers were, in particular, denied rewards for valour in the field of battle. This naturally irked the army. Uthmān was also insensitive to matters of religion and unnecessarily offended the orthodox. After the codification of the text of the Qur'ān, which was his singular achievement, he ordered other copies of the holy book to be burnt. His motive was commendable; but the manner in which he did it outraged the sentiments of the Muslims. His detractors exploited this later to whip up religious frenzy against him.

Uthmān ruled for twelve years. His first six years were marked by victorious campaigns which enhanced the glory of Islam. The second six years were characterized by internecine squabbles and rebellions. Uthmān did not have Umar's strength of character nor was his treatment of his opponents just and fair. Once he reproached them after the Friday prayers, saying: 'You blame me for things you bore cheerfully from Umar. He trampled on you, beat you with his whip and abused you. And you took it patiently from him, both in what you liked and what you disliked. I have been gentle with you, bended my back unto you; withheld my tongue from reviling and my hand from smiting you. And now you rise up against me.'[14] He forgot that it was his nepotism which had brought about the crisis. Umar was strict and stern but impartial; Uthmān was kind and soft but partial. Moreover, he lacked Umar's ability and courage. Faced with revolt Uthmān lost his nerve and desperately attempted to conciliate his detractors. He promised to change governors and abrogate disputed measures but he could not contain the growing resentment. More and more people, some from far-off Egypt and other provinces, came to Madīna, determined to oust him. He fought his enemies and argued that whàt God had given him no man could take away. His critics brushed aside his defence and said that he had forfeited God's trust. He was finally killed brutally by a coterie that numbered among its supporters many leading Companions including the Prophet's wife, A'isha. Her brother, Muhammad, played a leading part in the assassination.

His murder sparked off a series of civil wars in the nascent state. Arab families with tribal affiliations squared off against each other; each talked of saving the faith; but they were more interested in personal gains. Issues were feverishly debated but they became more confused and complicated as tension grew. The faithful were split into several sects; these in turn gave birth to various schools of thought; the Qur'ān and the hadīth were freely quoted to buttress the theories aired. In the end the faithful were divided between the Shī'as and the Sunnis: a divide which has remained unbridged to this day.

Ali, who had waited impatiently in the wings, was now catapulted into the centre of the action and almost forced to take charge of the besieged Caliphate. Earlier he had been eager to be the caliph but this time he hesitated. He was not sure that he would be able to lead the faction-ridden state. Therefore, when he was offered the position he declined; but when most of the leading Companions, including his rivals, Ṭalḥa and Zubayr, urged him not to refuse and save the Caliphate from disintegration, he reluctantly agreed. But no sooner did he assume office than his detractors, prominent among them Uthmān's cousin, Mu'āwiya, the governor of Syria, revolted against his authority and accused him of complicity in the murder of his kinsman. Ali's rule, therefore, faced opposition from the moment it began. Though he attempted to be conciliatory and fair, his opponents were determined to create trouble and so he was forced to fight civil wars—first at Kufa in Iraq, where Ṭalḥa and Zubayr, led by Ā'isha, turned against him; then at Siffīn in Syria, where Mu'āwiya's forces encountered his supporters. Ali found little time to deal with the administration of the state. Lamenting his lot he said that initially Abū Bakr had exacted the Caliphate for himself while he knew full well that his position in it was like that of a pivot in a mill. He had let that challenge to his authority pass though there was a 'mote rankling in my eyes and a bone sticking in my throat on seeing my heritage being plundered'. When Abū Bakr had nominated Umar, he had again accepted 'the severity of the ordeal' and the fact that 'people were afflicted by God, with stumbling refractoriness, capriciousness and cross-purposes'.

Uthmān was entrusted with the office in a manner, which was 'unmentionable'. After his murder, Ali explained how the faithful had come to him saying they wanted to pay homage to him, but he declined, saying to the people, 'I do not want it. I pulled back my hand but you stretched it forth. I tried to snatch it away from you but you seized it. You said, "we will accept no other but you, and we would not have gathered together except around you". '[15]

And so, said Ali, he had given' in. But now, the same Talha and Zubayr, who had forced him to accept the office, had joined forces with his enemies. Even the Prophet's widow, 'Ā'isha, who had earlier rebelled against Uthmān, had taken up arms against him. He said he could understand Mu'āwiya's rebellion; he could have put that down, but being betrayed by his own relatives and friends was unbearable. In the end the unhappy Ali was killed by one of his own men, a Kharijite, who accused him of betraying the Qur'ān. As the famous Indian jurist, Amir Ali, remarks,

> Wild, beneficent and humane, ready to help the weak and distressed, his life had been devoted to the cause of Islam. Had he possessed the sternness of Umar's character he would have been more successful in governing an unruly race like the Arabs. But his forbearance and magnanimity were misunderstood and his humanity and love of truth was turned by his enemies to their own advantage.[16]

The Islamic state that evolved out of these developments was an odd and volatile entity. The original religious and political base of the model state founded by the Prophet remained, but the power struggle that followed changed its structure. During the reigns of the first two caliphs, territorial conquests and the conversion of large numbers of non-Arabs to Islam brought in their wake new problems of administration which required innovative solutions. The Qur'ān and the hadith were there to guide the rulers; but even these had to be re-interpreted to suit the developments. More than religious compulsions, political necessity largely shaped the cast of the state. Under the third and fourth caliphs, internal rivalry and dissension created different kinds of problems. Each ruler had his own solutions and this led to a further distortion of the model state.

In subsequent ages, when Islam spread across the continents of Asia, Africa and Europe, it was subject to further stresses and pulls. The end result of the historical process was a State beset by contradictions. In order to understand the nature of these contradictions and the turmoil within Islam it is necessary to fully understand the Islamic State as conceived by the Prophet; and then to co-relate it to the conflicts that developed between the votaries of religious orthodoxy and temporal authority.

The main feature of the model state was the Prophet's emphasis on the supremacy of God in the affairs of men; he regarded all creatures as equal but struggled to make them follow the right path. Hence his community or umma encompassed everyone and he made every effort to include those of other faiths in it.

A State, by definition, must be sovereign; but in Islam sovereignty vests in Allah. This is repeatedly emphasized by the Qur'ān and was reaffirmed by the Prophet by his words and deeds. This emphasis on a Qur'ānic code had its genesis in the work of the Prophet as the ruler of Madīna; a number of the revelations that came to him were in the nature of directives about affairs of state. He was scrupulous in carrying them out. They also helped him to decide many issues and to settle many disputes. It was thus that the relevant Qur'ānic verses and the traditions of the Prophet came to be regarded as the guiding principles of an Islamic state. After the death of the Prophet, the troubled succession to the Caliphate compelled each caliph to adopt many measures not mentioned in the Qur'ān or covered by the traditions. Each group began to rely on its own judgement to meet whatever situation arose, resorting to ingenious interpretations of the Qur'ānic texts by the jurists. The result of all this was confusion on a large scale.

No one rule or system was followed even in the selection of the caliph, as I have already explained earlier. However, there was one important constant—the community at Madīna had to approve the succession each time, which had subsequently to be ratified by the faithful in other parts of the Caliphate. So there was some kind of popular sanction for the selected leader of the faithful.

Another striking feature of the Islamic State during this period, which the fundamentalists describe as the 'golden era' of Islam, is the respect for the rule of law and independence of the judiciary. The Prophet had treated everyone—high and low, rich and poor—alike. He had also encouraged judicial independence. But during the rule of the 'rightly guided' caliphs, the approach, though similar, was subjected to all kinds of pressure. The first two caliphs were able to resist them; the other two were not. Uthmān succumbed to them; Ali fought them but failed.

As to the shūrā or consultation, as enjoined by the Qur'ān, none of the four caliphs held regular council meetings. The Prophet took the counsel of his leading Companions on important issues and sometimes changed his decisions in the light of his discussions with them. His successors were much more in need of such advisers, because they had neither the Prophet's uncanny attributes nor his divine insight. Nevertheless there was much less consultation than at the time of the Prophet. Abū Bakr's tenure was too short for him to evolve the counselling system. Moreover, he spent much of his time quelling rebellions at home and prosecuting wars abroad. Umar occasionally convened the shūrā of the leading Companions and conferred with tribal chiefs, army commanders and governors. But the final decision always rested with him. Only Uthmān was amenable to the views of others; but eventually this went against him. During the time of Ali, the community was divided and he was embroiled in almost continuous civil war. After his death, the divisions among the various groups tore the state asunder.

Of the four caliphs, Umar alone was able to organize the administrative set-up. He is rightly acknowledged as the architect of the Islamic State. No aspect of its functions escaped his attention. The consultative council, provincial autonomy, military organization, independent judiciary, land reforms, regulation of commerce and trade, supply of goods and services to the people, safeguarding of weights and measures, the institution of a fiscal system, or protection of the rights and interests of the non-Muslims—all these came under his care and were fondly nourished by him. He also struggled hard to prevent Arab warriors from becoming landowners and the land-hungry Quraish from acquiring big estates; this worked as a very effective brake on the emergence of a feudal order. Unfortunately, his successors did not carry it forward.

Uthmān was too weak to resist the richer classes; Ali too kindhearted to overpower them. As Dr S.A.Q. Husaini has observed, 'The attempt at levelling and equalizing failed; the brotherhood of all believers was jeopardized; racial differences, tribal distinction and even discrimination between the old and new converts entered the scheme of things.'[17] At the end of the rule of the 'rightly guided' caliphs, the Prophet's dream of ushering in a new era of equality and social justice remained unfulfilled; more important, its unfulfilment changed not only the character but also the concept of the Islamic polity.

4

Imperial Expansion

The fight between Ali and Mu'awiya which gradually assumed ideological overtones, soon became a fight between religion and politics. As we have seen, it began with the death of the Prophet, and grew more intense during the time of Uthman His assassination gave it a bloody turn which affected all sections of the Muslim community. Thereafter, it became more complicated and irreversible. Ali represented the best in Islam. Not only was he a close relative of the Prophet, but he also had great strength of character. He had made untold sacrifices in the cause of Islam. Mu'awiya, on the other hand, was one of the latest converts to Islam and his father, Abu Sufyan, had fought the Prophet till the very end. Mu'awiya's mother, Hind, had exhibited her hatred of the Prophet by eating the heart of his fallen uncle, Hamzah, in the battle of Uhud; their conversion, in the final analysis, was one of convenience and not of conviction. When the Prophet returned victorious to Mecca and proclaimed a general amnesty, Abu Sufyan, along with members of the House of Umayyah, took advantage of it. The Companions doubted their sincerity and told the Prophet that they should not be accepted within the fold. But the Prophet refused to be vengeful and forgave Abu Sufyan and his relations and friends and pacified the faithful by reminding them that only Allah knew what was in the heart of man. The distrust of the Umayyads ran so deep among the Prophet's followers that even Uthman, the Prophet's son-in-law, was viewed with suspicion because of his lineal connection with Abu Sufyan and the House of Umayyah.

Hence, when Mu'āwiya raised the banner of revolt against Ali, ostensibly to avenge the murder of Uthmān, it was in reality an attempt to assert the superiority of the Umayyads over the Hashimites—the former were taken to represent the temporal leadership, the latter the religious. In this struggle, the orthodox sided with Ali; but the pragmatists, expecting Mu'āwiya to win, supported him. Ali's assassination cleared the way for Mu'āwiya to take over the Caliphate. He was aware that the House of Hāshim enjoyed the religious support of the believers. He was naturally upset when, after Ali's death, his supporters chose his eldest son, Hasan, as the new caliph at Kufa. Mu'āwiya sensed trouble and began to intrigue against Hasan. Although more powerful, Mu'āwiya did not want to take Hasan on and preferred to spread dissent among his supporters. He tried to persuade Hasan to abdicate voluntarily in his favour. This, ostensibly to avoid further bloodshed and preserve the unity of Islam.

The correspondence between the two, though full of polemic, gives us a fair idea of their views. Hasan's letter to Mu'āwiya talked of the usurpation of the Caliphate by Abū Bakr, Umar and Uthmān and stated how 'the birthright of Ali was snatched away' by them, 'even though they were men of excellence, possessed virtues and merits and were the forerunners in Islam'. His family bore this patiently. 'But', wrote Hasan,

> now what a great astonishment and shock it is to see that you, O Mu'āwiya, are attempting to accede to a thing you do not deserve. You do not possess any known merit in religion (deen), nor have you any trace (athar) of Islam in you. On the contrary, you are the son of the leader of the opposition party, from among the parties hizb min al-ahzab [the reference is to the 'confederacy' which, under Mu'āwiya's father, Abū Sufyan, made the last united effort to crush the infant state of Madīna] and you are the son of the greatest enemy of the Prophet from among the Quraish.

Hasan asked Mu'āwiya to give up his 'persistence in falsehood (batil) and enter into my homage as other people have done, for you are certainly aware of the fact that I am far more entitled to the Caliphate than you in the eyes of God and all worthy people'.[1] Mu'āwiya's reply indicates, unsurprisingly, a totally different point of view. He wrote,

'When the community had some disagreements after the Prophet concerning the leadership, it was not ignorant of your family's merits and priority and still chose Abū Bakr.' The same was the situation now, he told Hasan:

> Had I believed that you had a better grasp over the subject people than I did and that you were in a stronger position to safeguard the lives and properties of the Muslims and in outwitting the enemy than I, I would have done what you have asked me to do. But I have had a long period of administration, and I am far more experienced. I have better understanding of politics and also I am much older than you.

He requested Hasan not to persist in his claim, adding finally, 'if you enter into obedience to me now, you will succeed to the Caliphate after me'.[2] Later events proved how hollow this assurance was, but unfortunately Hasan succumbed to it; more disastrously, Mu'āwiya's pitch, which gave priority to worldly experience and relegated religious considerations, was given theological sanction by many of the jurists of the time. As a consequence, instead of highlighting the religious qualities a leader should have, Sunni ulamā have ever since stressed worldly qualities such as military prowess, administrative expertise, political acumen, the capacity to expand the dominion of Islam and the ability to protect the lives and property of Muslims. The vast majority of Muslims being Sunnis, they opted for the temporal considerations because they found it more practical and expedient. The Shi'ites, on the other hand, preferred to describe the Caliphate as an Imamate as they felt the caliph's religious qualifications were the primary consideration. In the process, there emerged sharp theological differences between the Sunnis and the Shi'as as regards qualifications for leadership.

Because of the inherent weakness of his military position, Hasan abdicated in favour of Mu'āwiya who managed to win most of the faithful to his side. A master tactician, he used every device at his disposal: some of his enemies were cowed by threats, others by war and the rest by tact and diplomacy. There was no election, no selection, no nomination; his was plain and simple usurpation of power by force, which he managed to legitimize by obtaining popular approval through diverse and not always honest means and by the juristic and theological sanction of a large majority of the religious divines, whom he managed to either win or buy over. Also, the zeal and determination with which he ran the Caliphate brought him more and more support.

He embarked on the expansion of the Islamic empire, which had stagnated for almost a decade. He annexed Herat, Kabul and Bokhara in Central Asia; his troops pushed on past Khurasan into the valley of the Indus. His armies advanced westward across North Africa to the Atlantic Ocean. He built the first Arab fleet of·battleships and used them successfully against the Byzantines, in what came to be known as the 'Battle of the Plasts' in 655. This naval engagement opened the seas for subsequent Arab conquests.

Mu'āwiya's twenty-year rule also brought an era of peace and advancement to the Islamic state. He made Damascus his capital (in order to undermine the importance of Madina where many of the Companions still lived and pontificated on religious matters) and developed it into a flourishing market centre. He adopted the Byzantine model of administration and took the ablest persons, whether Muslim or non-Muslim, as administrators. He employed Christians and Jews to streamline the management of revenue and finance. He also held consultations with Arab tribal chiefs and recognized their special status; but there was no regular shūra, as he discouraged any challenge to his authority. The natives of conquered territories, including neo-Muslims, were treated well but were subject to the overlordship of the Arabs; this naturally caused resentment.

In the selection of governors his policy was to appoint the strongest among the Arab chieftains, irrespective of their past affiliations. He was ruthless in his dealings with religious groups whom he suspected of fomenting trouble. To Basra, where the Kharijites were up in arms, he sent as governor, Ziyād, an erstwhile lieutenant of Ali,' who was known for his strong-arm methods. The first thing Ziyād did on taking up his post was to warn the turbulent factions: 'Many heads do I see tottering; let each man see to it that his own remains on his shoulders.' This put a stop to dissident activity and peace was restored. Mu'awiya believed in being lenient towards vanquished opponents. He was generous towards his friends and charitable towards enemies. He was lavish in his gifts to all and used the Bait al-Māl as if it was his personal property. When criticized he is reported to have replied that was worse than gifts as it cost much more. He laid no claim to any kind of religious leadership, but expressed pride in being a Muslim. The orthodox despised him for his opposition to the family of the Prophet and never accepted him as caliph. To them, he was a malik (king), who had destroyed the institution of the Caliphate. In place of religious ties, Mu'āwiya revived tribal bonds, and relied more on tribal chiefs than religious leaders. The result was that religion was sidetracked and political considerations given preference in affairs of state. Although Mu'āwiya cultivated Arab chieftains and remained wary of theologians, he did not give in to the tribal custom of selecting the chief (al-Sayyid) from among themselves. Nor did he follow the republican model of succession. Instead he chose the Byzantinian and Sassanid practice of dynastic succession and took pains to justify it. He considered the mulk or kingdom, with its fixed rule of primogeniture, to be far superior to the loose pattern of the Caliphate, which, he felt, had only led to disorder, dissension and disunity. So long as Hasan lived, Mu'āwiya not carry out his wish of appointing his eldest son, Yazid, as the successor because he had promised the Caliphate to Hasan.

Hasan died prematurely at forty; most Arab historians believe that he was poisoned by Mu'āwiya, who bribed one of Hasan's wives to do the deed. No sooner was Hasan laid to rest than Mu'āwiya began to plan Yazid's succession. He manoeuvred to get the acceptance of most of his governors and other leading temporal and religious leaders.

He was then eighty years old and well satisfied with the way things had gone; his empire extended from Arabia to Sind in the east, from Bokhara in Central Asia to the Berber territories in North Africa and further west to Spain. His writ ran everywhere in the Caliphate and, though his governors enjoyed quasi-independent powers and amassed enormous wealth, not one of them would have thought of revolting against the caliph. The one thorn in his side was the intransigence of the Companions who, despite his best efforts, remained opposed to him. He sought to countermand the impact of their opposition by patronizing poets who extolled his greatness and singers who praised him. He often remarked that people were more influenced by poetry than by piety. His policy was clear, as he himself explained once: 'I apply not my lash where my tongue suffices, nor my sword where my whip is enough. And if there be one hair binding me to my fellow-men, I let it not break. If they pull, I loosen and if they loosen, I pull.'[3] It was this policy, characterized by later Arab historians as

'Mu'āwiya's hair', which helped him in his fight against the orthodox; they could frighten the faithful about the consequences in the next world, but he gave them enough in this world to satisfy their appetite. Mu'āwiya showed a marked preference for the Arabs in his empire whom, unlike Umar, he allowed to own cultivable lands outside Arabia. They acquired large estates and made sizeable fortunes. These landowners then became the backbone of his empire. At the same time he did not neglect the neo-Muslims and sometimes gave them important positions; but they remained the maula or clients of the Arabs. He was also generous to the non-Muslims. He had no compunction in appointing Christians and Jews to high offices, provided he was assured of their loyalty.

His chief secretary was a Syrian Christian. His revenue and financial advisers were Jews and Christians; his favourite wife, Maysum, was a Yemenite Christian. In most respects Mu'āwiya played a significant part in the evolution of Islam, but his most decisive role was the manner in which he succeeded in separating religion from politics in the state he presided over. Prof. Syed Muhammad Zulquarnain Zaidi al-Huma of Government Degree College, Islamabad, who has done considerable research on Mu'āwiya, writes that the caliph had the unique distinction of having observed the Prophet at work and also functioned as a vital link with the 'rightly guided' Caliphate. He had therefore managed, despite heavy odds, to rise higher and higher in the government until he became the caliph; soon thereafter, he turned the Caliphate into a kingdom not by war but by diplomacy. 'Among Muslims he is the first king and the system of government that he formed proved to be so strong and stable that it has been prevalent in the Muslim world ever since. . . .He gave such a turn to the Islamic movement that he managed forever to separate religion from politics'.[4]

Yazid, who succeeded Mu'āwiya, was a weak ruler; he was contemptuous of friend and foe alike and made several enemies. A philanderer, he defied every tenet of the Islamic faith. His short rule was marked by an ugly exhibition of greed and misuse of power. He demanded allegiance from Ali's second and only surviving son, Husayn. When Husayn refused, Yazid began hostilities against him. In so doing he went against his father's advice to deal with Husayn gently, explaining that the latter commanded great love and respect because of his superior rights and close relationship to the Prophet.[5] Yazid did exactly the opposite. Instead of leaving Husayn alone, he had him and seventy members of his family and supporters massacred at Karbala. This single crime changed the entire course of Islamic history. It created an unbridgeable gulf between the Shiites and the Umayyads and the Sunnis, despite the fact that the Sunnis themselves were horrified by the cruel desecration of al-Bait (the family of the Prophet). Although all Muslims now claim Husayn as their first and most important martyr, it was the Shiites who first lauded him in legend and elegy and made 'vengeance for Husayn' their battle cry. It became the most important part of their creed and the basis of their hatred for the Sunnis.[6]

After the massacre at Karbala, three major attacks in quick succession were launched against the Umayyads. The first was in Iraq by a group of Shiites describing themselves as 'the army of penitents' because they had failed in their duty of protecting members of the Prophet's family. Their leader was Mukhtar representing Muhammad, Ali's son, through a wife belonging to Banu Hanifah. Though Muhammad was not a direct descendant of the Prophet, his lineal connection with Ali served the immediate purpose of angering the supporters of Husayn; but the real fight was waged by Mukhtar whose revolutionary zeal and oratorial prowess successfully roused the Shiites to religious frenzy. He defeated the ruling Umayyad caliph, Abd al-Malik's forces, killed their commander Ubayd Allah, who was responsible for the massacre of Husayn and his family, and threw his severed head at the same spot where Husayn's had fallen. Thus was the blood of the grandson of the Prophet avenged. Mukhtar occupied Iraq and ruled it for eighteen months but within that short period, he was able to create a religious order which kept alive the anti-Umayyad feeling among neo-Muslims, particularly those of Persian origin. He became the symbol of a new religious awakening. His growing influence among the people not only alarmed the Umayyads but even other rebel leaders, notably Abd Allah bin al-Zubyr who, despite sharing Mukhtar's hostility towards Umayyads, became apprehensive of his growing popularity.

Like Mukhtar, Abd Allah had sworn to avenge the blood of Husayn; but his appeal was broad-based. He established himself in Hijaz as the 'Protector of the Holy House' and organized both the Shiites and the Sunnis against the Umayyads. Yazid sensed the danger to his throne and dispatched a strong force against him. A fierce battle was fought at Haurah near Madina where Abd Allah's troops were routed. Yazid's army marched on Mecca, besieged the city and set fire to the Ka'ba. Before they could capture Mecca, news of Yazid's sudden death was received and the Umayyad forces hurried back to Damascus. Abd Allah, utilizing this unexpected reprieve, reorganized his forces and reinforced his supporters in Iraq. A bloody encounter took place between his lieutenant Muhallab, who had the support of the Bedouins, and Mukhtar, who had the support of the neo-Muslims. Muhallab surrounded Mukhtar's army and gained a decisive victory; among the slain was Mukhtar. Thus ended the short tenure of one of the earliest revolutionaries in Islam. His emphasis on racial equality and uplift of the poor inspired subsequent generations and considerably influenced the growth and development of Shiism. He was the first to effectively challenge Arab domination in Islam and also proclaim the advent of the Mahdi, 'the hidden imam', who would return to earth to restore righteousness and eradicate evil from the earth.

Earlier, the caliph, Abd al-Malik had been defeated by Mukhtar; hence when hostilities broke out between Mukhtar and Abd Allah, Abd al-Malik preferred to wait and watch, hoping his rivals would destroy each other. Already the Kharijites were giving him no peace as they continued their vendetta against the Umayyads. Masters of the art of guerrilla warfare, and fundamentalists to the core, they tolerated no compromise and showed no mercy towards their enemies. They thrived on violence and killed in cold blood those whom they regarded as heretics. In their eyes, the Umayyads were as sinful as Abd Allah and his followers. They were able to capture Basra but Abd Allah's governor managed to defeat them. It was thus that Abd Allah came to power, triumphing over both his rivals, the one (the Shiites under Mukhtar) at Kufa and the other (the Kharijites) at Basra. Proclaimed caliph at Madina , he took over the guardianship of Hermain Sharif, the Ka'ba and the prophet's mosque. By his victories in Iraq, the key province of the Caliphate, his leadership was endowed with both temporal and religious legitimacy; he was acknowledged by the orthodox as well as the common people as the amir al mu'minin or the leader of the faithful.

Abd Allah's victories made Abd al-Malik conscious of the great danger he faced. Consequently, he concentrated on building up an army that could take on Abd Allah and to this end even accepted humiliating terms from the Byzantines and made peace with them; then he consolidated his position in Syria, where Abd Allāh had failed to provide a strong administration. With his greatly strengthened army, the caliph marched on Iraq. By diplomacy and intrigue he won over many of Abd Allāh's supporters and defeated his brother, Mus'ab, who was commanding the rival forces. Abd al-Malik personally supervised plans for the final assault. He chose as commander al-Hajjāj, a school teacher turned soldier, known to have little respect for religion or the law. Al-Hajjāj led his soldiers into Mecca and destroyed the city. Even the Ka'ba was not spared. Many of the Companions perished defending it. Abd Allāh fell in battle; his head was severed from his body, impaled on a spear, and taken round to be exhibited at Madīna and Damascus.

Thus ended the fiercest rebellion of the forces of religion against temporal power in Islam; it resulted in the death of thousands of Muslims on either side, including most of the Companions, the bombardment of Ka'ba and the desecration of the Prophet's mosque, from where he had ruled for more than a decade. As Amīr Ali remarked,

> The city which had sheltered the Prophet, and which was sanctified by his life and ministry, was desecrated; and the people who had stood by him in the hour of his need were subjected to revolting atrocities which find a parallel only in those committed by the soldiers of the Constable of France and the equally ferocious Lutherans at the sack of Rome. The public mosque was turned into a stable and the shrines were demolished for the sake of their ornaments. . . .The Umayyāds thus repaid the clemency and forebearance shown to them in the hour of Islam's triumph. Its men were either killed or fled to safety into distant countries.[7]

Having frustrated the religious challenge, Abd al-Malik, and after him, his four sons and a nephew, who between them ruled from 685 to 743, consolidated the hold of their dynasty in different parts of the Caliphate. By a series of conquests they extended their territories from the Pyrenees in the west to coastal Sind along the Arabian sea in the east and inland up to Multan and the borders of China on one side and Transoxiana on the other; they had also taken over most of that part of North Africa bordering on the Mediterranean right into Spain. This was the greatest expansion of the dominion of Islam and made the Caliphate the biggest power in the world—greater than the empire of Rome at its zenith. However, this vast expansion made the caliphs indifferent to their religious obligations; some of them even outraged the religious feelings of the faithful by their open defiance of the Qur'ānic texts and the concoction of false traditions. In addition to this, the Ummayad caliphs' style of living incensed the orthodox. They abandoned the austerity of the 'rightly guided' caliphs and adopted a life of ease and luxury. They patronized courtesans, indulged in wine, women, music and dance and thus mocked the spartan simplicity of life which Islam enjoined upon them. Some caliphs arrived drunk for prayer; others shocked the faithful by delivering Friday sermons from the pulpit while remaining seated instead of standing as was the established custom. In short, they paid scant respect to the precepts of Islam, though they proclaimed their pride in being Muslims and took full advantage of the prestige that Islam gave them and used it towards the temporal advancement of their dynasty.

Despite the worldliness of the Umayyad caliphs, the message of Islam, in particular its emphasis on egalitarianism and racial equality, produced a powerful impact on subjugated and downtrodden people everywhere. It elevated them from their inferior status under earlier rulers to at least a notional equality with the ruling classes and offered them a better and freer social existence. The Umayyads were not interested in conversion because it deprived them of the taxes, non-Muslims paid. Indeed some of them even tried to discourage missionary activity. Quite apart from the mercenary aspect of this stance, it must be said that the Umayyads were not religious zealots; their outlook was secular. Still, they were not disloyal to Islam; to them it was 'a badge of united Arabism'. They issued coins with Islamic inscriptions; they appointed judges to enforce the sharī'ah and promoted Islamic brotherhood.

After the death of Ali, the Caliphate was in a ramshackle state; they reorganized and streamlined its functioning. Under the 'rightly guided' Caliphate, which the Ummayyads inherited, there was only one proper department, called the dīwān, set up by Umar, which maintained records of the assets of Muslims, the amount of pension granted to different categories of believers and the salaries of officers and soldiers. The Umayyads divided it into: the Dīwān al-khātam, which maintained official correspondence and State documents; the Dīwān al-barīd, which organized the postal service by relays of horsemen; and the Dīwān alrasa'il, which worked as the secretariat and received orders directly from the caliph and oversaw their implementation. There was no principal officer like the vizir or prime minister; the kātib or chief secretary performed the duties of such a functionary. Most of these departments were run along Byzantine and Sassanid lines and were manned by non-Muslims. Christians or Jews of Greek, Coptic or Persian extraction were often favoured for these jobs. Later, Arabs were trained to take over these responsibilities but non-Arabs continued to be preferred, who soon became proficient in Arabic, which was made the official language in place of Latin or Persian. However, the Arab lordship remained intact, its hold was not diluted. Another Umayyad innovation was the introduction of Arabic coins with Qur'ānic verses in place of Greek and Persian coins; these were made standard currency.

There is no record of the Umayyads convening the shūrā or holding regular consultations with religious leaders, theologians and tribal chiefs. Mu'āwiya was an autocrat; his consultations with tribal chiefs, if any, were of a patronizing nature. He never convened the shūrā as he was loath to share responsibility. He recognized no one equal to him in wisdom or experience. His successors inherited these traits. They were intolerant of dissent, and even vindictive towards their opponents. They exacted obedience and patronized sycophants. They used the Bait al-Māl funds indiscriminately to favour their friends and relatives, manipulated grants of pensions and gave these to undeserving persons, and generally ignored the rules. The only exception among the Umayyads was Umar II, who tried to restore the sanctity of the Bait al-Māl by regularizing records and making payments according to the established rules.

The Umayyads continued the judicial system which had obtained under the 'rightly guided' caliphs; but while maintaining the distinction between the executive and the judiciary they did not encourage too much independence on the part of either. On the whole the caliphs did not directly interfere in cases except those in which they were personally interested. Judgements were usually based on Qur'ānic tenets and the sunna. With the exception of cases where the caliph desired a particular judgement and the qadi concocted a tradition or two to give a doctored verdict, the Umayyads followed the shari'ah. Moreover, laws had not yet been codified, with the result that there was more latitude in the awarding of punishments and penalties. Yazid who was responsible for the massacre at Karbala was not condemned even by the theologians opposed to him as a kāfir (a heretic) but only as a fāsiq (transgressor). Likewise, Walid II was forgiven despite the fact that he had torn the Qur'ān to pieces by shooting arrows into it.

Religious rites and practices were not tampered with by the Umayyads, though some of the caliphs paid scant respect to them. Public prayers were held regularly, old mosques were kept in good repair; new and more magnificent ones were built; zakāt, ush'r, kharāj and jaziya were collected in the same way as before, though their disbursement, as we have seen, was often whimsical, nepotistic and corrupt. Friday prayers were properly conducted and the caliph himself led them at the main mosque in Damascus. Elaborate arrangements were made for the hajj; special officers were appointed to look after the requirements of the pilgrims. All these had little to do with the Ummayad caliph's innate religiosity but were done to boost his image as defender of the faith.

The Umayyads were past masters in the art of the possible. They were pragmatists untroubled by the lofty ideals enshrined in the Qur'ān and the traditions. They chose their relatives as governors of provinces and ignored the claims of better qualified or more pious persons. They also allowed considerable freedom of action to their subordinates, including deputy governors and others, who enjoyed the right of appointment and dismissal of officers and disbursement of local funds. They were not only authorized to collect taxes and levies; they could also, if they thought it necessary, levy new ones and spend them freely on works of public utility such as roads, mosques, government buildings, canals, schools, hospitals, etc., and on maintaining the services, including the disbursement of pensions, and the salaries of the staff, the police and army personnel.

The Umayyads were, however, particular about keeping the financial administration separate from executive and political control—a measure introduced by Umar, but which Mu'āwiya strengthened, despite resistance from his governors. For instance, when he asked Amr bin al-'As to effect the separation, the crafty governor objected, saying it was not fair that he should hold the horn of the cow and someone else should milk it. Mu'āwiya persisted and by the end of his rule, such separation had been effected in every province, with the financial controller, called sahib al-kharāj, being directly responsible to the caliph. Nevertheless, the amirs continued to be powerful. They influenced the affairs of the

Caliphate and played a significant role in decision-making. True, the influence of an amir varied from province to province. The amir of Iraq, the key province, and those of Egypt and Spain had far more power than the others. They were chosen by the caliph from among his most trusted lieutenants. Some of them later became so powerful that they defied the caliph, with disastrous consequences to the Caliphate.

Under the 'rightly guided' caliphs there was no need of a standing army to fight in the cause of the faith because every war was a jihād, a war for righteousness in which death on the battlefield ensured a passport to heaven. Things changed under the Umayyads who began to rely more and more on professional soldiers. They paid them well, looked after their comforts, and gave them extra rewards for hazardous tasks and expeditions. For instance, Yazid tempted his soldiers with an extra allowance of 100 dinars—a substantial amount in those days—for participation in the assault on Mecca and Madina. He also paid handsome subsidies to tribal chiefs for supplying fighting men for such 'heretical' wars. According to the historian Mas'ūdi, the chief of the Qahtānite tribe was paid 2,00,000 dirhams for providing 20,000 soldiers every year. The Umayyads preferred Arabs to mawalis (non-Arabs) for whose services they paid much less and they could treat them indifferently. For example, Umar II found that 20,00,000 mawalis in active service had hardly received any wages. Immediately, he put them on the regular payroll. Every able-bodied Muslim was supposed to enrol in the army, but not all did so. When the need arose, the Umayyads ordered conscription. Being the guardian of Mecca and Madina, the caliph could compel tribal chiefs in Basra and Kufa to supply him with 20,000 men each before assuring them facilities to perform their pilgrimage. He used these men to re-enforce his army in Persia and for advancing in Khurasan. The Arab cavalry relied more on camels than on horses or mules, which were preferred by the Romans and Persians. The terrain was more suitable for camel transport; many historians have opined that it was the camel which 'won indeed the victories of Islam'.

Under the Umayyads, every soldier was put through vigorous training and was selected with great care. He was also equipped with the latest machines and catapults, designed specially for different expeditions. Armour and arms, consisting of swords, lances and shields were made of the highest quality of metal. The Umayyads were also skilled in the art of warfare. They used their infantry for defence and their cavalry for attack and when required combined the two with admirable success. Their soldiers were divided into squadrons and divisions and taught how to unite and combine when the occasion demanded it. They had perfected this strategy with the result that their armed forces won remarkable victories. For the welfare of the soldiers, special garrisons were set up; this innovation was first introduced by Umar; the Umayyads improved upon it by making what later came to be known as cantonments. After conquering new territories, an Umayyad commander chose a suitable place for stationing his army. These camps were provided with all kinds of facilities including mosques, markets, schools and hospitals. In time these were developed into prosperous towns: thus were born al-Kufah, al-Basarah, al-Fustat (the modern Cairo) and Qayrawān.

Another area where the Umayyads improved upon the past was in their treatment of the non-Muslims. They did not only guarantee them religious freedom and protection of civil rights but also appointed them to some of the highest places in government. In many respects they were more trusted than the Muslims. Key departments such as finance, taxation, commerce and trade were usually manned by either Jews or Christians. Even the royal physicians were, in several cases, non-Muslims; the caliphs, their governors and commanders appeared happier handing their lives to non-Muslims than Muslims. This attitude created considerable resentment among the fundamentalists, who took it as an affront to the Muslims. Umar II reversed the process and dismissed many Christians and Jews from high posts, saying that the Qur'ān had warned the faithful that they should not be friends with them. His successors reverted to the old practice and brought back a large number of non-Muslims to positions of trust and responsibility.

By the end of the first century of Hijrah (722), the Umayyads had taken Islam to the four corners of the earth. In their temporal zeal, they had achieved more for the faith, in terms of territorial conquests, than any other dynasty before them. Their achievements were mostly in worldly affairs—in the reformation of the structure of the state and the machinery of the government, the patronage of art and literature, especially poetry (Umar ibn-abi-Rabiah, known as 'the Ovid of Arabia', was the most sought after poet; whose poems were full of romantic adventures); the encouraging of music and dance, which were taboo in orthodox Islam, and the reorganization and strengthening of the army.

In the religious field, except for the contribution made by Imam Abū Hanīfa, one of the founders of the four Sunni schools of jurisprudence, there was little theological development. No doubt, some outstanding jurists, such as al-Hasan, al-Basri and Shihāb al-Zuhri, made their mark, but their impact on Islam was not of a lasting nature. Nor were they patronized by the Umayyads who were more interested in hiring theologians who would cover up their misdeeds by concocting traditions, than encouraging genuine learning or scholarship.

This state of affairs, unsurprisingly, alienated the pious. The activities of the rulers scandalized the orthodox and made them more and more resentful of the Umayyads, who had corrupted the outlook of a large number of their subjects. Despite the lip service most Ummayads paid to Islam it would not be incorrect to say that under them Islam as a religion suffered, though its glory spread to the far corners of the earth. Even Mecca and Madina, the two holiest Islamic cities, did not escape from their baneful influence. These citadels of piety and orthodoxy became centres of music and dance, poetry and romance. The Companions, theologians and scholars confined their activities to their own small circles of disciples, trying to keep the flame of the original faith burning. They remained helpless spectators to the excesses and impiety of the Ummayads. To the Shias, in particular, they were worse than heretics, who deserved to be put to death; to the Kharijites, their place was in hell; to the orthodox Sunnis, they were, at best, a necessary evil in view of the fact that no other alternative seemed possible. It is true though that the Ummayads' determination to be materialistic rather than religious gave an impetus to the pursuit of science, including medicine. Much of the Islamic medicine of the time drew heavily from Greek and Persian sources. Architecture flourished; some of the most magnificent mosques were built during the Umayyad rule, including Masjid al-Aqsa, or the Dome of the Rock, in Jerusalem. Mihrab, a niche in the front wall of the mosque, and the minaret are architectural masterpieces. In sum, the emphasis of the Umayyads was on worldly affairs and even in religious matters they were more moved by temporal grandeur than by spiritual bliss.

Despite all the resentment against their practices, such as disregarding tribal custom in regard to succession and insistence on dynastic rule, it cannot be denied that it was the Umayyads who extended the frontiers of Islam far and wide. They were not devout Muslims, but they looked after the interest of the ordinary Muslims. Their quarrel was only with the religious zealots who wanted to overthrow them, not with the faith which they embraced unreservedly.

However, it was their betrayal of the concept of Islamic brotherhood, irrespective of race or language, that brought them down. Interestingly, the revolt against them had its beginnings among the mawali, the non-Muslims, consisting notably of Persians, Egyptians and Berbers, who formed the vast majority of their subjects. The more humiliated and ill-treated they were, the more resentful they became of the Umayyads, who subjected them to all kinds of racial discrimination. They were socially ostracized; intermarriage between them and the Arabs was discouraged; they were given lowly positions in the government and the army; at some places, separate mosques were built for them. The mawali knew that all these actions went against the tenets of the Qur'ān and the sunna, which guaranteed them equality of status and opportunity. Gradually their resentment turned into religious revolt backed by the Shiites, the Kharijites and the neo-Muslims, who combined to fight what they saw as a danger to the future of Islam. Helped by the ineptitude of some of the later Umayyads, the rebels finally succeeded in overthrowing the dynasty. It was the first major triumph of religion over politics in the chequered annals of Islam; but it proved shortlived, as we shall see.

5

Power and Glory

The savagery with which Abū al-Abbās, a distant cousin of the Prophet, brought down the Umayyads shows the bitter animosity that existed between the two families. His supporters butchered the caliph and members of his family and proudly dubbed their leader al-Saffah, the blood-shedder. His subsequent conduct was in keeping with his blood-thirsty nature. Whatever illusions the faithful had about a relative of the Prophet bringing back the golden era of Madīna was soon dispelled. The collapse of the Umayyads also saw the end of the Arab domination of Islam. Non-Arabs, who had played a decisive role in bringing the Abbasids to power, now slowly gained in power; the new caliph acknowledged this by issuing a da'wa (proclamation) that no distinction was to be made between Arabs and non-Arabs in matters of service and State patronage. One of the immediate effects of this was that non-Arabs began playing a decisive role in the management of the Caliphate. To start with, the Abbasids respected the sentiments of the fundamentalists by discarding the luxurious style of living at the court and disbanding the secular apparatus of administration. This was welcomed by the ulamā and the common people. Efforts were made to turn the Caliphate into a theocracy so that the aberrations and innovations which had crept into the body politic could be done away with and an Islamic state, in its truest sense, could be established.[1]

The theologians of the time were agreed that an Islamic state had to have a republican character. They held the Umayyads guilty of violating this principle by turning the republic into a monarchy. The Abbasids agreed and assured their subjects that this would be implemented soon.

There was, however, no consensus over the means to bring this about and so the monarchical system continued. As time passed it became more entrenched. Any protests against this form of rule were silenced as more and more of the faithful, including the Shi'ites, who had been in the forefront of the revolt to bring the Abbasids to power, were satisfied that what really mattered was that the Caliphate had at last come back to the family of the Prophet. They did not support the idea of electing the caliph or even his being selected, by consensus, through the shūrā. Some Sunni theologians insisted but they were silenced with offices and gifts. The opposition to the principle of hereditary monarchy gradually died down and the faithful were content that at last the heretical House of Umayyah had been replaced by the pious House of Hāshim, to which the Prophet belonged. The early Abbasids were also masters in the art of public relations. They portrayed themselves as the true representatives of Islam. The first Abbasid caliph donned the burda or the cloak (which the Prophet had worn on ceremonial occasions) every Friday, while leading the public prayers. He showed his respect for the theologians by consulting them on important issues. He was punctilious in the performing of his daily prayers and the observance of the fast during Ramadān. He also made arrangements for the imparting of religious instruction in mosques and schools. The orthodox did not ask for more as it seemed to them that fundamentalism had triumphed over secularism even though the system of administration had not changed; the end was more important than the means. Unfortunately their newly acquired power went to the head of the Abbasids and the ruling elite once more became sybaritic; corruption and nepotism became rampant in the court. The caliph called himself the Shah-in-Shah, the King of Kings, on the Sassanid pattern. A magnificent new capital was built at Baghdad. The caliph was no longer one among the believers but came to be accepted as 'the shadow of God on earth'. Even the Umayyads had been content to describe themselves as no more than vice-regents of the Prophet; the Abbasids claimed a direct link with God.[2]

The ulamā were ill at ease in this atmosphere which was more regal than anything that had gone before. But they were powerless as the caliph increasingly became inaccessible to the people, surrounded as he was by sycophantic courtiers and other hangers-on who carried out his bidding without question. In order to impress the absoluteness of his power, he took his executioner wherever he went to mete out instant justice.

After the death of al-Saffah in 754, Mansūr, who succeeded him, ruthlessly put down all opposition, including that of the Shi'ites, his erstwhile allies. He acknowledged no obligation to anyone and wanted to be free of any restraints, religious or temporal. He made no distinction between friends, loyalists and upstart sycophants. One of his courtiers, Ibn al-Muqaffa', advised him against alienating the landed peasantry and instead suggested he win it over to avoid potential revolts and to strengthen his military base. Instead of heeding this sane advice, the caliph was so incensed that he had Ibn al-Muqaffa' beheaded. His principal advisor was an unscrupulous kātib (scribe) who became the grand vizir.

Despite these shortcomings, Mansūr was a shrewd ruler; he lavishly rewarded his supporters and ruthlessly suppressed his critics. Through the collection of taxes from merchants and craftsmen and octroi on caravan routes—none of which had any sanction under the shari'ah—he kept his treasury full. He maintained an elaborate network of spies and informers who kept him posted on intrigues and conspiracies. He also created a number of consumer and credit facilities, which helped trade to flourish. He understood the power of money. He chose Baghdad as his capital because it was the most important trading centre in the Caliphate, close to the Fertile Crescent (the region comprising Syria, Lebanon, Iraq, Palestine and Jordan) as well as on the trade route to the neighbouring Arab regions of the Gulf and Iran. The capital became the commercial and cultural centre of the empire and attracted people from distant parts of the world. Finally, his encouragement of mercantilism among his subjects had an interesting effect: people became more interested in making money than saying their prayers.[3]

However, Mansūr, like the other Abbasid rulers, never tired of proclaiming his loyalty to Islam, observing of religious rituals, and honouring of the theologians. He styled himself al-Mansūr, the victorious fighter for truth. His son and successor took the name of al-Mahdi, restorer of the faith. Al-Mahdi was succeeded by his son, followed by Harūn al-Rāshid. All these caliphs made it a point to lead the Friday prayers and, as the heirs of the Prophet, donned his cloak. But outside the mosques they displayed their wealth in as ostentatious a manner as they could, accumulating expensive carpets, rare paintings and the

finest jewellery. They also entertained their friends lavishly, with courtesans, dancing girls and wine-goblets doing the rounds at their ban-
quets. Poets were better patronized than the ulamā, singers and dancers
more sought after than men of learning. Their beneficiaries included the
musician Ibrahim al-Mawsili (d. 904), and the poet Abu Nuwas (d.
803), a notorious philanderer and composer of bawdy songs. Scholars
of divinity kept their distance from the court. There were some notable
exceptions. The most respected was Abu Yusuf whom Harūn al-Rāshid
appointed as his chief qadi. He was a disciple of Imam Abu Hanifah,
whose pronouncements and dissertations on theology became the basic
canons of Islamic jurisprudence. Sharī'ah studies were, no doubt, encouraged but more importance was given to medicine, mathematics and
astronomy. Ma'mūn set up the Bait al-Hikmah (the House of Wisdom)
as a centre of secular research and learning. During his rule there was a
noticeable increase of the Persian influence in affairs of state and in social life. Persian became the language of the cultured elite. Persian
titles were suitably adapted and conferred by the caliph on the deserving;
Persian poetry was all the rage at the court and Persian songs and
dances became more popular than Arabic ones. Having a Persian wife
or a mistress was regarded as proof of high status. This all-pervading
dominance of Persian made everything Arabic appear rustic and primitive. It robbed the people of the fierce egalitarianism of Arab tribal society and replaced it with the fawning sycophancy that was the hallmark
of the Persian aristocracy. The replacement of Arab Islam by Persian
Islam transformed the pattern of public and private life; it brought in
not only more refinement but also more cosmopolitanism.

In this process the star role was played by members of an Iranian
family, the Barmakids, who were Buddhist monks before they embraced
Islam. Its founder, Khālid ibn Barmak was a scribe (kātib) in the courts
of al-Saffah and al-Mansūr. After him his sons and grandsons continued
in the employment of successive caliphs and rose to high positions.
Mansūr created the post of vizir (minister) and appointed Khālid to it.
In course of time, the vizir became the chief executive and appointed
his relations to important administrative positions. Despite this nepotism, the appointees, being competent and experienced, brought a certain refinement and skill to statecraft. They encouraged Ahl al-Qalam
(people of the pen) and patronized art, particularly fashion-designers and
interior decorators who furnished mosques with elaborately ornamented

lamps and chandeliers. The increasing hold of the Barmakids on the administration roused jealousy and hostility against them; their enemies finally succeeded in poisoning the ears of Harūn who cast all the Barmakids into prison and abolished the post of vizir, denouncing it as a Persian innovation and an anti-Islamic institution.[4]

Harūn and his successors replaced the vizirs with an elite of favoured officials, temporal and religious. They were largely drawn from the Hashimites. Another group associated with them consisted of renowned poets, musicians, qadis, mullās and scholars. A third, larger one, comprised merchants and tradesmen. The sūq or the marketplace became a beehive of social activity in every large town. It was in these marketplaces that common people rubbed shoulders with aristocrats and men of learning. Another meeting ground was the mosque. Foreign influences—Persian, Indian, Syrian, Egyptian and Greek—permeated the atmosphere. The emphasis was on good living, not orthodox Islam.

The trouble with the Abbasid caliphs was that though they posed as the guardians of orthodoxy and piety, hardly any one of them practised what they preached. Again, most of them were not of pure Arab blood which made their upholding of Arab Islam (whatever of it they chose to maintain) more a matter of convenience than of conviction. Mansūr was born of a Persian slave, Ma'mūn of a Berber; Wāthiq and Muqtadir had Greek mothers, while Muntasir was the son of a Turkish maid. Their claim that they belonged to the House of Hāshim of the tribe of Quraish was only correct to the extent that their paternal ancestor, howsoever remote, was a Hashimite; but their blood had, in between, become so mixed and diluted by marriages with non-Arabs that they had become hybrid.

Like the Umayyads, the Abbasids retained the Caliphate within their close-knit family. As we have seen earlier, the founder, al-Saffah, chose his brother al-Mansūr as his successor, who, in his turn, nominated his son, al-Mahdi, who selected his son, who was succeeded by his brother, Harūn, better known as Harūn al-Rāshid. Sensing trouble between his sons, Amīn and Ma'mūn , Harūn divided the Caliphate between the two as if it were a family inheritance. The division did not prevent the brothers from fighting it out. The war ended with the slaying of Amīn. Ma'mūn had also to contend with his uncle, Ibrāhim. It was only after Ibrāhim's death that Ma'mūn acquired full control of the Caliphate which he passed on to his brother, al-Mu'tasim, who was succeeded by his son, al-Wāthiq , the last of the Abbasid caliphs. Their rule lasted about 250 years (750–991).

What is important to remember is that all through this long period, unlike the Umayyads, every Abbasid caliph tried to assume supreme authority in both temporal and religious matters. They had their advisers, both temporal and religious, but none could circumscribe their orders: neither the ulamā nor the vizirs nor the amirs. The vizir looked after the administration; the amir, the provinces; the qadi, the judiciary and the hājib (the chamberlain), foreign affairs. Of them, the most important was the grand vizir or prime minister. This situation lasted so long as the caliph had the backing of the army. No sooner did the army become powerful, than the caliphs were reduced to the position of puppets. Until the time of Muqtadir (908–32) the vizir was the most powerful of all state functionaries; thereafter the amir-al-umarā' (commander-in-chief) played the decisive role. Earlier the vizir supervised the administrative set-up and presided over meetings of the Council of Advisers who were in charge of the different departments but accountable to him; of these the most important units were the Diwān al-kharāj, the Bureau of Taxes and the Bait al-Māl or the Department of Finance. This was the Sassanian pattern, in which the ulamā had no say.

Taxes were revised, as ordained in the Qur'ān, but their system of collection and disbursement varied from caliph to caliph. Like the Umayyads, the Abbasids also used these collections for the grant of personal favours or even for the buying of allegiance of important tribal leaders. In order to maintain their grip over finances the Abbasids also set up the Diwan-al-zimam or the Bureau of Audit to keep watch on income and expenditure. Their Diwan-al-nazar fi al-mazalim, or the Board for Public Grievances, kept the caliphs informed of the treatment their subjects received at the hands of officials. They also maintained a regular police force under the Diwan al-shurtah whose chief was designated the sahib al-shurtah and ranked next to the vizir. The muntaṣib or the inspector of markets and morals checked weights and measures as well as the morals of the people. Mawardi gives a list of his functions which included the checking of indulgence in alcohol, gambling, injury, illicit sexual relations and improper behaviour in public. From all this it is evident that the Abbasid public administration was as strict in enforcing secular regulations as religious laws.

The administration was divided for administrative convenience into twenty-four provinces each under an amir. Due to the far-flung nature of the empire and slow means of communication, the governors tended to assume more and more power and often acted as independent potentates paying allegiance to their sovereign. The unity of the Caliphate was maintained by force rather than through religious edicts. This policy later proved to be disastrous to the caliphs, for the governors, who paid their troops out of funds at their disposal instead of from the central exchequer, slowly succeeded in making their armies loyal to them instead of the Caliphate. In course of time each amir became a potential threat to the caliph and many succeeded in founding their own kingdoms.

Like the Umayyads, the Abbasids also showed considerable tolerance towards their non-Muslim subjects. With the abatement of religious fervour, privileges were conferred on many of them at the pleasure of the caliph. Although the ruling class was dominated by tribal chiefs, it was not unusual for Christians and Jews to be given high positions. Even Zoroastrians, Manichaeans, Buddhists and Hindus were favoured. In some respects, they were preferred to Muslims, particularly in the areas of revenue and finance. The Arab historian, Maqdisi, reported that most money-changers and bankers were Jews, while most officers and professionals at the middle and low levels were Christians. Likewise many women enjoyed special privileges and had an independent status of their own. Though they could not move about as freely as the men and had to observe certain norms of seclusion, they were able to achieve distinction in several fields, including literature, the arts and even the administration. Khayzurän, the wife of Mahdi, had enormous influence at the court as did Zubayda, the wife of Harün. Many women acquired renown for their poetical compositions and some were sought after because of their musical accomplishments. The most famous of them was Ubaydah al-Tunburiah, who became a favourite with the ruling elite. The ulamä disapproved of their activities on the ground that Islam encouraged neither poetry nor music nor the free movement of women, but the caliphs paid little attention to their protests.[5]

Gambling and drinking were common among the upper strata of society though they are described in the Qur'ān as 'acts of Satan'. No one was punished for indulging in liquor; the favourite drink was khamr, distilled from dates. According to Ibn Khaldūn, Caliphs Rashīd and

Ma'mūn preferred nabideh, made from grapes, raisins and dates.The chief qadi, Abu Yusuf, held that if the brew was not more than three days old its consumption was permissible; such was the liberalization of the rules of the sharī'ah done to suit the needs of the rulers and their courtiers.

Several Arab chronicles testify that the use of alcohol was common and was often openly indulged in by princes, viziers, judges, soldiers, artists, singers and poets. Abu Nuwas extolled its virtues in song, Ibn al-Mu'tazz showered praises on it in prose. Christians and Jews ran taverns for Muslim dignitaries and did a thriving business in illicit liquor. There were houses of gambling in big towns, including Mecca and Madîna. Favourite pastimes were chess (shaṭranj)) and backgammon (nard). For lovers of outdoor sports, there was horse racing and polo (jukan) played for high stakes. The Prophet had decried the display of wealth; but the Abbasids, more than the Umayyads, ignored this precept. They wore gold, diamonds, rubies, emeralds and other precious stones. They also preferred poetry, music and dance to theological pursuits.

The Abbasids encouraged a variety of intellectual pursuits. Medicine advanced greatly in their time. Despite the objections raised by the ulamā, doctors took to dissecting dead bodies to study human anatomy. The author of the oldest ten-volume treatise on ophthalmology was a Muslim, Hunayn Ibn-Ishaq. The Bakhtishur family produced many eminent physicians (hākims) starting with their founder, Jibril Ibn-Bakhtishur, who was the court physician successively to Harūn and his son Ma'mūn. Advances were also made in the use of drugs. The father of Arabic alchemy, Jabir Ibn-Hayyān, wrote his famous pharmacopoeia in 766.

Râzi (865–929) and Ibn-Sinā (980–1027) penned their famous dissertations during this period. Ibn Sinā was an eminent philosopher, who along with Kindi (801–73) and Fârâbi (870–950), mingled reason with revelation and broadened the scope of religion by harmonizing Greek philosophy with Islamic ideology. Fârâbi was influenced by Plato's *Republic* and Aristotle's *Politics*.

There also emerged during this period a group known as Ikhwān al-Safā (Brethren of Sincerity) who met regularly to question religious tenets. Though the group had limited influence, its meetings were attended, among others, by Abu'l Alā al-Ma'arri (d. 1057), who was denounced as an arch-heretic. Even Imam Ghazāli is said to have appreciated the epistles issued by the Ikhwān.

The famed al-Biruni (973–1050) flourished under the Abbasids. He travelled widely and was impressed by Hindu mystics during his sojourn in India. The Muslim contribution to astronomy is well-known and this science was greatly patronized by the Abbasids. Even astrology—frowned upon by the orthodox—for instance, the prognostications of Ma'shar (d. 886), known also as Albumasar, flourished and was even 'exported' to Europe. Another luminary of the time was the mathematician Muhammad Ibn-Mūsā (780–850), author of the oldest work on arithmetic. Muslims made notable contributions in the fields of chemistry and physical sciences, the greatest being the use of objective experimentation to test the veracity of facts. The achievements of Jabir Ibn-Hayyān (Geber) were outstanding and constituted, until the eighteenth century, the foundation of modern chemistry. The name of the anthropologist and free thinker, Abu Uthman Amr ibn-Bahr al-Jabir, (d. 869) is ranked amongst the most distinguished pioneers of this discipline. He was a radical theologian, whose books are still read for the elegance of his Arabic prose.

Despite the fact that theology received little patronage from the caliphs, it managed to produce many distinguished scholars including imams, jurists and scholars during the Abbasid period; the hunger for knowledge of all aspects of Islam had greatly increased and there was a constant clamour for more. The result was the founding of the four schools of jurisprudence by the four great imams, Abu Hanifa (d. 767), Mālik ibn Anas (715–95), Shāfi'i (767–820) and Hanbal (780–855) and the systematic compilation of the hadith by the six scholar-jurists, Bukhari (d. 870), Muslim (d. 875), Dāwūd (d. 888), Tirmidhi (d. 892), Ibn-Mājah (d. 886) and al-Nasai (d. 915). Of them, the sahih (or authentic) works of Bukhari and Muslim acquired a pre-eminence next only to that of the Qur'ān. These compilations along with the four schools helped significantly in the regularizing and systematizing of the practices and rituals of Islam. Each one of these schools, aided by the works of hadith compiled by Bukhari, Muslim and others, was instrumental in its own way in rescuing Islam from opportunistic accretions that had gathered on it and in reshaping it into a pattern that would withstand the vicissitudes of the times. Many of the imams suffered hardships; none of them received support from the State.

Nevertheless the intellectual environment all around and the hunger for knowledge inspired their works, which supplemented the guidance provided by the Qur'ān and gave to the faithful the necessary rules and regulations for the conduct of day-to-day affairs. In the process, they also curbed to some extent the unlimited use of State power by the caliphs and their coteries; they could not escape the moral pressure of religious edicts.

One of the Abbasid caliphs, Ma'mūn, encouraged free thinking among the faithful and patronized the Mu'tazilla, who were the pioneers in this field; he did not like the rigidity of the dogmas the ulamā propagated. He commended those with a rationalist and liberal outlook: unfortunately some groups, foremost among them the Mu'tazilla, in their enthusiasm to spread their creed, persecuted those who disagreed with them. The orthodox belief has been that the Qur'ān existed from the beginning with creation, being co-eternal with God. The Mu'tazilla, on the contrary, insisted that the Qur'ān was created by God, and, therefore, could be altered. They also emphasized that man was a free agent and must think for himself as against the orthodox view which maintained that all his actions were destined by God. Because of the backing of the caliph, many theologians meekly submitted to the Mu'tazillite doctrine; but there were some who refused.[6] Imam Hanbal was one of them. Ma'mūn flogged and imprisoned him. He set up a regular court—the first of its kind in Islam—to try dissenters. Every officer and judge had to adhere to the Mu'tazillite doctrine or lose his job. Those who protested were severely punished and some were even executed. Never before had there been such an inquisition in the history of Islam. Ma'mūn 's policy was followed by his successors until the time of Mutawakkil, who, due to mounting opposition from the ulamā and sustained resentment from his subjects, abandoned the inquisition.

The credit for this to a great extent must go to the teachings of Abu'l Hasan Ali al-Ashari (d. 935), who used the same process of free thinking to demolish the Mu'tazillite doctrine and show how the anti-dogmatists had become the worst perpetrators of inflexibility and rigidity. He founded a new school known as kalām or scholastic theology. He reconciled Islamic tenets with Greek thought and Christian beliefs and showed their universality. He was able to free orthodoxy of many shackles. Ghazāli , who is regarded as the 'father of the church in Islam', was much influenced by Ashari; even Thomas Aquinas and

Pascal came under his spell. Unfortunately, while Christianity broadened its approach under Protestantism, Islam remained glued to the same apparatus which Ashari had created and under its impact became impervious to the changes which took place subsequently. This was unfortunate. Likewise, the emergence of the four juristic schools and the codification of the traditions of the Prophet were significant developments which should have been used to streamline and enlarge the scope and depth of Islamic learning and theological understanding. On the contrary these were used to develop rigid adherence to rituals and rules which stultified the free flow of knowledge and hampered independent thinking. 'Enough of ijtihād', proclaimed the mullās, what Islam needed was taqlīd or imitation. The cry caught the imagination of the faithful who were tired of the confusion and contradiction in the religious laws, to which they had been subjected in the past. Even to this day Islam has not been able to get out of the stranglehold of taqlīd which has thwarted free thought and made reconciliation with the needs of the times more difficult. As a result, both the State and religion have been weakened and Muslim society has become stagnant. Liberalism and rationalistic tendencies have been curbed. More tragically, this attitude has divided the world of Islam into various schools of theologians feuding with one another. Territorial affiliations have taken precedence over religious loyalties and the ties of Islamic brotherhood, never strong in practice, have weakened Islam' due to power politics and internecine warfare.

6

The Decline of the Caliphate

Long before the Mongols sacked Baghdad in 1258, the rule of the Abbasids was subjected to a series of internal rebellions; the first eruption took place soon after the dynasty came to power when the young Abd al-Rahman, escaping the wholesale massacre of his fellow kinsmen, the Umayyads, fled to Spain with his supporters and founded an independent kingdom at Cordova, which, in course of time, rivalled the Abbasid empire. It lasted for more than seven centuries. The Moors, as they were called, never accepted the legitimacy of the Baghdad Caliphate and regarded their own kingdom as superior in terms of culture and civilization to that of the Abbasids. Their ulamā were emphatic in declaring the Moors as the true successors of the Prophet and defenders of the faith, and painted the Abbasids as usurpers. The rivalry between them expressed itself both in terms of politics and religion (which found expression in a spate of propagandist literature brought out by either side). The Abbasids and the Moors remained sworn enemies; they carried their past into their future.

Like Abd al-Rahman, Idris Ibn-Abdullah, a great-grandson of the Prophet's grandson, Hasan, also fled to Morocco, organized a revolt there against the Abbasids and established the first Shi'ite dynasty. An even more important development was the rise of the Fatimids, who in 909 founded a rival Caliphate in Tunisia. This was later shifted to Egypt. Then there was the emergence of Ibrahim b. al-Aghlab who, as a governor of the Abbasid caliph Harūn, assumed authority in al-Qayrwan in Africa Minor and set up his own independent kingdom. He passed it on to his sons who became a force in the struggle for power between Asia and Africa. Before the Fatimids, the short-lived Tulunid dynasty in Egypt and Syria (868–905) had also created another separate sovereign state in the valley of the Nile. Most of these states severed connections with Baghdad and became independent. Their individual ulamā accorded them the same legitimacy as their more respected counterparts did to the Abbasids. The common people were bewildered by the conflicting theological verdicts in different regions and reconciled themselves to the view that Islam enjoined upon them loyalty to whichever person actually ruled over them. The ulamā were mainly concerned with the implementation of the sharī'ah and so long as the ruler abided by it, they did not question his legitimacy. Consequently these rulers managed to obtain the necessary religious sanction. When they were ousted by others, the ulamā adopted the same attitude towards their successors and legitimized them.

In the West most of the sultans were Arab; in the East they were mainly of Turkish or Persian descent. The one-eyed Tāhir Ibn al-Husayn, a trusted general of Abbasid Caliph Ma'mūn, founded his dynasty in Khurasan. It was overrun by the Saffarids, whose founder al-Saffar, a coppersmith, spread his conquests to the borders of Persia and India. Another tribe, the Samanids, wrested Khurasan from the Saffarids, who ruled in Transoxiana with Bukhara as their capital. They also built Samarqand as a rival centre of art and learning to Baghdad. Then came the Ghaznavids who broke away from the Samanids to found their own dynasty in Afghanistan from where they invaded India; they were followed by the Ghoris and other invaders, who established their respective kingdoms in north India.

The Abbasid caliph, Mu'tasim (833–942), managed to check the growth of these independent kingdoms and to curb their power by raising an elite band of soldiers known as the Turkish Bodyguards. This army was utilized to suppress rebellious amirs. Some were overthrown; others were disciplined. The Turkish Bodyguards, who at first acted as a praetorian force, soon acquired political clout and became so powerful that they had it in their power to make and unmake caliphs, holding them prisoners, and even ridiculing some in public.

The situation changed after the death of Mutawakkil. The resistance to the Turks grew; the Berbers, led by the Shī'ite Buwayhids, overthrew them only to be overthrown a century later by another Turkish tribe, known as the Seljuqs. The Seljuqs were also from Central Asia but, being better organized, were able to check the decline of the Caliphate. They retained its form and glory but usurped actual power. As new converts they showed greater zeal for the faith and its hallowed institutions. They extended their authority over the whole of West Asia and restored the majesty of the caliph over the heartlands of Islam. Inevitably, the caliph became increasingly dependent on them; in reality they ruled in the name of the caliph. It was a unique combination under which a military group, exercising real control, acknowledged the nominal suzerainty of the caliph so as to conform to Islamic traditions.

The genius behind this arrangement was Nizām al-Mulk Ṭūsi who was the prime minister of the Seljuq Turks and the architect of the restoration and consolidation of Muslim power. He gave Islam a new dynamism by introducing realpolitik in its administration. Needless to say, the ulama did not approve of his views but there was little they could do about it. Ṭūsi's treatises, *Siyāsāt-Namah* (*Book of Politics*), and *Dustur al-Wuzara'* (*Document of Ministers*) are monumental contributions to the art of government. Unlike Western political theorists, Ṭūsi wrote about practical administrative problems in the light of personal experience. As the prime minister to the Seljuq kings he wielded enormous power and patronage. He was, it is said, 'A monarch in all but name'. In enunciating his principles, Ṭūsi combined Islamic tenets with the time-honoured practices and traditions of the kings of Persia and Central Asia. He evolved broad-based policies, which, while being faithful to the spirit of Islam, met the secular requirements of the time. He used ingenious arguments to justify hereditary kingship and avoided any reference to election or selection by explaining that 'God the Almighty selects someone from among men and gives over to him the charge of the well-being of the world and the comfort and tranquillity of the human race after duly furnishing him with the arts of government.'[1]

He wrote that a ruler was duty-bound to be just and fair to all his subjects and quoted the Qur'an and the hadith to support his viewpoint. He laid stress on the impartial dispensation of justice and issued Instruments of Instruction to all judges. Justice, he said, must know no fear or favour and should be independent of executive interference. Judges should be well-paid and not subject to government control. The executive should also consist of men of character, well versed in worldly affairs. He gave the highest priority to merit in the selection of officials. To quote his words, 'The wise have said that a worthy servant and an able slave rank superior even to one's own sons.'[2] He was against the employment of women in government service; they were, according to him, unsuited for politics and administration. Ṭūsī had very clear views on the security of the State. While advocating the necessity of accrediting foreign ambassadors, he warned rulers to keep a close watch on their activities. He wrote:

> We must remember that the real object of foreign envoys is not only that they should convey messages from their governments, but, if we were to look deeply into their purpose, secret information like the exact position and condition of roads, paths, valleys, canals and tanks; whether or not they are fit for the passage of troops and whether fodder is available anywhere near them. They also seek to know something about the ruler of the country, the exact state of the army and its equipments; the feelings of the soldiers as well as of the common people; and all about the wealth of the subjects and the comparative populations of different districts. They try to penetrate into the working of the government of the country and to know whether the ministers are honest or dishonest and whether the generals are experienced or not.[3]

It was more a secular than a religious exposition of the duties and responsibilities of a government.

In his *Document of Ministers*, Ṭūsī elaborated on the functions of rulers and advised them to pay special attention to 'men of the sword, without whom no throne could be stable and to men of the pen without whom no government could be run'. Despite his secular approach, Ṭusi was a devout Muslim, regular in his prayers. He fasted during Ramadan and observed the tenets and the rituals of his religion. He stood more for the spirit than the letter of the shari'ah, more for the inner core than the outer robe of religion. He abhorred fanaticism and encouraged humanism.

Ṭūsi was an assimilator who wanted Islam to advance with the times and to absorb in it whatever was good from every available source. He studied Hellenic and Persian histories and tried to incorporate the more positive aspects of their administrative systems into the Islamic system. He believed in the universal brotherhood of man which Islam propagated by breaking barriers of race and region. He invited Ghazāli, who was then in his twenties, to Baghdad and appointed him as the chief canonist. It was under the patronage of Ṭūsi that the foundation of Ghazali's thoughts, which later rejuvenated Islam, were laid. The future imam had learnt much from his mentor, al-Jwami of Hejaz, who also was persuaded by Tusi to come to Baghdad and preside over the famous Nizamia College, which soon rivalled al-Azhar, founded by the Fatimids as the centre of Islamic learning.

As a result of Ṭūsi's open-mindedness and pragmatism he earned the displeasure of religious bigots who regarded him as a heretic. Ultimately, it was an assassin belonging to the suicide squad of Hasan-i-Sabbāh (d. 1124) who gunned him down. Ṭūsi's death was a severe setback to the growth of liberalism in Islam as well as to the authority of the Seljuqs, who were soon plunged into a series of civil wars which doomed their rule.

After the assassination of Ṭūsi, Ghazāli, his disciple, left Baghdad heartbroken and wandered through Egypt and Syria, visited Mecca and Madina, and finally settled at Tūs, where he wrote his magnum opus: *The Revival of the Sciences of Religion*. The work was compiled at a time when Christian Europe was torn between the forces of the emperor and the pope. Although there was no such conflict in Islam, it had its own problems created by various theological schisms which threatened its very foundations. Like Ṭūsi, Ghazali also dreaded the disintegration of Islam and worked towards accommodating divergent views, whether held by orthodox theologians or the liberal ṣufis. He had a creative mind, opposed to dogmatism of any kind; within the broad framework of Sunni Islam he tried to bring about a harmonious mixture of spiritualism and materialism. He laid equal emphasis on a good life in this world and a secure future in the next. He insisted that while a ruler should be God-fearing and righteous, he should, at the same time, be tolerant and not bigoted; he should be absolutely neutral in his relations with his subjects irrespective of creed or race and pay equal regard to everyone, high or low, nobleman or slave; he should be ruthless in suppressing lawlessness and injustice. He cited the example of the great Sassanian vizir Buzurchimik, who gained the confidence of good people by becoming the nemesis of the wicked. He narrated the story of Alexander the Great, who believed that 'the secret of good government lies in the ruler's rising above his personal likes and dislikes. He should not decide without taking proper counsel, nor should he be influenced in his judgement by any other consideration except the truth.'[4] Ghazali's ideal was the Prophet, who fed his cattle, tied his camel, swept his home, milked his goat, sewed his shoes, patched his clothes and still found time to look after the needs of his people. He also drew inspiration from the first four caliphs: Abu Bakr, who was honest to the core; Umar, who defended the right against the wrong, Uthman, who was bountiful as well as modest; and Ali, who was the embodiment of faith and sacrifice. Ghazali emphasized that the sheet anchor of a Muslim ruler should be his virtues and not his power or wealth; on virtues alone, he declared, a true Islamic state could be built. He approved of kingship and tried to reconcile it with the canons of equality preached by Islam. He said that any kind of rule was better than no rule; order was always preferable to chaos. The full impact of his teachings, which gave a new impetus to the consolidation of Sunni Islam, was not felt immediately. But, in course of time, it revolutionized every aspect of the faith. He is, therefore, rightly regarded as one of the greatest builders of the Islamic community.

While Ghazali was disseminating his principles, forces both inside and outside the Muslim world were working towards the disintegration of the central authority. The Caliphate reeled under the attacks of the barbaric Mongols from the East and Christian Crusaders in the West. Even in this crisis, the Muslims failed to come together as one people. They had lost the old spirit which had once animated them to unite against the enemies of Islam. It was left to unknown warriors like Nuruddin of Syria and later Salahuddin (better known as Saladin) of Egypt, both common soldiers, to rouse the Muslims, bring them under the banner of the Crescent and to hurl back the Crusaders. The name of Saladin became a terror in Europe. He freed Palestine, which housed the third holiest shrine of Islam, the Mosque of Omar, from the clutches of the Christians. He destroyed the Shi'ite Fatimids in Egypt, who had degenerated beyond redemption because of rampant corruption and internecine warfare. He gave back to the Abbasids the sole authority, however nominal, which belonged to them as caliphs. He ensured that henceforth their position as the supreme rulers would not be challenged by local chieftains. It was thus that the Abbasid Caliphate regained its old status.

A brief account of the happenings before the advent of Saladin shows the turmoil through which Islam had to pass. There was no unity of purpose and action among the different Muslim rulers, no coherence in their approach, no adherence to any set of rules or principles. Many of them paid little respect to the values the Prophet had preached. There was no coordination between the secular and the religious orders, between rulers and theologians. Some rulers applied the shari'ah in their day-to-day dealings, but were lax in enforcing its various provisions; others used it to advance their personal interest. The Abbasids who came to power as the saviours of Islam left it in shambles. Other races tried to restore its sullied image; but, in the process, they also succumbed to worldly temptations. (And yet, it is a tribute to Islam that in less than fifty years after the sack of Baghdad, out of its wreckage arose three mighty empires: the Ottomans, the Mughals and the Safavids. The first two were Sunnite, the last, Shiite.)

Religiously, too, the interregnum was chaotic; innumerable sects rose among the Muslims. There were violent skirmishes between the Hanafis and the Hanbalis. Although the Hanafis continued to predominate in the Muslim world, and were more liberal in their outlook, the Hanbalis gained the support of the rabble. The Shafi'ies who came to prominence a little later remained confined to intellectual circles. The Shi'ites, though in a minority, were better organized and more fanatical. They refused to make common cause with the Sunnis, especially the Hanbalis, whom they despised. Each sect had its own sphere of influence. Religious Islam was as disunited as political Islam. Even jurists and scholars paid homage to conflicting power groups, causing more and more confusion. There were a few notable exceptions, such as Mas'udi and Zamakhshri, Kindi and Farabi. Their historical and philosophical treatises were a welcome change from the self-serving papers that were written during this period.

However, all that happened to Islam was not bad. The theological supremacy of the Mu'tazillites, though harmful in some respects, as explained earlier, was also of considerable value, especially because of their pioneering work in the furtherance of rationalist thought in Islam. It helped in the emergence of the 'Brothers of Purity' or Ikhwan al-Safa, who indoctrinated the petty rulers and their theological cohorts. The Ikhwan, surprisingly enough, received support from the self-indulgent rich, who were dissatisfied with the ruling clique, as well as from the ignorant poor, who were suppressed by it. The orthodox could easily whip up religious fervour to safeguard their interests. The Ikhwan advocated a rational understanding of the teachings of Islam. Their leader Zahid, who had his headquarters at Basra, opened branches all over the Caliphate. His followers met secretly to discuss religious and secular problems and find solutions which conformed to the spirit of Islam. The catholicity of their outlook was remarkable. In the conflict between orthodoxy and liberalism they always tended to be liberal. They thus helped considerably in the exhuming of Islam from the morass of theological mumbo-jumbo it had sunk into. All this took place at a time when Europe was still in intellectual darkness.

By the end of the thirteenth century, Islam was invigorated. The seventh of the Il-Khans, the successor of the dreaded Halagu, embraced Islam, and declared it the State religion of his realm. Likewise, while Halagu had destroyed many historic monuments of Islam and wiped out the traces of its once flourishing civilization, his great-grandson, Ghazan, who also became a Muslim, devoted all his energies to rebuilding them and restoring Islamic civilization to its old grandeur. The later Il-Khans also met the Crusaders in battle and threw them out of the heartlands of Islam. Later their kinsmen, the Ottoman Turks, burst on the world like a colossus and extended Islam's domains over new territories; they succeeded in establishing one of the most powerful empires in Islam and ruled from the fourteenth to the nineteenth centuries.

The Turks being non-Arabs were denied the aura and legitimacy of the Caliphate by the ulama. Their leadership of the Muslim world was acknowledged but religious sanction was withheld from them for a long time. They ruled the heartlands of Islam—from Arabia, Iraq, Egypt, Turkey, Iran, Central Asia to the eastern territories of Europe; nevertheless the ulama would not give them legitimacy. In India another non-Arab race—kinsmen of the Ottoman Turks—the Mughals, hoisted the banner of Islam; and another group of non-Arabs, the Shi'ite Safavids, founded yet another great Islamic empire. They were, in their own way, more powerful than the Abbasids but they remained sultans and never became caliphs.

Steeped in classical traditions, the ulama found it difficult to accept non-Arabs as caliphs; they had to be not only Arabs, but also Quraishis. Later, when they found that the Ottomans were firmly established in the heartlands of Islam and exercised authority over the Ka'ba as its custodians, the ulama quietly gave in and recognized them as caliphs. Though not religious zealots (they respected Islam) the Ottomans were more interested in conquests and the perpetuation of their rule. They did not hesitate to introduce innovations in their administrative systems, even though these did not strictly conform to the shari'ah or to the old classical pattern the ulamā were used to; the State was more important to them than the faith, barring to a few notable exceptions.

The Moorish empire in Spain, which followed a different drummer from its inception, carved out a special niche for itself in the edifice of Islam. Being part of Europe, it differed from the rest in many respects. Its rulers were enlightened and encouraged secular pursuits. During their rule some of the greatest men of learning in the Islamic world were produced: the physician Razi or Rhases (885–925), the philosopher Ibn Sina or Avicenna (980–1037), the scholar al-Biruni (973–1048) and the thinker, Ibn Rushd or Averrhoes (d. 1198). The very fact that the Moorish contribution was more cultural and literary than religious, explains its inherent character. The Moors' defeat at the hands of the Catholic King Ferdinand and Queen Isabella struck the final blow to Islam in Europe, annihilating the Arabs and destroying all the good they had done. Mosques were turned into churches and every trace of Islam was obliterated. As Stanley Lane-Poole has graphically observed: 'The Moors were banished; for a while Christian Spain shone like a moon, with a borrowed light; then came the eclipse and in that darkness, Spain has grovelled ever since.'[5]

From the theocratic point of view, the greatest challenge that the Abbasids faced, as we have noted, was from the Fatimids; the latter became so powerful that they proclaimed themselves the real caliphs and defenders of the faith. Under the reign of Abu Mansur Nizar al-Azia, their fifth ruler, they reached the zenith of their power. However, though the Fatimids had come to power as a result of their uncompromising fight against the corruption and moral degeneration of the Abbasids, they later lapsed into the same vices and failed to set a good example of Islamic piety, purity, simplicity or adherence to Qur'anic precepts and the traditions of the Prophet. They built lavish palaces for themselves and lived in great luxury. Their rulers took counsel not from Shi'a theologians but from their Christian ministers. They swore loyalty to Shi'ism but were guided by temporal considerations and were dependent upon their Turkish and Berber soldiers, mercenaries who cared little for Islam. The result was they succeeded in piercing the monolithic wall enclosing Europe that the Abbasids had created for more than three hundred and fifty years. They opened diplomatic relations with the Christians of the West but refused to parley with their co-religionists in Baghdad. Their Sunni subjects turned increasingly hostile to them and thus facilitated the task of Saladin to dethrone the Fatimids (after his spectacular victory over the Crusaders) and to restore Sunni Islam to its earlier majesty.

Apart from the Shi'a-Sunni conflict, there were also differences among the Sunnis which could not be reconciled. On the contrary, with the passage of time, they sharpened. Different groups, both political and religious, took full advantage of these differences, particularly the ulama, who because of their religious hold on their followers, began to interfere in the affairs of state. They clashed with the officials, who believed that they had to administer the kingdom by keeping in view practical compulsions and the requirements of the times. Even earlier this used to happen but then both the temporal and religious groups bowed before the authority of the caliph. Now, with the weakening of the central authority, officials became all-powerful; the ulamā revolted. There was a continuous tussle between the two; but as neither side was strong enough to subdue the other, the skirmishes continued endlessly. Finally the ulama, in disgust, retired into their shells with their small circles of disciples to preach and pray. Still they created enough unrest among the faithful and their activities led to intensive theological expositions. Some of the greatest minds flourished during this period: al-Mawardi (974–1058) was the earliest in applying rationalism to the conflict between religion and politics in Islam. He wrote a number of books expounding political theories to reconcile the demands of religion and the State. He explained the basis of a State as the rule of justice and truth and emphasized that its machinery should be able to sift the good from the bad, virtue from vice, right from wrong. That was, according to Mawardi, as much a political necessity as a religious requirement. The head of state should possess qualities of leadership, and acquire the strength to protect his subjects from oppression and injustice. He might be elected or nominated, but to justify his position, he must defend the faith, adjudicate fairly between his subjects, irrespective of their status, guard the stability and security of his realm, and administer it by appointing able and honest persons to assist him in the discharging of his duties. In a beautiful poem, he explained the duties of a Muslim ruler:

> For all his goodness, let Allah be praised.
> O' Faithful: Make that person your ruler
> Who is both benevolent and warlike.
> Who is neither upset by circumstances
> Nor acts rashly on the spur of the moment.
> Though wealthy, he takes no pride in his wealth.
> Ever vigilant, who does not hesitate to act
> When the occasion demands it.
> While heeding the advice of others,
> Who goes by his judgement
> And fulfils his task, firmly and resolutely.[6]

Mawardi elaborated at length the functions and duties of the organs of government. His emphasis throughout had been more Aristotelian than Islamic, more historical than religious. Even Ghazāli, who followed Mawardi, defined politics as a 'science which deals with the proper functioning of affairs of state', and which needed to be managed by 'men of special qualities, who should have attained a certain amount of knowledge, discretion and power of guidance'. Though it was not strictly in accordance with the shari'ah, he also approved of kingship, even that of an usurper, as he feared that, without some kind of a ruler, there would be 'continuous turmoil, a never-ending clanging of the swords, a recurring state of famine and cattle diseases and an end to all industries and handicrafts'.[7]

As a reconciler, Ghazāli tried to strike a harmonious relationship between faith and power. He described them as twin sisters, faith being the creator of goodness in human relations while power was the preserver of society. He stressed the need for a proper equilibrium between the two. In a classical passage, he described the functions of the State:

> My friend, consider the State as the body of a man. The king is its heart; the professions and trades its limbs; the magistrate its desire; the police its anger; and the mushir or adviser, its common sense.

The king needs the help of all; but if the magistrate, representing desire, resorts to injustice, and the police, representing anger, extorts revenues from the subjects, then the king must listen to his advisers, representing common sense, and control the magistrate and the police, representing desire and anger. Then only will the State run smoothly and properly. Otherwise, if he gives in to desire and anger, the whole body politic will be destroyed.[8]

Ghazāli's greatness lay in explaining, in Islamic terms, the requirements of the times and giving them a practical shape.

Ibn Taymiya (1263–1328) saw both the fall and the resurgence of Islam. His writings were, therefore, greatly influenced by both these developments. He was also distressed by the Shi'ite attitude towards affairs of state. He refuted it forcefully, especially the arguments of the great Shi'ite scholar, al-Hillī, who, in his work, *Minhajul Karamah*, asserted that the imam or caliph was a divine appointee and hence infallible both in his spiritual and secular conduct. He rejected the Sunni doctrine of ijmā or consensus because of the uncertainty of its outcome. Ibn Taymiya pointed out that neither the Qu'rān nor the hadīth laid down any systems of government; nor did they restrict the number of rulers. There was, therefore, no question of a caliph or a sole ruler of all Muslims. He also criticized the theory of election by an uninformed public or even by a small group of learned men. He contended that the Muslims never elected a caliph; what they did, even during the time of the first four 'rightly guided' caliphs, was only to ratify a fait accompli in each case. Ibn Taymiya also did not endorse the notion that a ruler had to be a member of the tribe, of Quraish; on the contrary, he asserted that he could be, according to a tradition of the Prophet, even an Abyssinian slave. He stressed that a ruler should concern himself with the rule of justice and the well-being of his people as ordained in the Qur'ān. The ruler was the representative of God on earth. He was, to use the words of Ibn Taymiya, like the guardian of orphans, or the mutwawalli (trustee) of a waqf and it is the duty of every one to act in such a way that there should be the greatest good of the greatest number put under his charge. He said that government should be carried out by shūrā or consultation but that these debates should not be endless and confined only to the ulamā. Though he approved of the right to private property, it had to be subject to the public weal and the conditions laid down in the Qur'ān. His doctrines seem to lie halfway between those of capitalism and socialism. He was no respecter of the ṣūfis and condemned the cult of personality. To him, any form of saint worship was a bidat or innovation. He wanted Islam to return to the puritanism of the Prophet and to the simplicity of the first four 'rightly guided' caliphs and to be free of all forms of mystical pantheism. A follower of Imam Hanbali, he fought against any compromise with the basic tenets of Islam. He frowned upon liberal interpretations of the Qur'ān and did not approve of any kind of innovation or adjustment to suit worldly interests. His teachings later inspired the Wahhābis, the disciples of Muhammad Ibn Abd al-Wahhāb, the mentor of King Ibn Saud of Saudi Arabia.

7

Bridge Builders

The collapse of the Abbasid Caliphate led to the mushrooming of small states, but surprisingly the process did not impede Islam's onward march. The chief reason was the widespread popularity of Ṣufism, which is the name given to mysticism in Islam. With the decline of central power, the people turned in greater numbers to the ṣufis, men of God, who taught love and compassion as the way to spiritual salvation. The ṣufis fulfilled the need of the times by their stress on purity and piety and a relaxed attitude to form and ritual. They freed the faithful from the shackles of orthodoxy and inculcated in them love of God and His creatures with an abandon unknown to them before. The ṣufis' spartan style of living evoked admiration; their spiritual devotion gave them almost a divine aura. Their popularity set alarm bells ringing in the courts of the rulers and the schools of the theologians. At the behest of the ulama, the State began to persecute them for straying from the accepted path. But the more they were persecuted, the more popular they became with the masses. Gradually, the rulers realized that the ṣufis did not pose any threat to law and order but were on the contrary an asset to the preservation of peace among the people. They were helped in coming to this realization by Ghazali whose contribution to Islam has been as valuable as that of St Augustine to Christianity. He gave the introspective attitude of the ṣufis the same importance within official Islam as the legalism of the theologians. As the result a rapprochement between the ṣufis and the ulama was brought about which greatly helped the work of the rulers.

Though unconcerned with affairs of state, the ṣūfis had a profound influence on the Muslim polity. They humanized its rigours and reduced the area of conflict between religion and politics. They gave Islam a broader base. Non-Muslims flocked to ṣūfi hospices in large numbers and in due course hundreds of thousands came into the fold of Islam. Unlike the ulamā, the ṣūfis did not indulge in worldly pursuits. They did not go to the rulers for favours. Rulers came to them for guidance, which they gave readily without asking for anything in return. Islam had not witnessed such a phenomenon before. As Ghazāli pointed out, after attaining his own realization, ṣūfis 'cannot be learned but only attained by direct experience, ecstasy, and inward transformation'.

By the beginning of the fourteenth century, large numbers of people, particularly in Central Asia and South and South-East Asia, had accepted Islam through the preachings of the ṣūfis. Under their impact, the Mongols, who had been the scourge of Islam, became patrons of Islam. They produced many great men, such as Rashīd al-Dīn of Tabrīz, who wrote a treatise on world history; the scholar, Saeed Taftazani; and intellectual giants like Nāsir al-Dīn and Ulugh Beg.

In Iran great poet-philosophers like Saadi, Hafiz and Jami' popularized Islam through their mystic tales and romantic poems. Despite the Islamic prohibition against making any form in the likeness of the human being, a school of miniature painters developed in Herat. Persian had already acquired the status of the second language of Islam; it now became the chief instrument of the spiritual revival in the eastern Islamic world.

After the Arabs and the Persians, it was the Mongol Turks, a third ethnic group, who infused fresh blood into Islam. Closer to the Persians in their general outlook and sensibilities, the Turks were considerably influenced by the ṣūfis' humanitarian outlook. This was more evident in the West, where the Seljuq Turks created a base in Asia Minor on which their cousins, the Ottomans, founded the greatest of all the Islamic empires. The Ghazanavids conquered northern India and opened the gates of the sub-continent first to the Turkish slaves, who founded an empire of their own, and later to the great Mughals. Many ṣūfi orders prospered during the long Muslim rule. In Central Asia Timur founded yet another empire stretching from Tashkent to

Mesopotamia. Here again the ṣūfis were much in evidence and influenced the course of events.

It should be borne in mind that during these periods of expansion of Muslim power, the conversion of the people in the newly acquired territories was due more to the missionary work of the ṣūfis and their disciples, who included traders, artisans and farmers, than to the sword of the rulers; the latter were more interested in the collection of the jaziya from non-Muslims than in the saving of their souls. In India, despite successive Muslim invasions and the founding of Muslim Sultanates, the Muslim population of the conquered region round Delhi and Agra never rose to more than ten per cent of the population, whereas in regions where the ṣūfis were active, there was a spurt of conversions. Again, as Muslim power waned, the hold of the ṣūfis waxed, with the result that more and more people flocked to their hospices and became Muslims. As the scholar, Prof. T.W. Arnold, has observed in his classic, *The Preaching of Islam*,

> The spread of this faith over so vast a portion of the globe is due to various causes; social, political and religious; but among these, one of the most powerful factors at work in the production of this stupendous result has been the unmerited labours of Muslim missionaries, who, with the Prophet himself as their great example, have spent themselves for conversion of unbelievers.[1]

He has proved, through facts and figures, that their endeavours were extremely effective. To quote him again:

> It is not the cruelties of the persecutor, or the fury of the fanatic that we should look for, but the evidence of the missionary spirit of Islam and more the exploits of that mythical personage, the Muslim warrior with sword in one hand, Qur'ān in the other, but in the quiet, unobtrusive labours of the preacher and the trader who have carried their faith into every quarter of the globe.[2]

Another point to be noted is that it was not the tradition-bound ulamā, patronized by the court, but the ṣūfis, with their message of love and compassion, who succeeded in spreading the message of Islam to far-flung areas. The ulama frowned on local customs and traditions and urged the populace to discard their beliefs and follow the shari'ah. The ṣūfis respected native traditions and customs and assured the people that Islam's liberalism could encompass their individualism. Unlike the ulamā they did not insist on adhering to the letter of the sacred law; they impressed upon their disciples the importance of the spirit underlying the system.

As Prof. G.E. Von Grunebaum writes:

> A community's law is, in the last analysis, precisely as elastic and as adaptive as the community would have it, and its criteria of admission are as catholic or exclusive as its identification implies. In Sunnite Islam, the community at large has, for many a century, been more cautious in putting the dissenter (who, in the Muslim environment, is often more significantly recognized by his practice than by his creed) outside the pale than the lawyer-theologian, who acts as its spokesman, and in a sense, its executive. In the general consciousness, the intention to be and to remain a Muslim counts far more than the failings that are observable in its implementation.[3]

Most Muslim rulers found the ṣūfi approach politically more useful than the stultified attitude of the ulamā, who were becoming increasingly unhappy at the loss of their hold on the establishment. In course of time, mainly due to Ghazāli, the ṣūfis and the ulamā patched up their differences with one another, agreeing to let each other pursue their objectives. The ṣūfis concerned themselves with the spiritual uplift of their adherents, while the ulamā concentrated on maintaining forms and rituals and punishing the guilty. Both accepted the shari'ah as the primary source of faith, but their approach to it was different. The ṣūfis tended to be tolerant of theological dissensions and local differences; while the ulamā thrived on them, each insisting on the correctness of their stand. The ṣūfis were happy to stay out of controversies. Their role was to unite, not to divide. However, despite the truce brought about by Ghazāli there were occasions when the ṣūfis had to confront the ulamā and the rulers. They refused to bow to the wishes of the court, did not join in Friday congregational prayers at royal mosques and preferred to pray in their own hospices. They declined the judicial and political posts offered to them. To the common Muslims the ṣūfis became the symbols of true Islam. Their piety, ascetic living and humility won the hearts of the poor and the downtrodden, irrespective of race or creed. The ṣufis did not mind borrowing from their theologies and incorporated aspects of Hinduism, Christianity, Judaism and Buddhism into their teaching freely; they took concepts such as moksa from Hinduism and nirvana from Buddhism. R.M. Zaehneer, an authority on mysticism, has interpreted the experiences of Abu Yazid Bistani (d. 874) as resulting from the Hindu influence, more particularly that of Shankara's Vedanta. Vedic advaita (non-dualism) and Vashist advaita (modified non-dualism) conform to the sūfi concepts wahdat al-wujud and wahdat al-shuhud, emphasizing the oneness of being. Again the ṣūfi doctrines of fana and baqa (annihilation and subsistence) correspond to nirvana with its positive and negative implications.

Sufism ran parallel to official Islam and lacked the grandeur and majesty attached to the latter. The word tasawwaf is from ṣū'f for wool and stands for the coarse woollen garments worn by the ascetics in pursuit of the divine instead of the muslins and silks worn by the rich, including the ruling elite. Hasan al-Basri (d. 728), probably the earliest ṣufi, disdained both riches and power and carried on a relentless fight against corruption in high places; likewise, the other ṣūfis had no love for worldly pleasures or gains. So disgusted were these men of God by the prevalent state of affairs that many of them retired from the world and took refuge in caves. As a woman ascetic hailing from Syria sang:

> They do not quarrel over this world's pleasure
> Honours, and children, riches and costly gowns
> All greed and appetite they do not treasure
> The life of ease and joy that dwells in towns.[4]

Many ṣufis suffered at the hands of their rulers and some of them even paid for their defiance with their lives; they were as averse to the misuse of power as to narrowness in religion. They stood for unity, both of God and of the human race, indeed, of all creation. Dhul Nunal-Misri (d. 861) was arraigned before Caliph Mutawakkil for enunciating the doctrine of gnosis; Hussain b. Mansur, better known as al-Hallāj, a wool-carder, was charged with heresy and beheaded because of his veneration of Jesus and the declaration 'I am the Truth.' Yahaya

Suhrawardi, the noted ṣūfi theoretician, was executed on the orders of the great Saladin because of his unorthodox attitude in matters of faith. It is paradoxical that though these ṣūfis refused to bow down to authority, their teachings made the task of governments, especially in states with mixed ethnic and religious populations, much easier. Had it not been for the environment of peace, goodwill and mutual understanding that they generated, Islam would not have become so readily acceptable to non-Muslims nor would Muslim rulers have been able to run their administration as peacefully as they did.

Ṣūfi liberalism had other important effects. While music and dance were anathema to the ulamā, these were encouraged in ṣūfi hospices. Their songs were full of passionate devotion to God, the unity of the soul and the body and the oneness of mankind. They indulged in samā', or the chanting of song and music, which led to hal, or a state of mystic exaltation. The theme is as common in the poems of Ibn al-Arabi and some of the Arabic poets as in the Persian compositions of such literary giants as Jalāl al-Dīn Rumi (1207–73), Farīd al-Dīn Aṭṭār (d. 1190) and Muslihuddin Saadi (1193–1292). One of the greatest ṣūfi saints of all time was Abd al-Qādir Jilāni (1077–1166), better known as Ghauth al-Azam or 'the Sultan of Saints' who preached in Baghdad. He was a disciple of Ghazāli and his eloquence was as soul-stirring as the radiance of his personality. He founded the Ghauth al order which spread to most parts of the Muslim world and may be regarded as the mother of all ṣūfi orders. According to H.A.R. Gibb, 'The Qadiri order is, on the whole, amongst the most tolerant and progressive orders, not far removed from orthodoxy, distinguished by philanthrophy, piety and humility and averse to fanaticism, whether religious or political.'[5]

Jilāni's emphasis was more on human values than on religious practices. He enumerated the following as the ten basic tenets of human behaviour:

1. Never swear by God.
2. Never speak an untruth even in jest.
3. Never break a promise.
4. Never curse anyone.
5. Never harm anyone.
6. Never accuse anyone of religious infidelity.
7. Never be a party to anything sinful.

8. Never impose a burden on others.
9. Never accept anything from human beings—God alone is the giver.
10. Look for in others the good points and not the bad.

Such humanistic teachings bridged the gulf between Muslims and non-Muslims. Much to the annoyance of the ulamā, ṣufis came to be venerated as intermediaries between God and His creatures. Around the tombs where ṣufi saints were interred sprang habitations where millions flocked to pray, sing and dance on death anniversaries.

Indeed, they gave 'a second youth to Islam' and injected a new spirit into it; their influence continues even today. Jilāni's tomb at Baghdad draws thousands of people from far and near; so does the tomb of his disciple, Umar al-Suhrawardi (d. 1234), the founder of the Suhrawardi order. In Iraq, the mausoleum of Ahmad al-Rifā'i (d. 1183), who founded the Rifā'i order, continues to be a centre of pilgrimage. Then there are the mausolea of Ruzbahan al-Baqli (d. 1209), the mentor of Muinuddin Chishti, the founder of the Chishti order. One is buried in Shiraz in Iran and the other in Ajmer in India. In Egypt, one of the most venerated mosques is that which entombs Abu'l Abbas al-Mursi, the successor of Abu'l Hasan al-Shadhili, a contemporary of Jilāni. More popular than his tomb are those of Ahmad al-Badawi (d. 1276) and of Umar b. al-Farid (d. 1235), who is regarded as the greatest ṣufi poet in Arabic. Abu'l Hasan al-Shadhili is buried in a desert in Egypt, but the cave in Tunis in which he meditated draws thousands of pilgrims every year. The patron-saint of Algeria is Shuayb Abu Madyan, a disciple of the legendary rebel Abd al-Qadir; while that of Morocco is Abd al-Salam b. Mashish (d. 1228), who inspired many a rebellion against the establishment, both native and foreign.

In Konya in Turkey lies buried the great Jalāl al-Din al-Rumi (1207–73). He was one of the most successful propagators of Islam. He is as much remembered for his poems extolling the virtues of Islam, as for his 'whirling dervishes', who danced and danced to achieve spiritual ecstasy. He lived through the trauma of the Mongol invasion; but there was not a trace of bitterness in him. His *Masnavi* is regarded as 'the Qur'ān in Pahlavi' or the Persian language; it gave a fresh perspective of Islam to the world. Through an unending chain of parables, Rumi meditated on different aspects of human behaviour. His poems depict the eternal tussle between good and evil, between right and wrong. The metaphysical in his stories is as important as the mundane and both are so intermingled that often it is difficult to distinguish one from the other. What the Qur'an taught in Arabic, the *Masnavi*, a more voluminous work, sought to do in Persian. Few works in the annals of Islam compare with it in terms of thought-content, melodious language and beauty of expression. Rumi loved music and dance and regarded them as essential instruments to reach the divine. The orthodox were very upset with him but none dared challenge his pre-eminence. He was regarded above dispute and universally hailed as one of the greatest exponents of Islam.

Most of the early ṣūfīs did not compromise with the practices and rituals of Islam but those who came later, and were influenced by local conditions, deviated from the traditional disciplines and tried to establish direct communion with God. They became, therefore, as much pantheistic as monotheistic in their devotion. What mattered was the goal, they emphasized, not the paths that led to it. Everyone was entitled to approach God in his own way. The field for speculation was left wide open. The precedent had been set in the times of the later Abbasids when free discussions among the different creeds was encouraged and their common objective highlighted. The later ṣūfīs carried the process much further. By the thirteenth century, Ṣūfīsm had assimilated the best in the various philosophies and religions and acquired an unassailable position by propagating broad humanism and spiritual upliftment. The two main planks of Ṣūfīsm could be summarized as: one, a deep and direct involvement with God, and two, a loving and compassionate attitude towards His creatures.

India played as significant a role as Persia in liberalizing Islam; the local traditions in both countries helped the process. The ṣūfīs who came to India did not behave as foreigners; they assimilated much of the philosophical outlook of the rishis and the practices of the swamis of the mutts. In this Khwāja Muinuddin Chishti led the way. He came from Khurasan but refused to settle down in Delhi or Agra, the centres of Muslim power. He travelled to Ambar in Rajasthan, ruled by a Hindu raja, and camped on the banks of the Pushkar, renowned for its sacredness. The ruler at first objected but soon was so impressed by Chishti's saintliness that he left him alone; Chishti then began his mission of removing bitterness between Hindus and Muslims, and opened his doors to everyone, irrespective of his or her faith, who sought spiritual well-being and communion with God. He did not ask them their religion nor did he force his devotees to become Muslims first. On the contrary, he encouraged Hindu bairagis to sing their hymns in his presence and prescribed the dark orange colour (held sacred by the Hindus) for the coarse robes of his devotees. They also carried a stick and a bowl, reminiscent of Vedic traditions. Further, he preached under a tree. By these means he came nearer to the hearts of people of every religion, particularly Hindus and Buddhists who began to venerate him as a man of God.[6]

His disciples, Baba Farid Ganj Shakar, whom the Sikhs revere as much as their own gurus and Khwaja Nizamuddin Aulia, who preached in Delhi, were indifferent to the lure of power. They concentrated on spreading the message of unrestricted love far and wide. They asked for no help from the State and took none. Nizamuddin Aulia is reported to have told his devotees, 'My room has two doors. If the sultan comes through one door, I leave by the other.'

Of the four leading sūfi orders, the Qadiris and the Chishtis kept themselves aloof from the seats of power, but the other two, the Suhrawardis and the Naqshbandis actively helped the Muslim rulers in maintaining peace and harmony in their realms and were sometimes duly rewarded for their services. In its own quiet way Ṣūfism acted as a counter-force to orthodoxy among the Muslims—to begin with as much among the Shī'as as the Sunnis, but later only among the Sunnis—against the rigidity of the teachings of the traditional theologians, who until then had dominated the faithful and were uncompromising in their outlook.

Though the ṣūfis maintain that the Prophet was their first shaikh, it is to Hasan al-Basri (born in Basra) that Ṣūfism owes its origin. He lived during the time of Umar and sat at the feet of Ali. He died at the age of eighty-six in 728. He took pains to explain to his devotees that religion was too good to be a part of the State. He said, 'He that knoweth God loveth Him and he that knoweth the world abstaineth from it.' The second great ṣūfi was a lady—Rabia al-Adawiyyah—again of Basra. She put spiritualism before materialism, God before paradise and asolute before relative. One of the early ṣūfis was Abu'l Qāsim al-Junayd (d. 910); his faith in God was so unshakeable that he said if his face was struck by a sword he would not feel it. But all these ṣūfis did not make an exhibition of their spiritual intoxication; they confined their preaching to their close circles, with the result that their activities created no problem for the State.

There were, however, some exceptions, the notable one being al-Hallāj, who provoked the authorities by his public utterances; these were misunderstood by the people and created a wave of unrest among the faithful. Ghazāli said that al-Hallāj's stance was wrong not in terms of its basic sentiment, which was in conformity with the ṣūfi approach, but in its public expression, which was bound to confuse an ordinary Muslim. But most ṣūfis took al-Hallāj's death as an affront to their devotion; it goaded them to challenge the authority of the state. Henceforth defiance of it became their slogan. They were convinced that the depth of their understanding of Islam was beyond the reach of the corrupt and immoral rulers, who were interested only in worldly pleasures, or of their stooges, the ulamā, who lacked the capacity to delve into the divine will. Moreover, they were disgusted with the general attitude of the ulamā who, in order to please their worldly masters, were only too happy to pass decrees against the ṣūfis. Ghazāli, who tried to bring the ulamā and the ṣūfis together, had to concede that 'those who are so learned about rare forms of divorce can tell you nothing about the simple things of spiritual life, such as the meaning of sincerity towards God or truth in Him.' It took a long time for the state to reconcile to this position; Ghazāli in his book, *The Saviour from Error*, explains how but for Ṣūfism Islam would have plunged into the abyss of scepticism.

As time passed, Ṣūfism took different forms, one of the most pioneering being the pantheistic speculation of the Spanish ṣūfi, Ibn al-Arabi (1165–1201). He is known as al-Shaikh al-Akbar or 'the greatest shaikh' and is regarded as the fountain-head of speculative thought in Islam. God, as the fundamentalists assert, is the source of everything; man can never become God or God man. However, the ṣūfis insist that through devotion man can reach God, and the basis of devotion can only be love. That was what al-Hallāj achieved and many others have tried since then. Their efforts were based on a theory propounded by Arabi which came to be known as wilayah or identification of man with God. This identification amounted to pantheism, in which distinctions between good and evil, existence and non-existence were dissolved. Arabi considered vice and virtue relative terms; consequently, distinctions between different religions were deemed superfluous. In one of his poems, Rumi expresses the same sentiments:

> In the adorations and benedictions of righteous men
> The praises of all the prophets are kneaded together.
> All their praises are mingled into one stream.
> All the vessels are emptied into one another.
> Because He that is praised is, in fact, only One,
> In this respect all religions are only one religion.
> Because all praises are directed towards God's light.
> Their various forms and figures are borrowed from it.[7]

The problem of rivalry in religious affiliation was mainly felt by the sūfis in India, where they were faced by the existence of conflicting creeds; the Muslim rulers gave preference to Islam and neglected the other faiths. This naturally created resentment in non-Muslim circles. The sūfis tried to contain it by respecting equally all religions. One of their greatest teachers, Mazhar Jan-i-Janan, who was responsible for all the sūfi orders—Naqshbandiyya, Qadiriyya, and Chishtiyya, stated in a letter to one of his disciples:

> You should know that the Merciful Being, in the beginning of creation, sent a book named Ved; this is apparent from the ancient literature of the Indians. This book is in four parts [and is] meant to regulate the duties of people in this world and the next through the instrumentality of the divine Brahma, who is omnipotent. Now it must be borne in mind that the Qur'ān says: 'And there is not a people to whom a warner has not been sent'; and further, 'To every land we have sent a warner.' Hence there were prophets in India as in other countries and their accounts are to be found in their books. How could God, the Beneficent and the Merciful, have left out of his grace such an extensive portion of the globe?

To the ulamā this was heresy. They could never accept that all religions were the same; nor that all prophets were divinely inspired. They did not approve of sūfi doctrines such as karmat (miracles), ta'bbud (renunciation), and qismat (predestination). Nor were they happy with the ṣūfi emphasis on fana (annihilation) or ta'ah (complete subservience of devotees to their shaikh).

The ulamā condemned these as anti-Islamic, because they glorified the individual as against the community and were hence destructive of the concept of the brotherhood of the umma, which was the bedrock of Islam.

Ṣūfism was essentially a Sunni phenomenon; it received a popular base under the Seljuqs, who were its patrons. During this period in other parts of the Muslim world also, as we have noticed, it gained millions of followers. Their orders were eagerly sought after by the poor and downtrodden. It is suggested that Seljuqs encouraged Ṣūfism as a counter-force to Shi'ism, which they had ruthlessly suppressed in the wake of the fall of the Buwayhids. The esoteric side of Islam, which the Shi'as glorified, was lacking in Sunni Islam; Ṣūfism tried to fill the gap. But as the Shi'a scholar Moojan Momen has observed, 'A more powerful stimulus towards the growth of Ṣūfism was probably that Muslims were beginning to despair of ever creating the perfect society through the leadership of the caliph and began to look to individual morality and the spiritual advancement of the individual.'

To begin with, the Shi'as frowned upon Ṣūfism because of its historical background; it was only after the Mongol invasion, when Sunni Islam was shattered, that the Shi'ites took to Ṣūfism. An early Shi'a patron of the ṣūfis was Abbasid Caliph al-Nasir. The Shi'a brotherhoods came to be known as futāwa (youths) and their hero was Ali, who symbolized Islamic piety and chivalry at its best.

The impact of Ṣūfism on Shi'ism during the short period when the two sects respected each other brought about a certain rapprochement between the two major sects of Islam. The Sunnis extolled the virtues of Ali and condemned the cruelties of Mu'awiya and Yazid, while the Shi'ias recognized the position of the Sunni shaikh in the ṣūfi orders, despite the fact that it compromised their stand on the supremacy of the imam. Ali was revered by both the Shi'ias and the Sunnis—a development for which the ṣūfis were largely responsible. In fact, some of the Sunni orders adopted the Shi'ite orientation, as for instance, the Kubrawiyya order in Khurasan; As-Simmani (d. 1336), a shaikh of this Sunni order, accepted Ali as superior to the first three caliphs and described him as the qutb or axis of the 'rightly guided' Caliphate. Al-Hamadhani (d. 1385), another Sunni shaikh, took the modified Ṣūfism, which was a mixture of Sunni and Shi'a tenets, to India; it also became popular among the later day Seljuq Turks, particularly the Turkománs. Likewise, the Khalwatiyya order of Anatolia was also pro-Shi'a. Husayn al-Kashifi, a Sunni theologian, was so influenced by these developments that he wrote a treatise called *Rawdat al-Shuhadá* or the *Paradise of the Martyrs*, glorifying Husayn's martyrdom; it was adopted by the Shi'as as a textbook.

In the emergence of the Safavid dynasty the ṣufis played a decisive role; its founder Shah Ismá'il became the shaikh of the Safavid order of the ṣufis, in addition to his primary position as imam. As the imam he was revered by the Shi'as; while as the shaikh he received the absolute obedience of his Sunni followers, the Qizilbashis, who later embraced Shi'ism. The ṣufi influence declined under the later Safavid rulers who gradually began to spread Shi'ism, especially after their wars with the Sunni Ottomans and the Sunni Moors. They were not prepared to countenance anything revered by the Sunnis. The Shi'a mujtahids resorted to open abuse of the first three caliphs and the Sunni ulamá. Some of them blamed the ṣufis for the weaknesses that had crept into the Safavid rank and file. Shah Ismá'il had made full use of the ṣufi orders to gain power; but when his son Shah Tahmásp, tried to underplay the anti-Sunni sentiment, he encountered much opposition from the Shi'a mullás. His successor, Ismá'il had to pay with his life for being tolerant towards the Sunnis. Shah Abbas, therefore, reversed the process, persecuted the Sunnis and vigorously pursued the spread of Twelver Shi'ism. He decorated Shi'ite shrines to demonstrate his loyalty to the creed. After his death, the arch theologian of Shi'ism, Majlisi, mounted a frontal attack on Ṣufism as a by-product of Sunnism and succeeded in expurgating it from Shi'ism. Ironically, with the disappearance of Ṣufism in Persia began the decline of Shi'ite power.

Under the Sunnis, despite occasional persecution, the ṣufis held their own until the rise of the Wahhábis, who began attacking them. In Saudi Arabia, where Ṣufism had earlier flourished, the ṣufis were denounced and imprisoned, their orders banned and the tombs of the earlier ṣufis desecrated and demolished. Their teachings were denounced as 'foul and hellish'. This was Wahhábism at its cruellest. Its bigotism created violent rifts among the Muslims, wherever the Wahhábis went. But their influence hardly penetrated beyond the Arabian frontiers. In

India it influenced Shah Wali Allāh and later the Deobandi School but, by and large, it did not appeal to the vast majority of Muslims. It is interesting to note that, in a way, it is the mother of modern fundamentalism in Islam and has permeated the thinking of religious leaders such as Maududi of the Jamā'āt-i-Islāmī and other fundamentalists.

Ṣūfism was considered by Ataturk is as an opium for the faithful and was banned by him but lately it has gained much ground in the rural areas of Turkey; even in the Asian Republics of the USSR the sūfi orders have shown some signs of revival. In other Muslim countries the ṣūfis, more the dead than the living, are still a force to be reckoned with; their tombs are venerated, promising to the spiritually starved and the materially-forsaken, who pray there, worldly prosperity and other-worldly bliss.

Government decrees in some of the Muslim countries, particularly Saudi Arabia and the Gulf shaikhdoms, have no doubt dampened the spirit of veneration of the saints; but it is far from dead. As a Western scholar has observed, 'The older sections in a changing society feel a nostalgic longing for elements of the past. The poetry and humanism of a Rumi influence many new men too. But these must be placed within the whole setting of the secularization of society. These are "survivals" from an old way of life; they are no longer ruling forces in men's lives.'[8]

Secularism with its emphasis on broad humanism has also taken its toll on Ṣūfism, which in many ways had fostered and encouraged a more humanistic and liberal approach to inter-religious understanding.

8

Revival and Resurgence

After the turmoil and bloodshed following the collapse of the Abbasid Caliphate, the Muslim forces regrouped eventually and went on to attain the zenith of their power. The flag of the Crescent fluttered in countries extending from the Western Sahara and the Niger Basin across Central Asia to South-East Asia where Muslim sultans replaced the Hindu rajas of Sumatra and Java. The most powerful Muslim empires at this time were those of the Safavids in Iran, the Mughals in India and the Ottomans in West Asia, North Africa and Europe. Their rulers were, by and large, good administrators. They built roads and canals, improved agriculture and encouraged the arts. They built mosques, palaces, and mausolea. Without surrendering any of their powers, they respected the ulamā and tried to take them into confidence in running the affairs of the state. As a result, royal decrees were harmonized with religious requirements and theological interpretations. Though the sultan's word was final, he had learned from experience that going against established Islamic tenets invited trouble. In this period the relationship between the two organs—religion and the State—was not hostile.

Of the three Muslim empires the most powerful and most enduring was that of the Ottomans. Apart from the heartlands of Islam, including Syria, Iraq, Palestine, the Hejaz and the holy cities of Mecca and Madina, its frontiers extended from Central Asia to Europe; its dominions included the Hapsburg capital of Vienna and stretched eastwards up to the Crimea. In the East it ruled Crete and the Ukraine, and in North Africa, Morocco and Tunis.

Murād I (1359–60) was the first great Ottoman sultan. Though a man of war, he devoted as much attention to administration as to soldiering. He was particularly concerned about his non-Muslim subjects. Though he prided himself on being a ghazi or warrior of Islam, he did not impose his faith on others. He had native Christians in his army, guaranteed them exemption from the jaziya and gave them usufruct of lands. From amongst those who converted to Islam, he picked the fittest to serve as his bodyguards. This elite corps came to be known as the janissaries (sacrificers) and became the mainstay of the sultan's court: they played a decisive role in managing the state. Their Islam was not orthodox; it was affiliated to an order of dervishes, initiated by a Christian convert, Hājji Bektash. They were intensely loyal to the sultan and were ever ready to die for his scarlet flag bearing the insignia of the crescent moon with the sultan's sabres crossing beneath it. Murād realized that the Turkish–Muslim system of administration would not be suitable for the many European lands which came under his sway, unless it was adjusted to suit the needs of these people. He initiated a process of assimilation between Muslims and Christians which was continued by his successors and thus created a multi-racial, multi-religious, multi-lingual society.

Muhammad II, who ascended the throne in 1441, was another ruler of significance. He encouraged the same secular approach in a more assertive way. He could do so because of the glory he had acquired by the capture of Constantinople in 1451. This victory ended for all time the Christian hegemony over Asia Minor. A generous victor, Muhammad did not impose Islam on the vanquished nations and tried to make his empire a model of inter-religious harmony. Although the Christian Church was subordinate to him, it enjoyed full autonomy in internal affairs. He organized religious minorities into millats or communities and enjoined them to observe their own laws and customs. The ulamā occupied a pre-eminent position in his court but the patriarchs of the Greek Orthodox and Armenian churches as well as the chief rabbi were accorded due respect. He showed so much deference towards the Christians and the Jews that some of them came to hope that the sultan might embrace their faith.[1]

Muhammad II was more a builder than a conqueror. While he added large territories to his kingdom, he fashioned them into a state which in some respects was unique. It was neither wholly religious nor wholly secular as it combined elements of both and established institutions, administrative, social and economic, which took care equally of the religious sentiments of Muslims, Christians and Jews, and at the same time promoted their social and economic well-being. He appointed a grand vizir to carry out the sultan's commands; he was named pasha, which literally means 'the sultan's foot'. Below the pasha was the chief qadi. Then came the daftardars or accountants. And lastly nishanjis.or secretaries. Finally, there was the army, the base of the sultan's power, with aghas or commanders to execute his ambitious designs.

This system was latter codified as *Qánún* or the *Book of Laws* based on the Qur'án and the sunna but supplemented by state laws to suit temporal exigencies. Though started by Murád I, it was carried forward by his successors until Muhammad II codified the various changes to form a compendium. He revised and modified it taking into account the commands of the various sultans and the fatwás of the ulamá, which were often given at the behest of the sultan. How religious precepts became subordinate to secular requirements is best seen in the way the 'Palace Schools' were run by the Ottomans. They were primarily designed to impart religious instruction; but they were also used to train students in administration as well as military science. Along with the ulamá, who taught religion, were scientists and technocrats, who gave instruction in secular subjects. The curriculum combined the teaching of theology with the liberal arts as well as physical and vocational training. Even music, both martial and otherwise, was taught. The aim was to produce persons who could be at once good Muslims, loyal soldiers and able administrators. Most of the grand vizirs were products of the Palace Schools.

Sultan Selim I (1512–20), who succeeded Muhammad II, tried to reverse the secular process. He was a Sunni fundamentalist who embarked on a war against what he believed was Shí'ite heresy, as represented by Shah Ismá'il of Persia. He succeeded in subjugating the latter's territories. Likewise, he invaded Egypt where the Mamlúks had usurped power, and made the Abbasid caliph, Mutawakkil, their puppet. He persuaded Mutawakkil to transfer the title of caliph to him; Mutawakkil agreed and gave Selím I the standard and cloak of the Prophet as the insignia of office and handed over to him the guardianship of the holy places of Mecca and Madina. Thus Selím I became the caliph, the first

Ottoman sultan to be so recognized. However, as he was a non-Arab, many ulamā refused to accord him religious sanction.[2]

The greatest of the Ottoman rulers was Süleymān, deservedly known as Süleymān the Magnificent (1520–66) because of the grandeur of his court and the magnificence of his palaces and mosques. He had little respect for the ulamā and concentrated his energies on building a strong army and a sound treasury, which alone, he believed, could ensure the stability of the empire. By his lights, the treasury had to be full for the people to be prosperous; if they were to be prosperous, there had to be justice all round. Where injustice prevailed there was bound to be iniquity and chaos. These ideas were too radical to be acceptable to the fundamentalists who went by established practices; they were not prepared to accept rulers who were neither Arabs nor Quraish as defenders of the faith. Consequently, the Ottomans' base remained mainly secular; for a long while it could not acquire any religious supremacy in the eyes of the faithful.

Süleymān was not bothered by the fundamentalist reaction and was eager to emulate the enlightenment that was spreading in Europe following the Renaissance. He also apprehended danger from the growing military power of Charles V in Austria, Francis I in France and Henry VIII in England, as all three were determined to checkmate the onward march of Islam in Europe. However, they failed to forge a united front against the Ottomans who were as adept in the art of diplomacy as warfare.

Süleymān fully deserved not only the title of 'Magnificent' but also that of 'Just'. To the faithful he was also known by a third title, 'Quānūni' or the 'Law Giver', because of the series of laws he enacted. He did not create a new legal system, but brought the existing one up to date by adopting the laws to new requirements. He regularized the division between temporal and religious matters, which had remained for a long while in a confused state. On the secular side in his set-up were first the members of the sultan's family, then the vizirs and dignitaries of the court, then the provincial governors and army commanders and their officers, the treasury executives, the standing army and, lastly, the bureaucracy. Their authority was confined to affairs of State. On the religious side were first the ulamā, then the qadis, scholars, teachers, the mullās and muftīs, who were the custodians and executors of the shari'ah. They were entrusted with the task of imparting knowledge and were also in charge of the religious affairs of state. The Ottomans were careful not to deviate from the shari'ah but through the ulamā and the muftis, hand-picked by them, they were able to liberalize most of these laws, under a compendium known popularly as *Multaqa al-Uther* or *Confluence of the Seas*, which was the result of intense discussions which the sultan's advisers had with theologians and scholars; it remained in force throughout the empire until the nineteenth century.

The sultan had already liberalized the laws and court procedures; these were now systematized. A more lenient attitude to crime was taken. Corporal punishment was replaced by fines. Even for offences like theft, armed robbery, murder, adultery and fornication, the Qur'ānic penalties of death and mutilation of hands and feet were rarely enforced. Interest on loans was allowed up to eleven per cent. Many other taxes, besides those sanctioned by the Qur'ān or the hadith, were levied. There were taxes imposed on the manufacture and marketing of goods. There was a sales tax and a form of income-tax on high incomes. The ulamā were not happy with these measures, as they lacked religious sanction. The sultan maintained a careful balance between his temporal and religious officers and did not allow either to lord it over the other. In matters of administration the grand vizir was his chief adviser and executor of his commands. In religious affairs, the grand mufti or shaikh al-Islām was the head, enjoying a status equal to the grand vizir. The grand vizir had the edge over the grand mufti, who possessed the authority to grant special privileges only to the ulamā and other religious persons, including immunity from taxation. Under him a hereditary class of theologians was created to whom learning could be passed from father to son. The sultan was generous to them and founded many schools and colleges to train religious teachers. The eight madrasas built around the main mosques were so well endowed that they came to be known as the 'paradise of knowledge'. It was in this fashion that Süleymān managed to resolve the conflicting claims of politics and religion. He combined temporal and religious powers in himself, and then adroitly delegated them to his subordinates and divided them between the temporal and religious functionaries. He managed to keep both sides happy—a feat which was the envy of many Western rulers.[3]

No sooner did Süleymān die (1566) than palace intrigues and administrative corruption began to take their toll. The army, which had enjoyed extra privileges and had maintained itself as a disciplined fighting force, became faction-ridden and failed to equip itself with new weapons or to learn modern techniques of warfare. Moreover, while Europe was rapidly changing from an agricultural to a capitalist economy the Ottomans stagnated with an agricultural economy. The ulamā played a very negative role, resisting every move to modernize commerce and banking, thus thwarting the policies of temporal officers trained in the West; they cited the Qur'ān and the hadīth to put the brakes on the various initiatives.

During the rein of Sultan Muhammad IV (1648–87) an attempt was once again made to bring in knowledge of modern development; his son, Sā'id, drew his attention to the enormous strides the hitherto weak Christian rulers had made through their application of the new methods of development. One of these, he told his father, was the printing press, which they had used to improve communications and especially impart training in new weapons to their armies. He wanted one to be installed in Turkey. The sultan asked his son to obtain clearance from the shaikh al-Islām. He appealed to the latter to permit his friend Ibrahim Muteferriqa to import a printing press from France so that the Ottoman soldiers could be fed information about arms, military techniques and the latest strategies. The shaikh al-Islām reluctantly agreed, provided the press would not print copies of the Qur'ān and other religious literature. Muteferriqa accepted the condition and in a short time set up the press and printed books and pamphlets in Arabic, Persian and Turkish, highlighting the new discoveries in Europe, and commenting on subjects as varied as physics, chemistry, geography, astronomy and cartography. He also published whatever he could find on telescopes, magnets, compasses and other inventions.

During the rule of Ahmad II (1691–95), a belated attempt was made at Westernization. He introduced some reforms in Islamic laws and jurisprudence and encouraged a scientific approach among his officials. He also overhauled the economic system so as to bring it in line with that in Europe. He organized his armed forces on the Western model. The movement towards modernization gathered momentum and found its emblem in the tulip as a symbol of the new era. In 1720 another Ottoman sultan, Ahmad III, sent an envoy to the court of Louis XV with instructions to 'visit the fortresses, factories and other works of French civilization generally and report on those which might be applicable to Turkey.' Then followed a succession of unimaginative and ineffective rulers who were unable to hold the empire together: Mustafa II (1695–1703), Ahmad III (1703–1730) Mahmud I (1730–1754), Uthmān III (1754–1774) and Abd al-Hamid I (1774–1789). Most of them were involved in warding off external threats rather than with internal reforms. The Russian empress, Catherine the Great, came forward as the defender of Christianity against Islam and the British prime minister, Gladstone condemned the Ottomans as barbarians. Even Voltaire hailed the Russian invasion of Ottoman territories as 'a war between reason and fanaticism, civilization and backwardness'.

Selim III (1789–1807), who succeeded Abd al-Hamid I, was a forward-looking young man, determined to rescue the empire. He realized that this could not be done on old, outmoded lines; new measures, borrowed from the West, had to be introduced among his people.

He had ascended to the throne in the year of the French Revolution, echoes of which had begun to be heard in Turkey. The new ideas of liberty, fraternity and equality sweeping through Europe affected Turkish towns and cities as well. The sultan, though sympathetic to these notions, had his problems. The empire was no longer a unified force—the local pashas were trying to defy the central authority and abuse their powers; in the provinces, native subjects were clamouring for greater autonomy. The deserts of Arabia were set on fire by the Wahhābis, followers of the puritanical leader, Abd al-Wahhāb, who wanted to free Islam from the 'heretical clutches of the Ottomans'. The Druzes were in revolt in Syria, the Arabs in Palestine. So also the Mamlūks in Egypt. These rebellions were not confined to Arab Muslims. Christian subjects of the sultan everywhere were more restless and in European territories clamoured for independence. The Ottomans had never before faced such a challenge to their authority in the empire.

The sultan saw the writing on the wall and quickly entered into an alliance with the new rulers of France, to forge a better understanding between the Turks and the French. The alliance was symbolized by the planting of a 'Tree of Liberty' in Istanbul. He then turned his attention to modernizing his army; simultaneously, he initiated sweeping educational reforms, so the new generation could face the growing challenge from the West. He sent young Turks to Europe to study modern methods of administration and new ways of social behaviour. On their return, they formed a new class, more secular than religious, dedicated to liberal ideas. The ulamā could do little to stem this tide from the West. Once freed of external dangers, the sultan decided to make radical changes at home. The ulamā rose in revolt against these changes. They were led by the grand mufti who declared that all these measures were the handiwork of infidels out to destroy Islam. Finally he issued a fatwā demanding the deposing of the sultan. The janissaries, whose own power was threatened by the Western-educated elite, responded to the call and forced Selim to abdicate, as he could not carry his soldiers or subjects with him on the pace of reforms. He was, therefore, condemned to die. Before he was taken for execution, he counselled his successor Mustafa IV not to commit the same mistake as he did of going in for secularization. However the reformists did not take their defeat lying down and re-grouped themselves under the leadership of Mustafa Bayrakdar and deposed Mustafa IV. They installed in his place Mahmud II (1808–39), who promised that he would carry forward the reforms initiated by Selim III and not listen to the ulamā. Bayrakdar was appointed the grand vizir and he introduced further measures of Westernization. The ulamā feigned approval but secretly conspired with the janissaries to overthrow the new regime. They set fire to the palace and Bayrakdar and most of his lieutenants perished. The forces of orthodoxy once again gained a gory victory over secularism and the movement for reforms received a big set-back. The new sultan, however, after some time managed to revive the processes of modernization. He first struck at the janissaries. This totally paralysed their collaborators—the ulamā. Then he reorganized his armed forces and won over some ulamā to his side. Eventually, even the grand mufti was persuaded to support him. When the disarrayed janissaries again rose in rebellion, the sultan appeared in person, holding the sacred standard of the Prophet in one hand and the fatwā of the grand mufti in his favour in the other. The impact was tremendous. The artillery pounded the janissaries, killing them by the thousands, with the populace cheering the onslaught. Besides being a victory for reformists against the reactionaries, it was also a triumph of modern weaponry over antiquated arms. The sultan decreed the abolition of the janissaries and banned the order of Bektashi dervishes who had plagued the Ottomans in the past. He then tried to build a new order more in accord with the secular requirements of the times.

Although with the loss of its European territories the empire had shrunk, Mahmud II was able to consolidate what remained of it by introducing radical changes aimed at Westernizing it and knitting his subjects into a multi-religious society. Towards this end, he demarcated the affairs of state from those of religion. The grand muftī's wings had already been clipped; the grand vizir's powers were also curtailed and delegated to different vizirs, aided by consultative councils. In course of time, ministries with specific charges came into existence. The execution of religious decrees was transferred from the office of the grand vizir to that of the grand muftī with the specific provision that they would apply only to Muslims. A new civil jurisdiction under a secular judge was created to deal with non-religious disputes. Hence, two separate courts came into existence—one dealt with religious matters; the other with secular disputes. Likewise, with the exception of mosques and some other religious institutions, schools and colleges were handed over to a secular Ministry of Education. The sultan also tightened his hold on the administration, especially its finances, awkaf, and so deprived the ulamā free access to these funds.

The grand vizir gradually became the prime minister and his Council of Ministers, the Cabinet; the grand muftī was left to deal with only religious matters. In either case, the ultimate authority vested with the sultan. Though not exactly democratic, these reforms helped to break down old, worn-out methods of governance and considerably diluted the exercise of autocratic rights and the privileges of powerful individuals. In the regrouping of departments prominence was accorded to the Department of Military Affairs and the Department of Judicial Affairs. Then there were the departments of education, commerce, agriculture and industry, which were jointly put in charge of one minister. The departments were collectively called the Board of Useful Affairs. All these were manned by educated members of the younger generation, mostly Western-oriented. Similarly, the provincial administration also acquired a new look; its officers were also from a new class, which did not depend for their appointment on lineage, influence or patronage. Nor was religious background or training given any importance; proficiency in secular pursuits was the determining factor.

Sultan Mahmud II also made fundamental changes in the system of jurisprudence. Though the sharī'ah and the qānūn remained in force, they were supplemented by royal edicts, which decisively changed the approach to the administration of justice. By this method, the sultan reinforced the concept of adālat or justice, which administered secular public laws, not connected with the shari'ah. Judges were made independent of the executive and directed to apply these laws strictly, irrespective of the status or position of the parties in the dispute. Public servants were made accountable. Punishment was prescribed by legislation and not left to the discretion of a judge. However, Muslim Personal Law was segregated from the common secular laws and left untouched, for example, the laws of inheritance, marriage and divorce, which were treated as sacrosanct. Even the sultan, with his passion for reform, could not tamper with them. However, education, which had for long been the preserve of the ulamā, was taken out of the control of the shaikh al-Islām; engineering, medicine and military science were taught on modern secular lines, untrammelled by any religious taboos. Despite protests from the ulamā, dissection and autopsy were made compulsory subjects for medical students. The study of French was also made obligatory and it soon replaced Arabic and Persian as the medium of instruction. Inevitably, the emphasis shifted from religion to secular knowledge. The annual report of the Board of Useful Affairs pointed out in 1838: 'Religious knowledge serves salvation in the world to come but science serves the perfection of man in this world.'[4] The sultan sanctioned the publication of a Turkish newspaper with a French version. It became required reading for public officials. He also introduced a postal service. Thus, out of the ruins of the Islamic Sultanate emerged a modern secular State, with many outward manifestations of change. Beards gave way to clean-shaven cheeks, divans and cushions to chairs and tables; long robes, turbans and slippers to tunics, breeches and boots. The fez cap was a compromise to which the ulamā reluctantly agreed; it was later turned into a symbol of Islamic solidarity.

Mahmud II was succeeded by his son Abd ül-Mejid I (1839–61), who was considerably influenced by the British ambassador in Istanbul, S.Canning, who goaded him to further secularize his state. On 3 November 1839, Mejid produced a constitution guaranteeing freedom of thought and expression, security of life and property and social and political rights, which his subjects had not enjoyed before. It came to be known as tanzimat or reorganization and was hailed as the Magna Carta of Islam. Even the sultan was made subject to the laws and no distinction was permitted between Muslims and non-Muslims, who were decreed to be equal in every respect. Lord Palmerston, the British prime minister, commended it as a 'grand stroke of policy'. It was welcomed by Mejid's Christian and Jewish subjects, who were exempted from paying the poll tax and given the right to employment in the armed services. The reaction of the ulamā and the Muslim bureaucracy and nobility was so adverse that they instigated street riots which were ruthlessly suppressed by the police. The sultan was unnerved; in order to appease the agitators he appointed the reactionary xenophobe Riza Pasha as grand vizir. Riza Pasha tried to turn the clock back but the secular forces ranged against him were too powerful for him to succeed. Soon he had to quit and his successor, Reshid Pasha, had to tread the secular path. He advised the sultan to call an elected assembly at Istanbul to which every province sent two representatives invested with certain legislative powers. Likewise, in every province, an elected council was established. A revised penal code was promulgated which once again made no distinction between Muslims and non-Muslims. A commercial code was formulated guaranteeing international transactions and free trade. Consequently, business undertakings, banks and insurance companies sprouted in Turkey. Their main beneficiaries were the Jews and Christians because Muslims did not take to these vocations readily, being accustomed to military and administrative jobs. They resented these reforms and were backed by the ulamā, who were against the secularization process. The old-fashioned traders and artisans also did not like the changes and soon there was a groundswell of disillusionment with the young sultan's policies; the ulamā fanned the discontentment with the result that there was widespread unrest, of which the external enemies of Turkey took full advantage.

Czar Nicholas I of Russia forged an alliance with the British against the 'heathen' Ottomans on the ground that they were harassing Christians. In such a hostile atmosphere, Abd al-Aziz (1861–76) ascended the throne on the premature death of his father Abd ül-Mejid I. He did not care for reforms and decided that might alone would save the Sultanate. Towards this end, he assumed despotic powers, much to the chagrin of large numbers of younger Turks, who formed an opposition group, with a bold programme of action. They decided to fight for hurriya or liberty, and asked for greater constitutional reforms, including the introduction of a proper parliamentary system with the sultan as its nominal head, on the lines of Britain and other democracies. The Young Turks dispersed to different parts of the Sultanate and organized clandestine cells. They did not believe in piecemeal reform like the tanzimat and demanded an overhaul of the entire administrative system. Many intellectuals joined them, the most outstanding being Nāmiq Kemāl, a journalist and author, who propagated in his writings love for both freedom and fatherland. He also tried to synthesize the teachings of Islam with the new secular upsurge and quoted chapter and verse from the Qur'ān and the hadīth to justify it. The British pattern, he believed, was the ideal and could be used as a model for a system of governance where Islamic and Western values could be fused judiciously. The people had to be the final arbitrators. The ulamā opposed him and stood by the sultan but the popular current was running against them. A prolonged drought, followed by severe famine, coupled with the outbreak of violence between Christians and Muslims created new difficulties for the sultan. To compound his difficulties, Muslims were massacred in some European countries and in retaliation Christians were killed by Turkish irregulars in the Ottoman territories. Religious hostilities between the two communities broke out on a wide scale; the czar took advantage of the deteriorating situation and persuaded the British and the French to impose economic sanctions on the Turks. The sultan was cornered; he could not withstand the blockade and surrendered to the West. His subjects were outraged. Thousands of students of theology of the three principal mosques of Istanbul came out on the streets and demanded the dismissal of his two main lieutenants, the grand vizir and the grand muftī, who had supported the sultan and implemented his orders. The police tried to control the mob but it led to bloodshed and many lives were lost. The sultan, shaken by the popular reaction, dismissed both the dignitaries. He promised to restore the status quo, to dedicate himself to the cause of Islam and to run his administration on the lines of the 'rightly guided' caliphs. He declared that he would function henceforth in accordance with the rules of the sharī'ah and provide for a shūrā composed of popular representatives. He also promised to punish the corrupt and indolent. No one, however, trusted the sultan and demanded that he be removed. The new grand muftī issued a fatwā to the effect that Abd al-Aziz suffered from 'mental derangement, ignorance of political affairs, diversion of public revenues to private expenditure and conduct generally injurious to State and community.'[5]

He was, in consequence deposed and his nephew, Murād V (1876), was enthroned. Nāmiq Kemāl was appointed secretary to the new sultan; other reformists were chosen for high offices. Midhat Pasha became the grand vizir. Murād V could not cope with the growing demands of the reformists and suffered a nervous breakdown. He stepped down in less than a year in favour of his younger brother, Abd al-Hamid II (1876–1909). The new sultan promulgated, immediately on ascending the throne, a constitution which guaranteed strict enforcement of the shari'ah for the Muslims and justice and fair play for the non-Muslims. The document was a compromise between fundamentalism and secularism and, therefore, did not satisfy either group, though it was not opposed by anyone in view of the sultan's ordering an immediate general election and convening the first Ottoman Parliament in March 1877, which consisted of 120 elected deputies and 25 nominated officials chosen from all over the empire. But soon the sultan found their deliberations inconvenient; he could not comply with their demands and satisfy their hopes and aspirations and, therefore, he dissolved the Parliament. An uproar greeted his decision and he was compelled to re-convene the Parliament. He avoided further confrontation with his people as the czar declared a war against Turkey, and the deputies agreed to give him their full support.

In the war, the Turks fared badly. Under the Treaty of Stefano, Turkey had to surrender most of its European territories. The deputies blamed the sultan for this loss, the sultan blamed the British and the French for having betrayed the Ottomans despite their treaty obligations. The sultan prorogued the Parliament and assumed autocratic powers. He declared: 'I now understand that it is only by force that one can rule the people', and added, 'excess of liberty is as dangerous as its absence.' Freed of international entanglement, the sultan began to consolidate his position at home. He dismissed grand vizir Midhat and sent him in captivity to an Arabian fortress, where he was murdered in 1884. He also got rid of the other reformists and chose ministers and officials loyal to him. The only redeeming feature of his otherwise authoritarian rule was his emphasis on education, which he completely secularized and expanded. He founded the University of Istanbul and encouraged it to be run on modern, secular lines.

Outside Turkey, the sultan's position became precarious. Tunis had already been taken over by the French, Egypt by the British and Central Asia by Russia; in West Asia the local Arabs organized themselves under Ahmad Arabi and demanded the ouster of the Khedive, who was the sultan's protege. This was the first popular Arab movement for independence from Turkish rule. The rallying cry was 'Egypt for the Egyptians'. Despite British support, the Turks failed to suppress the rebellion. Strangely enough, it took a secular turn against the religious Ottomans. Though the sultan was deprived of his European possessions, his Muslim territories had, till then, remained intact and supported him. Egypt occupied pride of place; its capital Cairo had been the spiritual centre of Islam for more than a thousand years. (It was in this city that the sultan's forbear Selim I was recognized as the caliph in 1517.) Consequently, the rebellion in Egypt left the sultan shaken. He blamed the Christian powers for instigating it and appealed to the Muslim world to save the honour of Islam. The Muslims of India and Central Asia responded to the call but not the Arabs who were eager to free themselves from the Ottoman yoke. Though he did not receive the expected support from many Muslims, there was an undercurrent of sympathy for the sultan. It later found expression in pan-Islamism, propagated vigorously by its ideologue, Jamāl al-Din al-Afghani (1838–97), who toured different parts of the Muslim world, trying to rouse Muslim sentiment against the West.

Meanwhile the international situation had also considerably worsened; Britain and France were ranged against Germany. The Ottomans were more drawn to the latter. Kaiser Wilhelm II paid a state visit and assured the sultan of his friendship; the Muslims were thrilled as they had come to distrust the British and the French. They believed that German help would be invaluable in consolidating Ottoman power and were enthused by the spirit of unity generated among their co-religionists, which came to be symbolized by the construction of the Hejaz railway running from Damascus to Madina, to which Muslims from many lands willingly contributed (indeed, the railway helped to boost the prestige of the sultan).

The Young Turks were as active as before and worked secretly for the abolition of hereditary monarchy. The support of the pan-Islamists to the sultan did not dampen their spirit; they continued with their agitation and formed the Committee of Union and Progress to achieve their objective. 'They were supported by a military leader, Enver Beg, and his young troopers. The sultan appealed to the shaikh al-Islām to issue a fatwā against them. But sensing that opposition to the sultan was growing among the people, he refused. The sultan cast about desperately for some way to curb the rebels but his ministers counselled caution, fearing that any precipitate action would lead to civil war. The sultan bowed to popular pressure and swore on the Qur'ān that a new constitution would be promulgated, guaranteeing freedom to the people, and a general election held to ascertain their wishes. He thus saved his throne. On 17 December 1908, the sultan opened the new Parliament which comprised equally of Turkish and non-Turkish deputies—a number of the non-Turks being Christians and Jews. He promised that henceforth he would abide by the Constitution and work to establish a multi-religious secular State.

This was resented by the ulamā, who instigated the regular Muslim soldiers in Istanbul to mutiny. The mutineers demanded the restoration of the shari'ah and an Islamic pattern of administration. Mobs joined them with cries of 'Down with the Constitution'. They forced their way into the Parliament chamber and the deputies had to flee. The grand vizir resigned. A more pliable substitute, who assured strict adherence to the laws of Islam, was found to be the sultan. The Committee suffered a set-back but its members reorganized themselves and met in Salonika, where they decided to march on Istanbul; many officers and soldiers joined them. They were able to capture the palace and the Parliament chamber, where the deputies were meeting in camera. Suspecting the hand of the sultan behind the counter revolution, they asked the shaikh al-Islām for his deposition. When he so decreed the sultan was dethroned and his brother Rashīd (1909–18) was installed in his place.

The real power in the result passed into the hands of the leading members of the Committee of Union and Progress, who received more and more support from the rank and file in the army. They took immediate steps to legalize their demands by incorporating them into a secular constitution; it was a half-hearted measure, however, and had little impact on the people. The new deputies were hesitant about accepting Westernization wholeheartedly; nor were they clear in their minds about the extent to which they should preserve their Islamic heritage.[6] The Young Turks again came to the fore and proclaimed their faith in

Turkish nationalism. They also demanded radical Westernization. A more moderate group known as the Party of the Liberal Union opposed the Committee of Union and Progress. A bitter tussle ensued between the two. In the midst of these internal conflicts, Turkey became embroiled in a war with the Italians who had occupied Libya. Then came the onslaught from the newly formed Balkan League. In the ensuing war, most Christians, except in Germany, took up arms against the Ottomans. Before the issue could be resolved World War I (1914–18) broke out, in which Turkey allied itself with Germany; with the defeat of Germany, the Ottomans lost their empire to the British and the French and their allies and were barely able to retain their Turkish homeland.

9

The Indian Impact

Four races were responsible for moulding the political aspect of Islam down the centuries: the Arabs, the Iranians, the Turks and the Indians. We have looked at the role of the first three; the fourth race played its part in the development of the Islamic polity after the Turkman Muslims entered India. The interaction between the two races gave a distinct character to both the Muslim polity and society. Here it should be borne in mind that, while in all the other regions conquered by the Muslims, the people were almost wholly converted to Islam, in India, despite almost a thousand years of Muslim rule, the people remained largely non-Muslim. Consequently, the practice of Islam here and its political manifestation was different from what prevailed elsewhere. In India, while Muslims and Hindus co-existed in amicable harmony most of the time there were occasional confrontations between the two. But the skirmishes rarely had their origin in religion. Whatever might have been the initial urge and intent of the Muslim conquerors, each of them—the Ghoris, the Khiljis, the Tughlaks, the Lodis, and the Mughals—established a pattern of administration which was different from what existed in other parts of the Muslim world. The invaders, no doubt, conformed to the rules of the shari'ah in the beginning, including the imposition of the jaziya on their non-Muslim subjects. But this was prompted more from a desire to enhance their revenue than from a sense of religious duty. Almost all the rulers who founded kingdoms in India gave little or no importance to proselytizing or conversion of their subjects to Islam; also they did not attempt to turn their empires into theocracies, for they were essentially soldiers eager to annex more and more territories and to consolidate what they had conquered. The Mughals who ruled India from the sixteenth to the eighteenth centuries were certainly more sophisticated than the Hindus but they were still willing to assimilate whatever they found attractive in India. Babur, the first Mughal emperor, was as rapacious an invader as Mahmud of Ghazna, but he did not much care for iconoclasm or religious fanaticism. The later Mughals settled in India, inter-married, and so mixed with the local population, that they became as much Indians as the people they ruled over. They discovered a great affinity with their erstwhile enemies, the Rajputs, who became their greatest supporters. Rajput generals and administrators soon became pillars of the Mughal empire, a relationship which Muslim fundamentalists abhorred but the common Muslims did not mind.

Earlier, in the pre-Mughal days, the sultans of Delhi were eager to obtain some kind of religious sanction; hence they tried and got farmāns from the Abbasid caliphs, sanctifying their rule. The recipients inscribed on their coins the name of the caliph along with their own. Even in khutbas at Friday congregational prayers, the names of the caliph and the ruler of the time were jointly mentioned. These formalities helped in reassuring the soldiers and Muslim subjects about their religious legitimacy. But some ambitious rulers tried to bypass the caliph. According to Ziyā' al-Din Barani, the noted Arab historian, Alauddin Khilji, founder of the Slave Dynasty, toyed at one time with the idea of declaring himself the caliph and even of founding a new religion; but he gave it up on the advice of his generals who thought it might offend Muslim sentiment.[1] Likewise, for a while, Muhammad Tughlak harboured the notion of proclaiming himself the supreme head of the Islamic world but he abandoned this in the face of fundamentalist opposition. Most pre-Mughal rulers preferred to style themselves sultans, in the Islamic parlance of the age, and acknowledged the titular overlordship of the Abbasid caliph without paying tribute or showing any other consideration to him. Another practice which these rulers honoured was baih or approval of the congregation in the main mosque of the capital, following their ascendancy to the throne. This again, though as much of a formality as recognition by the Abbasid caliph, helped to legitimize their rule in the eyes of the faithful.

Not many sultans bothered about the hereditary principle; the succession of the dynasty was often decided by the Turkish nobility at court or by the army commanders or both together. Although they tried to model their administration on the basis of the shari'ah, they soon realized that the problems they faced were often due to the methods of governance advocated by the ulamā: hence the sultans often ignored what the ulamā advised. In the Delhi Sultanate, for instance, the pattern of administration was, by and large, temporal. The chief administrator, known as khwāja jahān, enjoyed the status of prime minister, with control over the state's finances. He was assisted by two dignitaries: the mushrif-i-mamālik, or the accountant-general and the mustawfi-i-mamālik or the auditor-general. The army was managed by the āriz-i-mamālik or the military department. So was the intelligence agency known as the barid-i-mamālik. Royal correspondence was entrusted to a separate organization known as the dabir-i-khāss. These departments had little to do with religious norms; in fact, religious affairs were separated from temporal control and were put directly in the care of the ṣadr al-ṣudūr, who also functioned as the qāzi-i-mamālik, or the chief justice. He reported to the sultan who rarely interfered with his work or tampered with his judgements. Minor variations were made in this pattern by different sultans to cope with the growing requirements of their domains but the division between temporal and religious authorities was strictly maintained. The separation ensured that the administration of the state worked without a hitch; it also discouraged internal rivalries and jealousies. Hence, despite changes in dynasties, there were not many palace coups or religious uprisings. The armed forces were free of internal squabbles and presented a strong defence against external threat. Proof of this can be seen from the time when the Mongols overran the Abbasid Caliphate and dealt, to quote the words of the Arab historian Ibn al-Athir, 'the death blow to Islam'; contrary to the experience in other parts of the Muslim world, the sultans were able to repel these Mongol invasions and to preserve intact their Indian territories.[2]

The Delhi Sultanate was divided into provinces which were administered by nā'ib-sultans or walis, appointed by the sultan; below them were subordinates called āmils, entrusted with the administration of a purgana or district. Walis were answerable to the sultan acting through the khwāja jahān or the vizir.

An important factor in the stability of the Sultanate was the influence of the sufis who brought millions of Hindus into the fold of Islam. Their achievement was all the more remarkable if one considers the fact that it took place in a society where the local people prided themselves on the superiority of their religion. Of them, al-Biruni, who visited India in the first half of the eleventh century, wrote; 'The Hindus believe that there is no country like theirs, no nation like theirs, no kings like theirs, no religion like theirs, no learning like theirs. They are by nature niggardly in communicating that which they know and they take the greatest possible care to withhold it from men of another caste among their own people, still much more from any foreigner.'[3]

Given this sort of intransigence, the sultans worried a great deal about the manner in which to treat their Hindu subjects. Sultan Iltutmish (1210–36), acknowledged as the greatest ruler of the Delhi Sultanate, was constantly troubled by the problem. Discussing this, a distinguished Islamic scholar and member of the Pakistan Civil Service, Mr S.M. Ikram observes:

> Three out of four schools of Islamic law (the Hanifi was the expection) favoured the extermination of all idolaters, but the practice, initiated by Muhammad ibn Qāsim and maintained by the Ghaznawid, of treating idolatrous Hindus at least as privileged Dhimmis, proved more powerful. When the ulamā urged Iltutmish to give effect to the opinion of the majority of the founders of Islamic schools of law, he convened a conference and called upon his vizir Nizām al-Mulk Junaydi to explain the position. The vizir argued that since India had only recently been conquered, and since the Muslims were fewer in number than the Hindus, it would not be wise to attempt a course of action that might lead to disturbances. This argument was accepted and the status quo was maintained. The possibility of imposing the viewpoint of the majority of Islamic law was never again raised in the form urged by the ulamā.[4]

Thus the administration remained secular and as new people (notably converts to Islam) entered the administration, which had remained the preserve of men of pure Turkish descent, it became more broadbased and liberal.

Ghiyasuddin Balban (1265–87), a competent governor in the Sultanate, who usurped the throne, lusted so much after power that he proclaimed himself the vice-regent of God. He destroyed the power bases of both the secular nobles and the ulamā. He respected neither his colleagues nor the institutions he inherited. His ambition was to be a king in the majestic tradition of the ancient kings of Persia, who were obeyed as the shadows of God on earth. Barani complained that Balban had no 'fear of God'; all that mattered to him was his own interest 'whether it was in accordance with the sharī'ah or not'.[5]

The Khilji sultans behaved the same way. The founder of the dynasty, Alauddin, told the chief kazi, Mughisud Dīn, 'I do not know what is lawful or unlawful. Whatever I think for the good of the State or suitable for an emergency I decree.'[6] Neither the ulamā nor the Turkish nobility dared question him. He was ruthless in his pursuit of territory and power. He favoured the less privileged. He raised Mālik Kāfūr, a low-born convert to Islam, to the highest position in the empire and appointed Amir Khusraw, born of an Indian mother, poet-laureate. The Tughlaks, who succeeded the Khiljis to the Delhi Sultanate, followed the same policies. According to a contemporary chronicler, Farishta, they ignored canonical law, as expounded by the ulamā, and based their system on political expediency and worldly experience. Qur'ānic punishments were liberalized. Hindus were treated more humanely. Most sultans, observed a court historian, 'held the view that a combination of religion and kingship was not possible'.[7]

Even when the power of the Delhi Sultanate declined and relations between the Hindu officers and the Muslim ruling elite deteriorated, the general atmosphere of peace and harmony was but infrequently vitiated. In the capital there was occasionally some discord; but elsewhere the provincial satraps who had assumed independent power were able to maintain good relations between the two communities. The Bhakti movement also helped in this process. Two of its greatest exponents in northern India were Kabir (1455–1575), a Muslim weaver, and Nanak (1469–1539), the founder of Sikhism. Through songs in colloquial Hindi, Kabir tried to foster a spirit of harmony between the Hindus and Muslims. He preached:

It is not by fasting and repeating prayers and the creed
That one goeth to heaven;
The inner veil of the temple of Mecca
Is in man's heart, if the truth be known.
Make thy mind thy Ka'ba, thy body its enclosing temple,

Conscience its prime teacher;
Sacrifice wrath, doubt, and malice;
Make patience thine utterance of the five prayers.
The Hindus and the Mussalmans have the same Lord.[8]

Likewise, Nanak reminded the Muslims:

A Muslim's faith is to follow the Prophet
Caring neither for life nor for death;
To accept the Ordinances of God;
To believe He is the One and only Creator
And obliterate every thought of self.
Thereafter, O Nanak, if he extends his mercy to all
Treats all living beings as the same
Himself a Mussalman he can proclaim.[9]

And Nanak reminded the Hindus:

Not by talk you can achieve union
He who sees all mankind as equals
Can be deemed to be a yogi.[10]

And thus was peace and harmony fostered much, to the discomfiture of the ulamā. One outcome of this free intermingling between the members of the two faiths was the birth of a common language known as Khariboli, which later developed into Urdu. Also, there was a literary and cultural renaissance: poetry, music and the arts blossomed across northern India. Governors of provinces became patrons of this intercommunal fusion. Zayn al-Ābidin's rule in Kashmir was the high watermark of Hindu-Muslim fraternity; it was also fostered under the Husayn Shāhi dynasty (1493–1539) in Bengal and the Bahmanis in the South. The Ādil Shāhis of Bijapur (1090–1686), the Nizām Shāhis of Ahmednagar (1480–1686) the Imād Shāhis of Berar (1410–1568), the Barid Shāhis of Bidar (1580–1699) and the Qutb Shāhis of Golconda (1512–1687) also encouraged more harmonious relations between their Hindu and Muslim subjects.

Many of these rulers, who were Shi'ites, were finally swept away by the Sunni Mughals, but it is a matter of historical record that their administrations were, in many respects, more secular than that of the Mughals and more responsive to inter-religious rapprochement.

In this respect the contribution of the ṣūfis cannot be ignored; in fact until they came on the scene there was little meeting ground between the two faiths. The ulamā distrusted the Hindu pandits and since the raids of Mahmud of Ghazna and the destruction of the Somnath temple and other Hindu temples, the Hindus had developed what al-Biruni described as 'the most inveterate aversion towards all Muslims'.[11] Three centuries later, Ibn Baṭṭūta, after his travels throughout India, observed that no Muslim was either allowed to enter the house of a Hindu or given food in the same vessels as theirs. He wrote, 'If a Muslim is fed out of their vessels, they either break the vessels or give them away to the Muslims.'[12] The Muslims also looked down upon the idol worshipping Hindus and their caste system. Such was the hatred nurtured among them over the centuries, that saints like Kabir, Ramanand and Nanak on the one hand, and the ṣūfis on the other could manage to minimize, but not completely eradicate it.

The collapse of the Delhi Sultanate resulted in the establishment of petty kingdoms, both Muslim and Hindu, all over the north. They were not only independent but distrustful of one another. They could present no unity of purpose or action. Fragmented India offered an open invitation to the ambitious Bābur. On the battlefield of Panipat, he inflicted a crushing defeat to the last sultan of the Lodi dynasty, Ibrahim Lodi, on 21 April 1526. Flushed with victory he proclaimed himself the emperor of Hindustan. He was more a soldier than an administrator. But unlike other invaders, he was more humane and liberal towards the people he had subjugated. According to Tāriq Muhammad Shāhis, Bābur told his young son, Humayun, that to successfully rule India, he should make no distinction between Muslims and Hindus. Humayun followed his advice but found that the ulamā had conspired with one of his generals, Sher Shah, to bring about his downfall and to establish successfully his dynastic kingdom. Humayun had to flee the country but he soon returned to reclaim his throne with the armed assistance given him by Shah Tahmāsp of Iran. Six months later Humayun slipped on his library stairs and received injuries that proved fatal.

His son, Akbar, then only thirteen years old, took over as emperor; his father's close friend and commander Bairam Khan became the regent. Four years later, Akbar rid himself of Bairam Khan's tutelage and assumed full powers. In less than a decade, he extended the territories of his empire to almost the whole of India, from Kashmir in the north to Bengal in the east and across the Deccan plateau in the south. He did more towards secularizing the administration than any other Muslim ruler in India; his government was a model of religious tolerance and broad humanism. He reconciled his Hindu and Muslim subjects by his policy of sulh kull or peace towards all . He tried to bring about a synthesis of the two religions—Islam and Hinduism. In this he faced strong opposition from not only the ulamā but also the Hindu pandits but he persevered. First, he confronted the ulamā and asked them to reconcile their differences among themselves. He assembled them regularly in the 'Ibādāt Khāna (House of Worship) where discussions on Islamic tenets were organized. In such meetings the true nature of the ulamā was revealed: Akbar and his advisers saw how the ulamā, instead of trying to reach a consensus, were only interested in scoring points off each other; and often they used intemperate language. Having had his fill of the ulamā, Akbar invited scholars of other religions to expound their beliefs. Their disputations were as acrimonious. He then came to the conclusion that God would never want to divide His creatures; every true religion must aim at uniting them. He found little support for his views among the votaries of different religions who insisted that their faith was the best. So he propounded his concept of Dīn-i-Ilāhī—the religion of God. Prof. Rama Sharma in his thesis, *The Religious Policy of the Mughal Emperors,* is of the opinion that Dīn-i-Ilāhī was not a new religion; it did not renounce Islam as alleged by Akbar's critics. On the contrary, it was an attempt to bring together 'a band of enthusiastically devoted followers, some of whom, like the English murderers of Beckett, were prepared to give their all in the royal service.'[13] The charge of heresy levelled against Akbar was based on highly prejudiced accounts by bigots like Badayuni, who disapproved of Akbar's liberalism. The brothers, Abu'l al-Fazl and Faizi, in the service of the emperor, saw in Dīn-i-Ilāhī a new hope for the consolidation of the Islamic brotherhood. Some leading ulamā also supported Akbar as is evident from the fatwā they issued, accepting his supremacy in religious affairs. The 'decree of infallibility', as it is erroneously labelled, only re-stated the Islamic tenet that 'the rank of sultān-i-ādil (dispenser of justice) is higher in the eyes of God than that of a mujtahid (interpreter)'. It also stated that:

should. . .in the future a religious question come up, regarding which the opinions of the mujtahids are at variance, and His Majesty in his penetrating understanding and clear wisdom be inclined to adopt, for the benefit of the nation, and as a political expedient, any of the conflicting opinions, which exist on the point, and issue a decree to that effect, we do hereby agree that such a decree shall be binding on us and on the whole nation. Further, we declare that should His Majesty think fit to issue a new order, we and the nation shall likewise be bound by it; provided always that such order be not only in accordance with some verse of the Qurān, but also of real benefit to the nation; and further any opposition on the part of his subjects to such an order passed by His Majesty shall involve damnation in the world to come and loss of property and religious privileges in this.[14]

This fatwā has been faulted by many orthodox jurists; but Abu'l Kalām Āzād, the eminent Muslim divine, has explained that it was in conformity with accepted Islamic political theory, under which the ruler was supreme and subject only to the limitations placed on him by the Qur`ān and the hadīth. According to Āzād, the ruler enjoyed the right of ijtihad more than any other Muslim, however pious and learned. Nevertheless, at the time, some ulamā condemned the emperor's move as anti-Islamic. The charge that Akbar claimed divinity was made first by Mulla Muhammad Yazdi, who was a Shi'a. The chief kazi of Bengal also accused him of claiming prophethood. Another divine, Muzul Mulk, characterized Dīn-i-Ilāhi as a new religion and condemned Akbar's move as apostasy. Disgruntled elements found an opportunity to foment rebellion and tried to dethrone the emperor and replace him by his brother Mirza Muhammad Hākim. It is significant that none of these attempts to rouse religious frenzy gained popular support and were easily put down by the imperial forces.

Akbar was not a heretic and remained a Muslim till his death. His belief in one God, his reverence for the Prophet and Muslim saints, and his pilgrimages to the darghas of Muinuddin Chishti of Ajmer and Shaikh Salim Chishti, in whose honour he raised a new city, Fatehpur Sikri, show his devotion to Islam. Although he introduced innovations in the sharī'ah and passed a number of decrees which were unpalatable to the fundamentalists, he never pretended to be a prophet nor, as Vincent Smith has alleged, did he ever persecute Muslims. The charge of apostasy against Akbar received credence because of the diatribe against him by the Muslim savant Shaikh Ahmad Sirhindi, but it was born out of prejudice, mainly because the Shaikh was erroneously led to believe the report that, under Akbar, 'Hindus were demolishing mosques and building temples in their place.'[15] Sirhindi's rigid and orthodox outlook, moreover, could not stomach Akbar's liberalism and so he carried on a relentless campaign against him. His voice found ready acceptance in orthodox circles, which hailed him as the mujaddid-i-sani or 'reviver of Islam'. But it gathered some strength only after Akbar's death.

During Akbar's lifetime, his favourite adviser, Abu'l Fazl, had refuted, with cold logic, the charge of heresy as 'ill-informed and unfair' and explained that the emperor's liberalism, as reflected in his policies and regulations, was grossly distorted by the ulama, who had failed to find favour with him. However, it must be admitted that Akbar erred in mixing humanism with divinity, religious tolerance with royal patronage, and secular requirements with sectarian loyalty. His liberalism served a limited purpose but it failed to overcome the people's inborn prejudices against one another. It neither enthused his Muslim subjects nor reassured his Hindu subjects (who were happy with their own ancient religion and not ready to give it up). While his approach helped to broaden the base of his administration, with the recruitment of followers of all religions, and the removal of insidious discrimination against Hindus, it could not change anything but the surface manifestations of the deep divide between the religions. This despite the fact that Akbar himself practised what he preached. His harem was ruled by his Rajput wife, Jodhabai, who continued to worship her Hindu idols (and bore him his eldest son and successor, Jahangir) and his chief advisers were Mansingh and Todar Mal, both Hindu Rajputs. Mansingh, on his part, helped Akbar in the expansion of his empire and Todar Mal was responsible for its solid financial position.

On Akbar's death, his son Jahangir (1605–1627) succeeded to the throne. He was a complex character. Having Hindu blood in his veins, on his mother's side, he was even-handed in his dealings with his Hindu and Muslim subjects. However, there were instances of short-sightedness in some of his acts, of which the two most glaring ones were the murder of Abu'l Fazl and the persecution of the fifth guru of the Sikhs,

Arjun Dev, who succumbed to torture in prison in Lahore. Otherwise, as Francis Gladwin has remarked, 'from the beginning to the end of his reign, Jahāngīr's disposition towards his subjects appears to have been invariably humane and considerate.'[16] In his memoirs, Jahāngīr writes, 'The first order I gave was for fastening the chain of justice.' Like his father, he sought the company of men of different faiths and listened to their discourses. He remained a practising Muslim and came into conflict with the ulamā only once. Upset with Shaikh Ahmad Sirhindi for sending letters to leading Muslims, exhorting them to rescue Islam from the heathen policies initiated by Akbar and Jahāngīr, the emperor summoned the Shaikh to his court and at first tried to pacify him, but finding him adamant and unbending, imprisoned him. Later, repenting his decision, the emperor released him and showed him due reverence.

Jahāngīr was succeeded by his son Shahjahān (1627–1658) who, though more orthodox in his approach than either his father or grandfather, was attracted by ṣūfism. His bent was liberal. Consequently, his attitude towards his subjects, irrespective of race or creed, also changed for the better. He weeded out many Iranians, who under the patronage extended to them by his mother, Empress Nūr Jahān, had acquired considerable status in Jahāngīr's court, and replaced them by Indian-born Muslims. Rajputs occupied important positions in the emperor's army and a large number of Hindus found employment in the imperial secretariat. Aside from the ṣūfi influence, Shahjahān's liberalism can be credited to his eldest son Dārā Shikōh, who studied Sanskrit and the Vedanta. For a time, Dārā Shikōh's benevolent attitude found favour with some of the ulamā; Shaikh Muhibullah commended it on the ground that the Prophet advocated 'mercy to all mankind' and not the Muslims alone.   Mulla Abu'l Hākim issued a fatwā that it was wrong to build a mosque by demolishing a temple. Even Sarmad, the great ṣūfi poet, whom Aurangazēb subsequently beheaded, was influenced by Dārā, who in his book *Majma' al-bahrayn,The Mingling of Two Oceans* opined 'there were not many differences, except verbal, in the way in which Hindu monotheists and Muslim ṣūfis sought and comprehended truth.'[17] The battle for succession waged between Dārā Shikōh and Shahjahān's third son, Aurangazēb, can, in some ways, be seen as the battle between liberalism on the one side and fundamentalism on the other. The defeat of Dārā was a setback for liberalism.

Aurangazēb (1658–1707), being a puritan, reversed the process of secularism started by Akbar. Under the influence of the ulamā, he tried to reimpose both the jaziya and the pilgrim tax on Hindus and to put an Islamic stamp on the administration. However, he did not harass or ill-treat the Hindus, as is commonly believed, nor did he deprive them of official employment. On the contrary, the latest research shows that the number of Hindu employees in various departments under his rule was double that under Akbar. He also continued to give handsome grants to many Hindu temples and Sikh gurudwaras. Some of his senior administrators and trusted generals were Hindus. Nevertheless, the spartan pattern of Islamic rule that he tried to impose on his subjects had a stultifying effect on the people. He forbade the playing of music, discouraged poetry, painting and architecture, banned every kind of festivity, and even curtailed the practice of darshan or public appearance of the emperor.

There is a lot of uncertainty on the subject of Aurangazēb's dealings with the Sikh guru Tegh Bahadur. All that we can be certain about is that the guru was apprehended and executed in 1675 at Delhi. It is not known whether or not the emperor was at the time aware of the charges levelled against the guru and his subsequent conviction and execution. But the act caused great resentment amongst the guru's followers. Tegh Bahadur's son, Govind Singh, the tenth guru, turned the Sikhs from a religious reformist sect, advocating Hindu-Muslim unity, into a militant fraternity, determined to uproot Muslim rule from Indian soil. According to one account, there was an attempt at reconciliation between Aurangazēb and Guru Gobind Singh whose *Zafar Nama*, though bitter in its denunciation of Mughal tyranny, praised Islam for its humanity. Nevertheless, relations between the Sikhs and the Muslims continued to deteriorate as Sikhs ascribed the deaths of all the guru's four sons and the guru's own assassination to Aurangazēb.

Aurangazēb's treatment of Shivaji, the Maratha leader, also alienated the Hindus of the Deccan. His wars against the Shī'a kingdoms of Ahmednagar, Bijapur and Golconda widened the cleavage between the Shī'a's and the Sunnis. His strict adherence to the sharī'ah adversely affected inter-religious harmony and created a wave of resentment among the Hindus. Some of his Muslim officers, more to please the emperor than out of religious conviction, went out of their way to alienate people of other faiths. Historians are not agreed whether Aurangazēb's reversal of the well-established policy of tolerance of Akbar and his successors was done more to undermine the influence of his dead brother Dārā among the people or to pursue the dictates of religious orthodoxy, to which the emperor was undoubtedly attached. He ruled for more than fifty years but his policies sowed the seeds of destruction of the Mughal empire. As one Islamic scholar has aptly observed: 'Akbar disrupted the Muslim community by recognizing that India [was] not an Islamic country; Aurangazēb disrupted India by behaving as though it were.'[18]

After Aurangazēb, the great Mughal empire began to disintegrate. The invasion of Nādir Shāh in 1738 and the repeated incursions of Ahmad Shah Abdali destroyed whatever semblance of central authority had survived. Although eleven Mughal kings ascended the throne of Delhi after Aurangazēb, their empire kept shrinking until it extended no more than a few metres around the Red Fort of Delhi. In 1803, the British, for all practical purposes, became the rulers of India. The final blow was struck after the abortive revolt of 1857, when the last of the line of Mughal emperors, the poet Bahadur Shah Zafar, was exiled to Rangoon where he died in penury. Thus ended the thousand-year-old rule of Muslims in India, leaving behind shared values and attitudes among the Hindus and Muslims on the one side and their distrust and hostility of one another, arising out of the historic past, on the other.

10

The Shi'ite Experiment

The Shi'ites do not constitute more than ten per cent of the Muslim population; the rest are Sunnis. The Sunnis are spread over most parts of the Muslim world, while the Shi'ites are in the majority only in Iran, Iraq and Bahrain. But they have had, in the course of history, an influence disproportionate to their numbers. Unlike the Sunnis, who are not as dogmatic, the Shi'ites are absolutely uncompromising on the question of the separation of religion and State. For them the imam is the repository of all power—temporal and spiritual. Furthermore, they hold that only a descendant of the Prophet through his surviving child, Fātima, wife of his cousin Ali, can be his successor. This, the Shi'ites are convinced, is confirmed by the reference in the Qur'ān to the Ahl al-Bait or immediate family of the Prophet (33:33). The imamat, in consequence, passed on from Ali to his sons and their successors. Apart from this reference, the Shi'ites also maintain that the Prophet had implicitly nominated Ali as his successor before his death by describing him as his maula; the Sunnis contest this by interpreting the word maula to mean friend or kin and nothing more. Both Sunni and Shi'ite exegesists stick doggedly to their respective points of view; what is important to remember is that for the Shi'ites there can be no difference between faith and power; the two have to be merged into one.[1] The Sunnis are ambivalent about this. It is also important to note that the Shi'ites are not a homogeneous body but are divided by lineal affiliation into two factions: the line of Hasan and the line of Husayn. Out of these have arisen the Twelvers, Ithna 'Ashariyah, who believe in twelve imams; the Ismā'ilis or the Seveners, who accept only the first six and then Ismā'il, who is not acknowledged by the rest of the Shī'as. Flowing out of these two sects are the Druzes in Syria and the Lebanon and the Agha Khanis and Bohras, who are mostly found in India, Pakistan, Bangladesh and parts of Africa. There are many other Shī'ite sub-sects, but they are not of much significance.

By and large, the State and society on which the Shī'ites modelled themselves were religious, and, therefore, there were fewer conflicts between religion and politics among them than among the Sunnis. Such conflicts arose mainly between Shī'ism and Sunnism, each trying to assert its religious superiority over the other. For the Shī'ites the ideal State, as indeed the ideal religion, is what Ali stood for. His five- year Caliphate (656–61) is regarded by them, despite the civil strife and internal dissension that bedevilled it, as the golden period of Islam. For the Sunnis, Ali is one of the four 'rightly-guided' caliphs and as important as his three predecessors. The Shī'ites see Abū Bakr, Umar and Uthmān as usurpers; hence their rule could not be a model for an Islamic state. The Shī'ites remained in the wilderness for long, until one of their leaders, Idris Ibn-Abdullah, a great grandson of Ali's elder son, Hasan, tried to found, in 789, a Shī'ite state in Morocco. He had taken part in one of the recurring Shī'ite revolts in Madina, but on its being suppressed, fled to Morocco, where he founded the first Shī'ite state, which lasted for two hundred years (788–974). His dynasty came to be known as the Idrisi dynasty and was supported by the disgruntled Sunni Berbers, who, however, did not convert to Shī'ism. The Idrisis were later harassed by the Sunni Moors of Spain and the Shī'ite Fatimids, with the result that the western part of Morocco was annexed by the Moors and the eastern part by the Fatimids. Thus ended the first Shī'ite experiment in statecraft.

The Fatimids (909–1171), who are probably named after Fātima, the daughter of the Prophet, were better equipped and organized than the Idrisis; moreover, they took their Shī'ism—of the Ismā'ili brand—very seriously and worked assiduously to strengthen it through the instrument of the state. They entrenched themselves, first in North Africa and then in Egypt, which became the centre of their activities; from there they extended their domain to Syria and Palestine. They even wrested from the Abbasids, for a while, the guardianship of the holy places of Mecca and Madina. In many respects, their rule was different from that of the other Shī'ite dynasties—the Idrisis or their rivals, the Abbasids.

They did not ask for any sort of tribal or popular approval nor did they bother to appease the ulamā. They claimed their leadership by divine right. Strangely, the viziers, who were mostly Christians, became increasingly powerful under the Fatimids; they were treated with great indulgence. Even towards the Sunnis, their main enemy, their policy fluctuated. There were some periods of tolerance; but towards the Christians and the Jews they were favourably disposed throughout their reign. In fact, some of the highest offices in the administration were held by them and they were allowed to build churches and synagogues and worship in them freely, without any hindrance. The administrative set-up was highly centralized, with all the powers vested in the centre; unlike the Abbasids they gave little autonomy to the provinces. The result of this strict control was all-round prosperity and a much needed impetus to learning, the arts and the sciences. In their capital, Cairo, the Fatimids founded al-Azhar, the greatest centre of Islamic theology; they also set up Dâr al-Hakim or Hall of Wisdom for the exclusive propagation of Shī'ism with a department for copying manuscripts, a large library and several rooms for discussion and debate. They encouraged the study of astronomy, medicine and ophthalmology. They were also great builders; their architectural achievements were outstanding.

The reign of al-Hākim was the glory of their line; under it the Fatimids reached the zenith of their power. His supporters, the Druzes, called him the incarnation of God. The deification of the ruler led to a lot of unhappiness among the people and a new sect arose—that of the dreaded Assassins, who swore to exterminate their enemies, both among the Shī'as and the Sunnis, but particularly the Sunnis. They operated from the strong mountain fortress of Alamout. They used assassination as a weapon to further their cause. They were perhaps the first sect in history to publish a hit list and forewarn their victims. They killed many prominent leaders. Led by Hasan-i-Sabbāh, an Iranian fanatic, whom his followers revered as the Saiyidina or 'our lord', they consumed hallucinatory drugs and went on suicide missions. Nizām al-Mulk was murdered by them in 1092, while he was saying his prayers in a mosque.

Of all the Shī'ite kingdoms, that of the Fatimids was in many respects a model of Shī'ism. The Fatimids implemented the basic tenets of Shī'ism. As the legitimate heirs of Ali they behaved more as divines than rulers. They did not believe in being accountable to any worldly group; unlike the Sunnis (caliphs whom they detested and wanted to destroy) they were neither elected, selected nor nominated; leadership came to them by naṣṣ or the divine process. Hence they commanded and enforced obedience. They did not allow themselves to be controlled by any individual or institution. They did not ask for the baih or approval of the congregation; it led, they felt, to fitna or mischief. The Shi'as' precepts tried to use tradition and literature to guide their rule. Unfortunately their reign often degenerated into authoritarianism, which hampered the proper growth and development of institutions. It also led to corruption and nepotism which ultimately resulted in the fall of the Fatimids, though they had their share of contributions to Shī'ite art and culture.[2]

Along with the rise of the Fatimids in North Africa and Egypt, another Shī'ite family known as Buwayh established, out of the ruins of the Saffarids (873–900) and the Samanids (825–999), a kingdom in Azarbayjan and a part of Persia with Shiraz as the capital. Its leaders were three brothers, Ali, Hasan and Ahmad who belonged to Twelver Shī'ism. The young Ahmad, more ambitious than the others, marched on Baghdad in 945 and took over the government. The Abbasid caliph, Mustakfi, finding himself helpless to resist his attackers, made an adroit volte face and hailed Ahmad as his rescuer, conferring on him the title of sultan. In less than two years, Ahmad blinded Mustakfi and installed Muti' (946–41) as the new caliph; Muti' remained a puppet in his hands. This trend was followed by the successors of Ahmad, who made and unmade caliphs. This, because the Buwayhids did not want the Abbasids to escape from their clutches and become a danger to them from outside—for there was always the possibility that the Sunnis might rally round the Abbasids. The Buwayhids also cleverly avoided founding a separate dynasty as this might have provoked the Fatimids, who were Seveners, to attack them.

Each of these Shī'ite sects regarded the others as heretical. And so the Muslim world saw a unique experiment in statecraft in Baghdad with a Shī'ite family exercising de facto control and the Sunni caliphs enjoying de jure power—a peculiar Shī'a-Sunni combination, which lasted for a century.

The names of the Buwayhids were stamped on the coinage and mentioned along with the caliphs in khutbas. In reality, the Buwayhid sultan was, as Amır Ali observed, like 'Charles Martel under the

Merovingian king of France, for he was the virtual sovereign, whilst the caliph was merely his dependent, receiving a daily allowance of 5,000 dinars from the public treasury.'3

The Buwayhids maintained the Sunni character of the Caliphate but only in name; they enforced many Shi'a rites at the court and as a mark of their religious affiliation declared the tenth of Muharram as a day of national mourning to commemorate the martyrdom of Husayn. They also built out of public funds a shrine (mashhad) on the presumed tomb of Ali. They gave more prominence to Shiraz, the old capital of their family, with its preponderant Shi'a population, than to Baghdad. Withal they were not bigots; their contributions to art and culture were significant. They built an academy with a library of 10,000 books, a famous observatory, and encouraged freedom of thought and expression among members of the Ikhwan al-Safa.

More than half a millenium passed before the Safavids, who belonged to the Ithna 'Ashariyah or Twelver sect, founded their kingdom in Persia; they were, from the outset, aggressively anti-Sunni. Their Shi'ite state was in many ways different from that of the Fatimids or the Idrisis. To begin with, it was much influenced by the mystics. It endowed the young Shah Isma'il (he was barely 14 years old at the time), the founder of the dynasty, with a divine touch. His followers revered him and the sufi order he founded gave him a hold on them which was mainly responsible for the success of his campaign against the Ottomans. He also collected a powerful army under his command. Shah Isma'il hated the Sunnis because of the ill-treatment that the Shi'as had received at the hands of both the Abbasids and the Ottomans; even the Moors in Spain were hostile to them. Hence, he could never compromise with Sunnism, which he regarded as a great evil. The martyrdom of Husayn was a constant reminder of what a Sunni ruler had done to their hero. To the Shi'as, sacrifice in the cause of the faith was more important than material gain. After a bitter struggle the Safavids led by Shah Isma'il defeated the Turkoman rulers of Iran in 1510 and founded their dynasty in Tabriz. Shah Isma'il ruled from 1502–24. Both the Sunni Ottomans and the Sunni Moors of Spain were outraged at the emergence of a Shi'ite empire in former Ottoman territories and decided that it had to be destroyed as it posed a threat to Sunni hegemony beyond the eastern crescent. The war between the Safavids and the Ottomans dragged on until the Ottomans won a decisive victory at Chaldiran in 1514. This was a great setback to Shah Ismā'il, who as a result also lost the support of the Qizilbāshi tribes who formed the backbone of his army.

Shah Isma'il's son, Tahmāsp (1524–76) managed to win back Qizilbāshi support by offering members of the tribe ministerial positions and allowing them a say in the affairs of his kingdom. With their help, he was able to regain much of the territories earlier lost to the Ottomans. The prolonged Shi'a-Sunni wars and factional infighting caused much unrest among the people. However, when Tahmāsp's grandson, Shah Abbās I (1588–1629) ascended the throne, he succeeded in inflicting defeat after defeat on both the Ottomans externally and the troublesome Uzebegs inside Iran. His military leadership turned the tide in favour of the Safavids and made them the unchallenged rulers of their realm for more than two hundred years.

Shah Abbas was a devout Shi'a and concentrated on strengthening the Shi'ite state which his grandfather had founded. He put teeth into the Ithna 'Ashariyah form of Shi'ism and insisted that every one of his subjects cleave to its tenets. Already millions of Sunnis had been converted to this sub-sect and under official patronage became fervent devotees. He decreed that the twelve imams be given the highest veneration. The last one, Muhammad al-Muntazar, who had disappeared due to Abbasid persecution was deified. The Twelvers held that the hidden imam was concealed by God, his life miraculously prolonged until such time as he would reappear to restore virtue and eradicate evil; he would remain, however, in control of the world as Sahib az-Zaman; Shah Abbas proclaimed himself the hidden imam's deputy and demanded absolute obedience. Because of his powerful personality the ulamā gave in, and acknowledged his supremacy.

Herein lies the difference between the Shi'a and Sunni concepts of the State. The Sunnis, as we have seen, believe that State power is to be exercised through ijma or the consensus of the community; the Shi'ites, on the other hand, repose full faith in isma or the infallibility of their imam, with the ruler acting as his deputy. Shah Abbās so transformed himself that he was revered as the incarnation of the last imam and his word was, therefore, treated as a divine command. In this, he was, in fact, following the example of his grandfather, Shah Ismā'il, who was the first to proclaim himself the deputy of the hidden imam; but Shah Abbās could not obtain the acceptance of the Shi'ite clergy, with the result that he was not wholly effective. He also faced another difficulty. There were no guidelines in any of the Shī'ite scriptures to run a state. He searched in vain for precedents; he could find no theologians of stature to advise him. The only book which gave him some clues to statecraft was by Jamalud Din al-Hilli (1250–1325) in his work *Usul al Figh* but it was of a general nature and not sufficiently specific.[4] So he tried to get help from theologians outside Iran; in order to attract them Shah Isma'il created new posts. Those who held these positions would be called ṣadrs or propagators of Shī'ism, and would be responsible for the preparation of a text on the fundamental principles of a Shī'ite state. He was successful in obtaining the services of many ulamā from Iraq, Syria and Bahrain, who jointly prepared the framework of the Safavid state; unfortunately, this was too rudimentary to be a proper guide.

Shah Abbas was aware of the shortcomings of his rule but he was determined to overcome them. Furthermore, he realized that in order to survive hc had to be demonstrably anti-Sunni. He concentrated, therefore, on spreading anti-Sunnism much more vigorously than Shah Ismā'il or Tahmāsp. This earned him popularity among the Shī'ites, who had been so unhappy with the tolerant attitude of his immediate predecessor, Ismā'il II, that they had him murdered. The ulamā were thrilled with Shah Abbās' actions and gave him their whole-hearted co-operation. In return he heaped honours on them, loaded them with gifts and gave them much importance in his court. The tenth of Muharram, Āshūra, the day on which the grandson of the Prophet, Husayn, was slain by the Sunni Umayyad caliph Yazid, was declared a day of national mourning. Massive processions were organized in the cities and villages, the participants beating their breasts and slashing themselves with chains as penance for letting down the Ahl al-Bait, the house of the Prophet, and cursing (tabazzah) the first three caliphs and their followers for betraying Ali, Fātima, Hasan and Husayn. Shī'ite pilgrims went to Karbalā, where Husayn was murdered, showing the same reverence to this place as the Sunnis did to holy places in Mecca and Madina. The movement was given an Iranian twist with the discovery that the seventh imam, Mūsā al-Kazim, had married the daughter of Yazdigird III, the last Sassanian king. Whether it was so or not, the people at large readily accepted it; it provided Shī'ism with an imperial aura.

Again, Shah Abbās elbowed out the Qizilbāshis because of their Sunni past and their loyalty to ṣufigari. They had created a power base of their own which Shah Abbas destroyed. He replaced them by a band of his personal slaves (ghulams) whose loyalty was to Shahi Sivani (love of the Shah). He also executed a number of ṣūfis on the charge of collaborating with the Ottomans. He started ideological colleges in his capital, Isfahan, and made them the hub of Shī'ism. He obtained the services of Mulla Abdullah Shustari (d. 1612) who trained more than a thousand ulama. They actively helped the King in spreading Shī'ism. They were also instrumental in projecting him as 'the shadow of God on earth'—a title which the later ulamā denounced but by which Shah Abbās acquired a unique status and position. Apart from his zeal for Shī'ism, Shah Abbās encouraged the arts and sciences. He founded a new movement, known as Hikmat-i-Ilāhī, which combined science and divinity.

Shah Abbas was an autocrat to the core; he brooked no opposition or dissent from anyone, the ulamā included. Most of them readily swore fealty to him but in the last years of his reign, his authority was challenged by Mulla Ahmad Ardibili, who told him to his face that he had no right to usurp what legitimately belonged to the mujtahid, who alone could deputize for the hidden imam. The king could at best be the imam's trustee but his conduct was liable to be scrutinized by the mujtahid, who was the sole repository of the powers of the hidden imam. Shah Abbas ignored Ardibili, but after his death, the ulama were able to assert their claim to be the sole arbitrators in matters religious and temporal. The successors of Shah Abbas proved to be too indolent and weak to hold their own against the mounting onslaught from the Ottomans from outside and the growing opposition from the ulama inside. The later Safavids lost much of their territories to the Ottomans and gave in to the supremacy of the ulama in religious affairs. The king would remain the temporal head; but he had to listen to the ulama in all matters. They were above any secular law; their properties, which they received as gifts, could not be touched by the State nor could any tax be levied on them. Their centres and institutions had to be funded by the State and teachers and pupils in them were to be honoured.

From the time of Shah Sulaymān (1666–94), the ulamā had become strong enough to denounce the kings and condemn their immoral and corrupt habits and practices. For all practical purposes the mujtahid became the real rulers. This concept was sanctified by the name of naib or deputy and was formally put forth by Muhammad Baqir al-Majlisi (d. 1699) the most influential Shī'a ālim or scholar of his times. His book, *Bihār al-Anwār*, is revered by the Shī'ites next only to the Qur'ān and the sermons of the imams. He rose to prominence during the weak and colourless rule of Sultan Husayn Shah (1694–1722). His mission was three-fold; the eradication of Sūfism; the furtherance of Twelver Shī'ism; and the suppression of Sunnism. Sultan Husayn was so awed by Majlisi that he invited him to place the crown on his head—a recognition of the mullā's spiritual leadership. Majlisi agreed to do so provided four conditions were fulfilled: (1) The prohibition of alcohol; (2) a ban on pigeon flying; (3) the ending of factional strife and (4) the expulsion of the ṣūfis from Iran. The shah conceded these demands and issued the necessary decrees. To generate a greater religious fervour, Majlisi exhorted the Shī'ites to undertake ziyārāt or pilgrimages to the tombs of the imams, to discard the mystic teachings of the ṣūfis and to develop an abhorrence towards Sunnism. As a result, Twelver Shī'ism became more aggressive than ever before; it became rigid, completely divorced from Sūfism and shorn of all its philosophical content. Fortunately, there were some ulamā who disagreed with Majlisi and disapproved of his combativeness but it took time before they could undermine his hold. Unlike him, these ulamā advocated a more accommodative approach in both religious and temporal affairs.

The differences between the two groups of ulamās who were called the Uṣūlis and the Akhbāris led to mounting controversy. The Akhbāris insisted that Shī'a jurisprudence be based on the traditions (akhbār) and that it should be guided by principles (uṣūl).[5] It is important to note here that all these controversies conformed in more ways than one to the accepted Shī'ite religious pattern with anti-Sunnism as their base. Naturally this roused the wrath of the Sunnis—the Ottomans, the Moors and the Mughals—who began to mount a violent campaign against the Shī'as. Only the early Mughals were more indulgent towards them because Shah Tahmāsp had helped Humayun regain his empire. However, within their own territories, the Mughals were no less inimical to the Shī'ites than the other Sunni rulers and carried on constant campaigns against the Shi'ite kingdoms in South India. The Ādil Shāhī dynasty of Bijapur, which had declared Shī'ism as the State religion and lasted for more than two hundred years (1489–1686), was destroyed by Aurangzēb. Likewise, on the overthrow of the Bahmanids, Ahmad Nizām Shāh founded a Shi'ite kingdom in Ahmednagar in 1490 which lasted until 1633; it was also destroyed by Aurangzēb. Sultan Quṭb Shāh, an Iranian Shi'a, established another Shi'a kingdom in Golconda in 1512 which was taken over by Aurangzēb in 1687. Even earlier the Shi'a Chak kings of Kashmir were attacked by Akbar.

The Shi'a-Sunni conflict has, therefore, been a part of a continuing historical process which neither politics nor religion has been able to put an end to. Its causes are not only deep-rooted but have multiplied over the centuries. With the disintegration of the Safavid empire and the rise of Nādir Shāh and Ahmad Shah Abdali in Iran, Shi'ism suffered a severe setback. Before inflicting a crushing defeat on the Mughals in North India, Nādir Shāh had recaptured territories lost by the Safavids. He abolished the Ithna 'Ashariyah or Shi'a Twelvers and introduced a mixture of Shi'ism and Sunnism called Ja'fari, as a fifth school along with the prevailing four Sunni schools: Hanafī, Shāfi'ī, Hanbalī and Mālikī. This was a concession to the Afghan elements in the army who were Sunnis and on whose loyalties alone he could rely.

After Nādir Shāh's death, the Qājārs took over the empire and revived Shi'ism in its Twelver form. They acknowledged the supremacy of the mujtahids who, under the leadership of the imam, Vahid Bihbahani, restored the doctrine of uṣūl, thus eradicating the influence of the Akhbāris, whom Bihbahani condemned as heretics. He was hailed as mujtahid (or renewer of Shi'ism) and has been followed ever since by the Shi'ite ulama . Unlike the Safavids, the Qājārs did not claim to be the representatives or incarnations of the hidden imam. On the contrary, they designated the leader of the ulamā as shaikh al-Islām, who in turn defended the ruler.[6] His voice mattered. For example, Fateh Ali (1721–50), who laid the real foundation of Qājār dynasty and whom both the British and the French courted, declared jihad against the czar for ill-treating his Muslim subjects, knowing full well that it would spell disaster for Iran because Russia was far more powerful and was bound to retaliate; he did it because he was unable to resist the pressure of the ulamā.

Later the ulamā began to dominate national affairs more aggressively and their leadership continued to be unchallenged through various crises such as the uproar over tobacco concessions to the British in 1890–92, which they vehemently opposed, and the agitation for constitutional reforms in 1905–09 which they spearheaded. Having tasted so much power the ulamā could not be suppressed. The Qājārs accepted their supremacy; but the Pahlavis, who replaced them, challenged it. However, their kingdom did not last long and was overthrown by Khomeini, who reasserted, in a way more effective than ever before, the supremacy of religion over politics in Iran.

Khomeini has tried, at the same time, to dilute the anti-Sunni feelings among the Shi'as and to present Iran as a citadel of Islamic solidarity; not many Sunnis, however, are impressed by this. The historical background of ill-will between the two sects is so deep-rooted that it cannot easily be eradicated. The Sunnis resent Shi'ite attacks on the first three caliphs; the Shi'as can never forgive the Sunnis for their supposed betrayal of Ali. In more recent times the Saudi rulers of Hijāz, under the influence of their religious mentor, Muhammad bin Abd al-Wahhāb destroyed Shi'ite shrines including the grave of Fātima, the daughter of the Prophet; they also desecrated Karbalā and the tomb of Husayn and turned his mausoleum into a stable. To the Wahhābis the worship of tombs is anti-Islamic; to the Shi'as it is an integral part of their faith. The hostility between the two sects, as evidenced by the periodic flare-ups between Iran and Saudi Arabia cannot be wiped out easily; the damage to the Shi'a-Sunni relationship due to the Iraq-Iran war, which lasted more than eight years, is also colossal.

There is another fundamental difference between the Shi'as and the Sunnis, to which we have referred earlier but which needs to be emphasized here; it is the wide gulf that lies between the two doctrines of ijmā or consensus of the community and isma or the infallibility of the imam. Each is basic to the approach of each sect. The one is broad-based, democratic and liberal; the other, dogmatic, centralized and restrictive.

Prof. Arnold Toynbee has rightly observed in his *A Study of History* that while 'the Islamic society had inherited, from a precept enshrined in the texts of the Qur'ān, a recognition that there were certain non-Islamic religions which in spite of their inadequacy, were authentic partial revelations of divine truth', the Muslims 'signally failed to rise to this relatively enlightened level when confronted with differences between Sunni and Shi'as within their own religious community. Here they showed themselves in as bad a light as Christians whether of the "Early Church" or of the "Reformation period", in similar circumstances.'[7]

11
Resistance to Change

About the time the Muslim empires of the Ottomans, the Mughals, the Safavids, and the other local kingdoms were well entrenched, some of the European powers began their inroads into Asia and Africa. They came first as traders and with the money they earned, equipped their men with new weapons (brought from their own countries) which were far superior to the local ones. With these and through other means they managed to acquire territories and set up governments. The Muslim rulers who had given facilities to these Europeans became, due to indulgence and loose living, politically and morally degenerate; power had so corrupted them that they could not offer—weak, divided and disorganized as they were—much resistance to the onslaughts of the foreigners whose appetite was insatiable. A number of Muslim rulers collaborated with them in the hope of retaining their status and position. Surprisingly, it was the ulamā, the ṣūfis and the fundamentalists who came out of their spiritual shells and took up arms against the European intruders. They saw in the latter's machinations danger to Islam and its hegemony. They roused the faithful to stem the tide of Christian 'heathenism' which, they believed, threatened to engulf the Muslim world.

Foremost among the European invaders was Napoleon Bonaparte. On landing in Alexandria in Egypt in July 1798, he issued a proclamation 'in the name of Allah, the Gracious and the Merciful', assuring the Muslims that he would 'restore their religious rights and punish their enemies'. He declared, 'I respect more than the Mamlūks ever did, Allah, His Prophet and the Qur'ān'. He asked the Muslims:

By what wisdom, talents and virtues are the Mamlūks distinguished—only by the joys and pleasure of life, which they have arrogated to themselves. If there is good land, it belongs to the Mamlūks, if there is a pretty slave girl, or handsome steed or a good horse, it belongs to the Mamlūks. . . . In Egypt, there were once upon a time great cities, long canals and flourishing trade. The tyranny and covetousness of the Mamlūks have ruined everything.

Bonaparte invoked the help of the 'shaikhs, qadis and imams' and assured them that the French were 'true Muslims' and their real friends. He told them: 'Did we not march on Rome and crush the pope, who had urged the Christians to fight against the Muslims? Did we not destroy the knights of Malta, who claimed that God had ordered them to finish the Muslims? Have we not always been the friends of your Ottoman caliphs and enemy of their enemies? The Mamlūks, on the contrary, defy the authority of the caliph.'[1]

The proclamation had the desired effect; the French were warmly received by the theologians and al-Azhar. However, the French rule did not last for more than four years. But even in this short span of time, they left a permanent impress on the minds of the Egyptians. The British, with the help of a young Macedonian military officer of the Ottoman army, Muhammad Ali, who later became the founder of a modern secular state in Egypt, thwarted the efforts of Bonaparte and cleverly outmanoeuvred him. The rivalry between the French and the British did not help the natives; it only resulted in the parcelling out of territories between the two nations and the endangering of the freedom of the natives.

Expelled from Egypt, the French went into North Africa, took over Algeria in 1830, then Morocco and Tunisia; Czarist Russia was encouraged by their example, and penetrated into the Caucasus and Central Asia between 1865 and 1873. The British had already entered India and established themselves as traders in Bengal, gradually spreading their tentacles in the north and the south. By 1849 they had conquered most parts of the country, which extended up to Burma in the east and Sri Lanka in the south. Thirty years later they expanded their territories to the Malay peninsula, beyond the borders of India. The Dutch, thwarted by the British in Sri Lanka, took over Indonesia in 1840. Not to be left out of the race, the Italians occupied Tripolitania. The grabbing game reached its climax in 1920 at the end of World War I when British troops occupied Damascus and Baghdad, once the two most powerful centres of the Umayyad and Abbasid Caliphates. Everywhere Muslims found themselves utterly defeated and thoroughly demoralized. More shameful was their sense of religious subjugation at the hands of Christians, whom they had always regarded with contempt. The loss of political power was understandable; but what irked them was the superior behaviour of the new rulers whose forbears they had always vanquished in the past. As we have seen, the ruling clique quietly surrendered and it was the religious-minded Muslims, led by the ulamā and the ṣūfis who took up arms against the 'heathen' invaders. At first unorganized, they soon mapped out strategies and trained their armies. They faced heavy odds but they persisted in their rebellion. In Algeria, for instance, Abd al-Qadir, venerated as the imam by his followers, organized armed resistance against the French colonizers. He was hailed by the faithful as Nāsir al-Dīn, the champion of religion. He succeeded in driving out the French and became the 'dey' or ruler.

In Sudan, the rebellion against the British was led by Muhammad Ahmad (1840–45), who claimed to be the mahdi or 'the divinely guided one'. He vowed that he would rid the world of the Christian infidels and restore Islam to its original greatness. He became the master of the Sudan, defeating General Gordon, who was killed in the battle of Khartoum (1885).[2] In Libya, Muhammad Ali al-Sanusi (1787–1859), another fundamentalist leader, drove the foreigners from his native land. In Somalia, Muhammad Abdullah Hasan (1863–1920) spearheaded the movement against the British. They called him the 'mad mullā' because whatever the cost he never gave up. In Central Asia it was Shamil Waifi who inspired the Muslims to take up arms against the Czarist forces. This list is not exhaustive but it shows that while the secularists sat on the fence, it was the men fired with religious zeal who goaded the faithful to rise in defence of Islam against the 'heathens'. Although all these movements finally crumbled, the heroism with which the fundamentalists fought left an indelible mark in the annals of Islam.

Moreover, the manner in which they conducted their revolts was truly remarkable. They set up communal cells for their followers where strict adherence to the shari'ah was enforced along with rigorous training in military warfare. Their administrative set-up was based on the teachings of the Qur'ān and the traditions of the Prophet. Most of them belonged to the Naqshbandī order, which was directed in the nineteenth century by Khalid Baghdādī (1776–1827), who was inspired by the teachings of such spiritual savants as Shaikh Ahmad Sirhindi, the arch-rebel against Akbar's liberalism, and other ṣūfīs in India. Baghdādī imbibed the spirit of rebellion taught by Sirhindi and his disciples at Delhi and returned, charged with a new fighting spirit, to the heartlands of Islam in West Asia. He gathered together a large number of followers in Syria, Iraq and the Arabian peninsula. His fame spread to distant regions of East Africa and South-East Asia. His message was heard all over the Muslim world from Central Asia to the Caucasus and as far east as China. Unlike the old ṣūfī orders, which had preached asceticism and non-involvement in worldly affairs, Baghdādī exhorted his disciples to take up whatever weapons that they could find and sacrifice their lives for the cause of Islam. He turned ṣūfīs and maulvis into armed rebels and militant warriors.

The ṣūfī rebels fought on two fronts: against the foreign invaders, and against their own people, who had strayed from the right path as set out by the Prophet. Surprisingly, the Wahhābis influenced them greatly despite the fact that their teachings were against Ṣūfīsm. The spirit of rebellion that the Wahhābis inculcated among their followers also inspired the ṣūfīs to be militant. It changed the outlook of the rebels, particularly that of the Naqshbandīs. It had its impact as far away as Central Asia, where many Naqshbandīs and their disciples were engaged in establishing a purely Islamic state. Imam Shamil, a Naqshbandī ṣūfī, was both a religious zealot and an able guerrilla commander. He expelled Czarist troops from the Caucasus and ushered in 'the period of the sharī'ah' (1885). It lasted only thirty years till the Russians once again overran Shamil's kingdom and forced him to surrender. At about the same time, Bahal Din Vaishi (1804–93), another Naqshbandī ṣūfī, organized in Kazan a different kind of rebellion against the Russians. He found the Muslims cooperating with the Czarist authorities and in the process breaking loose from their Islamic moorings. He called upon Muslims to stop cooperating with the alien rulers by refusing to pay taxes or enlisting in the army or administrative services. Vaishi's movement was essentially non-violent, more or less on lines which Gandhi later adopted and made famous but when it spread among the

Tartars, known for their turbulence, the Russians were alarmed. Vaishi was arrested, declared insane and sent to a lunatic asylum. His henchmen were transported to Siberia and his followers tortured. Nevertheless, the torch that Vaishi had lit could not be snuffed out by repression. It flashed periodically for two decades and finally lit the path of Tartar nationalism.

In India, the role of Shah Wali Allāh (1702–62) was no less significant. He was an uncompromising fundamentalist, more inclined towards Ṣūfism than Wahhābism but influenced by both. He advocated armed rebellion to achieve an Islamic state, as a guarantee against 'heathenism'. Nothing was impossible, he said, if Muslims were true to the Prophet's message of equality and social justice and worked for a real brotherhood of the faithful. His writings were enshrined in his *Ṭarīqa-i-Muhammadīya* or the Way of the Prophet. He wanted an Islamic state to be established in every country where there were Muslims in substantial numbers; those states should then form an international Islamic brotherhood. One of his followers, Sayyid Ahmed of Rāe Barēli. (1786–1831), organized the mujāhidūn or migration movement. Like his mentor, his mission was also the regeneration of Islam by freeing it from the clutches of the infidels. He mobilized his followers in a war against the Sikhs, who had founded a powerful kingdom in the Punjab. They were, however, betrayed by their Afghan allies and defeated by Ranjit Singh, the Sikh emperor of North India. The Muslims of Bengal, who were the first to encounter the British, met an equally dismal end. Their leader, Hājjī Sharī'at Allah (1781–1840), fought valiantly but was eventually defeated. After his death, his followers carried on the struggle for many years, but it was a hopeless endeavour. Hundreds of them died without achieving anything.[3]

In China, too, the Muslims led by the Naqshbandīs declared a holy war against Manchu rule in Turkistān. There were five such holy wars: in 1820–28, 1830, 1847, 1857 and 1861. One of their military commanders, Ya'qūb Beg (1820–77), liberated the whole of Turkistān and turned it into a puritanical theocracy which he administered from 1867 till its disintegration ten years later. Other parts of China witnessed similar Muslim uprisings inspired by the ṣūfis. A legendary figure was Ma Ming-hsin (d. 1781) who rallied his followers round the green flag of the Prophet and called upon them to purify Islam of Confucian accretions. An erudite propagator of classical theology and jurisprudence, Ma Mua-Ming inspired several generations of Chinese Muslims to rebel against their non-Muslim overlords. Their devotion to Islam was so strong that they came to be known as the 'New Sect'; their spirit was kept alive by the hajjis—those who had returned after pilgrimage to Mecca. At one time, from 1862 to 1877, they became so belligerent that under the command of Ma Mua-Ming, they organized themselves as the vanguard of the shari'ah, determined to establish a true Islamic state. They fought valiantly but the odds were so heavily loaded against them that most of them perished in the struggle.[4]

In Yunan, under Tu Wenhsin, the Muslims defeated the emperor's troops and founded an independent Muslim kingdom, which lasted more than fifteen years. Tu Wenhsin assumed the name of Sultan Sulaymān and tried to Islamize the various departments of the State as well his subjects in general. He drew his inspiration from the teachings of Ma Teh'sin and was the first to translate the Qur'ān into Chinese; in this he was influenced by his contemporary, Shah Wali Allāh, who had translated the Qur'ān into Persian.

In Africa, the reaction of the Muslims to colonial rule was as aggressive and violent as in Asia. But while in Asia most of the rebel leaders were Naqshbandis, in Africa they belonged either to the Khalwatiya or the Idrisiya orders. The Khalwatiyas were activized by an eminent theologian, Mustafa al-Bakri (d. 1749); their order was based in Cairo and was extremely popular among the teachers and pupils of al-Azhar. One of its patrons was Muhammad al-Hifnawi, the rector of al-Azhar, whose preachings influenced Muslims all over the world; even Shah Wali Allāh of Delhi and Abd al-Wahhābi, the founder of Wahhābism, were impressed by the depth of his learning.

The Idrisiya order was founded by the Moroccan ṣufi, Ahmad Ibn Idris (1760–1837), who tried to reconcile Wahhābism with Ṣūfism. He mixed the puritanism and militancy of the Wahhābis with the devotion and piety of Ṣūfism. He fought bravely for Islam and propagated, like Sayyid Ahmad of Rāe Barēli, *Tarīqa-i-Muhammadīya* or the Way of the Prophet. There was another ṣūfism order, called Tifania, founded by Ahmad al-Tifani (1737–1815), which had also advocated armed struggle against non-Muslim rulers and their henchmen. This order rapidly won over the Muslims of Algeria, Morocco, Sudan and West Africa. One of its most colourful leaders was Hājji Umar Tali (1794–1864) who repelled a pagan incursion to found a theocratic state in western Sudan. He also conquered and annexed Senegal. In 1893, the French wrested Senegal from Tali's successors.

The ṣūfis of the Sammanya order were in the forefront of the jihād against the combined might of the Egyptians and the British. This order gained considerable popularity in Sudan, Eritrea and Ethiopia. The mahdi of Sudan belonged to it and after his victory over the British, tried to establish a Mahdist state, in which he tried to copy the pattern of the city state of Madina. He claimed to be a descendant of the Prophet and traced the ancestry of his lieutenants to the aṣḥāb or the Companions of the Prophet and called them anṣars (or helpers) who later played a significant role in the politics of independent Sudan. In Libya the rebel ṣūfi, Muhammad Ali al-Sannusi, who had successfully repelled the foreigners, inspired by the vision of a rejuvenated Islam, turned his people into devout and militant Muslims. Likewise, in Somalia, Muhammad Abu'l al-Hasan (1864–1920) led the Muslims to fight the British invasion of his country. In Black Africa, the newly converted Muslims were in the vanguard of the fight to save Islam, which gave them, for the first time, racial equality and a sense of belonging to a universal Islamic brotherhood. One of the most picturesque of the black ṣūfis was Samori Ture (1830–1900), who founded a purely Islamic state.

There were also many others whose revolts were of no less significance. They were, no doubt, sporadic and petered out after a few years, but they showed the determination of the faithful, under the leadership of the ṣūfis, to rescue their faith from the clutches of the infidels. They were not militarists or freedom fighters, but simply religious zealots to whom nothing in the world mattered except Islam. It is ironic that the ṣūfis, who were originally so liberal and tolerant towards followers of other faiths, should have been in the forefront of a militant jihād against them. Yet, this was understandable because they feared that the non-Muslims were bent upon destroying Islam by taking advantage of the ineptitude and weakness of corrupt Muslim rulers. Also, they were dismayed by the latter's cowardice and the readiness with which they surrendered to foreigners. As P.F. Francis Robinson has observed, 'As Muslim power crumbled from within, they [the sufis] strove to restore it, promoting the Islamic ideal. As old arteries began to harden they built new ones along which they pumped new vitality. As the community lost momentum and direction, they tried to place it once more on the sure base of revelation and the example of the Prophet.'[5]

However, no sooner did the ṣufis take to rebellion and power politics, than they lost much of their mystical strength and other-worldliness. They became hardened, coarse, and aggressive. However, it must be said to their credit that power did not corrupt them; even for the short duration that they acquired it they did not give up their piety, spartan living and care for the poor, though towards their enemies their attitude had hardened. This was best reflected in the code of conduct that Abd al-Qadir, the Algerian ṣufi rebel, imposed upon himself; in a public document he declared that it was his religious duty to despise wealth despite the power he possessed; be just and fair to all, irrespective of their rank or office; and lay down his life for Islam. He led an extremely frugal life and did not allow his companions to go astray.[6] They had to set an example to their followers. In fighting they were not to forget the obligations of piety and simple living which their religion enjoined upon them. Their war was on two fronts—one, against the external enemy who aimed at the subjugation of the Muslims and, two, against the cancer of luxurious living, social immorality and political corruption that was undermining the community. This was the common approach of most of the ṣufi rebels.

In this respect, they stood apart from the other rebels: they did not behave like worldly potentates; they were conscious of the fact that they were men of God and acted strictly in accordance with the Qur'ānic teachings and the traditions of the Prophet. The pivot of their rule revolved round the person of the leader who was the mentor, the executor and the exemplar. Hence he could leave no system behind; nor did the possibility exist of sustained popular support without him. In this lay the seeds of their downfall. The rebels were unable to regroup once their top leadership went down. This, coupled with their inability to wage modern warfare, proved disastrous. Moreover, the colonial powers had managed, by the use of force and graft, to weaken the rebel resistance. In many cases they also succeeded in winning over the secular elements among the Muslims who were enamoured by the achievements of contemporary science and technology. All in all, there was a systematic intellectual indoctrination by the West which the ulamā failed to counter and thus it was that the rebellion died.

To quote the Marxist scholar, Maxime Rodinson,

Christianity was made out to be by its very nature favourable to progress, and Islam to mean cultural stagnation and backwardness. The attack upon Islam became as fierce as it could be and the arguments of the Middle Ages were revived with up-to-date embellishments. The Islamic religious orders, in particular, were presented as a network of dangerous organizations animated by a barbarous hatred of civilisation.[7]

This onslaught inevitably led to the Western powers becoming more firmly entrenched in the lands of Islam.

The Western Onslaught

As the European powers occupied more and more Muslim territories, they inevitably influenced the way of thinking of the faithful. The fundamentalists could do little but helplessly witness the disintegration of the Muslim polity and society. Christian values were presented in a way which made many Muslims doubt whether theirs was, as the Qur'ān had proclaimed, 'the best community'. Having lost their freedom, they felt down-graded; and now their laws and practices were being ridiculed as archaic and immoral. 'What had gone wrong?' the Muslims asked themselves. In the past they had blamed their own rulers who had strayed from the path of the Prophet and the 'rightly guided' caliphs. Now their rulers—inept, cowardly and corrupt—had not only yielded power but were willing to adopt Christian values, laws and institutions. Indeed many of the popular leaders who came to the fore to guide the community began to impress upon their fellow-Muslims the need to befriend Christians and collaborate with the colonizers; they found religious texts to justify their stand. Asserting that there was no fundamental conflict between Christianity and Islam, they tried to bring about a rapprochement between the two. In the process Islam was pushed aside. Though they talked of reforming Islam, the aim of these leaders seemed to be to secularize it and, like Christianity, turn it from a community religion to one to be practised in the home.

When the new ruling classes, educated and trained in Western ideas, plumped for a reformed Islam, mainly in order to face the challenges of industrialization, they inevitably became unashamed admirers of Western-style democracy. This alienated the ulamā who could reconcile themselves to the rule of the colonizers but were not prepared to imitate their ways or institutions. Consequently, a conflict arose between the two attitudes among the Muslims and the battle between the fundamentalists who wanted to return to the past and the secularists who urged assimilation and transformation began to be waged with great fury. What tilted the scales in favour of the secularists was the patronage they received from the colonizers who realized that the fundamentalists would not be their allies. Besides the loaves and fishes of office, which they offered, the social and economic changes generated by the colonizers also brought immediate benefits to the secularists. But this did not last very long. As soon as the level of these benefits reached a plateau, the secularists asked for more. They became restless and turned agitators. Their appeal was different from that of the fundamentalists as, instead of demanding the glorification of Islam, they talked of the honour and freedom of the motherland. Even so, the occupying powers were more inclined towards the secularists than the fundamentalists, who advocated, as a panacea for all the community's ills, a new form of pan-Islamism which the colonizers felt was far more dangerous than nationalism.

Jamāl al-Din al-Afghani (1838–97) was the dominant figure of this movement. He tried to combine patriotism with religion by emphasizing, on the one hand, the unbreakable bonds of Islamic brotherhood and, on the other, the need for Muslims to rise and free themselves of the European yoke. He told them that the Western imperialists were their worst enemies and to collaborate with them in any way was a sin. During his visit to India, he chastized Sir Syed Ahmad Khan, the foremost Muslim leader of the time in India, for cowering before the British. He did not want Islam to go back to the days of seventh century Arabia and was as anxious as Sir Syed to take advantage of the new technological developments; but, unlike Sir Syed, he believed that this would be possible only if Muslims were freed of the Western stranglehold.[1] Afghani was not averse to science but thought it could be best used by his co-religionists only when they ceased to be slaves. He visited several Muslim countries, exhorting them to fight the colonizers. Soon he had enough support among the theologians and the common Muslims, but the Western-educated ones paid little heed to his pleas; they were happy to enjoy the crumbs that the new rulers offered and began to sing their praises. But, as we have seen, with the passage of time, Western ideas of liberty and equality began to permeate their thinking and they asked for more political rights. The imperialists resisted, occasionally throwing in a few more crumbs. A gulf, therefore, grew between the rulers and the Western-educated elite. Enamoured of the parliamentary system, these Muslims demanded a greater share in the running of their countries. Ironically, the fundamentalists did not like the growing power of the Westernized Muslims; they preferred the colonizers to, what they called, 'this hybrid breed of power seekers' among their own co-religionists. The latter, in turn, denounced the fundamentalists for their anti-patriotic stance and urged that religion be kept separate from politics. Similarly, they demanded changes in the shari'ah, particularly in the laws of succession, marriage, divorce, gifts, waqf, etc., which naturally infuriated the fundamentalists.

The early secularists, who tried to be loyal to both Islam and the Christian colonizers, avoided any sort of confrontation with rulers; they apprehended that it might cause further trouble and ruination to the Muslims. Sir Syed was one of the most notable of them. He stood for Islamic revivalism—but under the aegis of the British, whom he trusted. He said that Islam and Christianity had more in common than any other two religions. He also held that Christian values were quite compatible with Islamic tenets. Hence he urged the Muslims to shed their hostility to the Christians and be friends with them. Were they not referred to as 'people of the book' in the Qur'ān? he asked. He distrusted the Hindus, who, he felt, being in an overwhelming majority, were trying to replace the British as the rulers and were asking for parliamentary institutions only so they could dominate the Muslims and make them their slaves. Hence he opposed the introduction of these institutions. Afghani saw in Sir Syed nothing but an agent of British imperialism who aimed at the subjugation of Muslims by making them fight with Hindus. It was a sinister game of the British, he said, and Sir Syed was playing into their hands. He cautioned India's Muslims against it and asked them to join the Hindus in their fight against the British.[2]

In Egypt Afghani carried on a relentless war against the imperial designs of the British; he urged the Muslims to throw them out. At the same time he spoke of the benefits of science and urged to avail of them fully. There was no conflict, he said, between science and Islam; but imperialism was the enemy of both and so it had to be destroyed.

Afghani worked ceaselessly to mobilize the Muslims on a common platform against the colonizers and was greatly assisted in the beginning by Muhammad Abduh (1849–1905), who later became the chief mufti of Egypt and the rector of al-Azhar.

Abduh was more a rationalist than an agitator; he was impressed by Afghani's reformist slant but his anti-imperialist tirade left him cold. He agreed that the West posed the greatest danger to Islam but more religiously than politically. He, therefore, wanted to fight the West but in a constructive rather than a destructive way. He felt that Islam should absorb whatever good the West had to offer, without surrendering its basic tenets. He was also uncompromising on the question of preserving the Islamic identity; but unlike Afghani he was frightened of head-on confrontation and preferred to resolve disputes peacefully. Unlike Sir Syed he did not accept the superiority of the West; he believed that Islam was in every respect superior but Muslims had failed it and given it a distorted image. Abduh tried to present Islam in the best possible light by discarding its outmoded and outdated features. He concentrated on its moral and ethical precepts which were based on equality, fraternity and a broad humanism. His proposals for reform were couched in a language that avoided displeasing the orthodox but were still bold and innovative enough to please the newly-educated, Westernized Muslims. He argued forcefully that Islam was both rational and humane and asserted that every good modern concept could be reconciled with the injunctions of the Qur'ān. Instead of opposing the more liberal, political and social inroads the West was making, he maintained that there was nothing novel about them as these were essentially Islamic and had their roots in the Qur'ān and the hadith. His radical conservatism impressed Muslim intellectuals not only in Egypt but also in West Asia, India and South-East Asia. Attired in the garb of a mufti, he encouraged reforms in Islam, supported democratic rights, including the parliamentary system, and declared that these were in accordance with the precepts and practices of Islam. Despite his progressive outlook, Abduh remained at heart orthodox and his reforms were neither radical nor revolutionary. Though couched in modern terminology, they retained the old roots. Like his mentor, Abduh was shrewd enough to sense that no Muslim would accept innovations in the shari'ah; he, therefore, incorporated them rather ingeniously within the broad Islamic framework. But unlike Afghani, he wished to hasten slowly, he was afraid of revolt and disliked confrontation. The master broke with the pupil, accusing Abduh of being a defeatist.[3]

So Abduh went his own way and in the process was often misunderstood by both sides. His balancing act was too difficult to be imitated and he was sometimes maligned; a number of his disciples left him and began preaching their own credo. For instance, one of them, Qāsim Amin, created quite a stir when he condemned polygamy, easy divorce, and the use of the veil; on the other hand, another of his aides, perhaps the closest, Rashīd Rida (1865–1935), who edited Abduh's works, aligned himself more and more with the fundamentalists, pleading that Islam needed purification rather than adjustment. He was attracted to Wahhābism and stated that it was a more effective antidote to the evils of Westernization than piecemeal reform. His writings in *al-Manar*, which he edited after Abduh, glorified the role of Islam in human development and underlined its inherent greatness. He succeeded in putting a brake on the activities of the secularists, who were anxious to Westernize Islam and even Christianize it. Farid Wajdi, a colleague of Rashīd Rida, criticized Amin for his book, *al-Mar'a al-Jadīda (The Modern Woman)* and hit back saying that there was more equality for women in Islam than in the West; they were better protected and honoured than Christian women.[4] Then there were the Muslim apologists like Amīr Ali, an eminent Indian jurist, who insisted that polygamy did not have the sanction of the Qur'ān and that some of the prevalent forms of divorce among the Muslims were disapproved of by the Prophet. The ulamā were not impressed by his arguments, but the secularists took Amir Ali to their heart. Likewise, Dr Taha Husayn, the blind scholar of Egypt, who later became its education minister, demanded a wholesale assimilation of Western values; he was attacked by the ulamā for his heresy and nearly ostracized.

Undeterred by these attacks, the Westernized elite, with the tacit support of the colonizers, went ahead with their reforms; this, they thought, would also help them to obtain a larger share in the affairs of the state. When colonizers found that their political appetite had become insatiable it was already too late. The schools and colleges which the rulers had started and which they thought would produce only clerks and petty officials who would work for them, had begun to create a new generation of natives, fired by patriotic fervour and a nationalist urge, who demanded more and more political power. The higher their education, the more vociferous became their cry for independence. The enrolment of women further accelerated the process; they began to discard the pardah and the chudder, and opted for co-education and learned with the same zeal as the men. The more education spread among them, the more they asked for emancipation and sexual equality. Apart from the colonizers, who were shaken by this spirit of revolt, the fundamentalists were also upset at these developments and lamented the breakdown of age-old traditions. They were particularly piqued at the free mixing of men and women and the demand for the liberation of women. Already they were mortified by the replacement of the sharī'ah by European criminal and civil codes; but they found the interference in personal and family laws, as engineered by the Western-educated classes, intolerable. They had acquiesced in the replacement of Qur'ānic punishments for certain offences; and in the taking of interest on loans, but they could not stomach the tampering with of personal and family laws which threatened to destroy the whole social fabric. It must also be said at this point that the colonizers were playing a double game. As the rift between the secularists and the colonizers widened—at first the two were united on the need for reforming the sharī'ah—the secularists became more demanding and asked for changes on the European pattern. The fundamentalists opposed this. The colonizers played the one against the other—sometimes they gave in to the secularists and at other times to the fundamentalists. Both sides realized in time that the colonizers were friends of neither but just exploiters. They used the fundamentalists when it suited them and encouraged the secularists when it benefited them; divide and rule had always been their motto.

The point to be noted here is that the reluctance of the fundamentalists to collaborate with the secularists was largely due to their fear that Islam was in danger both from the pernicious influence of imperialism as well as the evils of nationalism. They saw nationalism as the greater evil; it was destructive of the spirit of Islam, which transgresses race and territory. Also, it was the mother of secularism, which was basically anti-religious. There was also the fear that in case the secularists succeeded, the ulamā would lose their hold on the faithful.

Ironically, the first Muslims to turn nationalist and consequently secularist were the Arabs, the founders of the faith. They revolted against the Ottoman Turks, who had denied them their rightful share in the administration, and secretly organized against them. Their aim was to secede from the Ottoman empire which had been the symbol of Islamic unity and the centre of Muslim brotherhood. So strong was Arab resentment against the Turks that they sided with those European powers who were hostile to the Turks and plotted to dismember the Caliphate. Britain and France actively helped the growth of a separate Arab identity, which, they hoped, would undermine Islamic supremacy under the Ottomans. Instigated by the British and the French, a group of Arab intellectuals met in Paris in 1905 and formed the League of the Arab Fatherland. They published a pamphlet entitled *The Awakening of the Arab Nation,* which was widely circulated; it contained the seeds of the separation of religion from politics. It demanded the establishment of an independent Arabic-speaking state, extending from the Euphrates through Syria, Iraq and Palestine to Egypt, under a sultan who would look after the political and administrative affairs and a caliph who would be only a nominal head. To counter the movement, the Ottomans sent out preachers who appealed to the Muslims to beware of the 'Christian conspiracy' to divide the followers of Muhammad and make them subservient to the enemies of Islam. The Ottoman caliph also invited Arab potentates to Constantinople. He cajoled them, looked after them lavishly, and showered favours on them. The most notable among them was Husayn ibn Ali, a scion of the royal family of Hejaz and a direct descendant of the Prophet. He occupied a pre-eminent position among the tribal leaders of Arabia and had four sons, Ali, Faysal, Abd Allāh and Zaid, who were active in the Arab nationalist movement. At the Ottoman sultan's invitation, the family remained in Constantinople for fifteen years, helping him to counter the growing anti-Turkish feeling amongst the Arabs and fostering a sense of unity amongst the Muslims.[5]

The outbreak of World War I upset the caliph's plans; his weakened position emboldened the rebels. They were aided by the British and the French who provided them with arms and other military support to fight the Turks. An Arab Congress, representing the various groups, had already met in June 1913 asking for an autonomous Arab state; they were encouraged now to demand complete freedom. The Ottomans were taken aback; even the Young Turks, who had earlier sympathized with Arab aspirations, were stunned. Then came the treachery of Husayn ibn Ali, whom the Ottomans had appointed the sharīf of Mecca; he entered into a secret pact with the British to work against the

Turks. With the military aid he received from them he organized revolts against the Ottomans in many places. This was because the British had said that if he succeeded in overthrowing the Ottomans, he would be recognized as the ruler of all the Arab lands then ruled by the Ottomans. However, when the Turks were defeated on various fronts and Germany surrendered to the Allies in 1918, the British went back on their solemn assurance, betrayed Husayn and instead divided the various Arab territories among the victorious Allies. They also promised the Jews a homeland in Palestine—a dagger in the heart of the Arab world. Husayn was badly betrayed. Disappointed, he sulked; but he lacked the courage to revolt. The Arab nationalists were furious at this double-crossing by the British; in desperation, they tried to patch up with the Young Turks, who had emerged as the most effective force in Turkey after the war. But it was too late.

The Young Turks no longer trusted the Arabs, nor were they in a position to confront the Allies. The rebellious Arabs discovered to their cost that they had only changed masters from fellow Muslims to alien Christians, who had no real love for them. This realization sent a wave of resentment throughout the Arab world; they felt forlorn and cheated but were too disunited and disorganized to fight back. They mourned the loss of power and prestige by their Turkish co-religionists and were plunged into despair and despondency. They had no alternative but to collaborate with the new rulers. An eminent theoretician of Arab nationalism, Sati al-Husri, has explained that they were caught on the horns of a dilemma, between nationalism and Islam, in which nationalism ultimately triumphed; it proved more profitable from the short-term point of view. Husayn, though bitter, had already reconciled himself to the fact that he now had to toe the British line; the other Arab potentates also bowed to the inevitable. To appease Husayn the British installed his two sons, Faysal and Abd Allāh, as rulers of Iraq and Transjordania respectively; in turn, the latter allowed a semblance of democracy to their subjects. But both had to function under the benign eye of the British, who gave them military protection. The rulers were Arabs; the popular representatives were Arabs but neither enjoyed any real power. They were dependent on British arms. The king was a showpiece; so were the newly created parliaments, where deputies could debate but not decide: shout but not act. A poet sang with cynical disdain:

In Baghdad a National Assembly was patched up
As would a ragged garment filled with holes
And so it collected all the handicaps;
The one-eyed, the blind and the bald,
Oh fate, how playful you have become?
What pleasure do you derive at these mockeries?[6]

The army played a crucial role during this period. Though largely comprised of natives it became the chief instrument of colonial exploitation and the base of the stability of their rule. Most of the officers came from rural areas, but they received training in cantonments located near the cities and were thus exposed to a Western style of living. Apart from training in the use of weapons, they were taught subjects which extolled colonialism. Islam was not prescribed for study. On their enlistment they usually wore their traditional costumes; but by the time they received their commissions, they wore Western uniforms, suits and hats and spoke in the European idiom. Their approach to both the State and religion underwent a radical change. Their politics was secular and their outlook thoroughly modern. In short, the colonizers not only replaced the Turks in the territories which were wrested from them but successfully trained the Arabs to fit into their political and social pattern. As a result Islam was remoulded by them in practice to suit their requirements; they kept the form but changed the texture. Moreover, as a result of the growing power of the army in the Arab world, a hiatus developed between soldiers and civilian agitators. The soldiers became mercenaries and fought for the colonizers and their stooges, who were thoroughly Westernized and pampered by the colonisers. The situation in the non- Arab world under the European colonizers was somewhat different. The Muslims there did not face the same problems. For instance, in Central Asia, the czarist regime was overthrown by the Bolsheviks who were not Westernized in the accepted sense; they were communists, who believed in no religion. Though they had assured Muslims in their area that Islam would be protected, that promise was never really honoured. Stalin's first Muslim collaborator in the Commissariat for Nationalities, Mullanur Vahila (1885–1918), believed that 'the influence of ancient Arab culture on the universal culture which would emerge as a result of worldwide socialist reconstruction would be immense', but he was sorely disappointed. He had dreamt that the new emerging culture would extend from the deserts of Arabia to the river Ganga, 'as great, beautiful and profound in its content'; but in reality it had turned out to be a nightmare, as much destructive of Islam as of Christianity.

In India, which was ruled by Muslim dynasties for more than a thousand years, the Muslims in the years after 1857 found themselves a minority without hope. Their problems were also different from other Muslims. They had not only to cope with British suspicion against them, but also with the rising tide of nationalism, which was essentially a Hindu phenomenon. (I shall deal with these developments, including the partition of the sub-continent, and the creation of Pakistan and its impact on the struggle between fundamentalism and secularism in Islam, in separate chapters.)

Similarly, in the countries of South-East Asia like Indonesia, which is predominantly Muslim, and Malaysia, which has a Muslim majority, the reactions of the Muslims towards the Dutch and the British differed. They were also inspired by nationalist fervour and influenced by the West, but their Islam, being of a later origin, had imbibed a lot from Hinduism and Buddhism and preserved much of the traditions of these religions; this made it more liberal and eclectic and, therefore, much more nationalistic. It also became less cooperative as time passed. After independence the fundamentalists did their best to reduce the influence of non-Muslim elements but the nationalists, who were more influenced by secularism than Islam, eventually triumphed and were able to usher in a more composite culture. The struggle in favour of fundamentalism that the Muslims—especially the two organizations, Muhammadiya and Sarekat Islam—in Indonesia waged against secularism was hardly effective in the liberation movement and never reached the dimensions which it did in India before its partition.[7]

The Fundamentalist Pattern

Fundamentalism, as we have seen, was a recurring phenomenon in the Muslim world down the ages, asserting itself whenever there was a feeling that Islam was in danger; however it did not have a uniform or consistent pattern but varied from situation to situation, and from time to time. There were two reasons for this. The first was that even among the fundamentalists there was never a common objective; and second, the Shi'a-Sunni divide was so basic that it negated chances of agreement on essentials.

Its present-day manifestations are also varied. There are today three Muslim states—Saudi Arabia, Pakistan and Iran—making strenuous efforts to enforce orthodox Islam in all respects. Saudi Arabia and Pakistan are mainly Sunni; Iran is predominantly Shi'a. A closer look at them will make their divergent stances clear and explain how they differ from one another in many important physical and spiritual spheres.

The Saudis subscribe to the puritanical teachings of Shaikh Muhammad ibn Abd al-Wahhāb (1703–92), who was influenced by Imam Hanbal and Ibn Taymiya and shared their disgust of the corruption and accretion that had crept into Islam. The shaikh waged jihād against corrupters and innovators and strove to purify Islam. Among those who came under his spell were Abd al-Aziz b. al-Sa'ūd (1880–1953), the founder of Saudi Arabia. To Abd al-Wahhāb, who came to be known as al-Shaikh, only the Qur'ān and the hadīth constituted the sharī'ah; everything else was counterfeit. All subsequent interpretations, additions and alterations made by the ulama, and the ṣufis were to be rejected. He was, in particular, against all forms of Ṣūfism and declared saint worship or homage to tombs to be heretical. Also he prohibited drinking and the use of tobacco. Likewise, he frowned upon the telling of rosaries as a form of prayer. He re-emphasized the unity and supremacy of God. His followers, who called themselves Ikhwān—or Brethren, helped al-Sa'ūd, who was then struggling to found a kingdom, to conquer the Arabian peninsula and to unite various tribes under him. On his victory al-Sa'ūd readily acknowledged the help the Ikhwān had given him and promised to fashion his rule on the lines of the teachings of al-Wahhāb.[1]

Al-Sa'ūd was a stern monarch and vigorously enforced puritanism in every walk of life. Fundamentalists hailed his emergence. As the custodian of the Ka'ba, he soon acquired a pre-eminent position in the Muslim world. His devotion to Islam and respect for the sharī'ah made him popular among pilgrims from different lands who looked to him as the new defender of the faith. The discovery of oil in his kingdom gave him the resources to further consolidate his position. Paradoxically, it was precisely his prestige as the ruler of Islam's holy places of Mecca and Madīna and the enormous wealth that his oil wells yielded that later created problems for him. Initially he resisted modernization, but compulsions of the State softened his attitude towards it; he had to let Westernization creep in through British and American involvement in the exploitation of oil. The Ikhwan protested vehemently but the king was unable to reverse the process. He realized that if Saudi Arabia was to be industrialized and to benefit from technical advances it had to provide a modern industrial infrastructure. Modern gadgets like radios, transistors and television sets found their way into the tents of the bedouins and ended their isolation, exposing them to the outside world. They began to enjoy riding in limousines rather than on camel-back. Custom-built Cadillacs, Mercedes Benzs and Rolls Royces became Arab status symbols. Behind the facade of spartan living, rich Saudis began squandering their fortunes with a vulgarity which horrified the Ikhwān. The distance between the king and the Ikhwān grew till it finally became a head-on confrontation. At the battle of Sabala (1929) the royal forces crushed the Ikhwan. This was one of the few instances in which fundamentalism, which had earlier triumphed over secularism, in the end was crushed by the very forces it had unleashed.[2] Though fundamentalism is still much in evidence in Saudi Arabia, it has lost its puritanical zeal; it has retained the shadow but lost much of the substance. The rituals are followed, but the vigour of the teachings of the founder of Wahhābism is gone.

By the time of the death of al-Sa'ūd in 1953, his desert kingdom had modernized many of its institutions; a pretence of puritanical simplicity was maintained but the overflow of petro-dollars had corrupted the ruling elite. Al-Sa'ūd's son and successor, King Sa'ūd, allowed such profligacy and laxity in the life-styles of the ruling family that he had to be replaced by his brother, King Faysal, who was a devout Muslim, steeped in Wahhābi fundamentalism. He was able to restore some of the old purity in administration and social life. He enforced the shari'ah in its totality and curbed the extravagance of the members of his family. He encouraged orthodox learning, both inside and outside his kingdom and came to be looked upon as the custodian of the Islamic heritage against the rising tide of Westernization on the one hand and Nasserism, a mixture of Islamic egalitarianism and leftist materialism, on the other. He received support from fundamentalists everywhere and was hailed as a redeemer.

However, there were limits to what he could do to stem the inflow of modern gadgets and equipment and the change in ideas that came in with them. For instance, he could not prevent the introduction of television in his country as it had become a necessary means of mass communication. This so enraged one of his fundamentalist kinsmen, Khālid ibn Musaid, that he planned to overthrow him. The conspiracy was detected in time and the conspirators, including Ibn Musaid, were beheaded. Ten years later, in 1973, Ibn Musaid's younger brother, Faysal ibn Musaid, avenged the execution by assassinating the king. Despite the wave of sympathy that Faysal's murder generated throughout the Muslim world it resulted in a set-back to his fundamentalist policies. Modernist elements in the royal family opted for more liberalization and technological advancement. His successor, King Khālid, lacked the religious passion of the late Faysal; so does his successor, King Fahd, the present ruler, who believes in adjustment to modern requirements, especially in the administrative and economic spheres. He is pragmatic in his approach to worldly problems and, despite the depletion in revenue from oil, has embarked on development projects in collaboration with the USA, Japan, Korea and other non-Muslim countries. He does not subscribe either to pan-Islamism or

Arabism. His chief preoccupation is to counter the impact of Shī'ite fundamentalism in neighbouring Iran. This he regards as the main threat to the Arab world and to Sunni hegemony. He has appealed to the ulama of all Muslim countries to modernize the sharī'ah through the application of ijtihād, and bring it in line with present-day reality. However, it must be stressed that despite all these efforts at modernization, the basic structure of the Saudi state has remained unchanged and only its superstructure has been given a gloss of modernity. The commercial law of the land had to be modified to conform to international requirements; but criminal and civil laws, particularly personal law, have remained unaltered. Women caught in adultery can be stoned to death though only a few cases have been detected. Criminals are publicly lashed and the hands of thieves amputated. The sharī'ah rules the land and there is no talk of modifying it or reforming it. Nevertheless the elite ignores it with impunity; only commoners have to suffer its rigours. The royal family wields absolute power; they do not speak against the sharī'ah but flagrantly defy its provisions; it is well known that their private lives, in many cases, are different from their public postures.

After the seizure of the Grand Mosque at Mecca in 1980, a high-powered committee was constituted to frame a democratic constitution ·to give the people both the asālīb (modalities of governance) and a majlis al-shūrā (consultative council). It was apparently meant to be a sop to assuage an outraged public but almost a decade has passed since the incident and there has been no effort on the part of the royal family to relinquish any of its arbitrary powers, with a view to implementing, even partially, the measures announced. On the surface everything seems placid but underneath resentment is developing, particularly among the newly educated class, which is denied any substantial share in the power structure; there is also disaffection among some sections of the ruling elite, hungry for more privileges. Dissensions are also on the increase in the royal family.

The king and the crown prince, in an attempt to curb this discontent, have inundated the Westernized Saudis with lucrative jobs and financial inducements; but they demand more say in the affairs of the state. However, the real threat to the established order is from the fundamentalists who refuse to be bought or silenced. They are known to be organizing themselves in secret, waiting for the proper time to raise their voice against the ruling family's betrayal of Wahhābism and its puritanical teachings. Several such organizations are known to exist and though no direct connection could be established between them and the executed Musaid brothers, the new Ikhwān, which gathered a sizeable following during the 1970s and the early 1980s, has made no secret of its revulsion for the life-style of the Saudi royalty; members of the royal family, according to the fundamentalists, are hand-in-glove with the British and the Americans (no friends of the Muslims) and are, on the contrary, helping Israel to hurt Islam. The takeover of the Grand Mosque of Mecca by Juhayman ibn Saif al-Utaybi was a desperate act by the fundamentalists to give vent to their anger. Although it did not succeed in creating a mass upheaval against the Saudi family, it shook the monarch and his ministers as well as the al-Shaikh family, the descendants of Abd al-Wahhāb. The two families have, through inter-marriage and adherence to a common ideology, merged religion and politics in Saudi Arabia and succeeded in establishing a kindred relationship. Al-Shaikh's family has, in effect, become the defender of the Saudi dynasty, putting its seal of approval on every governmental measure. This has enraged the new Ikhwān who condemn it as an 'unholy alliance' between the rulers and the ulamā against the larger interest of Islam. The demands of the fundamentalists include the abrogation of the monarchy which lacks, according to them, the attributes a ruler must possess, and its replacement by administrators chosen by the faithful and known for their piety. They also denounce al-Shaikh and his cohorts for their betrayal of Islam. The new Ikhwān demands implementation of all the directives and injunctions of the Holy Book and the enforcement of the sunna uncluttered by the devious interpretations of theologians who live on State patronage and produce edicts to please the establishment. The Saudi rulers, on their part, accuse the new Ikhwān of engineering unholy revolts, and in indulging in activities reminiscent of the Khawārij, who favoured assassination and terrorism and acted as saboteurs of Islamic solidarity.[3]

The membership of the new Ikhwān is confined to the Sunnis, but there are also Shi'as opposed to the Saudi royal family, whom they regard as the enemies of Ali and his progeny. Much smaller in number, they are largely concentrated in the eastern province where many oil wells are located. Since the rise of Khomeini in neighbouring Iran, Shi'a fundamentalism has gained much ground in Saudi Arabia. The

Ayatollah has condemned the Saudis as munafiqun or hypocrites. Despite the differences in their approach, the Sunni and Shi'a fundamentalists have made common cause against the Saudis. They even dress alike. Both sport long beards with clipped or shaven moustaches, have short cropped hair, white robes (thawb or gallabiya), a taqiyyad (rosary), and roam together in villages and towns, usually talking in whispers. So far they have not had much influence on Saudi public life; nor have they succeeded in weaning away the ruling elite or the educated class from the influence of the West, whose impact continues to be all pervasive. As George Linabury, a Western commentator, has pointed out: 'Not only the accumulation of material goods purchased with petro-dollars fuels the revolution of rising expectations but also the very presence of the Americans and other foreigners and the life-style they bring with them.'[4]

The Saudi attitude towards women deserves special notice; it shows, in effect, the subservience of politics to religious orthodoxy, which upholds male supremacy. Unlike in other Muslim countries, women in Saudi Arabia are obliged to veil themselves and are forbidden from driving cars or travelling alone. 'Nevertheless', Linabury writes, 'about 250,000 Saudi girls attend public schools and 11,000 are university students with half of the latter studying abroad.'[5] The number since then must have doubled. They can be chained physically, but no longer mentally, primarily because education breaks down many societal barriers. The emergence of a middle class consisting of bureaucrats, professionals, technocrats, teachers, and young army officers has also eroded the traditional pattern of Saudi society based on family ties and harem life. This middle class, Linabury predicts, 'may, in time, challenge the hallowed position of age and experience with a more lethal weapon: a modern, secular education.'[6] The extensive Saudi family which continues to multiply in geometrical progression and has been the principal source of strength of the regime, may soon become as much an irritant to the growing secular element as it has already become an eyesore to the fundamentalists; it may be besieged by both the sides—the secularists and the fundamentalists.

The most serious challenge to Saudi oligarchy, claiming allegiance to Wahhābism, has come from the southern tip of the peninsula, the Yemen, with Aden as its capital. It is commonly known as South Yemen, which, under the British, developed on modern lines with secular education and Western-type institutions. Soon after the British withdrew, the tribal Syeds who replaced them were ousted by a popular uprising and replaced by a revolutionary, Marxist group. The new regime completely transformed not only the economic, but also the social life of the inhabitants. The process was further accelerated by nationalist Arab fervour inspired by Nasser. The emergence of a democratic republic in South Yemen can be viewed as the beginning of the end of Saudi hegemony in that part of the world and a serious jolt to Islamic orthodoxy. Though South Yemen's Constitution declares Islam as the State religion and its leaders observe traditional religious rites, they are more committed to communism and have close ties with the Soviet Union. The other Yemen, known as North Yemen, with Sana as its capital, is aligned to Saudi Arabia and follows the same Islamic pattern of civil and criminal administration as its protector. There is, no doubt, growing modernization in the country's commercial sphere but otherwise the shari'ah, as interpreted by the Wahhābis, reigns supreme.

Although Saudi Arabia has considerable influence on the Gulf shaikhdoms, the latter are comparatively free of conflicts between the fundamentalists and the secularists. The five ruling dynasties proclaim their unreserved allegiance to the shari'ah, but in practice they are not as rigid as the Saudis; they allow considerable scope for modernism in social life, if not in politics. Their ruling cliques indulge in a conspicuous display of wealth and, unlike the Saudis, are much more tolerant towards their subjects. They turn a blind eye to many deviations from the shari'ah. Again, the large number of immigrants who come from such diverse lands as Egypt, India, Pakistan, Bangladesh, Sri Lanka and the Muslim countries of Africa, have helped liberalize the environment. They constitute almost 80 per cent of the population of these states and, though they are largely Muslim, their varied customs, rites and religious practices generate a kind of cosmopolitanism which loosens the shackles of orthodoxy. In addition, there are a large number of Palestinians occupying important positions in the administration, who are more modern in their outlook than the local Arabs; sometimes, because of their militant commitment to their homeland, these people become restless and pose a threat to the stability of these regimes; but such is the stranglehold of the ruling elite that none dare revolt or rebel. All these contradictory elements have made the various shaikhdoms a hotch-potch of modernism and orthodoxy, secularism and fundamentalism, with one trying to outdo the other in various ways. Oil wealth has given them the means to build high-rise buildings, highways, airports, factories and in increasing their agricultural output. But the fact remains that these developments have also created a certain measure of resentment as a reaction to materialism which the fundamentalists have been quick to exploit.[7]

The State apparatus in these shaikhdoms is on the same lines as that of Saudi Arabia, being tribal and monarchical. Family and tribal customs determine the mode of rulership with the ulamā providing the necessary legitimacy. There are no elections to choose the ruler; succession is decided by the shaikh and the crown prince. Advisers or ministers are drawn mostly from relations of the ruling family. Kuwait, the most modern and progressive shaikhdom, tried to establish a majlis al-shūrā or consultative council, with restricted membership and limited franchise, but the experiment was abandoned as it proved troublesome.

The ulamā are not a force in the Gulf states, as they depend for their livelihood on the rulers and toe the official line. In foreign relations these states are guided by the British and the Americans who guarantee their rulers protection from external enemies and internal revolts. The impact of the neighbouring Muslim countries is peripheral. The anti-communist outlook of the rulers has prevented them from cultivating friendly relations with Russia or China as they are entirely dependent on the armed support of America and Britain.

Despite the autocratic nature of these states, the spread of Western education has (as in Saudi Arabia) generated movements demanding more say for the people in administrative affairs. They are encouraged by expatriates from the Arab world, who include fundamentalists, liberals and leftists. While the liberals and leftists work surreptitiously, the fundamentalists have a powerful organization, with headquarters in Kuwait, known as Jam'iyāt al-Iṣlaḥ al-Ijtimā'ī or the Society for Social Reform. Its approach is much the same as that of the Muslim Brotherhood of Egypt. Though keeping a comparatively lower profile, the Society has issued warnings against the so-called 'secular pitfalls'. Their journal, *al-Mujtama*, is widely read; it supports the feudal apparatus of Saudi Arabia and the Gulf shaikhdoms and opposes the hybrid set-up of the Muslim regimes in Egypt, Libya, Tunisia and Algeria. It is known to enjoy the patronage of the Saudis and the Gulf shaikhs. The Jam'iyāt is Sunni. The Dār al-Tawhīd, also located in Kuwait, is an organ of Shī'ite fundamentalism and has received considerable inspiration and support from Khomeini's Iran. Shī'ite militants in the region are aggressively anti-establishment and have often been charged with subversive activities. The fact that Sunni fundamentalists have made common cause with their Shī'ite counterparts has forced the Gulf rulers to turn to liberals and secularists for support, placating them with jobs and other inducements.

Bahrain, which has a Shī'ite majority, is studded with dissidents who are known to be sympathizers of Khomeini and work against the ruling al-Khalīfah family which is Sunni. The main Shī'ite organization, Jabhāt al-Islāmīya li-Taḥrir al-Baḥrein (The Islamic Front for the Liberation of Bahrain) has been banned; its leader Hujjat al-Islām Hādī al-Mudarrisi, who was exiled in 1979, broadcasts regularly, inciting Bahrainis to rise against the shaikh and establish a Khomeini-type Shī'a rule in the country. Mudarrisi is equally hostile to the Saudis and calls upon Shī'ites everywhere in the world to revolt against Sunni hegemony.

The situation in the United Arab Emirates is somewhat different. Its rulers have shown greater accommodation, especially to the Shī'ites, who constitute more than thirty per cent of their population. Neither the fundamentalists nor the militants are persecuted but kept under control by gentler means such as official patronage and lucrative inducements. Shī'ite bankers and merchants are allowed to function freely. To appease them, the Emirates declared its neutrality in the Iran-Iraq war, which was welcomed by the Ayatollah and his government; of late, however, their attitude has hardened and become pro-Iraq.

Sunni fundamentalism is confined to the non-indigenous Muslim population, which is irked by the concentration of wealth and monopoly of power enjoyed by the ruling indigenous Arab elite. There is unabashed consumption of alcohol and womanizing among members of the ruling groups. Although this takes place behind pardah, it has caused widespread resentment among the common people, who talk freely—albeit privately—about the immorality prevalent among the rulers and their cohorts. Oman is the home of the Ibādi Muslims, who are the descendants of the Kharijites. Though they claim to be fundamentalists, like the Saudis, their approach to the State and society is different. The state is ruled by the Al-Bu Said dynasty. There have been many rebellions against it, including the Dhufar insurrection, which was ruthlessly crushed with the help of British arms. The father of the present King Qabus had to abdicate in favour of his son as the political and economic situation had rapidly deteriorated. Qābūs brought it under control and with his reforming zeal and passion for modernization, has turned the country around. His fight against the communist-led rebellion in Dhufar, which is aided by the Soviet-supported Democratic Republic of Aden, has greatly appeased the fundamentalists but they are still unhappy with him for his pro-British policy and lukewarm assistance to the Palestinians. There is no conflict between the religious and secular authorities, as King Qābūs has adroitly managed to maintain the balance between the two; both accept his overlordship. He has also lately moved nearer to his neighbours and given support to the cause of Islamic and Arab solidarity.[8]

All in all, the Gulf, though considerably menaced by the Iran-Iraq war and its aftermath, is not in imminent external or internal danger. However, if Khomeini's Iran and Qaddafi's Libya actively support the fundamentalists they may pose a threat to the ruling families. Kuwait and Bahrain, with large Shi'ite populations, are already facing a precarious situation accentuated by the unpredictability of the world oil market and the damage caused by the Iran-Iraq war. In other ways too the region is under pressure from resurgent Islam. For instance, it is not unlikely that in time, the different ethnic groups, subject to social and economic disabilities, will exploit religious sentiments and become a serious threat to the ruling elites, who, it must be said, have sensed this and have started ejecting them. The economy is also becoming regressive and can no longer bear the demands made upon it, especially by the expatriates. Even though Islam makes no territorial distinctions between the various ethnic groups, modern imperatives subject them to discrimination even in fundamentalist countries like Iran, Pakistan and Saudi Arabia. As the disaffection among these groups mounts the stability of the Gulf shaikhdoms could become a question mark.

14
The Nationalist Upsurge

The European occupation, after World War I, of the Arab territories ruled by the Ottomans, changed the political character of these lands completely; they became Westernized, though the process had begun much earlier, under the Ottomans. Egypt was the first Arab country to accept Western ideas and trends; this process was initiated in 1885 by Muhammad Ali, the founder of a new dynasty in Egypt. He embarked on the modernization of Egyptian society, albeit within a broad Islamic framework; his successors gave the process a secular twist. The main beneficiaries were the upper classes; the common people remained hewers of wood and drawers of water. The opening of the Suez Canal gave the colonial powers a vested interest in Egypt as it became the shortest waterway to their colonies in the east, particularly Britain's empire in India. It was not till 1922 that Egypt was conceded a measure of independence, though British troops remained there until 1936 and even thereafter the king relied heavily on the British presence. During World War II the British re-established their hold on the country and both the king and the ruling Wafd party willingly acquiesced in this. Then the ignoble defeat that Egypt suffered in the war against Israel (1947) created a wave of resentment among the people, which led to the revolt of the Free Officers under Nasser in 1952. It was a bloodless coup. Fārūq abdicated and went into exile in Europe. The old order collapsed. The triumphant Free Officers transformed Egypt into a centre of Arab revivalism, becoming in the process the new hope of the Arab world.

It is not within the scope of this book to go into the different phases through which the Egyptian freedom movement passed during the previous decades. All we need to bear in mind is that religion played only a marginal role and the struggle, all through, was motivated by patriotic fervour with strong secular overtones. The Egyptians, right from the time of Ahmad Arabi (1881–82), have been demanding Egypt for the Egyptians and not Egypt for Islam. The cry had its reverberations in practically every Arab country which opted for independence on the basis of nationalism. Because of its geographical position and its being the most populous Arab-speaking state, Egypt became the symbol of Arab awakening. Its newspapers and publications were read all through the Arab world and Arabs everywhere looked to the Egyptians for guidance and support. Egyptian poets, writers and scholars extolled the virtues of freedom and were enthused by the liberation struggle launched by the Wafd party under the charismatic leadership of Mustafa al-Nahas Pasha. Once in power, the Wafdists ceased to be revolutionaries and collaborated with the British. They distanced themselves from the common people. They lived luxuriously and encouraged corruption and nepotism in the administration. They even bought over the ulamā, who became passive spectators to the erosion of Islamic values and gave in to the replacement of Islamic laws by European codes. Even the Muslim Personal Law was codified. The fundamentalists soon had had enough of all this and one of their leading lights, Hasan al-Banna (1906–49), a school teacher, called on the faithful to resist the inroads being made into the shari'ah. There was no immediate response to this cry as the people were too frightened to act. The king and the Wafdists had an iron grip over them. Al-Banna had to struggle for many years before his Muslim Brotherhood acquired a sizeable following. From Egypt the movement spread to other Arab countries. It established branches in various towns in Egypt, Syria, Iraq and a few other Arab countries. Its propaganda began to have an increasing impact on the youth, who were nauseated by the loose living of the ruling classes and their indifference to Islamic tenets. The Brethren, as the members of the Muslim Brotherhood were called, wanted to wipe out every vestige of Western influence. Their motto was: 'Back to the Islam of the Prophet and the first four caliphs.'

Another aspect of the British and the French connection which disturbed the fundamentalists was the priority they gave to language as opposed to religion. This was welcomed by the secularists who propagated Arabism in place of Islam as the cementing bond. In the process Islam was relegated to a secondary position, though lip service to it was, no doubt, paid. However, secular Arab unity finally proved to be ephemeral as it fell to pieces under the Islamic onslaught with its emotional and fundamentalist overtones. As internal dissensions grew, Israel continued to encroach on Palestine; as the new state became a formidable military power, the Arabs lost their pre-eminence in West Asia. Still they had to rely on America for arms, which was pathetic because America was more committed to protecting Israeli interests than satisfying Arab aspirations. More than the secularists, the fundamentalists saw through this self-destructive game and struggled hard to strengthen the Muslim Brotherhood, which began to acquire a sizeable hold among the younger members of the bureaucracy and the armed forces. In Egypt, this led to the assassination of politicians suspected of links with the West.[1]

The king and his cohorts began to be hated and despised by the people. The younger officers in the armed forces, infected by the uprisings of the fundamentalists and the popular discontent, secretly plotted and staged a coup. The Brotherhood welcomed their coming to power as they regarded them as good Muslims eager to advance the cause of Islam. But it did not take it too long to discover that these free officers were more nationalist than religious, more temporal than spiritual. They were idealistic, energetic and incorruptible, but their dedication was more to Egypt than to Islam. Uppermost in their minds was the desire to avenge the humiliation the Arabs had suffered at the hands of Israel rather than to restore Islam to its past glory. Although Nasser in his *Philosophy of the Revolution*, published a few months after the October Revolution, gave equal importance to the 'Circle of Islam', he did not pursue it seriously. His concentration was more on the 'Arab Circle'.[2]

The Brethren soon became disillusioned with the Free Officers; the latter, on their part, were equally upset with the Muslim Brotherhood. They suppressed their activities and arrested their leaders. The gulf between the new government and the Brotherhood widened; it was never bridged while Nasser lived. The Brethren, in fact, plotted to kill Nasser while he was delivering a speech at Alexandria—on 26 October 1954.[3] As a result, more repressive measures were unleashed against them.

Their headquarters was razed to the ground and many of their members were tortured. With the years the hostility between Nasser and the Brotherhood further intensified and some of their leaders were sent to the gallows, the most prominent among them being Sayyid Qutb, who was hanged in 1966. Twenty-one others were shot dead by the police. Earlier, the consumptive Sayyid Qutb, who had been confined in a small unventilated cell, made a vitriolic attack on Nasser in his book, *Ma'alim fi'l Tariq* or *Signposts*. He portrayed the Egyptian leader and his henchmen as pagans who had to be eliminated if Islam was to be saved. In the Brotherhood differences arose on the methods to be adopted to rid Egypt of Nasserites; one section favoured assassination, the other was for persuading the people to rise against them. Though Sayyid Qutb's sympathies were more with the militants, he provided the inspiration for both groups. He was released on grounds of failing health; but even from his sick bed he continued his tirade against Nasser and was re-arrested in 1965, charged with complicity in the murder of the president, and executed.

On 30 August 1965, Nasser, while on an official visit to Moscow, denounced the Brethren as collaborators of the American CIA. Hasan Narwn, the shaikh of al-Azhar, condemned them as medieval terrorists. The Brethren called him a traitor. As the conflict escalated, Islam witnessed the biggest battle between faith and power in contemporary history. The fight was exacerbated by Egypt's ignominious defeat by Israel in June 1967. The Brotherhood blamed the rout of the Egyptian forces on Nasser's wrong policies; they attacked his socialist measures, such as the nationalization of industries, banks, insurance and other public utilities and foreign trade. Though the common people benefited from them, the Brotherhood condemned them as anti-Islamic, declaring that Islam favoured private ownership and individual enterprise. Strangely, even some of the greatest beneficiaries of these reforms, like university students, engineers, doctors, civil servants and army officers, sympathized with the Brotherhood. The government crushed them ruthlessly, which caused an increase in public resentment. To counter it, the government called upon the state-appointed ulama to denounce the Brotherhood and extol Nasser's policies as being within the Islamic framework. Apart from these repressive measures, the Nasserites sowed the seeds of dissension in the Brotherhood; they instigated divisions in their ranks and soon one section was advocating uzla or withdrawal to the mountains while the more militant were determined to fight the government to the bitter end. Eventually internal squabbles caused the Brotherhood to be torn apart. Some of them went underground and carried on their work clandestinely, while others gave up the fight in utter frustration.

The founder of the Brotherhood, al-Banna, was not an ideologue; except for his autobiography and a collection of letters he left behind no testament to guide his followers. In his writings he largely stressed the duty of fighting the British and Egyptian feudal oligarchy; there were no instructions to deal with the changed situation brought about by the Free Officers. Another reason the Brotherhood failed was that the ideology of the Brotherhood was expounded by Qutb, who was greatly influenced by Maulānā Maududi, the founder of modern fundamentalism in Islam. He called modern secular societies anti-Islamic and compared them with the jāhiliya, or ignorance, which prevailed in the pre-Islamic age. Qutb included in this category 'all the societies that now exist on earth'. These included the modern ones in the Muslim world, in which 'the highest sovereignty (ḥākimiya) is exercised in the name of the people or the party or whatever. From this they derive their organization, laws, values, judgements, habits and traditions . . . and nearly all the principles of their existence.' Like Maududi, Qutb preached that sovereignty vested in God and was, therefore, a guarantee against its arbitrary misuse by the ruler. He held that all legislation must conform to the Qur'ān, which alone was free of human error. To quote his words, 'The Muslim State is that in which Islam is applied. Islam means faith, worship of Allah, the legislation, social organization, and the pattern of behaviour, as prescribed by Him.' In his view, 'a society whose legislation does not rest on divine law is not Islamic, however ardently its members may proclaim themselves Muslim, even if they pray, fast and make the pilgrimage.' Further, he added, 'A society that creates a made-to-measure Islam other than that laid down by Allah and expounded by His Prophet, and called erroneously "enlightened Islam", cannot be considered as Islamic either.' He ridiculed Nasser's socialism, and described it as a betrayal of Islam.[4]

Nasser hit back with more socialist measures and greater modernization of Islamic laws and institutions. He had the support of the officially appointed ulamā of al-Azhar. Qutb denounced them as pharaonic pagans, who had no understanding of Islam; they were munāfiqun or hypocrites, who loved the pleasure of this world more than the life hereafter. The ulama reacted sharply to Qutb's views. The president of the Fatwa Commission, Shaikh Muhammad Abd al-Latif al-Sibk, quoted the Qur'an and the hadith in support of his condemnation of Qutb's 'inflammatory style' whose book, *Signposts*, the shaikh said, was a sinister attempt to delude simple-minded young Muslims into becoming fanatics. He decreed: '. . . that the message of the Brotherhood is no more than a plot against our revolution under the guise of religious zeal and that those who act to propagate it or who pay heed to it are seeking to prejudice the nation, to cause it to regress and to inflict calamities upon it.'[5]

Qutb was not an organizer; his forte was theoretical formulations. Throughout the sixties and seventies his ideas influenced the minds of young Muslims all over the world. They read avidly what he wrote and tried to implement his ideas in real life.

After the death of Nasser, his successor, Anwar as-Sadat tried to come to terms with the Brotherhood. He freed their leaders and removed the ban on the organization. His successful military operations against Israel in 1973, in which Egyptian forces liberated their territories across the Suez Canal, enhanced his prestige and endeared him to the Brotherhood. Its then supreme guide, Hasan Hudyabi expressed disagreement with the views of both Maududi and Qutb and pleaded for an understanding with the establishment. He denied that the Sadat regime was jahiliya and maintained that Qutb erred in making hakimiya a criterion of the State. Commenting on Qutb's use of jahiliya, Hudaybi wrote: 'There are some who base their faith on a term unattested by any passage of the Book or any of the sayings of the Prophet, a word of human fabrication, a word that is not sacrosanct and is, therefore, the repository of error and illusion.'[6] Many years later Qutb's own brother and other leading fundamentalist scholars like Talmasani declared that Qutb 'represented himself alone and not the Muslim Brethren'. However, extremists in the Brotherhood continued to be loyal to Qutb; to them he remained the spiritual heir of al-Banna and their pre-eminent guide.

One of Qutb's disciples, Ahmad Shukri Mustafā, advocated the destruction of the present jāhiliya society so that on its ruins a proper Muslim society could be built. His views influenced the hotheads of the Brotherhood. One of the Free Officers and the leader of the Egyptian left, Khalid Muhi al-Din, angered by the repressive measures taken by the police against the Brotherhood, applauded the tenacity with which the Brethren held on to their fundamentalist teachings and said they deserved to be cared for as they were the same people who had once been Nasserites and had even been sympathetic to socialism on the eve of the October Revolution of 1952.

Some Brethren, disgusted by attacks on them by the State-controlled press, organized themselves as al-Takfir wa'l-Hijrah or persons who 'spent and fly'. They found the whole social fabric anti-Islamic and urged their fellow-Muslims to withdraw into the mountains away from the corrupting influence of secularists, and lead lives of purity as good Muslims. They declared that all those who disagreed with them were enemies of Islam. They kidnapped Muhammad al-Dhahabi, a former Waqf minister, who had condemned their movement and executed him as an apostate. For this crime Shukri and five leading members of the Brotherhood were arrested, put on trial and hanged.

The trial, which was conducted by the military, evoked much public interest. In his defence, Shukri denounced both the traditionally orthodox and the secular modernists. Relying on the Qur'ānic verse that 'God knows and you know not' (2:216), he said that everything that came after the Qur'ān and the sunna was not binding on Muslims. He considered the four great schools of Sunni jurisprudence null and void; they were counterfeit and had no place in Islam. He said, 'Islam has been in decline ever since men have ceased to draw their lessons directly from the Qur'ān and the sunna and have instead followed the traditions of other men, those who call themselves imams.' The Qur'ān, he emphasized, was as clear as crystal. To understand its verses a Muslim needed a dictionary, not a commentary. He criticized the closure of the doors of ijtihad by the imams and said that they propagated the doctrine of taqlid instead because the ulamā were keen to make their own compilations objects of veneration by the faithful. He condemned the ulamā as asnām (idols) who put themselves up as deities as in a pagan pantheon, claiming to be the 'go-between' between God and the believers. He said the doors of ijtihād could never be closed and had always to be kept wide open so that each generation could think for itself and not be bound by fatwās which were tailored by the ulamā to suit the whims and caprices of the rulers. Shukri cited a number of examples to prove his point. Nasser had resorted to the same device as the kings and caliphs of yore, he contended. He quoted examples from history: Mahmud Shaltul, the rector of al-Azhar, had decreed that the taking of interest was Islamic; while the noted alim or scholar, Shaikh Sha'rwi, had pronounced that the issuing of treasury bonds was in conformity with the shari'ah. Even fornication was condoned as a measure of women's liberation. According to Shukri, whether in the past or the present, the history of Islam was replete with the ulamā's complicity with the rulers to permit the contravention of Islamic tenets and to condone these 'heresies'.[7]

After Shukri's execution, a group known as 'The Military Academy' came into existence in 1974; its sole aim was to recruit volunteers who would undertake suicide missions against traitors to Islam, both temporal and spiritual. A splinter group of this faction, calling itself al-Jihād, plotted the assassination of Sadat when he visited Israel in 1977 and later signed the Camp David Accord in 1979. They felt the accord betrayed the Palestinians. Sadat, they said, was a bigger enemy of Islam than Nasser. As one of their mentors observed, 'while Nasser had struck at Islam with a hammer, Sadat was trying to strangle it with a silken cord.'[8]

The role of the Egyptian journal *al-Da'wa* deserves mention here. Calling itself 'the voice of truth, power and freedom', it explained in its first issue (July 1976) that it was committed to the application of the shari'ah and the abrogation of all civil laws inspired by the Code Napoleon. It categorized 'four horsemen' as the enemies of Islam: Zionism or Jewry, the Crusaders or Western imperialists, communism and secularism. Any compromise with any of these four was treachery to Islam. As one of its editors, Talmasani, remarked: 'History will judge the present generation harshly, rulers and ruled alike, for having preferred material well-being to religion.' Though it had castigated the negotiations with Israel, it relented after the fatwa issued by al-Azhar, justifying the Camp David Accord on the ground that the Prophet had concluded similar treaties with the Jews, Christians and even the pagans. It quoted the Qur'ānic verse: 'If they incline to peace, make peace with them.' (8:61) It also condemned the use of violence to attain the desired objective:

Every honest man knows that the ruling regimes in this country and ourselves will remain on the opposite side as far as

programmes and orientations are concerned . . . until the day the
law of God is applied and His commandments are enforced. . . . But
if haraka (movement) means the burning of means of transport, the
looting of shops, and the pillaging of public properties, then we
shall not partake of that nourishment . . .

These belonged not to the head of state or the government but the
people. It also called upon the Muslim Brethren to enter the legislature
and bring pressure on the deputies to see that the shari'ah was strictly
enforced.[9]

Meanwhile, some student bodies began to organize themselves
separately on fundamentalist lines to counteract the spread of the leftist
movement in universities. A group known as the Jamā'at Islāmiya or
the Islamic Students' Association, was formed and accepted the
teachings of Qutb and Shukri as its guiding spirit. The Jamā'at propagated Islamic brotherhood and belittled nationalism. As one of its
mentors, Yūsuf al-Qardawi, said: 'Egypt is Muslim, not pharaonic; it is
the land of Amar Ibn al-As and not of Rameses . . . Egypt is not naked
women but veiled women who adhere to the prescriptions of the
shari'ah . . . Egypt is young men who let their beards grow . . . '[10]
They were reminded by one of their rising stars, Islām al-Din, a young
physician with a sharp tongue, that 'the Muslims have experimented
with Western-style democracy, with communism and socialism but
their fruits have been bitter.'[11] His prescriptions against the Western
influence were four-fold: the wearing of the veil by women, the wearing
of beards and white gallabiya by men, early marriage, and compulsory
attendance at public prayers. He demanded that the State enforce these to
bring about what Islām al-Din called iltizām, or the good, pious order.
He succeeded in capturing the student unions of the various Egyptian
universities which till then had been dominated by Nasserites and
Marxists.

Sadat had initially encouraged the formation of the Jamā'at as he
wanted to reduce the influence of the leftists and inject more religion
into politics. Initially the group stood by him and was enthused by
Egypt's victory in the war against Israel in 1973; but the situation
changed after Sadat's visit to Jerusalem, the Camp David Accord and the
treaty with Israel signed in 1979. He was then condemned as a traitor to
the cause of the Palestinians and accused of stabbing the Arabs in the

back. Sadat ordered the Jamā'at leaders to be arrested and placed restrictions on the organization. As the fundamentalists became more aggressive, their activities started frightening the non-Muslims, particularly the Christian Copts, who had always been more Westernized. Clashes between the two communities occurred and Copt leaders bemoaned the persecution suffered by Christians in Egypt. The government intervened and arrested leaders of the hostile groups. The Jamā'at accused Sadat of obeying the dictates of the White House, which is an extension of the Crusaders, and on relying on his administrative machinery, 'which is infiltrated by Christians'. Sadat realized 'the pernicious influence' of such propaganda on the Muslim masses. He countered it by exposing the extra-territorial connections of the Jamā'at and its anti-national activities. The members of the organization had no love for their country, he said. They fomented internal disruption and chaos so that, in the name of Islam, they could usurp power and reduce Egypt to the status of a satellite of some rich Arab country (by this he meant Saudi Arabia, from where they allegedly received funds).[12]

At this time a new preacher came on the scene. He was Abd al-Hamid Kisk. His fiery sermons were taped by his disciples and widely distributed throughout the country and abroad. He had been imprisoned by Nasser, but in the last years of Sadat he became a formidable force. His Friday discourses attracted huge crowds. He strongly criticized al-Azhar for having become a stooge of the establishment. In one of his sermons, he asked 'Who will be the next shaikh of al-Azhar? And answered sarcastically, 'I do not know, maybe an army general.' He demanded that al-Azhar should be made absolutely independent of the government. He wanted it to be financed by income from the waqf properties and not the State treasury.[13] Kisk did not relent even after the assassination of Sadat; Hosni Mubarak, who succeeded Sadat as the president of Egypt was forced to imprison him, though later Kisk declared himself satisfied with Mubarak's efforts to carry the fundamentalists with him. He told his followers to cooperate with Mubarak, who, in turn, gave him his freedom. He returned to his pulpit a much mellowed Muslim and began to preach against extremism and for the restoration of peace and harmony among the faithful. The other fundamentalists also kept a low profile; they feared a governmental backlash after Sadat's assassination. But this phase did not last long and they soon re-asserted themselves, taking over many mosques and using their pulpits to preach their doctrines. The police were unable to lay their hands on them as they slipped out of mosques wearing gallabiya and white skull caps. They were led by Shaikh Mahallawi, who was unsparing in his diatribes against the policies of the assassinated President Sadat. He said that Egypt had become jahali (pagan), and its government 'heretical'; he founded a new organization with the slogan: 'Egypt will be neither Jewish nor Christian . . . neither socialist nor capitalist, neither eastern nor western but Islamic.'[14]

In Cairo, another fundamentalist leader, Shaikh Hāfiz Salāma, harangued the faithful from the pulpits of one of the largest mosques, asking them to go back to puritanical Islam. The government tried to take over the mosque. When it was frustrated in its attempt to do so, it arrested Salāma. His infuriated followers attacked the police and denounced them as 'the champions of the depraved and the prostitutes and the persecutors of the propagators of the message of Allah'.

It would be useful at this point to highlight some of the differences between the Sadat and Mubarak regimes. Sadat was particularly harsh with the Jamā'at, which was involved in over 300 violent incidents during his tenure. Mubarak was much more lenient with them, until a large amount of arms, stolen from army barracks, were recovered from the universities; then he clamped down on them. Later on, when he discovered that the Jamā'at was being funded by Egypt's oil-producing neighbours out of secret funds channelled through their diplomats, he gave them no quarter. There were other differences between the Sadat and Mubarak regimes—in particular the lifting of restrictions on the press by Mubarak, which Sadat had enforced in the wake of the Camp David Accord and Mubarak's overtures to Arab and Muslim countries, whom Sadat had greatly alienated.

Sadat's economic policies had mainly benefited the rich; they hardly brought any relief to the mass of the people. He was also hated by the fundamentalists for his reformist zeal; they were particularly irked by the changes he made at the instance of his wife, Jehan, in the Muslim Personal Law by granting more rights to women in respect of marriage and divorce. Mubarak modified some of these reforms, but he refused to go the whole hog and replace these by the old and outmoded provisions in the shari'ah.

Mubarak has balanced the opposing forces in his country but continues to lean towards secularism. He has been wary and hesitant in his approach, hoping that Cairo will be able to recapture its past glory and become once again the centre of Arabism. He fondly recalls how the first Arab university was founded in the city in 1925; and how the Egyptian press, with more than 200 Arabic newspapers and journals, had become the authentic voice of the Arab world. Since the 'betrayal' by Sadat of the Palestinian case, Cairo has lost the position it once held, which Mubarak is now struggling to restore.

Unfortunately he does not have any strongly held convictions and has basically tried to follow a policy of appeasement; the result is a hotch-potch, with no direction. Though his heart is with the secularists, he easily gives in to the fundamentalists. Take, for instance, his gradual climb-down on the question of women, who have now been stripped of several rights which both Nasser and Sadat had given them. Again, the manner in which he has allowed the State-controlled radio and television to be used by the fundamentalists has caused concern among the secularists, especially the televising of the weekly sermons of the charismatic preacher, Shaikh Netwali Sharawi, who is heard by millions of Egyptians. During the last elections, Mubarak's National Democratic party, though claiming to be secular, had the crescent moon on a green ground as its symbol. Its party paper is named the *Islamic Banner*. Rightly, Dr Nawal Sadawi, one of Egypt's leading secularists, has observed: 'Who is paving the ground for these Islamic groups? It is the government itself and the first victim will be the government.'[15]

Despite mounting fundamentalist activities, Mubarak has not acted against them. This is possibly because they are able to gain much public sympathy by the exhibition of their unbounded devotion to Islam and the president feels that to confront them may be to invite more trouble for himself. This is not to say that Egypt has been almost taken over by the fundamentalists; there are also signs of a secular awakening, though this is not as strong yet as the fundamentalist groundswell among the devotees; one example is the publication of a book, *Before the Fall*, by a young activist, Faraq Foda, in which the author skilfully exposes Islamic fundamentalism as a pernicious product of Saudi petro-wealth and a betrayal of Egyptian nationalism.[16] Another popular intellectual, Ahmad Baha al-Din, whose syndicated newspaper column is read all over the country, attacks in his characteristic style, the ill effects of fundamentalism. He blames not only Sadat but also Nasser, who while popularizing education, did not provide enough funds for it, with the result that there were schools without teachers, textbooks and even blackboards; the students who came out of them were semi-literate and consequently unfit for any worthwhile employment; frustrated, they eventually ended up in the ranks of the fundamentalists who only too gladly took them under their wing.[17]

Foda writes of them, 'Allured but frightened by what they saw, they could not enjoy or afford what Cairo had to offer.' Others have also challenged the weak government policies that have helped the fundamentalist cause. A former chief justice, Said al-Ashmawi, has warned that unless the government wakes up and takes care of the youth, the battle will be lost. Unfortunately, instead of heeding these warnings, the secularists continue to be as wishy-washy as before; they have no plan of action to woo the youth; on the contrary, they are more interested in appeasing the fundamentalists. Wafd has entered into an alliance with the Muslim Brotherhood; other political parties have also given a fundamentalist colour to their programme. Fortunately for Egypt, the people are still afraid to hand over power to the fundamentalists; they applaud their dedication but do not vote for them. In the last election, Mubarak's secular-minded National Democratic party was returned with an overwhelming majority; whether this was due to its being the ruling elite or because of its secular character it is difficult to say; what is certain is that the fundamentalists will not go away even if they lose an election or two, for they are convinced that even if they are not successful in this world, their reward is assured in the next. This is what Mubarak will need to realize and take into account when he attempts to work out the direction his country needs to take in the near future.

15
The African Pattern

In the struggle between religion and power in Islam, Sudan occupies a unique place. It is the largest country in Black Africa and covers an area of one million square miles. Its people are a mixture of Muslims, Christians and Animists; it has a pivotal location astride the Nile which links the sub-Saharan regions to the Arab world. The majority of its population, largely concentrated in the north, are Arabic-speaking Muslims; a substantial minority, consisting of Christians and Animists, inhabit the south. The integration of these communities has been one of the biggest problems faced by Sudan. Disputes between them have surfaced periodically before and after the country became independent in 1953.

It is instructive to look at the long and chequered history of Sudan's struggle for freedom, which was led by two ṣūfis, Sayyid Abd al-Rahman al-Mahdi, who founded the party of the Anṣars (so named after the people who helped the Prophet in Madīna) and Sayyid Ali Mirghani, who belonged to the ṣufi order of the Khatmiyya. These two men fought the Ottomans and then the British. As time passed their hold on the faithful increased and they became a force to reckon with. During British rule, a Western-educated class, enamoured of the parliamentary system of government, emerged and snatched the lead in the liberation movement from the ṣūfis, who were supported by the fundamentalists. But the Western-oriented elites were not able to sustain their initiative, with the result that in the first free elections that followed independence, the fundamentalists again forged ahead and were able to capture a majority of seats in the newly-established parliament in 1956.

The Ansars formed the government; the less politically-minded Khatmiyyas kept out but cooperated with the Ansars. The Ansars had no experience of governing nor did they have an economic programme. Consequently they were unable to cope with the mounting problems of the newly independent nation. This led to popular discontent and, in November 1958, the Ansars themselves asked the army to take over the government. The chief of army staff, Ibrahim Abbud, agreed reluctantly. He restored order and brought a certain measure of normalcy to the administration. However, as time passed, and the situation improved, the Ansars, finding themselves in political wilderness, became restless. They regarded themselves as the true representatives of the people and did not like being out of power. Their new leader, Siddiq al-Mahdi, urged the end of military rule and the restoration of the parliamentary system. He enlisted the support of more than twenty religious leaders and in a memorandum demanded that the army return to its barracks. This was repeated, year after year, with greater and greater public backing. The army refused to give in, arrested the rebels, and interned them in a place called Juba while their leader, Siddiq al-Mahdi, was put under house-arrest. On al-Mahdi's death in 1961, the leadership of the Ansars was split between his brother, al-Imam al-Hádi al-Mahdi, who took over religious matters, while the political wing, known as the Umma party, came under the control of Sadiq al-Mahdi. However, the two groups were united in their demand that military rule should end. Surprisingly, the communists joined them and manoeuvred to take over the leadership of the protest movement. They gained the support of the Western-educated Sudanese, as well as disgruntled workers and peasants.

Under their combined pressure, Abbud and his colonels abdicated and a new government with strong popular backing was ushered in. It was a leftist-oriented government but the experiment did not work. The fundamentalist forces regrouped themselves, mounted a campaign of vilification against the leftists and forced elections in May 1965, in which the religious groups, headed by the Ansars, once again gained the majority and formed a government. However, they could not maintain unity in their ranks and factional squabbles broke out. The two wings of the Ansars fell out and even the Umma party split between the supporters of Sadiq al-Mahdi and the more senior Muhammad Ahmad

Mahjub. The Khatmiyyas, who had so far kept away from politics, could not resist sharing in the spoils and organized themselves into the Democratic Unionist party. Trouble broke out between them and the Anṣars. After some time a reconciliation was effected between Sadiq and Mahjub and an agreed constitution, suitably amended, was adopted; under it Sadiq became the prime minister and Mahjub the president; the formula helped the Anṣars close ranks. But soon cracks developed in the united front of Anṣars and Khatmiyyas; there were quarrels between ministers and party functionaries, and the Anṣars and the Khatmiyyas levelled charges against each other. The alliance collapsed. A period of instability followed. Finally, on 25 May 1969, a young and ambitious army officer, Ja`far al-Nimeiry, supported by disillusioned members from all the factions, including the communists, staged a coup and assumed power. The imam of the Anṣars, al-Hadi, refused to submit to such 'heathen' rule and gathered some 40,000 of his followers on Aba Island. Nimeiry's air-force bombarded the rebels, killing more than 12,000 zealots, including the imam. Mahjub has described the scene as ' . . . a brutal massacre; ruthless, senseless and without precedent in our history. With little protection and no defence against air attack, the people were slaughtered in the streets and fields.'[1] Sadiq al-Mahdi left Sudan and remained in exile for many years, striving to build an anti-Nimeiry front composed of all opposition forces, irrespective of their political affiliations, including the Khatmiyyas and the Muslim Brotherhood. In this he was encouraged by Saudi Arabia and Qaddafi's Libya.

Nimeiry soon revealed himself as an opportunist. He played one group against the other, sometimes favouring the communists, sometimes the fundamentalists, and adopting the time-tested policy of divide and rule. He concentrated on appeasing the south, where the Christians and the Animists had been constantly at war with the Muslims of the north and eventually managed to end the civil strife and bring about a truce between the warring forces. This was a feather in his cap. To further consolidate his position, he founded the Sudanese Socialist Union, on the same lines as Nasser's Arab Socialist Union. It advocated a mixture of Islam and socialism.

Nimeiry also signed an accord with Egypt and later openly aligned himself with Nasser in his struggle against fundamentalism. However, the fundamentalists secretly began infiltrating the Sudanese armed forces and managed to organize a coup against Nimeiry in 1971. Though it failed because of timely Egyptian help, it shattered and demoralized Nimeiry, who realized that he had to come to terms with the rebels, notably the Anṣars, if he were to survive. He, therefore, proclaimed that he would henceforth work for 'national reconciliation' and invited Sadiq al-Mahdi and Sharif al-Hindi, a prominent ṣūfi and supporter of the Khatmiyyas, to return to Sudan and become partners in his government. Sadiq accepted the invitation but Sharif declined. Nimeiry and Sàdiq met at Port Sudan on 8 July 1977 and signed an eight-point agreement, which guaranteed the restoration of political rights and civil liberties and a general amnesty to all those in exile or in prison. Sadiq returned to Sudan. After major electoral changes in the constitution, a general election was held in February 1978. Out of 304 seats in the People's Assembly, 60 seats were won by the Anṣar and Khatmiyya candidates, 20 by the Muslim Brotherhood and 60 by independent candidates sympathetic to the fundamentalists. Nimeiry and Sadiq tried to honour the accord but there were forces in both camps who sabotaged its smooth functioning. These included the anti-Nimeiryans, on the one hand, receiving help and encouragement from Libya; and the secularists and the Christians on the other, who did not like the return of Sadiq and the Anṣars, as they apprehended a reversal of Nimeiry's socialist policies and the re-imposition of Islamic rule at the behest of Sadiq.

Nimeiry played his usual game: favouring one side against the other. When the Christians in the south rose against him for appointing a commission to determine the manner in which Sudanese laws should conform with the sharī'ah, he ensured that the Islamic fundamentalists in the north rose en masse in his support. The Christians and the Animists, incensed at this development, ran amuck. They characterized Nimeiry's action as a clear breach of the Addis Ababa Agreement of February 1972 by which the civil war between the Muslims and the Christians had been brought to an end. Indeed the agreement had specifically stated that no attempt would be made to make Islam the religion of the State or to Islamize its political institutions. Though his Islamic supporters, notably Sadiq and his Anṣars, cooperated with Nimeiry initially, they could not prevent the government's stability from being shaken. Then Sharif, who had always been wary of Nimeiry's motives, came out in the open against him, as did the Muslim Brotherhood. Ultimately, even Sadiq gave up in despair and backed out of the accord.

The die was heavily cast against Nimeiry. Popular discontent, mainly fanned by the fundamentalists, mounted; Nimeiry tried to placate the Muslims with increased Islamization of laws and institutions. Qur'ānic penalties were imposed. The hands of thieves were cut off; fornicators were publicly flogged; gambling and the sale and consumption of liquor was prohibited; the taking and giving of interest was banned. This gimmickry worked for a while, due to extensive publicity. For instance, the proceedings of the shari'ah courts were televised under a programme called 'Decisive Justice' which showed women adjudged guilty of fornication being publicly flogged along with men. One Islamic tribunal ordered the flogging of two Italians caught with Eritrean women on the road in 'a rather endearing manner' for the offence of 'contemplated adultery'. The male hair-dressers of Khartoum were rounded up and given twenty-five lashes each for cutting women's hair. However, the people could not be fooled for too long; they realized that Nimeiry was playing tricks with them and exploiting the Islamic sentiment to serve his own ends. As a critic put it, 'At one moment he is the most Marxist of the Marxists and at another the most Muslim of the Muslims.' Moreover, the fact that his actions were creating dissent both among the various Muslims groups of the north and the Christians and Animists of the south was deplored by all sections of the population. The functioning of the so-called Islamic courts became so scandalous that a highly respected religious leader, who claimed to be an exponent of humanist Islam, condemned Nimeiry as an enemy of Islam. He accused him of distorting Islam's tenets and giving the religion a bad name. He was sent to the gallows. His execution sparked off a mass stir and a wave of bitterness among the faithful.

Famine and the north-south conflict added to Nimeiry's difficulties. Riots broke out, in which the secularists took a leading part. There were widespread strikes, dislocation of transport and communications; even the army, infiltrated as it was by the fundamentalists, turned against Nimeiry. So did his erstwhile supporters, the Muslim Brethren. Such was the public outcry against Nimeiry that no one dared stand by him. He was denounced as a tyrant by both the secularists and the fundamentalists. Finally, there was a spontaneous mass revolt, led by professionals—doctors, lawyers, engineers, civil servants, university teachers—and supported by their relatives and friends in the army. Nimeiry was deposed in a bloodless coup. A new military ruler, Suwaı al-Dahab, was installed in his place. Al-Dahab declared that his government would modify the Islamic code and humanize its 'draconian enforcement'. Public lashings and summary executions were stopped; married couples, who were formerly arrested for not providing instant proof of their marriage, were released; the chopping of hands of thieves was replaced by imprisonment; the televising of court proceedings was stopped; more cultural programmes, including songs and dances, were shown on the media.

The diehard fundamentalists had been so thoroughly discredited that they dared not protest and they joined the secularists. Their leading light, Sadiq al-Mahdi, who had pampered them so far, had to publicly condemn Nimeiry's rule as a slur on Islam and his policies as a travesty of Qur'ānic teachings. When democracy was restored to the country, Sadiq became, once again, prime minister, but he was no longer as zealous a crusader for Islamization as he had been in the past. In his book, *The Shari'ah Punishments and their Position in the Muslim Social Order,* he reopened the debate on the role of the shari'ah in a modern Muslim state. He cited rulings to expose the contradictions in the approach of different juridical schools and questioned the basis of some of the commonly accepted punishments. He doubted whether the Qur'ān prescribed the stoning of women for adultery; the Prophet, he said, had approved of it before the revelations in *Surat al-Nisa* (15-16) and *Surat al-Noor,* which prescribed flogging and not stoning. Sadiq has also not accepted the double standard that the classic jurists adopted in distinguishing married from unmarried offenders. On other matters also he has been equivocal. This has naturally infuriated the fundamentalists, but they are lying low and Sadiq has cleverly managed, by his tightrope walking, to keep the situation under control.[2]

Sudan is a typical example of the conflict between secularism and fundamentalism in Islam; its experience has been different from that of the North African states such as Algeria, Libya, Tunisia and Morocco, where Islam arrived with triumphant Arab armies and whose people, on conversion, began to speak Arabic. The Muslim states of the Black continent, namely Mauritania, Guinea, Niger, Senegal, Nigeria, Somalia, Sierra-Leone and Mali, though predominantly Muslim, were not conquered by Arabs and their inhabitants did not give up their native tongues. Likewise Gambia and Uganda, which have a thirty to forty per cent Muslim population. Their brand of Islam is different; it is an odd mixture of Islam and tribalism, which tries to reconcile temporal local requirements with the Arabian faith. This was also the result of historical development; to these Africans Islam came through contact with Muslim traders and the teachings of the sufis. No doubt they took to Islam devoutedly and helped greatly to spread the faith, discarding whatever they could from their animistic teachings, but much of their ancient traditions and practices remained intact and continue even today.

With the advent of colonialism, Muslims in these countries became increasingly fundamentalist and helped convert a large number of Animists to Islam. The policy of apartheid pursued by the colonial settlers also accelerated the process of Islamization. Further, the principle of equality of all believers attracted blacks to Islam. Moreover, under the British and French administrations, Muslim officers treated the Africans with much consideration; they promptly redressed their grievances and went out of their way to ease the difficulties of newly-converted Muslims (by reconciling their traditions with the requirements of their new faith). This has been graphically brought out by the noted Orientalist, I.M. Lewis, in his analysis of the studies which were presented and discussed at the fifth International African Seminar, organized by the Ahmadu Bellou University of Zaire in January 1964; he points out that 'one of the most interesting and significant facts of the introduction and assimilation of Islam in tropical Africa has been that of the interaction in the field of social organization and personal relations between the provisions of the shari'ah and the canons of customary legal procedures.'[3]

At the same seminar it was shown how the theoretical regulations of the shari'ah had been much modified by the recognition accorded to local customs and rituals; as Lewis explains:

> . . .as long as traditional beliefs can be adjusted in such a way that they fall into place within a Muslim scheme in which the absoluteness of Allah remains unquestioned, Islam does not ask its new adherents to abandon their accustomed confidence in all their mystical forces. Far from it. In the voluminous Qur'ānic storehouse of angels, jinns, and devils, whose number is legion, many of these traditional powers find a hospitable home.[4]

The fundamentalists may not be happy at this accommodation; but African Islam has thrived because of it. As a result its faith in divination, magic, witchcraft and sorcery has not been completely abandoned but Islamic norms and forms are gradually replacing them. I.J. Trimingham, a well-known authority on African Islam and a participant in the same seminar, reported that many African mosques were built on the old sacred graves in order to show their conjunction with the new trends and also to stress the pre-eminent position of Islam now. It is in such ways that Islam in Africa has married and assimilated tribalism, with its many gods and devils, with the monotheism of Islam, with one God, one Book and one Prophet.[5] The reconciliation between the two was brought about under the names of adab and urf, and took place under the protecting umbrella of Islam. As C.K. Meek, another scholar of renown, has said, 'Islam . . . has converted isolated pagan groups into nations before our eyes, forming themselves into nations'.[6] Islam provided them with a coherence which they lacked; it gave them a unity of strength which they had never possessed. On its part Islam had to accommodate, as mentioned before, many African rituals and traditions, which it has frowned upon elsewhere; therein lies the uniqueness of Islam in the Black continent.

Its impact in a broader sense has, however, been felt more along the Sudan belt, especially in Mauritania, Senegal, Nigeria, Niger and Somalia, than elsewhere, although the driving force in the political arena has been nationalism rather than Islam. Many instances can be cited of non-Muslims acquiring a predominant political position in these states; they are popular among the people and respected by tribal chiefs. Muslim leaders do not hesitate to declare that religion should not be mixed with politics. For many years, the head of government in Senegal was a Catholic. Another interesting case is that of Gambia, about which H.A. Gailey, an expert on Africa, observes:

There are three reasons for this odd separation of religion from politics in Gambia. Politics have so far been personality-oriented and thus the popularity of the leader has been far more important than his religion or his political platform. Secondly, the extended family system overrides religious differences. One can change his beliefs and still retain his position within the group without loss of popularity or prestige. Thirdly, there is little connection between

Gambian Muslims and any outside pan-Islamic movement which equates Islam with political goals.[7]

This is equally true of other Muslim states in the sub-Saharan region of Africa. Though proud of their Islamic affiliation, African Muslims are not prepared to give up their secular outlook; they find no contradiction in this.

The fundamentalists have, therefore, not been able to make much of a dent in the ranks of the Muslims of Black Africa; neither the large number of hajjis (pilgrims to Mecca) nor those who have come back after studying at al-Azhar or other Islamic centres in the Arab world have much altered the social or political outlook of these peoples. The petro-dollars and linkage with Saudi Arabia and the Gulf shaikhdoms have, of late, marginally altered the situation but not in any significant way. African Muslims do seem more responsive to a reconciliation between Western secular ideas and the religious mix of their local traditions and Islam than Muslims elsewhere. The best example of this is to be found in Senegal, where the Murids, an offshoot of the Qadiriyya ṣūfi order, have mixed the local African heritage with Islamic tenets and the secular values of the West. The outcome has not always been smooth; it has given rise sometimes to what the fundamentalists call 'heresies'; but despite protests by the latter, these so-called 'heresies' have persisted. As recorded in the *Cambridge History of Islam*:

> Muslim separatism in Africa is an attempt to maintain a balanced relationship between the faith and the practical circumstances in which the faith exists. If the faith seems too foreign, it will be adapted; if too acclimatized, it will be reformed. In the nineteenth and twentieth centuries, the practical circumstances have included both the African traditional heritage and the Christian, colonial and Western presences. National independence changes the detail of the practical circumstances somewhat, but in no way removes the tension between them and the ideal faith.[8]

16
Turkey's Retreat

The Turkey of today is more European than Asian and more secular than Islamic. But in the past it played a historic role in the establishment and spread of Islam. For six centuries, starting from the fourteenth and ending with the twentieth, it made its presence felt in Europe, Asia and Africa. Its leadership of the Islamic world had a profound political and spiritual impact on Muslims around the world. Until the collapse of the Ottoman empire and the abolition of the Caliphate in 1924, most Muslims (except the rebellious Arabs), looked to it for guidance. The Turks were not only conscious of their Islamic identity, they were also proud of it. It gave a greatness to them which they had never enjoyed before. Even the revolutionary movement of the Young Turks, and its leader, Kemāl Ataturk, initially drew inspiration from Islam. It was later that Ataturk abandoned any pretensions towards Islam and turned Turkey from being the epicentre of Islam into a modern, secular republic. His volte face shocked Muslims everywhere and they ceased to look upon Turkey as their spokesman. It was only after the death of Ataturk in 1938 that the fundamentalists roused themselves to try and bring Turkey back into the Islamic orbit.

No discussion of the politics of Islam can ignore Ataturk; after his spectacular victories against the Western powers and the Greeks, soon after the end of World War I, he turned his attention to the problems of his country. He concluded that Islam was the main cause of Turkey's difficulties and believed that its regeneration as a nation could come about only through rapid Westernization. He rammed secularism down the throats of his people and declared that religion would no longer be allowed to interfere in affairs of state. Though Ataturk proclaimed that his aim was to make Turkey 'even more religious in all the purity of faith', his actions belied his declaration. He secularized administration and education; he replaced the shari'ah by European civil and criminal codes; he introduced the Roman alphabet in place of the Arabic; he banned the wearing of fez caps by men and discouraged the use of chudder by women. He lifted the ban against liquor (which he liked) and ball-room dancing (which he enjoyed), both anathema to the orthodox. Within a few years he gleefully announced to the Grand National Assembly in 1932, 'we are by now a Western nation'.[1]

The process of transforming what was, in effect, a theocracy, into a secular state, was by no means smooth. Despite the despotic powers that Ataturk assumed, he had to tread warily lest he roused the wrath of the mullās or hurt the sentiments of the devout. But this was not new to him, for the Young Turks had never dared belittle the importance of Islam, as they were fully aware that the majority of the populace of the empire was Muslim. In their battles against Greece and the Allied powers they found it expedient to fight in the name of Islam. It was only after Turkey's defeat in World War I and its loss of its Muslim territories that the Young Turks began to think more in terms of the country than Islam and Islamic solidarity. This was also because the revolt of the Arabs, and their alliance with Britain and France had shattered their faith in Islamic togetherness; it left the Turks with little choice but to concentrate their energies on rebuilding their country.

Ataturk's victories over the Greeks had given him the aura of the saviour of the nation; he fully exploited this. As soon as he assumed the reins of power, he put an end to the Sultanate. Though his proposal was debated in the National Assembly, with the ulama and some of the old guard opposing it, he told them bluntly:

> Gentlemen, sovereignty and sultanate are not given to anyone because scholarship proves that they should be; or through discussion or debate. Sovereignty and sultanate are taken by strength, by power and by force. It was by force that the sons of Osmān seized the sovereignty and sultanate of the Turkish nation; they have maintained this usurpation for six centuries. Now the Turkish nation has rebelled, has put a stop to these usurpers, and has effectively taken sovereignty and sultanate into its own hands. This is

an accomplished fact. The question under discussion is not whether or not we should leave the sultanate and sovereignty to the nation. That is already an accomplished fact—the question is merely how to give expression to it. This will happen in any case. If those gathered here in the Assembly and everyone else could look at this question in a natural way, I think they would agree. Even if they do not, the truth will still find expression, but some heads may roll in the process.[2]

No one was prepared to risk losing his head. The final rites of the death of the Ottoman Sultanate were performed by the Grand National Assembly on 1 November 1922. Thus disappeared the Sultanate; the Caliphate still remained. When the reigning sultan fled to Malta, the Assembly appointed his cousin Abd ül-Mejid as caliph, as he was 'in learning and character most worthy and fitting'. Then Ataturk dissolved the old Assembly and called for fresh elections. His newly formed People's party won a comfortable majority. Ataturk was elected president of the Republic. One of the burning issues he faced was the future of the Caliphate. Most of the deputies were in favour of retaining it. The influential newspaper *Tanin* underscored their sentiments in an editorial and castigated the opponents of the continuation of the Caliphate. The abolition of the Caliphate, it wrote, would result in 'the loss of all importance of Turkey in the world of Islam', and it would 'sink to the rank of a petty and insignificant state. The Caliphate was acquired by the Ottoman dynasty and its retention in Turkey was thus assured for ever; deliberately to create a risk of losing it is an action totally incompatible with reason, loyalty and national feeling.'[3] One of Ataturk's own confidants said to his friends: 'This man Mustafā Kemāl had proved up to now that he had superior vision, but has he suddenly gone mad now?'

The Muslim world had similar feelings. In India, the Muslim leaders not only pleaded for the Caliphate's retention, but agitated for it with the support of Gandhi and his Congress (their agitation was called the Khilafat movement). Ataturk turned a deaf ear to all such pleas; he was convinced that the Caliphate, being the last bastion of orthodoxy, had to go. Despite strong opposition he coerced the Grand National Assembly, on 3 March 1924, to depose the caliph, abolish the Caliphate and banish every member of these Ottoman family from

Turkey.[4] He followed it up by abolishing the highly respected office of shaikh al-Islām, banning the ṣūfi orders, closing down the department of sharī'ah, disbanding sharī'ah courts, and shutting down all religious schools and colleges.

Ataturk then turned his attention to abrogating the whole sharī'ah, including the Muslim Perṣonal Law, which he replaced with the Swiss Civil Code. He had made his objective clear in a speech delivered on 5 November 1925:

> The negative and overwhelming force that has condemned our nation to decay, that has ultimately broken and defeated the men and their initiative and drive, whom our fecund nation has in no period failed to produce, is the law that has hitherto been in your hands, the law and its faithful followers. . . .It is our purpose to create new laws and thus to tear up the very foundations of the legal system. . . .[5]

Within a few years he Europeanized all the Turkish laws, drawing from the French, Roman and Swiss codes. Polygamy was banned; divorce made restrictive; equal rights were given to women; Qur'ānic penalties were abolished; licences for the sale of liquor were freely given; the distinctions between Muslims and non-Muslims were removed and both Muslim men and women were given the freedom to marry non-Muslims; apostasy from Islam was no longer made a punishable offence.

These measures, enacted by the Assembly on 17 February 1926, were indicative of Ataturk's zeal to bring Turkey on a par with other European nations to enable it 'to achieve, in essence, and in form, exactly and completely the life and means that contemporary civilization assures to all nations.'[6] He was not satisfied with the substance of transformation and was anxious that it be paraded to the rest of the world so that everyone could see that the Turks were a transformed people. He had already selected the fez as his target; on 25 November 1925 he decreed that wearing a fez cap would be punished as a criminal offence. Explaining the reasons behind it, he said,

> Gentlemen, it was necessary to abolish the fez, which sat on the heads of our nation as an emblem of ignorance, negligence, fanati-

cism and hatred of progress and civilization; to accept in its place the hat, the headgear that the Turkish nation, in its maturity as in other respects, has accepted, in no way diverges from civilized social life.[7]

The compulsory wearing of hats spread dismay among Turkish peasants and Muslims elsewhere. The rector of al-Azhar issued a fatwā against Ataturk, declaring that a Muslim who dressed like a non-Muslim was 'an infidel'. He added, 'Is it not folly to abandon one's own national way of dressing in order to adopt that of other people, when this desire for limitation can lead to the disappearance of our nationality, the annihilation of our own identity in theirs, which is the fate of the weak. . .?'[8] Ataturk ignored such criticism and went ahead and denounced the veil as 'a barbarous posture' and encouraged women to mix with men.

After crushing religious and political opposition Ataturk held general elections in 1927. Only candidates of his People's party were allowed to contest. One of the earliest measures the Assembly took on 10 April 1928 was the deletion of a centuries-old provision from the Constitution—namely, the 'religion of the State is Islam.' All citizens, irrespective of their religious belief, were made equal in every respect. Turkey became in law, as it was already in fact, a secular state; its authority was made supreme not only in temporal but also in religious matters. In a speech lasting thirty-six hours, Ataturk explained why he had transformed Turkey from a citadel of Islam into a modern European state. It was a devastating indictment of the harm which he believed religion and religious institutions had done to Turkey. He was eager to make the final break with the Islamic past. Later, even the azan, the Muslim call to prayer, universally recited in Arabic, was by decree ordered to be intoned in Turkish. Islamic names such as Bey, and Beyan (originally given as titles) were disallowed and substituted by Turkish surnames. He gave up his name 'Mustafā' because of its Islamic connotation and took on the name of Ataturk—father of the Turks. However, when he died on 10 November 1934, he was buried according to Islamic rites with the imam reciting Qur'ānic verses. This was insisted upon by his sister. Likewise, in 1954, she held a mewlud recital in her brother's memory at the Sulaymāniya mosque in Istanbul for the peace of his soul and absolution of his sins.

For almost two decades Ataturk tried his utmost to transform the Turks into modern, secular Europeans. But no sooner had he been laid in the grave than Islam began to raise its proud head. The poor and downtrodden, especially in the villages, had remained immune to Ataturk's radical, secular changes. Even in the urban areas there was a noticeable resurrection of Islamic traditions; it took a decade or two, but the process could not be stopped. Finally, after many ups and downs, the People's party, committed to undiluted secularism, was forced into the background and, in the 1971 elections, the opposition, spearheaded by the Democratic party, under Sulaymân Demirel, made Islamization an election issue and won a majority of seats to the National Assembly and formed the government. Religious education was reintroduced in schools; the University of Ankara was entrusted with the training of religious leaders; new mosques were constructed; old mosques were repaired; the ban on pilgrimage to Mecca and Madina was removed and facilities provided for intending hajjis; schools for the training of imams were started; and even the restrictions on the ṣūfi orders, including visits to the tombs of saints, were lifted. Though the religious sphere was kept apart from politics (the government passed an act forbidding 'the use of religion for political or personal gain'), religious groups began to manifest their presence in politics. The ruling Democratic party, sensing the mood of the people, made an alliance with an Islamic organization called the 'Followers of Light', founded by a noted Sunni theologian, Sayyid as-Nuri (1867–1960). His programme included the return of Turkey to the Islamic fold, the abandoning of secularism, the restoration of an Islamic character to the republic and the reintroduction of the sharî'ah. As the ruling Democratic party was predominantly Sunni, and its activities had Sunni overtones, the Shî'ites became apprehensive of their future and formed their own Party of Union to protect their sectarian rights. Instead of accommodating the Shî'as, the Sunnis sunk their own internal differences and united under a new political party, known as the National Order party with an Islamic scholar, Prof. Nazimuddin Erbakan as its leader. Fearing internecine warfare, the government promptly outlawed the party; but it re-emerged under another name: the National Salvation party. Though it moderated its anti-Shî'ite stance, and even refrained from demanding the re-establishment of an Islamic state, it continued to propagate vigorously for the restoration of Islamic values and the Islamization of political and social institutions within the Sunni framework.

The 1970s were times of turmoil for Turkey. Fundamentalism, ethnic separatism and political opportunism erupted in many parts of the country. The Khomeini revolution in neighbouring Iran gave a further fillip to Islamic fundamentalism and the demand for more Islamization was vociferously raised, thus generating political instability. The armed forces, which remained committed to Ataturk's secular philosophy, became alarmed. In September 1980, a military junta seized power. The fundamentalists, including their leader, Erbakan, were arrested. Once again, by force of arms, Turkey was brought back to the secular path.

The martial law administration, under General Evren, managed to keep the political turmoil in check. The people acquiesced in military rule as they were fed up of political intrigues, the general economic malaise and the collapse of law and order. The army banned all political parties but allowed certain civil liberties and promised a new constitution. Evren had it drafted by experts and placed it before the people through a referendum. It was ratified by an overwhelming majority. Simultaneously, Evren was also confirmed as the president of the Republic for the next seven years.

Though he and his newly formed National Democratic party stood for the continuation of Ataturk's secular politics, other parties—the pro-Islam Motherland party and the leftist Populist party—which were allowed by him to contest the general elections in 1983, opposed him on varying grounds. They published separate manifestos. The Motherland party stood for moderate Islamization and relied heavily for support on the ranks of the disbanded National Salvation party with its avowedly fundamentalist programme. Its leader Turgut Ozal had had connections for a long while with National Salvation party and made no secret of his love for Islam; but being a realist he showed more concern for the economic betterment of the Turks than religious requirements. His party secured 212 seats out of 400 in the elections in 1984 and formed the government, and Ozal became prime minister. One of the first tasks he undertook was the appeasement of the fundamentalists. Liberalizing religious freedom, he gave many more facilities for the revival of Islam and tried to develop closer ties with Muslim, particularly Arab, countries. All these measures, to some extent, silenced the fundamentalists but the secular roots of the army, bureaucracy, professionals and intellectuals were so deep-rooted that they had penetrated every aspect of Turkish life, especially in urban areas. Ozal had, therefore, to tread cautiously and go about his task slowly, in more a persuasive than confrontationist manner. He and his government made strenuous efforts to get the Turks to realize that while a complete break with Islam had rendered them rootless, Westernization, in turn, had brought them economic and political stability. Turkey had, no doubt, been reduced to a fourth-rate power subsisting on American aid; but the remedy, according to Ozal, lay in an adjustment between the two forces, which could prove useful for Turkey in the long run. He was aware that Turkey had become neither European nor Oriental but a hybrid and that it had to be reshaped both by retaining its Islamic heritage and by absorbing the Western trends, especially in the economic and political fields.

Hence along with economic and political reforms, he also encouraged, as I have mentioned earlier, religious revival. New madrasas were opened, more mosques were built, and encouragement was given to renewal of interest in the sūfi orders. Also he allowed any number of newspapers, journals and books on different aspects of Islam to be started. Once again Muslims heard the muezzin's call to prayer in Arabic.

No restrictions were placed on women wearing chudder. Pork became taboo and halāl meat popular. Religious texts with Turkish translations were sold in hundreds of thousands and commentaries on the Qur'ān, the traditions of the Prophet and other classical books on Islam were published, such as those by the Dargha publications. There was marked interest in Maulana Rumi; *Islam*, an organ of the Naqshabandi sūfis, soon had one of the largest newspaper circulations in Turkey. Earlier, the National Salvation party had founded two Islamic dailies, *Yeni Devir* (*The New Age*) and *Milli Gazette* (*National Gazette*), which acquired a wide readership.

Seeing the inroads these publications were making on the public mind, other political parties also toed the line by bringing out their own Islamic publications. However, the secularists, realizing the danger ahead, reacted and started their own newspapers and journals to counter the fundamentalist propaganda. Also the established newspapers like the *Cumhuriyat* and *Tercuman* came out aggressively in defence of secular values and pooh-poohed fundamentalist arguments, exposing their absurdities in the modern age. President Evren encouraged them. A secularist to the core, he was determined to see that Turkey did not lapse into religious obscurantism and lose its valuable link with the West. The fundamentalists continued with their tirade against secularism; they were no longer so weak and disorganized as to allow Turkey to go back to the so-called 'Thermidor period' (1924–49), when every manifestation of Islam was banned.

Since then the tussle between fundamentalism and secularism has continued unabated, sometimes erupting in violence. At times the secularists, despite popular support, develop cold feet in the face of the fundamentalist onslaught; they lack both courage and conviction. Even Marxist scholars have made a turn-about. Take, for instance, the case of the poet-philosopher, Ismet Ozel. He gave up Marxism and opted for the kingdom of God. When questioned about the transformation, Ozel explained, 'Man looks either after his freedom or his security. But he cannot achieve one without the other. All my life has been a search for ontological security. I am convinced that I have found this security in the Qur'ān. Islam is a healing for me.'[9] His book, *The Three Problems*, is widely read and has considerable influence on the younger generation.

Ali Bulae is another luminary on the intellectual horizon. Though a secularist, he has also become an ardent advocate for the revival of Islam. To quote his words:

> We are not for or against Kemalism. That does not concern us. We are much more concerned with the question of science and values, the relevance of technology to our society, the ecological and environmental problems of Turkey, the social and economic betterment of the vast majority of our people, the provision of absolute justice, the spread of equality, the epistemological basis of our civilization, the reconstruction of a critical Islamic tradition, the flowering of our art and culture, poetry and fiction. We seek Islamic alternatives to these issues. And it is precisely these issues which concern university students and young academics, Muslims and non-Muslims, throughout Turkey.[10]

However, despite these reactions, it does not seem likely that Turkey will ever adopt the Saudi Arabian or the Pakistani pattern of administration or at any time want to return to the era of the Ottoman

Caliphate. The desecularization of Turkish politics seems to be, therefore, out of the question. It can at best be liberalized, granting greater religious freedom and thus becoming more acceptable to the rest of the Muslim world. It is never likely to sever its links with the West which provides security to it and turn to its Muslim neighbours, either Iran or the Arabs, who are militarily of little help though they may be able to give some financial aid or increase in trade. The Turks are trying to resolve this paradox: if they succeed in reconciling the material advantages of secularism with the spiritual upliftment which religion provides, then they may show the way to the other Muslim countries.

Meanwhile in the last election that Ozal called, a year before schedule, in November 1987, he challenged the old politicians both of the left and the right (who were imprisoned by the army after its take-over but were released by Ozal's government after getting the people's approval in a referendum), to test their electoral strength. In a free and fair contest, Ozal's Motherland party won 294 of the 450 seats in the National Assembly, after more than ninety-one per cent of Turkish voters had cast their votes. The second place went to the left-wing Social Democrat party, with ninety-four seats. Sulayman Demirel, the chief spokesman for the Muslim fundamentalists, whose party in 1970 had won a majority of seats, came third, with his new True Path party winning only fifty seats. Ozal has demonstrated that Islam need not be an obstacle to progress and that it can be used effectively for more political democratization and better economic growth. He has not only outwitted his mentor, Demirel, but out-manoeuvred the secularists by carving out a middle way between religion and the State, where both can coexist with each other and enjoy a position of honour and popular acceptability.

17
The Socialist Patchwork

The Arab world, with its chequered historical past, has become a curious patchwork of fundamentalist and secular states. Saudi Arabia and, to a lesser extent, the Gulf shaikhdoms and Sudan, are fundamentalist; secularists, with a strong nationalist grounding, are in the ascendant in other lands. Egypt, the most populous of them, showed the path to secularism and has remained so despite the constant onslaughts it has faced from the fundamentalists. Syria and Iraq, which were once the centres of the Umayyad and Abbasid Caliphates respectively and also the fountainheads, by and large, of dissent and opposition against the orthodoxy, have turned to a form of socialism, which, in a way, is an advance on secularism. In the others, there is a curious amalgam of fundamentalism and secularism; sometimes traces of this are to be found even in the so-called socialist states.

Egypt was the first to be exposed to Western ideas in the wake of the Napoleonic wars in the mid-eighteenth century and the growing British inroads into its territories as a result of the opening of the Suez Canal in 1869. Though the rebellion led by Ahmad Arabi and later by Saad Zaghlul Pasha was against the British, it was motivated by secular trends and aspirations. Saad Zaghlul wanted to lead his party, the Wafd (which means delegation), to the Paris Peace Conference but the British instead exiled him to Malta which, contrary to their expectations, had the effect of turning him into a national hero. Saad Zaghlul Pasha was always more secular in his demands than religious; in fact at no time did the Egyptian rebels use Islam to buttress their cause. Until the Free Officers, the rebel group of young army officers under Gamal Abd al-

Nasser (1918–70), took over the reins of government after the coup in 1952, the Wafdists under Mustafā Nahas Pasha (who succeeded to the leadership after Saad Zaghlul Pasha) and other political groups, cooperated with the British and ran a Western form of government, with its attendant evils of corruption, nepotism and so on. They had ceased to be revolutionaries, with the result that popular discontent mounted against them, leading to the successful revolt by the Free Officers, who, though initially supported by the fundamentalist Muslim Brotherhood, were secular and more patriotic than religious. The Free Officers however had no economic base.

The situation in Iraq and Syria was somewhat different; the rebels in these countries who spearheaded the liberation movements were much influenced by Marxist ideology. Unlike the Free Officers in Egypt, who had no political background and only revolted because they were tired of the corruption and nepotism in government and wanted to see it eradicated, the Ba'athists wanted to transform the whole system. They were more enamoured of Marxism than Western ideas of liberalism. The revolutionaries in both these countries, had a lot in common, particularly their hatred of the West and its native collaborators. Indeed, both groups of revolutionaries reserved their greatest scorn and loathing for their own countrymen who were apologists for and sycophants of Western powers. They also had some strategies in common; for instance both the Nasserites and the Ba'athists planned to infiltrate the army and the civil services and indoctrinate young officers with revolutionary ideas. Once successful, they used military power to political ends. Nasser and his fellow officers were trained by the British; the Ba'athists trained under the French. But the Ba'athists wanted to change the whole system of government; the Nasserites, to begin with, were content to usurp power and establish their own rule. Neither were motivated by religious fervour. And although circumstances later forced Nasser to adopt socialism it must be noted that neither he nor his colleagues were initially inclined towards it.[1] Paradoxically, many of the leaders of the rebellions in Syria and Iraq, though hardcore socialists, were practising Muslims; they were trying to give 'Marxism in Islamic cup'.[2]

The revolutionaries in Syria organized themselves into two groups: the Parti Popularire Syrien (PPS) and the Ba'ath Socialist party which was founded by two French-educated intellectuals, Michel Aflaq, a

Christian academic, and Salaheddin el-Bitar, a Muslim school-teacher. While the PPS was less radical and somewhat pro-West, the other Ba'athists were entirely anti-West, with a leftist orientation. On the religious front, both were for reforms of the shari'ah to bring it in line with progressive ideas from the West. Of the two, the Ba'athists were more aggressive and better organized. Their position was further strengthened after another group led by Akram Haurani, who had built a strong base among the poorer peasantry, joined them.

In the struggle for supremacy, the Ba'athists ousted the PPS and formed a united front, consisting of Ba'athists and a section of the old nationalists with leftist leanings. This group did not mind enlisting the help of even the communists. Along with other revolutionary groups, the Ba'athists opposed the military alliance with the West, known as the Baghdad Pact.[3] At the same time they were critical of Nasser's ambition to lord it over the Arab world. However, after the Egyptian leader signed an arms deal with the Soviet Union, and favoured some kind of a leftist approach to the solution of Egypt's economic problems, the Syrian Ba'athists came round to accept Nasserism and agreed to the Union of Egypt and Syria in 1958. The Union lasted only three-and-a-half years. It floundered because the Ba'athists found Nasser too over-bearing; Nasser, in turn, accused the Ba'athists of being self-centred. Ironically, the ones who had initiated the Union were the first to sabotage it. A disillusioned Nasser did not try to stop the dissolution of the Union and thus ended one of the most imaginative attempts at Arab unity, though in this case, the cause for the failure had more to do with a clash of temperaments than of ideologies or even policies.[4]

In the welter of recriminations that followed, the Ba'athists accused Nasser of being a capitalist stooge. Determined to prove them wrong, Nasser embarked on an aggressive more socialistic programme. He arrested leading capitalists, confiscated their properties and nationalized major industries. Always suspicious of the hold of the pashas and the beys, whose power he felt was being perpetuated by Egypt's parliamentary system, he decided to change the composition of the Parliament. Out of a total membership of 1750, he reserved 375 seats for peasants and 300 for workers. The rest were divided among industrialists, professionals, civil servants, professors, teachers, students and women. This was close to the one-party political system, so dear to the communists; but it irked not only the Ba'athists, who were anti-communist, but also the fundamentalists who condemned it as totalitarian and heretical. However, al-Azhar, which had been taken over by the government, welcomed it as a herald of true Islam; it presented Nasser as the real friend and protector of the downtrodden. The Muslim brotherhood mounted a frontal attack against Nasser and described al-Azhar as the 'devil's workshop'. Nasser retaliated by arresting their leaders and banning their organization. Later, some of them were executed for conspiring to murder Nasser.

Despite their socialist measures, the Nasserites were never accepted as genuine socialists by the Ba'athists; instead they were dubbed opportunists. The Ba'athists claimed that they were the only true leftists. In the 1950s and the 1960s the Ba'athists took up the cause of the peasantry and received enthusiastic support from the rural youth. They also gained a following among young army officers, recruited from the peasantry who were keen to see the emergence of an egalitarian order, as also among the minorities who hoped to get a better deal from them. The Sunnis, who were concentrated in the cities and the towns, feared the Ba'athists' anti-urban policies, and pro-peasant orientation and opposed them. Likewise, the ulamā also attacked their secular policies and characterized them as anti-Islamic.

In 1962, the Ba'athists came to power in a military coup. They gave more representation in their administration to the minorities, particularly in the army and the bureaucracy; the Sunnis, who formed the vast majority of the population, were sidelined. The ulama rose against the Ba'athists, but they managed to remain in power with the support of the rural population, the middle classes, the minorities and the young army officers indoctrinated by them. This far, there have been three Ba'athist governments in Syria—1963–66, 1966–70 and from 1970 to the present. The government's edifice rests on three pillars: one, the party cadre, two, the military and the police and three, the bureaucracy. The ulama figure nowhere. The Ba'athists have consistently refused to give them special powers, although some of them have been appointed by the government to specific posts which involve the leading of congregational prayers, the teaching of theology and the performing of religious rituals. What makes the Ba'athists acceptable to the faithful is their pro-Arab militancy and uncompromising hostility to Israel; the military, which is predominantly Shi'a Alawites, is also solidly behind them. In recent years, the Ba'athists in Syria have also made some concessions to the Sunnis and are slowly winning them over. Only the fundamentalists continue to oppose them as they are more inclined towards the Sunni majority than the Shi'a minority.

The situation in Iraq, which is also ruled by the Ba'athists, is different. The majority of Iraqi-Arabs are Shi'ites, whereas the opposite is true of Syria, but it is the Sunni minority living in and around Baghdad, which rules the country. When the Ba'athists came to power in Iraq through a military coup in 1968, they tried to suppress the (mostly Shi'ite) Kurds who constitute a fifth of the population and who have constantly clamoured for autonomy. The situation has worsened since the Khomeini revolution in neighbouring Iran, for it has made the Kurds more restless and aggressive. They now demand a separate Shi'ite state in central and southern Iraq where they constitute the majority; these areas are adjacent to and have close links with the Iranian Shi'ites. The conflict between religion and the State in Iraq has, therefore, acquired Shi'a-Sunni overtones. The ruling Iraqi Ba'athists have managed to placate the Shi'as by introducing several welfare schemes for their exclusive benefit but their emotional bonds with Iran continue to fuel their disenchantment with the government.

A quick survey of Iraqi history shows that the Shi'as have never accepted Sunni domination; their resentment goes back to the days of the British, who used to patronize the Sunni minority. King Faysal, who was installed by the British, tried to win over the Shi'as; he gave them increased representation in the administration and even appointed some of them as his prime ministers. He also looked after their economic interests. This appeased the Shi'as to some extent; but when Nūri al-Said became the prime minister he began to favour the Sunnis over the Shi'as. In time the Shi'ites revolted and, in 1958, Brigadier General Abd al-Karim Kassem, a Shi'ite, overthrew the Sunni Hashimite dynasty. His regime was short-lived. He was overthrown by Colonel Abd al-Salam Arif and the pro-Sunni Ba'athists. They were supported by the Iraqi Nasserites and refugees' from Ba'athist Syria. It was during this time that Khomeini took refuge in Basra in Iraq; despite the hospitality that he enjoyed there, the Ayatollah did not soften his attitude towards the Ba'athists. He regarded them as munafiqun or 'hypocrites' and their socialist creed as anti-Islamic, and particularly harmful to the Shi'ites.[5]

The emergence of Saddam Husayn as the supreme leader of the Ba'athists further intensified Khomeini's hostility to the socialist regime. He opposed the land reforms which adversely affected the holdings of the Shi'ite clergy. He was also upset with the totalitarian methods used by President Husayn to suppress the Shi'ites and harass their clergy. The Ayatollah feared that the Ba'athists, in their secular zeal, might desecrate the Shi'ite holy places at Najaf, Karbala and Kazimayan. Though ill-founded, these fears ensured that Husayn and his Sunni officers were even more unacceptable to the Shi'as. Khomeini and the Shi'ite ulama were also unhappy at the agreement that the Shah of Iran entered into with Husayn over the disputed Shatt al-'Arab waterway; they regarded the pact as a betrayal of Iran and of the Shi'ite cause.[6] As time passed Khomeini and his followers in both countries secretly planned to overthrow both Saddam Husayn and the Shah, whom they regarded as the stooges of America and inimical to Islam. To make matters worse, Husayn, at the instigation of the Shah, expelled Khomeini from Iran; he had to flee to France. This infuriated the Shi'ites. They organized massive protest marches which resulted in widespread rioting. President Husayn came down hard on the protesters.

After a period of exile in France, when Khomeini returned triumphantly to Iran in 1979, Iraq's Shi'ites openly defied the Ba'athists and demanded a separate Islamic state of their own in eastern Iraq. They also gave their whole-hearted support to the Khomeini revolution. Baqir al-Sadr was their leader; he was arrested, put on trial and executed for treason. His death enraged the Iraqi Shi'as; they hailed him as a marji'iya (supreme leader), who had sacrificed himself for Islam. They also called him a shahid or martyr—the highest commendation for a Shi'ite—and pledged that every Iraqi Shi'a would die to uphold the cause for which al-Sadr had so valiantly laid down his life.[7]

Al-Sadr was one of the most respected theologians of Shi'ism; his work on the Islamic State is regarded as a masterpiece of Shi'ite theocratic philosophy. Al-Sadr maintained that God alone was sovereign, and in God alone vested all authority—spiritual as well as worldly. From God power and authority flowed to the umma, which was bound by His commands, as enshrined in the Qur'ān and the sunna; the imam alone could interpret God's commands and no one else. And, in his absence, the marji'iya, who acted as the deputy of the imam (hidden, according to Shi'ite belief). As the marji'iya was the repository of both religious and secular powers, he alone could be entrusted with the leadership of all matters in the state. His word was sacred and infallible and he was best suited to look after the interests of the faithful. He was the sole arbitrator not only in the appointment of the clergy but also in the selection of candidates to elective, executive and judicial posts. It was his right to select governors and army commanders. In his work, he could be assisted by a supreme council of one hundred clerics, preachers and teachers. The marji'iya might listen to their views, but his decision in all matters was final and binding on all. In case of a contest between aspirants for a particular post, al-Sadr recommended reference to the faithful, whose verdict would be honoured by the marji'iya.[8]

In al-Sadr's scheme of things there was not much delegation; Khomeini allows and encourages it. But where the essentials are concerned there is no difference between the two. Both emphasize the supremacy of the imam in all matters and the unflinching obedience of the Shi'ites to the commands of the marji'iya. Saddam Husayn is dubbed a satan or yezid by both the religious leaders and his collaborators, the Ba'athist apostates and their destruction is held to be the religious duty of every Shi'a. Al-Sadr paid for his views with his life. Khomeini had vowed to succeed, but in the Iran-Iraq war, which ended in August 1988 after eight years, Iran has suffered much more than Iraq in every respect.

Algeria falls into a different category than Syria and Iraq though its leanings are also broadly socialistic. Situated in North Africa, its bloody freedom struggle took birth in the womb of fundamentalism; but later the Western-educated socialists came to the fore and took over the leadership from the fundamentalists. Their leaders Ben Bella, Ben Khedda, Muhammad Khider, Boumedienne and Benjadid gave the battle against the French as they were better organized than the fundamentalists. More than six million Algerians died before the country gained independence. Ben Bella, who became president, proclaimed that the mission of equality that Islam preached could not be implemented without socialism, and embarked on socialist measures to rebuild the shattered economy. The task demanded hard decisions; Ben Bella was unable to take them. He was, therefore, replaced by Boumedienne, who proved a tough ruler. He opted to modernize the country and declared that his decision was compatible with Islam. He persuaded a large number of theologians to support his government. So armed, the socialists denounced the fundamentalists and accused them of being interlopers between God and His creatures and of creating a class of priests, who acted as agents of foreign exploiters and native collaborators. The officially-appointed ulama supported the socialist regime. After the death of Boumedienne, his successor, Benjadid, has pursued the same course, though its vigour has been considerably diluted.

Algeria today pursues a modified socialist form of government; it has not nationalized all its means of production and distribution; nor has it taken an avowedly anti-religious stand. It permits Qur'anic schools, madrasas and institutes of higher theological learning. The State appoints imams, muftis and other religious functionaries. It discourages dissent but does not suppress it, unless it threatens to become violent; its declared aim is to build a 'commonwealth of citizens, workers and peasants' with equality of status and opportunity irrespective of class or race; it also tries to interpret the Qur'an and the sunna in such a way as to give socialism a certain legitimacy. Indeed, Algeria's rulers maintain that their way of functioning is a much better example of true Islam than the feudal and capitalist regimes prevailing in Muslim countries such as Saudi Arabia. But this is not to say there is no dissent in Algeria. The fundamentalists continue to denounce Algerian socialists as heretics and accuse them of exploiting Islam through State-appointed ulama who propagate secularism and socialism. They call them 'war yuharr-iman al-halal', or people who reverse religious edicts, under whom it is sinful to line up for prayers.[9]

In recent years fundamentalism has gained some following in Algeria as a result of the Khomeini revolution in Iran; but its impact is not yet significant. The government is aware of the mounting discontent fanned by the fundamentalists and has slowed down the pace of socialist measures, especially those which aim at women's emancipation. It has stopped making any further inroads into Muslim Personal Law and has slackened the programme of population control which has been opposed by the fundamentalists. There is a spurt in the building of mosques by the people, some of which are said to have been financed by Saudi Arabia. Nevertheless, the government has not given up its programme of socializing society and bringing about a more equitable order. Bashkir Hajj Ali, a celebrated poet, proclaims that there is nothing wrong for a Muslim to hold the Qur'an in one hand and *Das Kapital* in the other, because the two complement each other—the one aiming at spiritual upliftment and the other, material well-being.[10]

In order to gain some insight into Arab socialism, it would be useful to discuss one of the many books that have influenced radical young Arabs. Khālid Muhi ud-Dīn's *Religion and Socialism*, has, in fact, served as a textbook for Islamic socialists as much in Algeria as in Egypt, Syria and Iraq. A lieutenant of Nasser and a Marxist, he argues that social justice, which is the foundation of Islam, was undermined by the Umayyads, who corrupted religion with the help of hired ulamā, and turned it into an instrument of economic exploitation to enrich a small upper class. This was against the collectivist spirit of Islam. The early Muslims, he wrote, who rebelled against the Meccan aristocracy, like the Prophet and the first four caliphs, were true social revolutionaries. Nothing moved them more than the plight of the poor; nothing motivated them better than the urge to fight against social injustice and economic inequality. They abolished the distinctions between man and man and ushered in the concept of human brotherhood which was a forerunner to the socialist commonwealth of workers and peasants. Muhi ud-Dīn's appeal to his co-religionists was that while the Qur'ān enshrined moral precepts, the people had to put them into practice, by means of socialism, to better their lot.[11]

The other country in the region with its own brand of socialism is Libya. Libya's socialism, as propounded by its supreme leader, Mu'ammar al-Qaddafi, is more radical than that of Syria, Iraq or Algeria. Interestingly, Qaddafi accepts only the Qur'ān as legitimate and rejects all others, including the hadith. In one of his Green Books, entitled *Socialism, the Solution of the Problem of Economy*, he calls upon the people 'to play a leading role in preaching the Islamic revolt, the new socialism'. What is this new socialism? Nothing beyond what the Qur'ān preaches, he maintains. He quotes chapter and verse in support of the abolition of capitalism because they (the capitalists) 'desire to be God on earth' and advocates the advent of socialism, which 'is equality and joint participation of the citizens in the wealth of the country'. The rich have denied this to the poor, 'their religion is the dollar. They smuggle out of their own country money, gold and foreign exchange. They do not worship God or serve their own people or cultivate the agricultural land they have laid to waste, but only look after their own interests. One owns a building with one hundred apartments, yet another lives in a shack. One has concubines, yet another is unable to secure a loan from a bank to marry a woman. One owns a luxury car which he replaces every month, yet another has to go barefoot. Is Islam palaces, gold and silver?'

Qaddafi asks. 'Didn't God say, "But those who store up gold and silver and spend it not in God's way give them glad tidings of grievous woe" (9:34)?' continues Qaddafi. 'And did not the Prophet say that "my people are like the teeth of the comb?" ' Qaddafi questions, 'if one lives in a shack, and another in a palace, are they equal? One has so much money, he does not know what to do with it and smuggles it out to Europe, while another does not have the money to feed his children, so he works twenty-four hours a day. Are they like the teeth of the comb?' Hence exploitation of man by man has to be ended, says Qaddafi and points out that all previous efforts in this direction have failed because the solutions offered were either of a 'cosmetic nature' or 'merely acts of charity'. His solution is 'the abolition of the wage system and a return to the law of nature, which provides for equality among the factors of production, namely, raw materials, the instruments of production and of the producers'. Ownership is of no consequence; what is important is the role of the producer.[12]

Qaddafi is not against private ownership, but he wants it to be restricted. More important to him is socialist ownership which must be jointly held by the producers. Everything productive, industrial or agricultural, has to be owned by all. He insists that the State guarantee four things: food, housing, clothing and transport. There are other norms for individuals: an individual may own the house in which he lives but he must not rent it out. Similarly he may own the means of transport which takes him from his house to his place of work. 'There are no wage earners in a socialist society. There are only partners. Your livelihood comes from a partnership in a production unit, or the use of agricultural land or the performance of a public service.'

In Qaddafi's ideal society there will be three kinds of people: the self-employed, partners in a socialist corporation and public servants. But a citizen's earnings must not exceed his needs, because 'any amount he acquires in excess of his needs is actually taken from the needs of others'. Moreover, 'the disabled and the insane have the same share as the healthy'. The surplus belongs to society; only the industrious, the skilful and public servants can claim a higher share, commensurate with their performance; but accumulation of wealth is not permissible. The final step in this socialist set-up will be the disappearance of both money and profit.

Qaddafi believes that the more profit is increased by socialist production, the sooner it will disappear, because it will lose the value scarcity gives it. He has taken steps to implement his ideas. People living in rented houses have been granted ownership; no one owns more than one house; factories have been taken over by workers who manage them as joint partners; agricultural lands have been re-distributed among cultivators. Qaddafi's view is that the creation of plenty is the key to answering society's ills—the more one can have of anything the less he desires it. Lately he has allowed private enterprise in certain sectors to be established—particularly shops and establishments—though a strict control on prices is kept.

In his personal life, the one thing matters to Qaddafi is his religion; this faith consequently is reflected in his public stance. As with the economy, so with politics. Though Qaddafi claims to be committed to democracy and socialism, his version of these is different from the archetype; he regards Western-style democracy as spurious and believes that political parties, elections, representative assemblies and the other organs of parliamentary democracies do more harm than good. He has no faith in the institution of the opposition, for it 'keeps watch over the ruling party, only waiting to replace it in power'. He stands for people's congresses, which will select the leader by consensus, who in turn should act on the dictates of the people. In short, what Qaddafi advocates is direct democracy with no intermediaries. To use his words: 'In such a system, the people become the system of government and it becomes the truly socialist system'.[13] Too utopian to be practical, the ulama outside Libya have found it not only incompatible with Islamic norms and the traditions of the Prophet, but in many respects antagonistic to them. Qaddafi's exclusive emphasis on the Qur'ān, to the exclusion of the hadīth, which he does not recognize, has alienated him not only from the ulama but also most other Muslims. Even Khomeini's Iran, which Qaddafi supports, accepts neither his interpretations of the Qur'ān nor his new-fangled theories. And, indeed, even in his town country, his rule over his people continues only because of the military power he wields. In one of his Green Books he admits that 'in real life it is always the strong who rule'. Qaddafi is neither a revolutionary in the accepted sense of the world nor a classical socialist; he is a confused thinker, eager to do good to the poor and the downtrodden, but unable to see through the contradictions of his ideas. The main thing about his vision that makes sense to the interested observer—perhaps the only aspect that is valid—is his determination to destroy the West's hegemony over the Arab world; that, in many ways, is his strength. It is also his achievement, for which he will be remembered.

18

Pakistan's Ambivalence

Pakistan, which separated from India in 1947, with the intention of becoming the biggest Islamic state in the world, is still struggling to become one; various experiments in state-craft have been tried by successive governments, but none has produced the desired result. Curiously enough, the creator of Pakistan, Mohamed Ali Jinnah (1876–1948) did not support the idea of an Islamic state; he opted for a secular Pakistan. This became evident when he inaugurated the Constituent Assembly in Karachi on 11 August 1947 and told the representatives: 'You are free, you are free to go to your temples, you are free to go to your mosques or any other place of worship in this state of Pakistan. You may belong to any religion or caste or creed—that has nothing to do with the business of the State.'[1] It was strange that a man who had fought for an Islamic state would, at the first opportunity he got (on the eve of its formation), impress upon its citizens the virtues of secularism. He declared unequivocally that all citizens, irrespective of their religious beliefs, were equal in every respect. He said, 'Now I think we should keep that [equality] in front of us as our ideal and you will find that in course of time Hindus will cease to be Hindus and Muslims will cease to be Muslims, not in the religious sense, because that is the personal faith of each individual, but in the political sense as citizens of the state.'[2] Later, while addressing a public meeting at Dhaka on 21 March 1948, he elaborated his concept further: 'Pakistan is not a theocracy or anything like it.'[3] Subsequently, he told his lieutenants in the Muslim League that he had no intention of allowing the mullās to interfere in the affairs of Pakistan.[4]

Jinnah's successor, Liyaqat Ali Khan (1875–1951), was not so unequivocal; consequently the ulama succeeded in getting some Islamic concepts incorporated in the Objectives Resolution moved by him as prime minister in the Pakistan Constituent Assembly on 25 March 1949. This was a triumph for the fundamentalists and the ulama who were campaigning for an Islamic state. Later Maududi took the lead; he had earlier opposed the creation of Pakistan on the ground that territorial nationalism and Islam could not go together; however, since Pakistan had been created, he wanted to make it a model Islamic state. It could not be secular because that would be a negation of its creation. He expressed his disaffection with the half-hearted inclusion of Islamic concepts in the Objectives Resolution and demanded that a new constitution should be framed, based exclusively on the shari'ah.

The ruling Muslim League, grounded in the British tradition, ridiculed the maulānā as a 'turn-coat' and went ahead with its proposed apparatus. Maududi unleashed a wave of religious frenzy through his Jamā'āt-i-Islāmī and attacked the framers of the Constitution. Soon his followers found an explosive issue in the matter of the Ahmaddiyahs, a sect of Muslims, who revered their founder, Mirza Ghulam Ahmad (1839–1908), as a prophet. The Jamā'āt and their collaborators demanded that the Ahmaddiyahs be declared non-Muslims as they did not accept Muhammad as the last Prophet.[5] The government refused. They then took to the streets, killing the Ahmaddiyahs and looting and burning their property; riots broke out in many places; many lives were lost and much damage was done to property. The authorities came down with a heavy hand on the rioters and jailed the ulama who had instigated these riots. An enquiry commission under the chairmanship of Muhammad Munir, chief justice of the Supreme Court of Pakistan, was appointed. After months of labour and investigation, the Commission presented its report.[6] The document, which is a classic exposition of the conflict between religion and politics in Islam, points out that even on the fundamental question of who is a Muslim, there was no agreement among the ulama. The government used this lack of unanimity to curb the activities of the fundamentalists and prevented Pakistan being turned into a theocracy. Some sops were no doubt provided to appease the fundamentalists. For instance, there was the incorporation of a provision into the Constitution which stipulated that even if one member objected to a bill on religious grounds, the bill would be referred to a board of five members 'learned in theology'; as it turned out this served no practical purpose as the ulamā differed on every issue. The Constituent Assembly tried in vain to obtain a consensus on at least the fundamentals; but its efforts failed. After haggling for many years, a sort of consensus was arrived at on the 'Basic Principles of the State'; it took another six years before a new Constituent Assembly could approve them and finalize the Constitution. However, apart from a few such provisions, the Constitution was, for all practical purposes, as secular as that of India, as both were modelled on the Government of India Act of 1935, enacted by the British.[7]

The ulamā contemptuously dismissed the Constitution as a betrayal of Islam; they could not accept it as Islamic because Islam did not recognize the sovereignty of the people, only that of God. They held that no parliament had the right to legislate on issues; Allah, they said, had already made his decrees in the Qur'ān. According to the fundamentalists most legislators were unqualified to interpret God's laws as they were not learned in theology; they were also not pious. The entire governmental apparatus was composed of, what they called, 'bogus Muslims'. How could such people usher in an Islamic state?

The ruling elite in Pakistan, on their part, claimed to be better Muslims than the fundamentalists, whom they condemned as antiquated fanatics, who had no idea of modern imperatives; they argued that Islam was broad-based and had always adjusted to changing circumstances. They also quoted from the Qur'ān and the hadīth in support of their stand. And so the controversy dragged on, each side advancing its arguments with vigour and refusing to work out a compromise. Meanwhile, the political situation deteriorated and the people began to resent the corruption and ineptitude of the government; a short while after this, the commander-in-chief of the armed forces struck and seized power. On 8 October 1958, General Ayub Khan (1907–74) imposed martial law throughout Pakistan. He was a progressive leader who believed that 'religion is for man and not man for religion'. He maintained that 'an Islamic constitution did not mean that the Pakistan nation should revert to backwardness. Islam is a progressive religion and a religion for all times and people.'[8]

Soon, he abrogated the Constitution and concentrated all the powers of the State in himself. He also set up a panel of scholars and experts to give him a new constitution according to his wishes and directives. The abrogated Constitution which had been finalized during the premiership of Chaudhary Muhammad Ali, had included a statement of intent to usher in an Islamic state, 'wherein the Muslims shall be enabled to order their lives in individual and collective spheres in accordance with the teachings and requirements of Islam, as set out in the holy Qur'ān and the sunna.' It designated Pakistan as an Islamic republic and stipulated that the head of state should be a Muslim. It incorporated the principles of liberty, tolerance and social justice, as enunciated by Islam, and provided that the governance of the state and its laws and regulations would be modified in accordance with the sharī'ah. Most of these provisions were pious declarations, unenforceable in a court of law; for instance, it stated that the State would endeavour, where the Muslims of Pakistan were concerned, 'to make the teaching of the holy Qur'ān compulsory, to promote the unity and the observance of Islamic moral standards, to secure the proper organization of the zakāt, the waqf and mosques; to prevent the consumption of alcoholic beverages and to eliminate riba [usury]'. But all these high sounding ideals remained only on paper, for the government was unable to implement them. Its administrative service ignored the provisions, nor did the ulama, who were strangely lacklustre at this point in time, press for their implementation.[9]

In May 1962 (almost four years after the imposition of martial law), the General promulgated Pakistan's second Constitution in which much of the old was retained. The word 'Islamic' was omitted. Although there were references in it to the Qur'ān and the sunna it was much more secular than the earlier one. Ayub Khan retained the provision for constituting an advisory council of Islamic ideology, but broadened its scope to include, besides the ulamā, lay scholars, lawyers and administrators. He also set up an Islamic Institute under a modernist, Fazlur Rahman, now a professor at Chicago University. The ulamā viewed this as an affront to them and an encroachment on their rights. Despite his dictatorial powers, the General could not suppress the rising tide of opposition from fundamentalists who denounced his Constitution as anti-Islamic. Under its restricted franchise General Ayub contested the election for the presidentship; he was opposed by Fātima Jinnah, sister of the founder of Pakistan; she was backed by the ulamā, led by Maududi, who had earlier declared that no woman could be the head of an Islamic state. Ayub's supporters were quick to expose the second 'about face' of the maulānā—first, they said he had accepted Pakistan, after opposing its creation; and now he was actively campaigning for a Muslim woman for the presidentship, when he had earlier decreed that a woman could not head a state or even take part in politics.[10]

Ayub won the election by a comfortable margin and ruled Pakistan for almost a decade. He introduced many progressive measures which further alienated him from the fundamentalists, who vowed to bring him down. When Ayub ultimately fell, however, it was not because of them but due to corruption and misrule. He was replaced by another military dictator General Yahya Khan, who abrogated the Ayub Constitution and promulgated his own 'legal framework order' which was, in effect, a third constitution. Under its provisions, elections on the basis of adult franchise were held in 1970 in both the wings of Pakistan; these were the fairest elections held in Pakistan to date. Once elected, the representatives were to be asked to frame their own constitution by replacing 'the legal framework order', provided they adhered to 'the Islamic ideology which is the basis of the creation of Pakistan'. Though the elections went off peacefully, there was much skirmishing between the two major parties contesting the elections, Zulfikar Ali Bhutto's Pakistan People's party and Shaikh Mujibur Rahman's Awami League. The first won the majority of the seats in the West and the second swept the East. Yahya Khan tried to patch up the differences between Bhutto and Mujib but failed. Fearing an all-out confrontation, he did not convene the National Assembly. Despite this the conflict between the two parties worsened and finally exploded into civil war in which India got involved on the side of the East Pakistanis. There was fierce fighting, which ended on 16 September 1971, when the Pakistani army capitulated and an independent state called Bangladesh came into existence.

In the western wing, which continued to call itself Pakistan, Yahya Khan was removed as the president and Bhutto took his place; in Bangladesh, Mujib became the president. The break-up of Pakistan struck a severe blow to the fundamentalists who had never imagined that the bonds of Islam could prove so feeble. Chief Justice Munir hit the nail on the head when he declared, 'There can be no doubt that it was Mujib's nationalism that won the day and Islam proved to be too tenuous a bond to keep the wings together.'[11] Though President Bhutto was no less responsible for the dismemberment of Pakistan, he presented himself as its saviour and promised that he would avenge its defeat. He blamed India and vowed to wage a thousand-year war against her. A man of enormous energy and guile, he plunged himself into the task of rebuilding his dismembered nation. He reorganized the badly shaken army, instilled in it a new confidence and assured his stunned people that out of the country's ruins he would build a better and stronger Pakistan. One of the earliest tasks he undertook was the framing of an interim constitution. On 21 April 1972 he convened the National Assembly, consisting of members elected in 1970 from the four provinces of West Pakistan; most of the representatives belonged to his People's party. He tabled before them the draft of the interim constitution which would be in force until a new constituent assembly could be elected. The National Assembly approved his draft and invested the president with more power than what was wielded by the British viceroys. President Bhutto then called an all-party committee to draft a permanent constitution, which would embody the basic features of an Islamic state. The ulama welcomed the move; they were hopeful that the president would try and inculcate a true Islamic spirit among the ruling elite and that the new Constitution would reflect the traditions and values of Islam. Further, they expected it to be faithful to the requirements of the shari'ah. The members from the North-West Frontier Province and Baluchistan insisted that the Constitution should include Qur'ānic punishments and a ban on the taking of interest, the sale and consumption of liquor and gambling of every kind. A few asked for the compulsory wearing of the veil by women. The president was taken aback by these demands as he felt that their fulfilment would turn Pakistan into a theocracy. He cleverly sidetracked the various issues while assuring the people that every provision of his Constitution would breathe the Islamic spirit. In order to win popular support he also emphasized the plight of the poor and talked of Islamic socialism which would ensure every Pakistani had food, clothing and shelter: *roti, kapda aur makan*. In the new elections that he called his People's party won an overwhelming majority of seats in the National Assembly, which approved and adopted the new Constitution—the fourth one.

Though proclaimed as more Islamic than the Yahya Khan one, the new Constitution was, in many respects, more secular. True, like the earlier ones it also declared that sovereignty vested in Allah and further that Pakistan would pursue an Islamic way of life and uphold Qur'ānic

values; it held that Islam would be 'the religion of the State' and stipulated that 'all existing laws shall be brought in conformity with the
injunctions of Islam as laid down by the holy Qur'ān and the sunna. It
said that 'no law shall be enacted which is repugnant to the injunctions
of Islam'. The ulamā hailed the document; the fundamentalists welcomed it. They were unable to see through Bhutto's game; if they had
analysed the Constitution closely enough they would have seen that the
secular provisions were mainly mandatory whereas the Islamic ones
were merely pious declarations. There was no change in the administrative or judicial set-up; it remained, more or less, as before. The Islamic
Council was of an advisory nature; it was accountable to the government. The bureaucrats continued to rule the roost; the army remained as
powerful as before. But the president's Islamic pretensions—the organizing of an Islamic Summit at Lahore in 1974, for instance, or the
incorporation of a special article in the Constitution which stated that
the State 'shall endeavour to preserve and strengthen fraternal relations
among the Muslim countries based on Islamic unity'—helped to give
his leadership an Islamic aura. In actual practice he pursued secular
policies with the same vigour he had shown right through his career,
though he now couched his policies in Islamic terms and spoke of
Islam's greatness. He befriended the king of Saudi Arabia and the Shah
of Iran and established a close relationship with Qaddafi of Libya—all
of them none too friendly to each other but friends all of Bhutto. In
time these friendships led to a massive infusion of Arab petro-dollars
into Pakistan. Bhutto also endeared himself to the Pakistani masses by
his public postures as a champion of their cause. However, it must be
said to his credit that he took some radical measures to improve their
lot; he ensured better working conditions for labour; more remunerative
prices for farmers; more housing for low and middle income groups and
so on. He also hounded the rich for violating various laws and
nationalized their businesses and industries and even confiscated the
properties of some of them. But while all these measures made him
popular, they also masked a strong authoritarian streak; ultimately,
more than anything else, it was his own lapses that led to his downfall.[12]

His popularity also began to wane because he was unable to implement all that he had promised. He was distrusted by the bureaucrats;
even the top brass in the army, which he had rebuilt, disliked his meth-

ods. Gradually the people lost faith in his leadership. Taking advantage of the popular unrest, the fundamentalists demanded full Islamization. In desperation, Bhutto gave in. He declared Friday, instead of Sunday, a holiday, prohibited the making and imbibing of liquor, banned cabarets and stopped all forms of gambling. He declared the Ahmaddiyahs non-Muslims and conceded the opposition demand for fresh elections. Fearful of the results, he rigged the elections and managed to obtain an overwhelming majority for his People's party both at the centre and in the provinces. The outcome of the elections enraged the people who rose in revolt. Once again the army stepped in and Bhutto had to quit. General Muhammad Ziaul Haq, the commander-in-chief, ironically a Bhutto nominee, who was appointed superseding the claims of six senior generals, took over and imposed martial law. The General promised elections within three months, but kept postponing them on one pretext or the other. He also decided to remove Bhutto for ever from the political scene; he charged him with the murder of the father of an opposition legislator, put him up for trial before the courts, obtained the final verdict against him and executed him.

In the years that he was in power, General Zia proved to be an extremely wily ruler. First, he appointed himself the chief martial law administrator and, after 1984, by means of a controlled election, president. We need not concern ourselves with his political manipulation except to note the manner in which he used Islam to strengthen his position and his hold over the faithful. He successfully enlisted the support of the ulamā in this task; they believed that he was a true Muslim who had come to rescue Pakistan from the clutches of secularism. Soon after he assumed power, he took advice from Maududi and his Jamā'āt-i-Islāmi about the manner in which to run the state. At their bidding he embarked on a programme of Islamization, which came to be popularly known as the Nizām-i-Mustafā or 'Administration as run by the Prophet', though it was officially described as the Nizām-i-Islām or 'Administration of Islam' (which in effect means the same thing). To start with, some of the programme's religious aspects were vigorously implemented, an easy task given the fact that the country was under martial law. Then Zia began to emasculate the political opposition, declaring that party politics was anti-Islamic. In 1987, under Measures to Enforce Nizām-i-Islām, an adjunct to the first programme he had announced, he banned political parties on the ground that the concept was a Western innovation antagonistic to the Islamic notion of rulership. This was obviously designated to undermine the influence of secular groups; it also provided him with an excuse to nominate a majlis as-shūrā or council of advisers, in accordance with a Qur'ānic text, which Zia interpreted as meaning shūrā or consultation and not an elected assembly. In so doing, the General was able to associate a large number of ulamā with his administration despite their lack of electoral support.[13] To appease the minorities, he entrusted their representatives with the management of religious, social and cultural affairs. By another decree known as the Introduction of Islamic Laws (issued in 1979), drastic changes were made in the fiscal and legal structures in the country. Of the four taxes recognized by the Qur'ān (zakāt, us`hr, kharāj, jaziya) Zia imposed two—the zakāt and the us`hr—on the faithful, retaining at the same time the existing taxes, which he could remove only at the cost of the exchequer.[14] Despite all this, his continuation of secular measures annoyed the fundamentalists. In order to mollify them he talked in terms of banning interest on loans (the basis of modern banking), and introduced some profit sharing on investments, but he generally left the fiscal system untouched. Where the judiciary was concerned, he introduced punishments as prescribed in the Qur'ān for certain crimes, but these were rarely carried out. The Criminal Procedure Code, based on Anglo-Saxon law, was modified to suit Islamic requirements but its basic framework was largely left unaltered. This irritated the fundamentalists. Also, the establishment of sharī'ah benches in the various high courts and the Supreme Court did not fully satisfy them as the sharī'ah was not given the veto in all matters; just before his death, and soon after he sacked Junejo as the prime minister, Zia issued an ordinance providing for such a veto. There were protests by many sections, particularly lawyers and women, but before Zia could oversee its implementation, he was gone.

Zia had also started Islamizing textbooks and reorganizing the educational system so as to make it conform as much to spiritual as to worldly requirements. In this respect also the secular-minded bureaucracy did not cooperate with him; his orders were diluted and never fully carried out. It was the same with many of his social and cultural strictures such as the prohibition of alcohol, gambling, horse racing and dancing in places of public entertainment. Many of his trusted generals and top civilians indulged in them to the knowledge of Zia, but there was little he could do to stop them.

Meanwhile, his opponents began challenging his authority; they demanded an end to his dictatorship. After her return from exile, Benazir Bhutto, the daughter of the executed prime minister, attracted huge crowds everywhere. They asked for Zia's dismissal. The president moved quickly to counter the threat; he was also under pressure from Washington to hold immediate elections. First, he called for a referendum on his programme of Islamization and simultaneously asked the people to confirm him as the president. The referendum was opposed by the opposition parties; they appealed to voters to boycott it. The turnout was, therefore, poor; but he managed to get enough votes to be confirmed as president.

Emboldened by the success of his manoeuvres, Zia subsequently called elections to the National Assembly and the four provincial assemblies; none of the political parties were allowed to participate but their members contested as individuals and won hands down. The poll results were an eye-opener. The secularists trounced the fundamentalists everywhere. *The Times*, London, wrote:

> The new National Assembly may not be quite ready to do the General's bidding as he would like. Despite the ban on political parties contesting the election, the successful candidates included a large number of former members of parties wholly opposed to the Zia regime. The one party that had sided with Zia in the past, the fundamentalist Jamā'āt-i-Islāmi, took a beating at the polls and lost many of its prominent figures.[15]

In the previous elections also the Jamā'āt candidates had not fared any better; as Prof. Fārūq Hasan, a scholar of some repute, has pointed out:

> This party has been considered by all accounts to be the most well organized party in the country. It has various tiers of administration, and the priests in every mosque, commonly called mullās, are its principal workers. But despite its massive organization this party has never been able to win, politically, any election in the history of this country. The fate of the other fundamentalist candi-

dates has been no different; it is mostly the secularists, in every
contest in Pakistan, who have won power electorally.[16]

After the elections the president lifted martial law and allowed new
bodies to function with limited powers assigned to them under the
Constitution. Zia even diluted somewhat the implementation of the so-
called Islamic injunctions he had so relentlessly pursued. As a result,
sartorial habits in ruling circles began to change; the newly-elected legislators and popular ministers started appearing in ties and Western-style
suits instead of the shalwar kameez and other Islamic attire. The prime
minister, the Oxford-educated Muhammad Khan Junejo, though a
devout Muslim, talked less of Islamization and more of mundane,
secular matters. His government concentrated on economic and welfare
measures; it did not bother much about the shari'ah, which consequently
receded into the background. Even measures relating to banking and
taxation were not pursued. Welcoming the change, one of the leaders of
the opposition, Asghar Khan, president of the Istiqlal party, suggested
that there should be a separation between theocracy and Islamic
ideology. (He was afraid to characterize it as one between religion and
the State.) Likewise, Benazir Bhutto emphasized in her speeches the
urgent need to grant real economic and political rights rather than the
bogus Islamic 'doses', which were 'a hoax played by the General to fool
the poor and the downtrodden'.[17]

The president did not want a confrontation with the newly-elected
bodies; he sensed the popular mood and slowed down his Islamization
programme, to the chagrin of the Jama'at and other fundamentalist organizations. They felt let down and their leaders openly attacked Zia,
calling him a hypocrite.[18]

One of his deputies explained Zia's predicament: 'Now with parliamentary pressures and more complex decision-making in the absence of
arbitrary powers Islamization will probably suffer a temporary set-back.'
The fundamentalists hit back; they were not prepared to allow the
president to abandon the path he had hitherto followed. Even in the new
legislature, a member of the Senate belonging to the Jama'at introduced
a private member's bill, under which the shari'ah would be the supreme
law of Pakistan; it was a warning to the secularists. As Muhammed
Ya'qub Ali, a former chief justice of Pakistan said, if it was enacted it
would enable even a subordinate court to declare the Constitution

'repugnant to the shari'ah and as such void and of no legal effect'. Further, as Zia's close friend and leader of the Muslim League, Pir Pagara, told him, the move was dangerous as it would open 'a Pandora's box of sectarian rifts'. Among other things it also stipulated that Muslims who did not say their prayers regularly or refrained from keeping the month-long Ramadan fasts would be prosecuted and jailed. Also, women would be confined to their homes and the whole fiscal system of Pakistan would be overhauled.

Junejo and his Muslim League opposed the bill; other parliamentarians were equally against it. Meanwhile, the then prime minister called for elections to the local bodies to test the popular mood. The results, once again, proved the hollowness of the claim of the fundamentalists. In cities and towns either Junejo's candidates or those of Benazir Bhutto's Pakistan People's party won. In the rural areas, Bhutto's candidates swept the polls in Sind, in Punjab and the North-West Frontier Province, while Junejo's candidates triumphed elsewhere. The Jama'at candidates won only 20 seats out of 200 in Karachi and 6 out of 150 in Lahore; in other places they fared worse. The fate of the other fundamentalist candidates was no better; everywhere they were trounced. These results boosted not only the leadership of Benazir Bhutto, but also gave a shot in the arm to Junejo. Zia was naturally worried; he feared a threat to his position not only from outside but also from within. His strength had all along been in keeping alive the forces of fundamentalism; their death might have meant his end. Hence, he tried to clip Junejo's wings; the prime minister resisted it. Apprehending an open confrontation with Junejo, Zia sacked him and dissolved the National Assembly; in order to contain popular reaction he simultaneously promised fresh elections and subsequently fixed the date on which they would be held—16 November 1980.

On 17 August 1988 came the air crash in which Zia, along with five of his seniormost generals and the American ambassador to Pakistan, Arnold Raphel, died; the chairman of the Senate, Ghulam Ishaq Khan, a former defence secretary and a protege of Zia, took over as the acting president and promptly assured the people that the elections would be held as scheduled in accordance with the Constitution.

Four days before the air crash Zia had said, 'I want history to judge me objectively'; whatever be the verdict of the historians one thing is indisputable. Zia used Islam, as no other politician in recent times has done, to sustain himself in power without a popular base for eleven long years; but did he really succeed in purging the 'impurities' in the land of the pure? Questioned about the 'formidable legacy of Islamization' that Zia left behind, Benazir Bhutto said: 'He talked about Islam, Islam. But shorn of the rhetoric, what Islamization has really taken place? In fact, the brutalization of society was going on. Zia's Islamization just boils down to amputation of hands, stoning of people to death and discriminatory laws against women. He raised a hysteria. If anyone took Zia to task on constitutional issues, he would reply by saying it is un-Islamic. I remember a passage from V.S. Naipaul's *Among the Believers*. He went to the Ministry of Religious Affairs and asked them to show him Islamization in action. They showed him pilgrims going to hajj. Now pilgrims didn't start going to hajj from Zia's times. They have been going there from Hazrat Muhammed's times. It was just amazing how Zia got off the hook on Islamization.'[19]

However, 'Islamization' will continue to haunt Pakistani politics, Zia or no Zia; but Benazir Bhutto in a recent interview, has perhaps best expressed the general trend in Pakistan: 'We are all Muslims, we will all remain Muslims. But within the Muslim context, we believe that secularist policies should be followed.'[20]

In her whistle-stop, hurricane election tour Benazir campaigned from one end of the country to the other, harping on the same theme; her opponents lambasted her as an enemy of Islam. However, when the results came in, her Pakistan People's Party emerged as the largest single group with ninety-two out of 205 seats as against fifty-five of Islami Jumhoori Ithihad, a loose alliance of Zia's supporters and Junejo's Muslim Leaguers. After some hesitation, due to popular pressure at home and fear of adverse reaction (in case of a contrary decision) from powerful democratic elements abroad, particularly the US, the acting president, Mr Ghulam Ishaq Khan nominated the daughter of the executed Bhutto as the prime minister. The event signalled an incredible phenomenon; it brought in a woman at the helm of affairs in an Islamic state with the promise of a modern secular future for the people. And the unprecedented massive response to her appointment exploded the oft-repeated myth that fundamentalists, due to the vigorously pursued Islamization programme of Zia, had come to stay in Pakistan's corridors of power.

Composite Nationalism

Besides Pakistan, there are three major Muslim states in Asia: Bangladesh, Malaysia and Indonesia. Although until 1971 Bangladesh was a part of Pakistan, it had more in common with its neighbours across the sea—Malaysia and Indonesia—than with any other Muslim country. All the three have sizeable non-Muslim populations and, despite fundamentalist pressure, continue to treat them as equals. The Muslims in these countries are liberal in their outlook and the society more cosmopolitan.

Bangladesh, which is the youngest of the three states, hived off from Pakistan in December 1971 as a result of a successful nationalist revolution with Indian support. It was not a happy or peaceful parting but was accompanied by months of savage repression by Pakistani armed forces on the hapless Bengalis. In the end Pakistan lost not only a major portion of its territories but also the sympathy of much of the world.

Though most Bangladeshis are deeply religious, their attachment to the Bengali language and culture is equally deep. Pakistan's rulers failed to realize the strength of this attachment and this was a major reason for Bangladesh's separation from Pakistan. Prof. Peter J. Bertocci, a scholar specializing in Bangladesh, has explained the phenomenon thus:

> Islam has sunk deep roots in Bengali soil. But Bengali Muslims also share, along with the Hindus and a far smaller number of Buddhists and Christians, a diverse cultural and social pattern which is distinctly Indian, most saliently marked by common usage of the

Bengali language and inheritance of its literary traditions. Thus, Bengali Muslims are the bearers of what may be seen as a composite cultural identity, uniting both 'Muslimness' and 'Bengaliness'.[1]

This can be easily observed in their social customs, modes of thought and literary traditions, which in turn have created a strong commonality with non-Muslims, especially the Hindus, and a distinctive Bengali ethnicity, which, as Prof. Bertocci has put it, 'finally produced the national state of Bangladesh itself, and continues to mould the Bangladeshi response to our contemporary world.'[2]

Shaikh Mujibur Rahman (1920–75), the founding father of Bangladesh, had the difficult task of finding a fitting place for Islam in his scheme of nation-building. Bangladeshi Muslims, with their affinity towards the Bengali language and culture, which cut across religious affiliations, were averse to any sort of inroads into their traditional style of living. After a year of deliberations, the new leaders of Bangladesh opted for a parliamentary type of constitution which incorporated secularism as one of the cardinal objectives of State policy. No community was to enjoy special privileges and religious groups were barred from taking part in political activities.

However, in the euphoria of their newly-won independence, the country's enthusiastic secularists had forgotten that there were still well-entrenched cliques of fundamentalists in Dhaka, particularly in the army, secretly working against the new regime. On 15 August 1975 they murdered the Banga Bandhu (or the father of the nation), Shaikh Mujibur Rahman, and members of his family. The whole nation was stunned. The murderers, a group of army officers with Pakistani links, gathered round one of Mujib's own ministers, Mushtaq Ahmad, swore him in as the president and declared Bangladesh an Islamic state. The country was plunged into chaos and it was only the timely intervention of the commander-in-chief, General Ziaur Rahman, which prevented the situation from deteriorating further. People gathered in thousands everywhere and demanded instant retribution. The pro-Pakistani groups went into hiding, fearing reprisals. Ziaur Rahman sensed the popular mood against the fundamentalists and avoided any reference to Bangladesh as an Islamic state in his speeches, though he declared that the country would be guided by 'absolute trust and faith in the

Almighty Allah'. He also emphasized that he would 'endeavour to consolidate, preserve and strengthen fraternal relations among Muslim countries, based upon Islamic solidarity'.[3] This was a concession to Saudi Arabia and the Gulf shaikhdoms, which had earlier refused, under Pakistani pressure, to recognize Bangladesh. The ploy worked; petro-dollars started to pour in. In the general elections held in 1979, General Zia's Bangladesh National party, which was as secular as Mujib's Awami League, won a landslide victory; the Islamic Front, a coalition of Muslim religious groups, which had fielded candidates for most of the 300 seats, won only 20, receiving a bare 10 per cent of the popular vote.

President Zia worked hard at cultivating the other Muslim countries and succeeded in obtaining substantial financial aid from them. This he used to stabilize the economy. To the fundamentalists' demand for Islamization he paid little heed. In fact, he was averse to overhauling the legal system, especially the criminal and civil codes which had been introduced by the British. He was also an admirer of many of Ayub Khan's progressive measures, including the Muslim Family Law Ordinance. Because of all this, the fundamentalists hated him, as did the pro-Pakistan elements. He was to become their next target and on 3 May 1981, he was assassinated by a disgruntled major general and a small group of army officers. Once again the country was plunged into a crisis. General Ershad, the army chief took over to fill the vacuum. He has continued in power since then, first as martial law administrator and now as the elected head of the republic. He remained as secular in his policies as his predecessors until recently, when he found that without playing the Islamization card he would not be able to continue in power. The secularists, who are still dominant in Bangladeshi politics, have refused to have anything to do with him; he has, therefore, begun to align himself increasingly with the fundamentalists. To placate them his hand-picked Parliament declared Bangladesh an Islamic state.[4] Among other things, he has lifted martial law, removed the ban on political parties, contested elections for the post of president and held general elections for the National Assembly; in this his main opponent has been Hasina Wajed, Shaikh Mujib's only surviving daughter, whose Awami League won one-third of the seats and she emerged as leader of the opposition. The fundamentalists and the ulamā are not happy with these developments but they have been unable to challenge the secular forces, spearheaded on the one side by Hasina Wajed and on the other by Begum Zia, the widow of the assassinated General, who is equally determined to oust Ershad and strengthen the values propagated by her late husband.

Malaysia

Malaysia, which is the name for what was formerly Malaya, a peninsula which extends southward from the Asian mainland, is approximately fifty per cent Muslim; the other fifty per cent of the population includes Chinese Buddhists (thirty-seven per cent) and Hindu Tamils (thirteen per cent). Until the spread of Islam, these territories alternated between the control of Hindu and Buddhist rulers; according to Marco Polo, by the beginning of the fourteenth century, one of these, Parlaks, came under a Muslim sultan. It was mainly through trade and inter-marriage that conversions to Islam took place. Sayyid Fayyaz Mahmud, a Pakistani historian, has said that inter-marrying first took place between the merchants, who had settled in the port towns, and the local inhabitants; and, next, between the Gujarati and Bengali Muslim merchants, who travelled between the two countries and the natives—'the wealthier among these merchants rose to positions of importance and became local rajas.'[5] Thus Islam gradually entrenched itself in these territories, replacing both Hinduism and Buddhism; the first to become Muslim was Malacca in the fourteenth century, to be followed by some twenty more Muslim kingdoms, which vigorously spread Islam and applied the shari'ah to the new converts. All these kingdoms were brought under British administration one by one during the late nineteenth and early twentieth centuries. The sultans were retained as nominal rulers but actually power passed into the hands of the British administrators.

The Hindu and Buddhist influence in the peninsula was too deep-rooted to be wiped out, especially because the economy was largely controlled by the Chinese and Indians. After the arrival of the British, many more Chinese Buddhists and Hindu Tamils came in and settled in the territories, which explains present-day Malaysia's multi-racial character. Under the British the relationship between the various groups, though strained, was under control; but since attaining independence in 1953, Malaysia has been bedevilled by racial, ethnic and even religious conflict. The original Malay inhabitants, all Muslim, are supporters of the 'sons of the soil' theory and press for privileges in every sphere of national life. The fundamentalists have supported them by turning the ethnic issue into a religious one and demanding the establishment of an Islamic state. The ruling party, the United Malay National Organization (UMNO), though predominantly Muslim, has rightly turned down the demand, but the Muslims, being 'sons of the soil', continue to ask for special treatment in order to better their lot, which, when compared to the Chinese and the Indians, is not very happy. Moreover, they are sensitive about their Islamic heritage. As Prof. Fred P. von der Mehden of Rice University, Houston, has observed, 'To the Malay it is almost unthinkable to be anything but a Muslim . . . within Malay society there is an integrated perception of religion, traditional values, and village and family life. It is difficult for a Malay to disentangle himself from this whole.'[6] For this reason, it has been easy for the Muslim fundamentalists to turn every ethnic issue into a religious one, which the non-Muslims have naturally resented. Fortunately, the influential leaders of the Muslims have opted for the secular character of the state; their UMNO has managed to win every election, whereas the fundamentalists, grouped originally under the Pan-Malayan Islamic party (PMIP), but now known as the Partie Islam Se Malaysia (PAS), have failed to make a dent in the political structure of the state.

Despite their pressure, the government has, all along, attempted to be fair in its dealings with the minorities; right from the beginning, the UMNO has aligned with the Malaysia Chinese Association (MCA) and the Malayan-Indian Congress (MIC) and formed a broad national front. The fundamentalists' main successes have been on the social, cultural, and educational fronts. They were able to force the government to formulate an educational policy which favoured the Malay Muslims. Likewise, they have managed to obtain special privileges for their co-religionists in several other fields; this, unsurprisingly, has caused much resentment among the Chinese and the Indians. To placate them some compromises have been attempted from time to time; but these have not allayed the fears of the non-Muslims. Occasionally tension has mounted between the Muslims and the other religious communities and there have been, at times, even large-scale rioting, particularly between the Malays and the Chinese. The Hindu Tamils have not had the same strained relations with the Muslims, as they are mostly labourers, unlike the Chinese who are flourishing traders. In the 1960s the UMNO agreed to declare Islam the State religion; this was a sop to the fundamentalists but at the same time the State guaranteed to the followers of other religions the right to manage their own affairs, to establish and maintain their religious and educational institutions, and to order their lives according to their beliefs and traditions. The Muslims were assured that their personal and family laws, as prescribed by the shari'ah, would not be tampered with, including all laws pertaining to succession, testate and intestate, betrothal, marriage, divorce and dowry, maintenance and guardianship, gifts, partitions and public and family trusts (aukaf). In addition, the government recognized and allowed specified Muslim organizations to collect and distribute the zakāt, the fitra or charity and to administer the Bait al-Māl; no restrictions were placed on the construction and maintenance of mosques and certain Qur'ānic punishments for specified offences were permitted to be imposed on Muslims by the shari'ah courts.

This process had in fact begun, albeit sporadically, soon after independence. The first prime minister, Tenku Abdul Rahman, who remained in power from 1957 to 1970, showed considerable tact in handling the situation but was nevertheless criticized by the PMIP. Even some hardcore members of his own party (UMNO) accused him in Parliament of evading the Muslim demand for more Islamization. He had, for instance, refused to declare Friday a holiday on the ground that it would have an adverse effect internationally on Malaysia's export trade of tin. He also refused to impose a ban on liquor to prevent the loss of State revenues. Though he did a balancing act for much of his tenure, on some issues he stood firm. When Muslim fundamentalists demanded that he make the shari'ah the law of the land, he told them bluntly: 'Our country has many races and unless we are prepared to drown every non-Malay, we can never think of an Islamic administration.'

The 1970s were a time when Islamic fundamentalism was on the rise around the world due to the burgeoning coffers of the Arabs who controlled much of the oil production in a world hungry for fuel. Malaysia was impacted by the Islamic revival too and it responded by doling out money to build new mosques, including the biggest and grandest in the capital, Kuala Lumpur. It also commisssioned radio and television programmes whose sole aim was to propagate Islam. Ministers made it a point to be seen at Friday prayers and vociferously supported the cause of the Palestinians. Muslim Malay students demanded closer ties with other Muslim countries and asked for even more privileges to enable them to take on the more prosperous and industrious Chinese and Tamils. The student movement was taken over by lawyers, teachers and other professionals, many of whom, though educated in Britain or America, became enthusiastic supporters of fundamentalism. Some of them even grew beards; women took to the veil or the chudder and resorted to khalwat or seclusion. Some of the more fanatic among the Muslims went to the extent of asking for the closure of television, which they condemned as an instrument of the devil. The Khomeini revolution gave a further fillip to the Islamic upsurge, as did the influx of many theologians and scholars from Pakistan who extolled the virtues of Islam, in particular of fundamentalism.

Tenku Abdul Rahman's successor as prime minister, Abdul Razak, was alarmed at these developments; he felt that these would disrupt the multi-religious character of the State. He was a firm believer in secularism and as the home minister in Tenku's cabinet had blocked proposals to turn the State into a theocracy. The government had done, he had said then, 'all that we could within our power to maintain the Islamic religion', but he could not go along with the mullās and alienate the non-Muslims. The fundamentalists were, however, equally determined to pursue their goals; their chief political organ, the PAS, renewed its attack on Razak after he became the prime minister, and denounced his policy of appeasing the non-Muslims. After Razak, Husayn Onn became the prime minister. He inherited the same problems, but did not have the guts and determination of his predecessors. Mild and soft-spoken, he soft-pedalled or ducked most of the disputes which arose, with the result that relations between the various communities worsened. The present prime minister, Dr Mahathir Muhammad, is tough, aggressive and quite decisive. An urbane, sophisticated, Western-trained medical practitioner, he is a modernist; the fundamentalists accuse him of being more enamoured of the technological advancement of Japan than the glorious heritage of Islam. On his part, he has shown little regard for them and has instead taken the battle to them. He called general elections earlier than scheduled in 1986 and challenged the fundamentalists to test their strength. The gamble paid off handsomely. His policies were endorsed and the coalition party he led, the multi-religious National Front, was returned to Parliament with a greater majority than ever before. His party won 148 out of 177 seats and 228 out of 240 in the state legislatures. The PAS got only 1 parliamentary seat, compared to 5 in 1982 and only 15 seats in the states compared to 18 in the past.

The fundamentalists, however, are not dismayed and continue with their campaign for more Islamization; Dr Muhammad has also become more vulnerable. He has recently faced trouble from senior leaders of his party—in fact it has split[7]—and, because he needs support from every quarter, has softened towards the fundamentalists and even agreed to implement the recommendations of the National Fatwa Conference, attended by muftis from all over Malaysia, which interalia, has asked for the imposition of Qur'ānic penalties for certain offences, including flogging in public for the consumption of liquor, theft, fornication and slander. The prime minister has had a hard time trying to explain his *volte face* to the secularists; an aide justified it recently on the ground that it was done so that Malaysia's laws for its Muslim citizens would be in line with those obtaining in other Muslim countries. He also attempted to explain the new penalties thus : 'The punishment to an offender has to be commensurate with the gravity of the offence.'[8] Though the measures do not affect non-Muslims they are understandably perturbed. They apprehend quite rightly a further widening of the gulf between them and the Muslims, a development which can only endanger the ethnic balance and harmony in the country.

Indonesia

Indonesia is the largest Muslim country in the world, with a population of more than 120 million Muslims; it is also, next to Turkey, the most secular Muslim state. However, unlike Turkey, it is not fully Westernized. Indonesian Islam has, therefore, a unique identity of its own.

Islam came to Indonesia in the fourteenth century with the sūfis and traders from Arabia and India. The locals accepted it readily but retained their rites, rituals and mystical beliefs, which were interwoven with the new faith. For instance the Indonesians found nothing wrong in accepting the oneness of God and at the same time sticking to their old belief in advaita or non-duality, which is based on the Hindu and Buddhist concept of no God. The fundamentalist proselytizers were naturally disturbed at this 'heretical' approach; but the Indonesians stuck to this belief even after their conversion to Islam, which insists on monotheism. Likewise, they persisted (like the Hindus) in regarding their earthly existence as illusory (maya) and the eternal as the real. The division between the actual and the ideal, the physical and the spiritual, was not only accepted by them, but it influenced both their political outlook and religious rites and practices.

The fundamentalists have been trying hard, over the centuries, to reform Indonesian Islam but they have so far failed to make much of an impact on the ordinary Muslims. Their loyalty to Islam, as they understand it, is nonetheless intense; they are proud of it and will do nothing to undermine it. It was, in fact, a constant rallying point in their struggle for freedom, generating a sense of brotherhood among them.

This Islamic sense of togetherness extends far into antiquity: it was first witnessed when the Muslims ousted the Hindus and the Buddhists and took over the administration from them. In later times, when the Dutch colonized the country, it was Islam which helped to unite the ethnically and linguistically scattered islands and to create a sense of cohesion and national consciousness among them. The Dutch perceived this as a threat to their rule quite early on. Indeed, a pioneer of Orientalism, Dr C. Snouck Hurgronje, advised his countrymen not to interfere with the religious or social life of the indigenous people and to concentrate only on political and administrative matters. The advice was well taken by the authorities, who thereafter refused to take sides between the secularists and the fundamentalists, who have had a long history of conflict behind them. Finally the secularists gained ascendancy over the fundamentalists and took over the leadership of the liberation movement. About this time the fundamentalists realized that it was in the national interest not to confront but to cooperate with the secularists. Another reason the fundamentalists decided to join hands with the secularists was because they had limited popular support. Even today, they are only heard among the merchants and traders and religious groups; on the common people in the interior their impact has been negligible, as the latter still cleave to atavistic rituals and animistic beliefs.[9]

Nowhere has this been more reflected than in the indifferent response to the fundamentalist demand of making Indonesia an Islamic state; it was first raised by a small section in the wake of the surrender of Japan in 1945, when a militia known as Hifzullah established Islamic rule in some islands. When Indonesia became free and a national government under the charismatic Sukarno (1901–70) was formed, the State began to function on modern, secular lines. In 1948 a more serious challenge was posed by the fundamentalists, who liberated West Java, and proclaimed Nagara Islam Indonesia or the Indonesian Islamic state. The fundamentalists also took over Aceh, the northernmost part of Sumatra and Celebes in southern Sulawesi. The rebels distrusted the secular outlook of the Javanese-dominated leadership of the country and agitated for its overthrow. For many years its leaders held their own and carried on a guerilla war against the new republic. Many leading Muslims, including some belonging to the political organization known as the Masjumi party and the religious body known as Nahḍat al-Ulamā supported them. But the new rulers of Indonesia, whether democratic or military, were not prepared to turn their country into a theocracy. True, they were keen to retain their links with Islam, which made them popular with the people, but they were not prepared to allow the ulamā entry into the corridors of power. In this they had much in common with the old sultans of Indonesia, who, before independence, had put their spiritual majesty to good use, but had continued to administer their domains through laws and rules that owed their composition to traditional and colonial structures. As with the sultans, so was it with the modern rulers who ruled with a hotch-potch of laws and regulations based on a mixture of religious and secular codes. Unfortunately, this disorganized method of government left the door open to all sorts of agitations; the fundamentalists were quick to seize the opportunity and asked for more sharī'ah, while the secularists urged more modernization. In between lay the largely passive illiterate and semi-literate masses scattered over hundreds of islands, who continued to follow their own mix of Islamic and traditional codes of conduct and worship. This division between the State and religion has been a continuing problem in the politics of modern Indonesia.[10]

The Masjumi party and the Nahdat al-Ulamā have been dominated by the fundamentalist santri, while secular parties like the Parta National Indonesia (PNI) and the Parta Komunis Indonesia (PKI) have received support from the ruling elite, who are associated with the secular abangan. Sukarno was the first to rein in the two groups by the sheer force of his personality and the loyalty he inspired in his supporters. It was his efforts which gave his newly liberated country a national identity. He refused to turn Indonesia into an Islamic state and encouraged secular values. His 'Guided Democracy' (1959–65) with its emphasis on the supremacy of the leader as against the popular will and commitment to the Panchsheel (the five principles of coexistence between various groups) as the basis of national life were major factors in moulding the new nation. These infused a sense of unity among the warring factions. Though Sukarno was ousted from power largely because of his alliance with the communists, he was neither a leftist nor a rightist. He played the varying forces in his government skilfully to strengthen his leadership but he never compromised with the fundamentalists.

General Suharto, who replaced him, has turned out to be as secular as his predecessor. Many of the president's lieutenants have been avowed abangan who have tried to counter the religious fanaticism of the santri. In 1973, the 'New Order' promulgated by him recognized the abangan as a separate religious group. This upset the fundamentalists, who condemned it as kufr or heresy; they had helped to oust Sukarno because of his communist alliance but Suharto has proved worse. He is no Muslim, according to them (his Golkar party, however, won a comfortable majority in Parliament at its very first electoral test in 1971, though the fundamentalists opposed him). Indeed, the president has managed, with the passage of time, to purge the political scene not only of them but also of the leftists. It is interesting to go a little deeper into the methods Suharto has used to nullify the fundamentalists. First, he has managed, with the passage of time, to set up a Ministry of Religion, ostensibly to look after the religious requirements of the Muslims, but in reality designed to control Islam politically rather than to allow it to meddle in affairs of state. This was in line with what Sukarno had done (his first minister for religious affairs was Wahid Hashim, the leader of the orthodox Nahdat al-Ulamá and the son of one of the most respected Muslim theologians of the country, Háshim Aasi). President Suharto has behaved much worse than his predecessor, according to the fundamentalists. He appointed instead of a theologian, a known secularist, albeit a scholar in Islamic history and culture, Makti Ali, as his minister for religious affairs. Makti tried to bring about some kind of accommodation between the State and religion without compromising the supremacy of the State. The attempt failed but again, instead of appeasing the fundamentalists, the president replaced Makti by a General with little understanding of Islam. The president then created a hierarchy of consultative councils, supervised by a Council of Theologians, hand-picked by him, who were supposed to guide the State in matters of religion. It was a camouflage. Suharto had neither the time nor the inclination to listen to religious discourse or to allow his policies to be influenced by them.

This came as a shock to the NU, who had gone to great lengths to accommodate the secular requirements of the rulers; but it had no stomach to revolt and therefore preferred to concentrate on providing religious training to thousands of pupils in their peasantren or school; in order to be free of any State control they refused to accept any grants. Their teachers, known as kiyayis, came from old religious families, highly respected among common Muslims. Suharto dared not touch them. He has not. Hence the NU continues to be a force; so far it has not interfered in day-to-day politics but what will happen in the future no one knows. The president appears, however, determined to retain the secular character of Indonesia and is not prepared for any adjustment with the fundamentalists. He has shown more guts in this respect than any other secular leader among Muslims the world over. There is a touch of Ataturk in him, though he is more cautious. Nevertheless he has worked hard to get his Panchsheel or Five Principles accepted by all parties and groups. It is a new version of Sukarno's Panchsheel, as incorporated in the Jakarta charter of June 1945. No party can contest elections unless it accepts Panchsheel as the basis of the State. Its five principles as modified to suit present conditions are: (1) Belief in one God; (2) National unity; (3) Humanitarianism; (4) Democracy; and (5) Social justice.

The fundamentalists have refused to accept it; they perceive it as a threat to Islam. Indeed, when the president first enforced his Panchsheel through the promulgation of what came to be known as his 'New Order', riots broke out; but Suharto stood firm and refused to compromise. The secretary-general of Golkar, his party, declared that the five principles of the 'New Order' were the weapons by which alone a free and open society could be built in Indonesia. In keeping with this attitude, it is not surprising that orthodox Islam and its votaries, whether in the political or the religious field, have been placed under some sort of restriction by the government, which is not prepared to allow religion in any form to influence the affairs of the state. Further, to counter their hold, Suharto has started establishing State Institutes for Islam

(Institute Agma Islam Negeri) to train graduates in Islamic theology fully in religious dogmas and practices and at the same time to equip them with modern, Western ideas. They will be the vanguards of Panchsheel and the custodians of secularism.[11]

20

The Indian Muslims

Muslims form the largest religious minority in India. Though they constitute a mere twelve per cent of the population of the country, they number over ninety million; in terms of actual size they are next only to Indonesia, and are the largest group of believers in any one country. Before the partition of the sub-continent in 1947 they constituted almost a third of the total Muslim population in the world.

Islam came to India more than a thousand years ago. Though the Muslim dynasties which ruled India were not a part of either the Umayyad, Abbasid, or the Ottoman Caliphates, they governed according to the shari'ah. The ulamā and the ṣūfis played a decisive role in the affairs of state without being directly involved in them. Even after these dynasties went into decline, one after the other, Islam continued to be the dominant influence, in the lives of Indian Muslims—whether Turko-Iranians, Afghans or converts from Hinduism.

The British, who colonized the sub-continent in the nineteenth century, realized to their cost the grip Islam exercised on its followers, particularly when Indian soldiers in the British army revolted in 1857 and proclaimed their allegiance to the last Mughal emperor, Bahadur Shah Zafar. To counter this phenomenon, the British persuaded the Ottoman caliph, Sultan Abd ül-Mejid, to issue a fatwā, enjoining the Muslims to remain loyal to the colonial masters. Nawab Salar Jung, who rose to become the prime minister of the princely state of Hyderabad, described the place of Muslims in India at the time of the British vividly:

England has in India some fifty millions of Muslim subjects, including in their mass the most war-like of the native races. . .and England is not likely to forget that it was these very races who, in 1857, at the bidding of their caliph, the sultan Abd ül-Mejid, gave their united support to the British connection at the supreme moment when their defection might have cost the life of every white man and woman in India. My late father frequently assured me that the whole influence of the Caliphate was used most unremittingly from Constantinople to check the spread of mutiny, to rally round the English standard the Mussalman races of India--and that in this way the debt that Turkey owed to Great Britain for British support in Crimea, was paid in full. And the time may come again when the devotion of the Mussalmans to their Caliph and the shrine of St Sophie may be not less necessary to Great Britain than in 1857.[1]

But the British were not kind to the Muslims in the wake of 1857, as they considered them, in the final analysis, untrustworthy. Syed Ahmad Khan, a junior officer in the British East India Company, who later became one of the greatest leaders of Muslims in India, was apalled at the plight of his co-religionists and worked hard to bring about a rapprochement between them and the British. He appealed to the Muslims to cooperate with him in this task. Such collaboration between the Muslims and the Christians, he said, was commended by the Qur'ān and the traditions of the Prophet. He pursued this mission through a number of pamphlets and books and prayed that the British raj should last till eternity. The ulamā did not approve of his stand and denounced him as a kāfir. But gradually his pleas had an effect on the community and moulded the course of their lives, making them loyal to the British.

However, when Turkey entered World War I (1914–18) on the side of Germany, the British attitude to India's Muslims changed. This enraged the Muslims; consequently, when the Ottoman caliph called on the faithful to fight against the British, he found many among the Indian Muslim community eager to respond to the fatwā signed by the shaikh al-Islam, Effendi:

The Muslims in general who are under the oppressive grasp of the aforesaid tyrannical governments in such places as the Crimea,

Kazan, Turkistan, Bukhara, Khiva, and India, and those dwelling in China, Afghanistan, Africa and other regions of the earth, are hastening to join in this great jihad to the best of their ability, with life and property, alongside the Ottomans, in conformity with the relevant holy fatwa.[2]

The fatwa was ignored by most Muslims around the world (the Arabs, in fact, preferred to support the British), but India's Muslims organized one of the biggest mass movements the world had ever seen—the Khilafat—for the preservation of the Ottoman Caliphate. The Ali brothers, Mohammad and Shaukat, whipped up religious fervour throughout the country; thousands of Muslims were imprisoned for their support of the Turkish cause and several hundred others left India because in their eyes India under British rule had become a dar al-harb or house of war. These Muslims headed for Afghanistan, but the amir refused them entry. Frustrated, they returned to India; many died on the way; many more found themselves in British jails.

Mahatma Gandhi lent his support to the Khilafat movement in the hope that it would forge Hindu-Muslim unity in India's struggle for freedom. For a short period it did. But the movement collapsed when Kemal Ataturk abolished the Caliphate in 1924. Two Indian Muslim leaders, the Agha Khan and Justice Amir Ali, pleaded with the Turks to retain the centuries-old Caliphate, but Ataturk refused, accusing the Agha Khan and his colleague of acting at the behest of the British. Other Muslims, particularly the Arabs, neither lifted a finger to save the Caliphate nor shed a tear over its demise. Indian Muslims were thus alienated from the young Turks as well as from the resurgent Arabs.[3]

The British were in no mood to listen to the Indian Muslims demands and they came down hard on the agitators. The Hindus too began losing interest as their collaboration seemed to be serving no useful purpose. In several parts of the country Hindu-Muslim riots broke out. In disgust, the Ali brothers, the leaders of the Khilafat agitation, severed their link with the Hindu-dominated Congress and joined hands with the fundamentalists, who now turned to the British to obtain as many concessions from them as possible. Secular Indian Muslims, however, continued to side with the Congress, believing that the future of Indian Muslims lay in collaboration with the Hindus and in working for a free, united and secular India. The fundamentalists immediately began maligning the secularists as heretics; the secularists, in turn, portrayed the fundamentalists as stooges of the British.

The tallest among the secular Muslims was Maulānā Abu'l Kalām Azād (1888–1958). He was the son of a Muslim divine and was born in Mecca. By the age of sixteen he had learned Arabic, Persian and Urdu. Being both a gifted writer and a powerful orator he moulded the thinking of many generations of Indian Muslims. He impressed upon them the need to be accommodating and liberal in their religious outlook. He refused to be chained by traditional interpretations and dogmas and in terpreted the Qur'ān in keeping with the requirements of the times articles and books, including a commentary on the Qur'ān, are no for their profundity as well as passion to build a composite nati the basis of inter-religious understanding. Though steeped in orth learning, Azād was a forward looking Muslim; his thesis o reconciliation of Islam with the needs of a free India is as origina is masterly. It was for such stands that he earned the ridicule of the damentalists. When he opposed the two-nation theory, pointing out tha Hindus and Muslims, despite following separate religions, have a common history and composite culture and are bound by geographicali- ties, its arch proponent, Mohamed Ali Jinnah, denounced him as a traitor to Islam. Azād stood firm by his conviction. In his presidential address to the annual session of the Congress at Ramgarh in 1940, he declared:

> I am a Mussalman and am proud of that fact. Islam's splendid traditions of thirteen hundred years are my inheritance. I am unwilling to lose even the smallest part of this inheritance. The teaching and history of Islam, its arts and letters and civilization are my wealth and my fortune. It is my duty to protect them. As a Mussalman I have a special interest in Islamic religion and culture and I cannot tolerate any interference with them. But in addition to these sentiments, I have others also which the realities and condi- tions of my life have forced upon me. The spirit of Islam does not come in the way of these sentiments; it guides and helps me for- ward. I am proud of being an Indian. I am a part of the indivisive unity that is Indian nationality. I am indispensable to this noble edifice and without me this splendid structure of India is incom-

plete. I am an element which has gone to build India. I can never surrender this claim.[4]

Azad made rich contributions to the development of a secular outlook among the Muslims; so did some other Muslims, in particular, Hakım Ajmal Khan and Dr M.A. Ansari, who also presided over the Congress. Theirs was, indeed, a formidable task, with most Muslims distrusting them. On the one side they had to deal with the Hindu-dominated Congress, some of whose leaders were known to be hostile to the Muslims; on the other, there were the Muslim fundamentalists who were patronized by British officials.

Secular-minded Muslims, in consequence, found themselves in an unenviable position. They had to steer clear of both these forces, working in opposite directions, in order to bring about a reconciliation between religion and nationalism and make it acceptable to their co-religionists. Fortunately, in the forefront of the secular forces was the premier organization of Muslim divines, the Jam'iyyat al-Ulama-i-Hind. Founded in 1919 by Maulānā Maḥmud al-Ḥasan (1851–1921), it drew inspiration from the Dār-al-Ulūm, the well-known theological seminary at Deoband in U.P., which was founded by Rashīd Ahmad Gangōhi (1828–1905). He issued a fatwa in October 1888, justifying Muslim participation in the activities of the Congress.[5] His successors at Deoband followed his lead and impressed upon their followers that Hindu-Muslim cooperation was in the larger interest of Indian Muslims. The Jam'iyyat worked with the Congress for a free secular India, in which Muslims would have the same religious freedom as Hindus. Its leaders and workers took part in the various satyagraha movements launched by Gandhi and suffered much hardship at the hands of the British. Though fundamentalist in their religious outlook, they were secular in political affairs. They cooperated with secular Muslims and opposed their denigrators. They accepted the leadership of Azad and the North-West Frontier leader, Khan Abdul Ghaffar Khan (1890–1988), better known as the 'Frontier Gandhi', who organized, under Gandhi's inspiration, what came to be known the Red Shirt movement. The Red Shirt volunteers, known as Khudai Khidmatgars, or 'Servants of God', made the Frontier Province a fortress of composite nationalism opposed to the two-nation theory of Jinnah s Muslim League. In the oath the Khudai Khidmatgars took with the Qur'ān in their hands they pledged, among other things, that they would regard 'Hindus, Christians, Parsis and Muslims' as 'the creatures of one God' and would 'always protect the oppressed from the oppressors'. They were the toughest opponents of the Muslim League, which, despite its ascendancy in the rest of India, was unable to disloge the Khudai Khidmatgars from their dominant position in the Frontier.[6]

In their battle against the secular Muslims, the fundamentalists won their greatest victory when they won over the arch-secularist Jinnah to their side; his conversion changed the whole course of Indian politics. Indeed, until the advent of Gandhi on the political scene, Jinnah had been hailed as 'the best ambassador of Hindu-Muslim unity'; the mixing of religion with affairs of state had always disgusted him and he had been contemptuous of the ulamā dabbling in politics. He also did not like the involvement of the uneducated masses in political affairs, which he believed was better handled by educated, Westernized Indians. But after years of struggling for Hindu-Muslim unity and of repeated failure to bring the Congress and the Muslim League together, Jinnah finally gave in to the fundamentalists. He came to the conclusion that the Hindus and the Muslims needed separate homelands for the fulfil- ment of their hopes and aspirations. The Muslims overwhelmingly backed him, with the result that the sub-continent had ultimately to be divided and Pakistan created. The division came as a shock to the Muslim secularists; more so since it had been brought about by a man who was a champion of secularism, but had abandoned it in the evening of his life to give the greatest impetus to the forces of fundamentalism.

On the creation of Pakistan in 1947, the Muslims were reduced to a hopeless minority in India. They had to undergo a long period of humiliation at the hands of the Hindus for what was seen as their part in the destabilizing of the sub-continent. Isolated and helpless, they gave up several things, particularly their cherished demand for separate electorates and the reservation of seats in Parliament and the state legis- latures. Their only hope was that the Hindus would not harm them and that the newly enacted Constitution would protect them. As time passed, they realized that their position was becoming worse with every electoral contest under the new dispensation; their representation in every sphere—legislative, executive and judicial—went on dwindling. Today, neither in Parliament nor in any of the other elected bodies like the state assemblies, zilla parishads, panchayats or municipalities is their representation either adequate or effective. The same is true in regard to employment, whether in agriculture, trade or industry. In the police and armed forces their numbers are negligible. In the Indian Foreign and Administrative Services, the percentage of Muslims is abysmally low; as it is in the other public services. They have hardly any share in the management of public-sector undertakings and even less in the private sector, which is largely owned by non-Muslims. All in all, the condition of Indian Muslims has considerably deteriorated after partition.[7]

The recurrence of communal riots allows the Muslims no respite; the police gives them hardly any protection. Also, being vastly outnumbered in most areas, their sense of insecurity is enhanced with every passing disturbance. The fundamentalists exploit this situation, whip up communal passions and inculcate in them a ghetto feeling, which further isolates them from other Indians, particularly their Hindu neighbours. Secular Muslims are dismayed at the steady decline in their influence among co-religionists, but there is little they can do; they are not trusted any more and whatever little they can do is vastly outweighed by the social and economic factors which are primarily responsible for sustaining communalism among them. Again, with the worsening of the law and order situation, a fatalistic tendency is developing in them, especially among young Muslims.

It is undeniable that the Muslim community in India has some grounds for its disaffection. For instance, they feel strongly that their culture (and, by extension, their religion) is in danger. They have fought for decades for an honourable place for Urdu; despite their protests, however, the language has continued to languish. Though not a language of Islam—it has more Brij Bhasha and Persian words than Arabic—it is a storehouse of Islamic religious literature and is written in the Arabic alphabet. It has almost ceased to be taught in India except in Jammu and Kashmir where Muslims are in a majority. Elsewhere it has been systematically weeded out; the Muslims are trying to preserve it by teaching it in their own madrasas and schools, but without proper governmental support and official patronage it has little chance of survival. According to the last census (1981) Muslims themselves have begun giving it up, especially in the north where they have taken to Hindi, primarily because of economic compulsions. The late Dr Zakir

Hussain, the former president of India (1967–69), once organized a mass signature campaign for the protection of Urdu. It had little effect on the authorities and gave no better deal to the language.

Another cause of unrest among the Indian Muslims is the minority character of the Aligarh Muslim University. The Supreme Court in one of its judgements held that as the university was not founded by Indian Muslims, but by the British, it could not be considered a minority institution. Both the secularists and the fundamentalists asked for the restoration of the minority character of the university. At first the government opposed it but later relented and passed the necessary legislation; it has satisfied the Muslims emotionally but made little difference to their educational backwardness.

There is also the question of Muslim Personal Law. Though most of the major political parties have declared that they will not meddle with it, the Indian Muslims remain unhappy with a directive principle in the Constitution which requires the State to enact a common civil code. This unhappiness found expression in the celebrated case of Shah Bano, an aged divorcee, who had sued her husband for maintenance and in which, while decreeing for her, the chief justice of the Supreme Court had passed some unfortunate remarks against Islam; this caused an angry outburst among Muslims throughout India. The fundamentalists demanded a reversal of the court order and succeeded in getting the necessary relief through Parliament, which enacted a special law to conform to the interpretation of maintenance as given by the classical jurists.[8]

The secularists were unhappy at the development and some of them even spoke openly in favour of the judgement and against the new law, incorporating the injunctions of the shari'ah as demanded by the fundamentalists. The voice of the secularists was drowned in the popular clamour to abrogate the judicial verdict. The fundamentalists won the day but the victory was won at grave cost: the Hindus were aghast at the whole business and many of them felt that the government should not have bowed to Muslim pressure which gave Hindu communalism further impetus.

Another issue which has strained Hindu-Muslim relations is that of the Babri masjid in Ayodhya. The Hindus contend that the mosque was constructed at the instance of the first Mughal emperor, Bābur, on the ruins of a temple built to commemorate the birthplace of Lord Rama.

The Muslims refute it and say that there is no historical evidence of Rama having been born there. Though the matter was sub-judice a local magistrate allowed Hindus to occupy a part of the premises, instal idols on the site and establish a temple. Religious feelings in both the communities were whipped up and clashes occurred between them on this issue in many towns and cities. The Muslim fundamentalists say that it is not the question of just one mosque that upsets them; there are thousands of such mosques all over India which might at one time have been temples; they say once they surrender the Babri mosque, the others would meet the same fate. The development has sinister implications. As M.J. Akbar, editor of the *The Telegraph*, Calcutta, after an on-the-spot survey of the situation at Ayodhya, explains:

> There is a great subtlety in this. If there is any symbol of the rule of perfect justice and tolerance it is Ram Rajya; when Gandhiji dreamt of Ram Rajya he was promising the minorities and the untouchables a state of equality and freedom. And Bābur was one Muslim emperor whose broad tolerance has not been challenged by even the fanatic historians. If Hindus can be convinced that even Ram cannot get the respect of Muslims, then their sentiment can be much more easily roused. And, if even Bābur cannot be considered acceptable, then the Muslim in turn feels desperate—what more must he do to become acceptable? Become a Hindu?[9]

Behind these actions and reactions lie the same age-old prejudice which bedevils the relations between Hindus and Muslims; the fear of a minority being absorbed by the majority and that of the majority being stabbed in the back by the minority. Unless this vicious circle is broken, there will be neither communal harmony nor political stability in India. The secularists are struggling to bring it about but the fundamentalists continue to thwart their efforts; never before, since independence, have the relations between the two communities been so bitter and the danger to secularism more serious.[10]

As always in the past the mass of the Muslims are caught between two conflicting forces—the one is the religious which is in the hands of the fundamentalists who never tire of appealing to the Muslims to be prepared for sacrifices in the cause of Islam; the other is the political, spearheaded by the secularists, advocating that the future of Indian

Muslims lies in reform and change in accordance with the demands of the times and in active collaboration with the Hindus. The secularists among the Muslims have always been apologetic about their stand; the fundamentalists, on the other hand, act boldly and aggressively. In this conflict between the two, the common Muslim suffers. He is suspected by the State and distrusted by society both of which are dominated by Hindus. That is the dilemma he faces: can he really build a future on his own inner resources and faith, as the fundamentalists tell him, or should he integrate within the larger, multi-religious whole, as the secularists suggest? No other Muslim in any part of the world is faced with such a dilemma or finds himself as confused and helpless.

21
The Challenge of Communism

Religion is anathema to communism, but no religion has resisted the imposition of communism on its followers as doggedly as Islam. The struggle which the Soviet Muslims have put up against communist rule and the fight that their Chinese brethren waged on the eve of Mao's take-over speak eloquently of this. To begin with, the communists gave the Muslims in both countries all sorts of assurances, but as they consolidated power Islam, like other religions, was stamped out. At times, some compromises with religious practices were made but this was for either tactical reasons or to curry favour with the Muslim world. The policy of the communists was to indoctrinate the younger generation against theism and no communist regime has deviated from this dogma. The ruling communists have allowed some groups to retain their cultural heritage, which in most cases is rooted largely in religion. This has given a disinterested observer the impression that the communists have softened thier attitude to religion but this is a wrong view.

Central Asia, encompassing five republics of the Soviet Union—Uzbekistan, Kazakhistan, Tajikistan, Kirghizia and Turkmenistan—and the Caucasus, is the most important Muslim region of the communist world. Although Sunnis predominate, there is a sizeable number of Shi'as, including Isma'ilis, among them. Under the czars, efforts were made to convert the Muslims to orthodox Christianity; but the Muslims resisted stubbornly. The Bolsheviks were on firmer ground, since they wanted to abolish all religions. They started by secularizing society and taking over religious establishments. This was followed by a rigorous programme of indoctrination using Marxist ideology, including atheism. It was done cautiously at first, by assuring the Muslims that they would be much better looked after by the new rulers. Lenin was aware of Muslim hostility to the czarist regime and was eager to enlist their support for the revolution. He and his comrade-in-arms, Stalin, issued an appeal in December 1917 wherein the Muslims were reminded that their 'mosques and prayer houses had been destroyed' and their 'beliefs and customs trampled upon by the czars and oppressors of Russia'. They told them that 'henceforth your beliefs and usages, your national and cultural institutions are forever free and inviolate,' and urged them to 'organize their national life in complete freedom'.[1]

Following the assurance, the Muslims of the various regions collaborated with the Bolsheviks. But as soon as Lenin was firmly in the saddle he declared war on all religions. Addressing the Second Congress of the Third International in 1920, he spoke inter alia about '. . .the necessity to struggle against the clergy and other reactionary and medieval elements, which have influence in backward countries. : .the necessity to combat pan-Islamism and similar currents', which strengthen 'the position of the khans, large landowners, mullās etc'.[2]

This was translated into action first by withdrawing State support to religious organizations, and then by instructing communist cadres to free the Muslims from the clutches of the mullās. The orthodox Muslims resisted this intrusion into their religious affairs and organized Basmachestov, the 'armed revolt' of the Muslims, which took the Soviet rulers by surprise because their experience with the Christians had been different; the latter had meekly submitted. Lenin, therefore, cautioned his colleagues in the Seventh Congress of the Central Committee of the Communist party to be careful in dealing with the Muslims, 'who till this day are under the influence of their mullās'. Impatient to usher in the new order, the Soviets, nonetheless went ahead with the confiscation of waqf properties, the closure of adalat and shari'ah courts, the reorganizing of madrasas and schools, and the discontinuation of religious instruction. These measures provoked violent outbursts. Lenin once again cautioned party workers 'to proceed tactfully and not to offend the religious sentiments of the Muslims'.[3] But as soon as resistance subsided, the same policy was renewed. After Lenin's death, Stalin, in 1927, declared the shari'ah invalid, abolished the Islamic judicial, educational and religious institutions and came down heavily on the mullas, many of whom were imprisoned and denied civil rights. The Muslim rites of marriage were abolished; so were their divorce laws. Stalin even created a new class of clergy known as novomechetniki (the 'new mosque') to fight reactionary mullas. They campaigned against the payment of the zakat and the wearing of veils by women. No one was allowed to go on hajj, the pilgrimage to Mecca; many mosques were turned into museums. According to a leading Soviet historian, N. Suviznov, 'Counter-revolutionary elements were utilizing the Qur'an and were attempting to manipulate the religious sentiments of the believers. . .[in order]. . .to hinder socialist construction. . . [and]. . .to inflame national and religious hostility with a view to splitting the single front of the toilers of the Soviet Union.'[4] Every Soviet citizen, irrespective of his religion, was subjected to the same secular laws; no exceptions were permitted.

By 1939, the Soviet authorities had convinced themselves that Muslim religious organizations and mosques had become centres of anti-Soviet activities. A party pamphlet noted that 'the enemies of the people carry on their treacherous work under the flag of the defence of religion. . . .The activity of the counter-revolutionary Muslim clergy in the USSR is directed by the Japanese secret service'.[5] The onset of World War II (1939–45) and the destruction it brought to Russia compelled the government to appease the mullas, who, in turn, mobilized the Muslims in defence of the fatherland. A more cordial relationship was established between the Muslim 'clergy' and the State, and was formalized in 1943 at a conference of the mullas at Tashkent where a 'Spiritual Administration for the Muslims of Central Asia and Kazakhistan' was formed with Mufti Isban Babakhan as chairman. For the Shi'ites, a special administration was set up at Batu, and for the European Muslims at Ufa. All three centres were directed and controlled by the Council for Religious Affairs, presided over by a member of the Politbureau; its task was to make use of religion to communize society and to cover up communist indoctrination in State-run schools and colleges. This was followed by the collectivization of agriculture and rapid industrialization, where the peasants and the workers were taught communist ideology. Again, through the 'social engineering' pursued since World War II, the Muslim bourgeoisie was shorn of their privileges and, in some cases, eliminated. The ulama, who did not cooperate with the authorities, were ostracized and deprived of their means of livelihood by being forbidden to teach religion.[6]

The situation has not changed very much since then except that recently, in order to placate Muslim sentiment elsewhere, Islamic cultural achievements in the Central Asian Republics and the Caucasus are being displayed through Muslim Spiritual Boards. These Boards appoint muftis to manage 'working mosques' and guide believers, but the priests are more mouthpieces of Soviet propaganda than of Islam. Their activities are severely restricted and they can neither complain against the anti-Islamic tirades of the communists nor ask for the right to propagate their faith. Despite the many international Islamic conferences convened in Tashkent and the delegations of Soviet Muslims sent to the Arab and other Muslim countries, the official approach remains basically atheistic. This is obvious from the fact that fifty million Soviet Muslims have less than 150 'working mosques' in the whole of Central Asia. There are two madrasas—one in Bukhaara and the other in Tashkent—maintained as showpieces; there are a few religious periodicals, such as *Muslims of the Soviet East*, which are mostly circulated abroad. Beautiful editions of the Qur'an are printed solely to be presented to visiting Muslim dignataries. Likewise, copies of the hadith of Imam Bukhari, who was a resident of Bukhara and in whose name one of the two madrasas was established, are published for distribution outside the Soviet Union. *The Great Soviet Encyclopaedia* (1953 edition) had explained the communist viewpoint candidly.

> Like all religions, Islam has always played a reactionary role being an instrument of spiritual oppression of the toilers in the hands of the exploiting classes and was used by foreign colonizers for the enslavement of the peoples of the East. . . .After the victory of the Great October Revolution in Russia, during the armed foreign intervention and the civil war, Islam was utilized by the internal counter-revolution and foreign imperialists for the struggle against the Soviet state. . . . During the period of socialist construction in the USSR, the remnants of the exploiting classes strived to utilize Islam for the struggle against socialism. The Muslim clergy as agents of these classes conducted a struggle against Soviet laws on family and marriage, against the emancipation of women, for the retention of chudder and the pardah. . .for the struggle against in-

dustrialization and committed terroristic acts. Especially actively were the Qur'ân and the sharī'ah employed. . .for the struggle against industrialization and collectivization. . . .In the USSR Islam exists [now] only as a survival of one of the forms of ideology of the exploitative society. . . .The American-English imperialists utilize Islam for the purpose of struggle against the revolutionary and national liberation movements in the Muslim countries. . . . [7]

There has been little change in this attitude, except under Brezhnev when, from 1964 to 1982, he reversed the repressive measures against the Muslim 'clergy' reintroduced by his predecessor, Krushchev, who, between 1959 to 1964, had closed down thousands of mosques and banned religious teaching. Brezhnev welcomed the resurgence of Islam in the world at the Twenty-Sixth Congress of the Soviet Communist party and hailed it as a progressive force. He said, 'The banner of Islam may lead to the battle for liberation.' But since the advent of Gorbachev there has, once again, been a revival of the old hostile attitude towards Islam though its manifestation is more subtle.[8]

However, despite official denigration and sustained atheistic indoctrination, Islam has not disappeared from the Soviet Union. Soviet Muslims may not practise the five fundamentals of their faith, but they have not given up Islamic rites and customs. Officials have learnt from experience that it is wiser to allow religious ceremonies during marriage or death and let the Muslims celebrate festivals such as Behram or Id al-Adha than prohibit them, since they are more social than religious events.

There are two other sources of Islamic influence which the authorities have not been able to eliminate. One is the tribal court, dominated by erstwhile tribal leaders, which is still rooted in the Islamic tradition. Many of these leaders continue to speak and read Arabic and possess a rudimentary knowledge of theology. The other wellspring of Islam in the USSR is the clandestinely organized network of sūfi brotherhoods which has been popular in Central Asia since medieval times. These continue to exercise considerable influence on the Muslims. Of these, the Naqshbandīya is the most popular, followed by the Qadirīyya (mostly in the Caucasus) the Khalwatiya (in Turkmenistan or Turkmen SSR), and the Yasawiya (in Uzbekistan, Kirghizia and Kazakhistan). The Soviet authorities are aware of the potential of these institutions for religious revival but have so far left them alone, since suppressing them in the past had only inflamed fundamentalism. Nevertheless, Communist party workers have been actively decrying what they call 'parallel or unofficial Islam', as opposed to official or State-controlled Islam. They also point to the benefits the State has given the Muslims, contrasting this with their apalling living conditions before the Bolshevik revolution. It is undeniable that the Soviet Muslims, cut off as they are from the rest of the Muslim world, are vulnerable, but memories of their 'splendid past', of the splendour of Samarqand and Bukhara, remain a powerful force that bind them to their faith. Even as late as 1967 it was admitted by the Soviet authorities that religious 'prejudices' among them were still alive; the Soviet press repeated that 'the instructions of the shari'ah are frequently adhered to in all the Central Asian republics. Religious traditions and customs are observed not only in rural areas but also in towns and even by non-religious people, including members of the national intelligentsia, who are members of the Communist party.'9

The Soviets continue to regard Muslims as a potentially destabilizing force and so allow only a few to go on the hajj pilgrimage; also Friday congregational prayers are largely restricted to 'the working mosques', which are not easily accessible to the majority among the Soviet Muslims. After the Khomeini revolution in neighbouring Iran and the Soviet intervention in Afghanistan, the party leadership has become even more apprehensive about unrest erupting among the Central Asian Muslims. The general secretary, Mikhail Gorbachev, warned that the communists must be more vigilant and active in countering the possible impact of foreign religious influences, which he described as 'reactionary', and the work of 'foreign spies and agents' in league with anti-Soviet elements. On his visit to Tashkent in November 1986, the Soviet leader made a frontal attack on Islam as 'an instrument for the spiritual oppression of the workers and for the subjection of the people of the East', and issued an order barring party members from visiting mosques. The long-standing programme of Russification has also seen no let up. In fact, communist intellectuals are now coming round to the view that 'religious groups' should not be equated with nationalities as what had so far been done can be legitimately encouraged under Leninist dogma.

China

The Chinese communists share the same basic attitude as their northern counterparts to Islam, but are infinitely more flexible in practice. According to the population statistics of 1936, the then Kuomingtang Republic of China had an estimated 48,104,240 Muslims, who were described as one of 'five great peoples of China'. Since then the number must have increased considerably; but as no figures are available it is difficult to assess their strength. Soon after the communist takeover in 1949 the Mao government divided the Muslims into 'nationalities' on the basis of their ethnic origins: their total number then was estimated to be about 10 million. One wonders what happened to the other 40 million. All kinds of theories have been suggested by detractors of the communist regime, including mass extermination, but to this day no official explanation has been given.

The Chinese communists recognize eleven ethnic groups as Muslim, mostly Sunnis of the Hanafi school. Nine of them were originally Central Asian and lived in the province of Xingiang, which is adjacent to both Soviet Central Asia and North-West China. They speak different Central Asian dialects. The largest group are the Huis of Arab or Iranian descent. They speak Chinese, follow the Chinese Han ways, but are also proud of their Islamic heritage. They are strict in the observance of the religious rites. They do not eat pork and avoid 'Han food' which is cooked in lard. There are non-pork restaurants and Hui stores all over China. In factories and offices special arrangements for Hui food are made. As compared to the Muslims in the Soviet Union, Chinese Muslims are, by and large, more liberally treated and are not subjected to atheistic or anti-Islamic indoctrination, perhaps because China has cordial relations with Pakistan, Iran and the Arab world. Unlike the Soviet Constitution, which does not allow freedom of religion, the Chinese Constitution of 1954 specifically provides for 'freedom to believe and freedom not to believe'. Mosques in China are permitted to function without official hindrance. In Beijing alone, there are sixty-seven 'working mosques'. During the Cultural Revolution, many mosques were damaged or closed down; but since then the policy has changed and China has become more tolerant of religious practices. It has, for instance, established many Islamic organizations and institutes' though, as in the Soviet Union, most of these are for show. The

Islamic Theological Institute has branches in all the eight predominantly Muslim provinces (these are Ningxia, Gansu, Xinjiang, Qunghai, Hebei, Henqn, Shandong and Yunnan; there are also large numbers of Muslims in Beijan and Tiqnjin). There is also the Central Chinese Islamic Association. Both the Institute and the Association receive government grants and patronage. The Association endeavours to project a favourable picture of Chinese Muslims. It has published the Qur'an in Mandarin and organizes receptions in honour of visiting Muslim dignitaries. It also arranges hajj pilgrimages to Mecca and Madina, though the number of hajjis is restricted and the selection is officially screened and controlled.

There is little conflict between religion and the State in China but occasionally riots have broken out when the authorities have tried to curb religious practices—for instance, when waqf properties were confiscated and some mosques and darghas forcibly occupied. The Chinese Muslims have also resented officially sponsored campaigns against ahongs or traditional religious leaders and their denunciation as reactionaries and anti-people. In Honan province in 1953, Muslims came out en masse in the streets and proclaimed an 'independent Islamic kingdom' and pledged that their first loyalty was to Islam. Although the rebellion was suppressed, the vehemence of the popular reaction was unmistakable. Again, during the Cultural Revolution, there were many Muslim revolts which were ruthlessly suppressed.

The Muslims fear that they may be assimilated into the Chinese mainstream and lose their identity. But there is not too much friction even on this score between the State and the Muslims because the Chinese are much more subtle in their dealings than the Russians. This trait in the Han character has yielded rich dividends in the past; and the Chinese hope that they can make it possible for their Muslims to settle down within the communist framework. Since the rise of Deng Xiaoping and his group, there has been greater tolerance towards the Muslims and other religious communities.[10]

This has been admitted by the Soviet official organ *Izvestia*, which wrote that China's interest in its thirteen million Muslim citizens 'is by no means fortuitous. It is dictated by the leadership's pragmatic approach to the fluctuations in the politics, economics and socio-religious movements in the world'.[11]

Eastern Europe

The communist regimes in Eastern Europe treat their Muslim minorities more or less on the same lines as the Soviet Union does. The only difference is to be seen in Yugoslavia, which is not a member of the Warsaw Pact. It has also a much larger Muslim population than any other East European country, except Albania, in which, at one time, Muslims were an overwhelming majority but which is now completely 'Sovietized'. In Yugoslavia every sixth citizen is a Muslim. The Muslims are powerful politically and otherwise because the Constitution of Yugoslavia gives proportional representation to all ethnic nationalities. Though not based on religion, the system enables Muslims, particularly in Bosnia and Hergovina, to obtain substantial strength in elected bodies and in the bureaucracy. Yugoslavian Muslims enjoy far greater freedom to practise their religion and to organize their life in accordance with their culture than elsewhere in the communist world. Mosques are well maintained and frequented. No official restrictions are placed on the performance of prayers or rituals. Every town or village with a substantial Muslim population has its own Muslim burial ground. There are Islamic community centres, where congregations and religious functions are held. Islamic landmarks are preserved as historical monuments or utilized for educational or cultural purposes. Muslim children are taught the fundamentals of their religion at the primary school level; there are also madrasas where the Arabic script and the Qur'ān are taught. Religious education is imparted in two centres of higher Islamic learning—the Madrasa-i-Husrefbey in Sarajevo and the Madrasa-i-Alauddin at Pristina—to more than 500 pupils in each. At the apex is the Islamic Theological Faculty, started in 1977, which gives specialized instruction in the Qur'ān, the hadīth and different aspects of the sharī'ah. Some Muslim students are also sent to the Arab world and Pakistan for higher studies in Islamics.

One of the important libraries in Yugoslavia is the Ghazi Husrefbey in Sarajevo which has thousands of rare manuscripts in Arabic, Persian and Turki. It was founded by Ghazi Husrefbey, a religious scholar and poet, who established several Islamic centres. He also built the mosque named after him—which is a splendid example of Islamic architecture. It is maintained by the State. The network of religious institutions, including mosques and madrasas, is financed primarily through public subscriptions or the collection of the zakāt or the sale of qurban meat and skins. All employees are paid from these funds. They have their own trade unions known as Il Umiga associations, which are affiliated to the Socialist Association of Working People. The State also gives grants to religious bodies. In Yugoslavia, there is little conflict between religion and the State, though when the occasional skirmish occurs it is ruthlessly suppressed by the government.[12]

In the final analysis, though the communist world is not conducive to the preservation, much less, the promotion of Islam, in the last two decades the clout of petro-dollars and the international importance of Muslim countries has softened communist hostility towards the religion. Nevertheless the communists' basic stand—the encouragement of religion in any form leads to the disintegration of society—remains unchanged. Interestingly, though both Afghanistan and South Yemen are ruled by Soviet-backed quasi-Marxist governments, they do not follow the party line on religion. We are not concerned here with the merits or demerits of the Soviet armed intervention in both these countries, but are only interested in the impact of Marxist ideology on these Muslims. While the ruling parties in both countries are composed either of communists or fellow-travellers and their policies are directed towards strengthening institutions and movements which are anti-religious, they have been cautious enough to hide their intentions and have taken public postures which are seemingly Islamic. In countries with an overwhelming Muslim majority anything else would have been unthinkable.

Afghanistan

In Afghanistan, the process of transformation from a feudal Islamic society to a modern, communist one has been slow. But from the very beginning, when Soviet troops moved in, the administration was taken over by two leftist parties, the Khalaq and the Parcham. The assassination of President Daud and his colleagues and the elimination of several high officials were aimed to change the political system and reverse the socio-economic decline of the society. There was no difference of opinion in this between the three top leaders of the revolution—Noor Muhammad Taraki, who became prime minister, and Hafizullah Amin and Babrak Karmal who were made the deputy prime ministers. They tried to play down their Marxist commitment and called upon the people to support them in rooting out corruption, distributing wealth equitably and eradicating poverty, disease and unemployment. They intended to reduce the hold of religion among a people known for their fanatical devotion to Islam. Taraki explained this clearly:

> Some people mix politics and religion and make use of the true religion of Islam as a political tool. After the Saur (April) Revolution there is absolutely no room for such practices. We respect our mullās and other religious figures. As repeatedly emphasized, when they do not dabble in politics and do not stand opposed to the Saur Revolution, we will honour and respect them. But should they engage in demagoguery, deceive the masses and don the veil of religion to rise against the Saur Revolution, we will not permit it. Every class has its own theoreticians. . . .We the theoreticians of the working class will not permit the theoreticians of other classes to make the slightest move against the interests of the workers and the peasants.[13]

Tribal leaders, landlords and mullās were hard-hit by the land-reforms the Marxist government proposed. They exhorted the faithful to rise in defence of their religion and organized an armed resistance movement, which received substantial support from Pakistan and Saudi Arabia. The rest of the Muslim world was also sympathetic to their cause, as of course was America, for reasons of its own. The result was sustained resistance by the Islamic fundamentalists led by Ustad Burhanuddin Rabbani with learnings towards the Jama'āt-i-Islāmi and Gulbuddin Hekmatyar of the indigenous Hizbi Islāmi. The rebellion was backed by Pakistan, which opened its doors to the mujāhidūn or fighters in the cause of Allah, and provided them with arms and ammunitions supplied for the purpose of America. The mujāhidūn waged a ceaseless battle over the years and were able to restrict the control of the Marxist government to the larger cities and towns, while holding most of the country in their hands. Battles between the two forces, each backed by a super-power, continued to be fought with fierce intensity. Finally, as a result of the agreement between Reagan and Gorbachev, to which Zia of Pakistan was a party, the Soviets agreed to pull out of Afghanistan; but the mujāhidūn have continued their guerrilla warfare. Will they succeed in toppling the communist government headed by Dr Najibullah? Time alone will tell, but one thing appears clear; without military backing it is not possible to sustain an anti-religious regime in a predominantly Muslim country for long. This was the main hurdle the Soviet Union faced in Afghanistan; Najibullah realized it, though late, and made every effort to bring about, what he called, a 'national reconciliation'. The mujāhidūn leaders spurned his effort. He has begun to woo the mullās and even them given financial inducements. He has also provided stipends to Qur'ān readers and undertaken the repair and maintenance of mosques and payments to imams and muezzins. He permits a large number of Muslims to go on hajj and has stepped up religious programming on radio and television. In an interview to the American magazine, *Newsweek*, Dr Najibullah has explained the reasons for some of these changes:

> Our society is an Islamic society. But in the first phase this point was not taken into account. For example, the lands belonging to the holy mosques were included in the reforms. Also, according to Islam, children inherit the land of a person who dies. In the first phase this was ignored. Now utter respect is being paid to the beliefs of the people.[14]

But it is doubtful whether these gimmicks will pay off and the religious-minded Afghans will believe in his government; if they do it will be the most spectacular triumph of secularism over religion, though finally Najbullah's communist grounding may push Afghanistan into the communist fold.

South Yemen

The circumstances which led to the formation of a Marxist-oriented government in South Yemen differ considerably from those in Afghanistan. The leftist National Liberation Front (NLF) won the civil war following the withdrawal of British troops from the territory and embarked on creating a 'new, rational, socialist society'. The Soviet Union came forward with financial and military aid. The fundamentalists resisted the efforts of the Marxist government to restructure their society using the model recommended by the Soviet Union. Their belief that the Marxist leaders intended to destroy Islam was reinforced when they dispossessed the local sultans, tribal chiefs and religious leaders of their lands and assets and tried to wean away their followers, condemning them as 'guardians of religious obscurantism'. They also eliminated the private sector, nationalized trade and industry, took over lands and properties without compensation and introduced many other Marxist measures. A media campaign was unleashed against merchants, landlords and property owners, vilifying them as 'parasites' and 'reactionaries'; the struggle intensified and thousands of the so-called bourgeoisie fled the country. Peasants, workers, students, women and writers were organized into cadres and every attempt made to undermine the hold of Islam on the faithful.

These actions aroused widespread resentment in the Arab countries. In the face of this, the government decided that it would be more politic to modify its anti-Islamic stance. It channelled the income from waqf properties (which it had confiscated) for religious purposes and provided funds for the salaries of imams and other 'clerics'. Marriages and divorces were allowed to be performed by qadis, according to the shari'ah, though they had to be registered with the appropriate authorities.

These policies have since been further strengthened. Mosques have been repaired and facilities for prayers and fasting in the month of Ramadān provided. The Qur'ān is taught in schools, but its verses are given a 'progressive' and secular interpretation. Friday sermons are delivered according to official directives, which emphasize social justice. A typical example is the sermon delivered in one of the mosques in Aden, the capital of the Republic, in 1984: 'The essence of Islam is equality and the end of class exploitation and the establishment of a prosperous and just life, the promotion of democracy and social justice and a society free from social contradictions and exploitive relationships.'[15]

Despite such subtle propaganda, the Marxists have not so far succeeded in dislodging Islam from the hearts of the southern Yemenites. Even officials, both ministers and civilians, have made a strategic turnaround and have taken to describing themselves as practising Muslims. They can be seen praying in mosques and observing fasts during Ramadān. However, on the question of the role of women, the government has remained steadfast. It encourages them to give up the veil and participate in civic activities. They are given employment in educational institutions, factories, the police and the army. The Family Law of 1974 protects them fully in every respect and is broader than any such law enacted anywhere in the Muslim world. Women are adopting Western styles of dress; some of them are even going on stage as singers and dancers. Radio and television have opened up further avenues of employment for them.

The government seems to have succeeded to some extent in its balancing act. The concessions to the fundamentalists have abated the rigour of the so-called 'socialist order' and an uneasy truce now prevails. As the former president of the Republic, Ali Nasir Muhammad, admitted, 'it is natural that there are contradictions or conflicts' (between the old order and the new, much more so between communism and Islam). That attitude has not changed despite several changes in the top leadership: it is very likely that there will be further conflict between Islam and the State, for all evidence points to the fact that despite their concessions to religious practices the Marxists remain as committed to a communist transformation of the State and society as before and in this confrontation with Islam seems inevitable.

22
Conclusions

It will be evident from the foregoing survey that the portrayal of Islam by Western and other non-Muslim scholars as an uncompromising, monolithic and fossilized faith is far from accurate. Muslims are no more bigoted than others in their devotion to their faith nor have they been more militant in spreading or preserving it. Every religion must be judged in its historical context. Buddhism spread more than a thousand years before the birth of Islam; it would be incorrect to view its development without taking into account the factors which brought it about. Likewise, Hinduism, Christianity and Judaism, each flourished under certain circumstances and this, in turn, affected their respective characters. All through history, as we have seen, Muslims, like the followers of other religions, had to face innumerable problems of adjustment and solved them in their own way just as the non-Muslims did.

However, unlike other religions, Islam became a power within the lifetime of its founder. This simplified problems to start with, but when he was gone it made for complications. His jurisdiction was confined to Arabia; but his immediate successors had to deal with the extensive territories they had conquered, each with its own historical background and cultural affinities. Inevitably the conquerors encountered new administrative, judicial, fiscal and social problems and had to resort to ijtihād (independent judgement) to solve them. When the Prophet was alive, he had two advantages: divine guidance and his own intuition. He was acknowledged to be the best judge there was and his decisions could not be questioned. None of his Companions could measure up to him nor were they blessed with celestial attributes. The Qur'ān and the sunna alone were their rule books, which they had to use to derive methods of governance and solutions to changing situations. This was not an easy task. The Qur'ān was not codified, and the sayings and traditions of the Prophet were scattered.

Furthermore, the speed with which Islam expanded created various difficulties, which could not be resolved on the basis of general rules. Conditions differed vastly from place to place. Egypt was different from Syria, Iraq from Iran; each had its own historical roots. The habits of their peoples varied, their languages were not the same. Despite being faced with such a difficult situation, the first four caliphs, inspired by the faith they inherited from Muhammad, spread Islam and consolidated their rule with admirable skill.

It was impossible for them to be rigid in administration; they had to interpret the Qur'ān and the sunna in the light of the varying circumstances they faced. This was, in fact, the foundation on which the 'rightly guided' Caliphate was run; it encouraged not only ijtihād but also ikhtilāf (disagreement).[1] They took their cue from a saying of the Prophet: 'Difference of opinion among my community is a sign of the bounty of God.' It must be said, though, that at times it was taken to such ridiculous lengths that each Companion had his own interpretation of a Qur'ānic text or an action of the Prophet.

Through the course of Islam's development, various rulers naturally took advantage of this plethora of opinions and functioned as they deemed best in the larger interest of the state. Their actions were in most cases justified by the ulamā, hired by them, and approved by the general mass of the faithful; but the minority who differed gave their disapproval or defiance religious overtones. The major division which took place between the Sunnis and Shī'as, though political, took on a sectarian character and even dissent was hallowed with a religious colour. The theologians of each sect prided themselves in turning their differences into virtues and even went to the extent of glorifying sectarianism. This sort of thing happened not only under the Umayyads, whom the Sunni fundamentalists abhorred and the Shī'as hated, but also under the Abbasids whom both these groups helped to instal in power. The situation did not differ much under the Ottomans, the Safavids or the Mughals, who asserted their authority over their hired religious functionaries and managed the affairs of state in the manner the rulers wanted, irrespective of theological considerations or the views of the classical jurists. The secular authorities, no doubt, usually respected the theologians but more often than not the theologicans toed the secular line and not vice-versa, unless there was a patent violation of the rules of the shari'ah.

*

Islam is a simple religion; it requires of its followers two things. One, a belief in the unity of God; and two, a belief in the prophethood of Muhammad. Iqbal has said, 'As long as a person is loyal to the two basic principles of Islam, i.e., the unity of God and the finality of the holy Prophet, not even the strictest mullā can turn him outside the pale of Islam even though his interpretations of the law or the text of the Qur'ān are believed to be erroneous.'[2] Islam does not recognize any intermediaries between man and God. But throughout history, the fundamentalists have arrogated to themselves the right of excommunication, even though there has been no consensus among the ulamā as to what makes a Muslim. The Munir Commission of Pakistan (referred to earlier) asked each of the eminent ulamā who appeared before it to define a Muslim; there was such acute divergence of views that the Commission observed, '. . .if considerable confusion exists in the mind of our ulamā, on such a simple matter, one can easily imagine what the differences on more complicated matters will be.'[3]

In our study, we have concentrated on politics and its interaction with religion and nowhere has this relationship been more relentlessly acrimonious as between fundamentalists and secularists: that is, in our definition, between those who are more concerned with spiritual matters and those with exclusively worldly interests. The conflict between the two, in most cases, was decided in favour of the secularists. Interestingly, Islam did not suffer as a result of this: rather its influence increased worldwide. This is amply borne out by history. Take, for instance, the Mongol invasion and the sack of Baghdad in the thirteenth century; it cast such gloom on the world of Islam that a contemporary Arab historian characterized it as the 'wrath of Allah' for the sins of the Muslims; but out of the ruins arose three powerful empires—the Ottomans, the Mughals and the Safavids. Islam, which was brought to its nadir by internecine warfare, religious disputes, and corrupt and immoral practices, emerged more mighty and glorious than ever before.

The conflict between the fundamentalists and the secularists did not cease; it resumed more feverishly, but the outcome was no different. And though there has been conflict in one form or the other all through history, the fundamentalists have never achieved the upper hand. The face-off continues today, though its characteristics are not the same and its implications and flavour have changed.

In order to understand the nature of the conflict it is necessary to have a clear idea of the relationship between religion and politics in Islam. The first issue that bedevilled the faith, as we have noted, was that of succession to the Prophet, on which hinged the question of the leadership of the faithful. The Prophet had left no specific or clear-cut instructions; subsequent theories, even by the Shī'ites, were either matters of interpretation or downright concoctions. In the crisis that threatened the nascent state, Abū Bakr was hurriedly nominated by Umar and approvéd by a meeting at Saqifa, a central place; neither the character of the gathering nor the manner in which the selection was made could be said to have been representative. Umar later admitted that he would not like the same procedure to be followed in the future. He himself was nominated by the dying Abū Bakr and his choice was ratified by a congregation in the capital. Uthmān was selected by an arbitrator and Ali was forced by various groups, under the pressure of the crisis following Uthmān's murder, to accept the Caliphate. Mu'āwiya usurped the Caliphate by trickery; he was not qualified for the position.

He turned the republic into a mulk or kingdom. The Abbasids overthrew the Umayyads with fundamentalist support but used secular methods to remain in power. The Ottomans relied on their might and utilized it fully to expand their empire. In each case, a different procedure was followed in determining succession. Moreover, after the first four caliphs, every Muslim ruler until recent times has been a king, basing his authority either on a family or tribe or army; some ulamā objected to such usurpation of power but the majority not only acquiesced in it but also approved of it. Abu'l Hasan al-Mawardi, the political theorist (d. 1058) did not object to such usurpation (even by a governor or a military commander owing allegiance to the caliph) and commended it as 'the path of compromise'; Ghazāli, who was criticized by his contemporary Ibn Rushd (1126–98) for his compromising nature as 'all things to all men', justified it on practical grounds. Ibn Taymiya (d. 1328), the most orthodox of the early theologians, went to the extent of saying that 'sixty years with an unjust ruler are better than one night without a ruler'. He quoted Ali, who is reported to have said that the people could not do without a ruler, whether pious or sinful. When questioned, the fourth caliph replied, 'Yes, even sinful because highways are to be kept secure, canonical penalties are to be applied, holy war is to be fought against the enemies and spoils of war are to be collected.'[4]

Political realities more than religious requirements were, therefore, the determining factors for the onward progression of Islam. No one has analysed better the phases through which historical Islam had to pass than the eminent Arab historian Ibn Khaldun (1333–74). He makes a clear distinction between the ideal—the Madinian state of the Prophet—and the reality, which was dynastic rule (mulk) based on asabiya or the spirit of kinship rooted in a family or tribe.[5] Except during the time of the Prophet and the first two caliphs asabiya prevailed. Uthman fell victim to it; so did Ali, their murders intensifying the age-old conflict between the House of Hashim and the House of Umayyah. The triumph of Mu'awiya was, in a sense, the victory of the stronger tribe. Since then the annals of Islam have been full of family and tribal warfare. And thus it came about that the emergent Islamic state was more asabiya than a mirror to the advancement of Islam. Ibn Khaldun explains this development graphically. He goes back to the earliest times and traces the history of each kingdom and shows its connection with asabiya; whenever one kingdom replaced another it was because of the war between tribes and families.

Strictly speaking, there are no specific directions in the Qur'an or the hadith to warrant the appointment of an elected head; but Maududi has said that from the Qur'anic injunction about shura or consultation 'the Companions rightly inferred' that the 'head of the Islamic state had been left to the elective discretion of the Muslims'.[6] He however, admits that this was never followed in practice. Maududi restricts the elective principle to a close circle of pious and practising Muslims. Iqbal is more liberal; he leaves it open to all. He has said 'The republican form of government is not only thoroughly consistent with the spirit of Islam, but has also become a necessity in view of the new forces that have been set free in the world of Islam.'[7] There is no gainsaying the fact that the whole basis of Islam is democratic; in it kings and dictators do not fit in. Unfortunately neither the classical nor the modern jurists, by and large, have done anything to enforce it. On the contrary, quite often the democratic principle has been overthrown and even the theologians have quietly complied with the dictates of the ruler. Mawardi, Ghazāli, as well as judges in modern times have been guilty of this. The Supreme Court of Pakistan, for instance, has validated time and again the military takeover of democratically elected governments on the ground of necessity.[8]

The situation in many other parts of the Muslim world is no different; might continues to be right. And the ulamā have rarely hesitated to accord legitimacy to kings and dictators who have had no electoral base. This is certainly not in accordance with Islam, which stands for democracy in action; it has never preached kingship or dictatorship. One of its cardinal principles is the equality of believers, irrespective of status, position or race. In his farewell address, a few months before his death, the Prophet had made this clear: 'All Muslims are brethren unto one another. They form one brotherhood and are equal in every respect. Nothing which belongs to one Muslim is lawful unless freely given by the other out of goodwill.'[9] D.S. Margoliouth, a former professor of Arabic at Oxford University has observed: 'The equality of all Muslims was, we have reason to believe, a fundamental doctrine with the Prophet, and the earliest interpreters of his ideas were probably right in thinking that he intended that rule to be absolutely without exceptions.'

Authoritarianism, in any shape or form, cannot, therefore, be justified in Islam; yet the majority of jurists have not hesitated to glorify it. However, in recent times, Maududi has spoken unreservedly against it. No man, he maintains, has any rights over the others. To quote him, 'The basic principle of Islam is that human beings must, individually and collectively, surrender all rights of overlordship, legislation and exercising of authority over others. No one should be allowed to pass orders to make commands *in his own right* and no one ought to accept the obligation to carry out commands and obey such orders.'[10] True, Maududi does not agree that even elected representatives of the people have the right to make laws because he asserts that God alone is the law giver and quotes the Qur'ān: all authority belongs to God alone. (3:154). The legislators are only to implement divine commands and the government appointed by them or the electorate has to see that these are properly implemented. Unfortunately, Maududi confuses God's omnipotence with political sovereignty. Consequently, while he rejects every form of authoritarianism, he also disapproves of popular democracy. He is, in effect, for theocracy, though he explains that

> theocracy is something altogether different from the theocracy of which Europe has had a bitter experience wherein a priestly class, sharply marked off from the rest of the population, exercises unchecked domination and enforces laws of its own making in the name of God, thus virtually imposing its own divinity and godhead upon the common people. Such a system of government is satanic rather than divine. Contrary to this, theocracy built by Islam is not ruled by any particular religious class but by the whole community of Muslims including the rank and file.

However, as we have seen, such an ideal hardly ever obtained in the Islamic kingdom. Who among the Muslim kings fulfilled Maududi's basic conditions—individual liberty and social justice? Very few indeed!

Again, in Islam a ruler, government, or state has to strictly follow Islam's ideology; the Prophet took over the government in order to propagate and nourish the faith. How many Muslim rulers were really so motivated? Most of them fought for territorial aggrandizement and ruled for personal glory. A Muslim ruler, according to all theological canons, is required to be endowed with certain qualifications. Of these piety is universally regarded as the most important. But how many of the rulers were really pious? Indeed, the whole business of the character of Islamic rule and of those who are equipped to rule has been a vexed question right since the death of the Prophet. Apart from the points mentioned earlier, a good ruler (according to the jurists) had to have good character, a sense of equity and justice, a capacity to defend the faith, commitment to uplift the poor and the downtrodden and so on. The jurists in every age were also insistent that the ruler must be a member of the Arab tribe of Quraish, with the result that all non-Arabs were excluded. Until the thirteenth century even non-Quraishi Arabs were unacceptable. This was accepted even by the general populace as an unalterable requirement. Only the Kharijites had differed and asserted that every pious Muslim was entitled to be a caliph.

The most graphic description of a Muslim ruler has been given by the celebrated theologian, Hasan al-Basri in his reply to the question posed to him by the Umayyad caliph, Umar bin Abd al-Aziz, whom the fundamentalists regard as the fifth 'rightly guided' caliph: 'The just ruler, O, Commander of the Believers, is like a herdsman, solicitous for the camels he tends, desiring the sweetest pleasures for them, driving them away from any dangerous grazing place, protecting them from beasts of prey and shielding them from harms of heat and cold.'[11] The Ottomans, being non-Arabs, were denied legitimacy for a long time despite the unparalleled glory and power they brought to Islam and despite the fact that they were in control of Mecca and Madina and exercised custodianship over the Ka'ba. It was as late as in the eighteenth century that they were accepted by the faithful as true caliphs. Most of the ulamā still dithered; even today there are many who insist that leadership of the faithful must go to the tribe of Quraish. For instance, the noted Syrian theologian, Abd al-Rahman al-Kawakibi (d. 1902) suggested in the wake of the abolition of the Caliphate by Ataturk in 1924 that the Caliphate should be given to a Quraishi Arab with headquarters in Mecca.[12] As far as the Shi'as are concerned they believe that the leadership of a nation must vest in a member of the Prophet's family.

Maududi is one of the few among the modern fundamentalists who rejects any such pre-condition based on family, tribe or race. He considers it a violation of the Qur'ānic verse: 'Allah has promised to those among you who believe and do righteous deeds that He will assuredly make them succeed [the present rulers] and grant them vice-regency in the land just as He made those before them to succeed others. According to him Islam stands for equality of the believers; to quote his words, 'There is no reservation in favour of any family, class or race . . . . the Holy Prophet has said, "Every one of you is a ruler and every one is answerable to his subjects." ' He also quotes another oft-repeated dictum of the Prophet: 'An Arab has no superiority over a non-Arab or non-Arab over an Arab; neither does a white man possess any superiority over a black man nor a black man over a white man, except in point of piety.' Also the hadith: 'Listen and obey even if a negro is appointed as a ruler over you.'[13]

Every virtue was included in the list of qualifications enumerated by the classical jurists for a person fit to rule; indeed one who possessed them all would be a saint. Unsurprisingly, given the reality from age to age hardly any saints became rulers. Rather, military commanders and tribal chiefs were seen fit the bill. One of the most successful—albeit autocratic and ruthless—Muslim rulers was Süleymän the Magnificent. He wrote a poem on the qualities of a ruler:

> To be charitable and kind
> Is the glory of the throne.
> Remember, O Süleymän,
> And make these qualities your crown
> In counting your subjects
> To make them happy,
> Do not think to be better
> Than the least of them
> And know that many of them
> Are better than yourself.
> Every man is a brother
> And as a brother you must love him.
> For a true Muslim, O Süleymän,
> This precept is sacred.
> As soon as you conceive a wise idea
> Act upon it with an invincible face.
> Protect the good and be terrible
> To the evil doer.
> To be tyrannical
> Is to be a Tatar Khan
> And not a Sultan.
> Not to act at all
> Is a guilt as serious
> As to do evil.
> The king who sleeps on his throne
> Is similar to the brutes.
> As the fate of the universe
> Is in our hands,
> We should strive
> To deserve
> The respect and the love of men.[14]

*

As we have seen, many of the ulamā were only too ready to compromise and waive canonical compulsions to meet the exigencies of whichever time they were part of; there were some notable exceptions, who insisted that every word of the Qur'ān, irrespective of its context, and every action of the Prophet, irrespective of its historical context, was sacrosanct and should be implemented. They arrogated to themselves the right to interpret the texts and to advise on the correct course of action. Dedicated to the cause as they perceived it, and sincere in their conviction, they claimed to be the real custodians of the faith.

The modern fundamentalists are their inheritors; unmindful of what happened in the last fourteen hundred years, since the time of the Umayyads, they are as determined as their forbears to go back to the earliest era of Islam and if possible to undo all that has taken place, especially in the political sphere. In short, they want to wipe out almost the whole Islamic history. As the highly respected divine, Maulānā Ihstishamul Haq of Pakistan has put it:

> The Qur'ān is the sacred word of God and embodies His divine Guidance, who has the fullest knowledge and embodies prescience of every minor event of every period and every epoch from the beginning of time to its end. He knows all the infinite varieties of human relationship which can happen in any period or epoch in all futurity. Hence His revealed book and His appointed Prophet with prophetic wisdom, all are based on the truth that until doomsday all teachings and injunctions of the Holy Qu'rān and the sunna shall be the authoritative guidance and final word for all the infinity of events that may take place in this Universe.[15]

The only concession that the venerable maulānā makes to practices like ijtihad is that the faithful should seek guidance in order to understand the true import of the Qur'ān and the sunna from the ulama, who being experts and specialists' can alone interpret their meaning and content. However, as we have seen, the ulamā became active much later. Before them the caliphs and the Companions—none of whom claimed to be experts or specialists—acted according to their own lights. They, in fact, freely exercised ijtihād; they also welcomed ikhtiláf or differences among themselves. Their judgements form an important part of the corpus of Islamic jurisprudence; they moulded these, as I have explained, to suit the secular requirements of the times. In the process the unscrupulous rulers got even the hadith concocted and turned ijtihád into license. In course of time this inevitably led to disenchantment with ijtihád, and gave way to taqlíd, with the result that free thought was throttled. It also resulted in intellectual stagnation which enveloped not only religious but also social and cultural affairs. The emphasis shifted from the spirit of Islam to rules for daily living—what to eat and drink and how to dress and walk. This was taken to such a ridiculous extent that even the study of foreign languages and the wearing of foreign dress was declared heretical. The substance of the Prophet's teachings was lost in the pursuit of these shadows. Iqbal was so disgusted by their clutter that he penned a poem to express his frustration. He entitled it 'A Mullá in Paradise':

> Being present myself, my impetuous tongue Could not to silence resign.
> When the order from the God of admission Above was handed that reverend divine.
> I humbly addressed the Almighty: Oh Lord, Excuse this presumption of mine;
> But he'll never relish the virgins of Heaven, The garden's green borders, the wine;
> For Paradise isn't the place for dogmatics To quarrel and argue and jangle;
> And he, worthy man, second nature to him Is the need to dispute and to wrangle,
> His business in life was by fuddling their wits To put nations and sects in a tangle:
> In the sky there is neither a Mosque nor a Church Nor a Temple; poor man, he will strangle:[16]

On this earth, however, he did not strangle; the mullá tried to strangle others, not only the secularists but also his theological opponents. As we have noticed, in the course of our survey, on none of the basic issues involving religion and politics, was there at any time consensus among the ulamá. Their views depended on the exigencies of the situation; theories, therefore, clashed and caused even canonical chaos. Who should rule? What sort of a person should the ruler be? How should he be chosen? What should be the pattern of government? On all these questions there was considerable divergence of views among the ulamā. Take the Qur'ānic injunction about shūrā, which is regarded, almost universally, as the basis for democratic functioning; what does it connote? An elected council, a representative legislature, or just a group of advisors. Again is the opinion of the shūrā binding or merely advisory? What was it really like in practice? Maududi has admitted, 'after the period of the "rightly guided" caliphs, the institution of shūrā disintegrated.'[17] The Qur'ānic text in this respect has been variously interpreted by different jurists to cover different situations; some of them had even extolled the virtues of sycophants for being appointed as advisers. The ulamā gave their consent to every such shūrā; their opinions were so confounding that when Jamāl al-Dīn al-Afghani was asked for his interpretation, he chose to remain silent. His disciple Abduh was one of the first Muslim divines to equate the shūrā with Western-type democracy; but Abduh's disciple Rashīd Rida differed and restricted its composition to a small group of theologians. Dr Taha Husayn, the blind scholar of Egypt, said that the shūrā stood for an unadulterated parliamentary system; while the Turkish poet, Zia Gokalp, and the Egyptian author, Mustafa Kamil, gave it the broadest base by making adult franchise its basic feature. The noted judge Ali Abd al-Raziq opined that Islam recognized complete separation of power and faith and said that all governmental institutions should be run on secular lines, without any interference by religious authorities. His views, expressed frankly and boldly in his work *al-Islam wa Usul al-Hukm* or *Islam and the Bases of Government*, created a storm in al-Azhar, where he worked. He was expelled from the university and removed from judgeship.[18] As against this, Muhammad Abd al-Wahhāb, the founder of Wahhābism, hailed the hereditary, dynastic form of government as the best and said that the shūrā should be confined to the orthodox ulamā. His teachings have inspired many leading modern fundamentalists.

*

How should an Islamic state be run? The fundamentalists have always held that it should follow the pattern of the Madinian state, which was the 'kingdom of God'; in it no changes were either necessary or justified. But even the immediate successors of the Prophet, as we have seen, made innumerable changes and resorted to several innovations. So did the other caliphs who followed them. It is an inalienable fact that they were all proud of their Islamic heritage and worked for the glory of Islam. They applied the shari'ah to their subjects after making such alterations as became necessary. None of them practised entirely what the precepts demanded of them. Most of them followed either their tribal customs or more often than not secular compulsions. In our survey this comes out vividly. Rulers, whether in the past or today, are motivated by practical considerations; their concerns are more worldly than otherworldly.

Again the classical jurists are all confused about the removal of a ruler; when and how should this be done? Even when rulers were tyrannical, lazy, indolent, impious and unfaithful to the dictates of religion, the ulama, by and large, did not suggest their removal. On the contrary, most of them advised obedience, basing their opinion on the oft-quoted saying of the Prophet: 'Obey those in authority over you.' No one has put the case as it has prevailed all through the historic process since Mu'āwiya installed himself as the king, defying all religious canons, better than the celebrated theologian, Badr al-Dīn Ibn Jama'ah (d. 1332):

> Force is the last alternative on which a government may be founded. When there is no legitimate leader present, or when none capable or competent to assume the leadership seek the leadership, and someone takes possession of the government by force, and even though there has been no election nor transmission of sovereignty to him (by any of the recognized methods), he is to be acknowledged as ruler and is entitled to obedience; and this is, indeed, to keep Muslims together and to avoid the growth of parties. It matters not if the ruler is ignorant or godless. But if one has seized the government by force, and another rises against him and conquers him, the conqueror is to be acknowledged as the rightful leader and this for the reasons already given.[19]

Ibn Taymiya, no doubt, advised the removal of a tyrannical or immoral ruler; but he prescribed no method. This is also true of his adherents who support popular revolt or rebellion. They are emboldened now due to the democratic environment obtaining in most parts of the world and time after time some of them have encouraged the masses to revolt. Incensed with the policies of Nasser, Sayyid Qutb, for instance, asked the faithful for his head and paid for saying so with his life; likewise Maududi directed his followers to revolt against Bhutto. The leaders of the Muslim Brotherhood instigated their members to assassinate Sadat; they joined the forces which ousted Nimeiry from power.

What Maududi, Qutb and their ilk, who espoused 'limited political sovereignty', failed to take into consideration is the historical development of Islam. Didn't many kings of the past behave much as certain rulers today—autocratic to their fingertips, posing as shadows of God on earth? God does not interfere in the daily affairs of man. He does not formulate policies, issues orders or execute them. He does not send criminals to jails, flog them, or amputate their hands. Given that man does everything, what guarantee is there that even if he does it in the name of God he will do it right? And who can right such a wrong and punish the wrong-doer, when the wrong-doer happens to be a mighty ruler? Ibn Taymiya gave no solution; Maududi has provided none, except spontaneous, unorganized revolt by the faithful. But such revolts can be easily suppressed unless backed by the military. That was exactly what happened when Bhutto was ousted; the army took over and the populace, once again, was left high and dry. The jurists could prescribe no constitutional or legal remedy. The fact is that except for the time-tested Western democratic method of control and removal by an elected body, the head of a state or government can rule with impunity and no religious considerations are going to make him step down. It is unfortunate but true that popular institutions have yet to take deep roots in most Muslim countries; there is no democratic functioning in most of them and the entire governmental set-up is carried on according to the whims and caprices of the army junta.

*

There are many other matters related to politics on which the fundamentalists have taken an ambivalent attitude. I shall deal with four of these, which were burning issues in the past and which are very much alive today. One, the position of non-Muslims in an Islamic state; two, the power of taxation of the state; three, the nature of punishment for certain offences mentioned in the Qur'ān; and four, the implementation or otherwise of the concept of Muslim brotherhood.

As regards the non-Muslims, most ulamā favoured discrimination against them in sharing power; but neither the Qur'ān nor the sunna support this. There is, in fact, no basis for such discrimination in temporal affairs, as ably brought out by several scholars, notably Dr K.G. Saiydain and Dr Sayyid Abdul Latif.[20] The celebrated translator of the Qur'ān into English, Marmaduke Pickthall, has rightly observed, 'Many Muslims forget that our Prophet had allies among the idolators, even after Islam had triumped in Arabia' and further, that 'he never failed to fulfil his treaty obligations towards non-Muslims'. Maududi's contention that as there were no non-Muslim advisers in the Madinian state, no Muslim can be associated with the running of an Islamic state, is a travesty of history. Despite occasional protests by some leading ulamā, Muslim rulers, by and large, adopted a liberal attitude towards their non-Muslim subjects. In fact their treatment of them was far better than what prevailed in medieval Europe; non-Muslims enjoyed religious liberties and civil rights. No less an authority than Mahmud Shaltout. Shaikh al-Azhar, has testified that non-Muslims in an Islamic state 'who live in cooperation and peace are looked upon by Islam as equal to Muslims'.[21]

The Umayyads relied more on non-Muslims than Muslims in many spheres of administration, particularly revenue and finance. This was also the case with the Abbasids and the Ottomans. Instance after instance can be quoted of non-Muslims occupying the highest positions; a typical case was of Abduh bin Sayyid, a Christian minister under the Abbasids. He went once to see a Muslim judge, who was a highly respected theologian. The latter stood up and greeted him. Some of the Muslims present objected. The judge replied, 'The Qur'ān does not forbid you to deal with those who have not fought against your religion or driven you out of your home (60:8). The Christian minister looks after the affairs of the Caliphate. He is an appointee of the caliph. To honour him is our duty.'[22] A Copt, Ibn Sagha, was the finance minister under the Ikshid rulers in Egypt. Similarly, the Fatimids were so generous towards the Jews, that a poet wrote:

> The Jews of this age have attained their highest hopes and grown
>   strong.
> Power is theirs and wealth. From them is chosen the counseller by
>   the King.
> Men of Egypt turn Jews, I advise you; The sky has turned Jew.[23]

Under all these Muslim rulers, bankers, merchants and traders, were invariably Jews; clerks and officials were mostly Christians. Non-Muslims were ministers in many states but they were even military commanders in some. There are also instances of Jews holding posts of the highest confidence at Caliphate courts. Kings chose their physicians from among Jews and Christians. It is true that several Muslim rulers did not treat their non-Muslim subjects fairly and justly; some even persecuted them and destroyed their places of worship. It is also true that they did all this in the name of Islam. But it was a part of medieval behaviour; rulers everywhere used religion for selfish ends. Mahmud of Ghazna looted the treasures of Somnath; he did not care to convert Hindus to Islam. Likewise several sultans preferred to recover the jaziya to converting non-Muslims to Islam; the latter would have resulted in financial loss to the treasury.

Again, take taxation; as I have earlier explained, the Qur'ān mentions only five taxes but even in this narrow orbit, there have been 'disputatious casuistry', each school giving its own interpretation. Even in regard to the zakāt, where the Qur'ānic injunction is clear, much confusion prevails. Hardly any Muslim ruler collected it in the manner in which the Prophet did; in fact history bristles with controversies about its mode of collection and distribution. Even now, after a lapse of fourteen hundred years, the ulamā are not unanimous about it, nor are they agreed on who should collect it or how much should be collected. Some say that it is for every Muslim to personally set aside the requisite amount for charity; others say that it should be done by the State. More disputed than the amount or means of collection is the disbursement of the zakāt. Some jurists maintain that a person is free to decide how his zakāt will be spent; others hold that the ruler is the proper authority to disburse it. In Pakistan the Shī'as strongly protested against an official zakāt law promulgated by Zia, saying that it violated their belief. He had, therefore, to exempt them. Even some of the Sunni ulamā objected to it on various grounds. The same is true of the other taxes such as the kharāj, the land tax (or, as some theologians call it, crop tax); it is much more complicated both in its levy and mode of collection than the zakāt. The jaziya was abandoned a long time ago. Modern forms of taxation, such as income and wealth tax, sales tax, property tax, are increasingly levied by Muslim countries; some of these did not exist before and none are mentioned in the Qur'ān or the hadīth.[24] Even in the past resort to such taxes, not authorized by the sharī'ah, had to be taken. For instance, in 764 the Abbasid caliph, al-Mansūr levied several such taxes to build Baghdad. He appointed the ulamā to collect them; they resisted at first but then gave in. These taxes came to be known as mūkus. In order to give them religious colouring most of these taxes pertaining to tolls, customs, tariffs, imports, excise, property, etc., were grouped under the zakāt. Mūkus were in course of time legitimized. No Muslim ruler either in the past or now has been able to dispense with such taxes in view of the increasing cost of administration; indeed they may have to devise more taxes in the future to meet new exigencies.

A similar situation obtains where the enforcement of civil and criminal law is concerned; modifications, alterations and even innovations in them had to be made to run the state. These were done by all the rulers—from Umar to the last Ottoman caliph; their actions were justified by the jurists. The ulamā, by and large, approved the new measures, though it is true that there was opposition from the hardcore fundamentalists—however, their voice, especially in medieval times, when the ruler's word was law, was neither heard nor was it effective. The Umayyads resorted to large-scale judicial innovations; fundamentalists, both Sunni and Shi'a, denounced them as heretics but their decrees later became part of Islamic jurisprudence. Likewise the Abbasids, who claimed to be the true inheritors of the Prophet, took many liberties with the implementation of the sharī'ah. Again, under the Ottomans radical changes were made to the classical approach to the sharī'ah and comprehensive reforms were introduced. Under colonialism, changes on Western lines were made, altering the whole legal system. This was quietly acquiesced to by the faithful everywhere. After independence most Muslim countries opted for reforms. Ataturk and Bourguiba went, of course, the whole hog, but other leaders though cautious were no less reformist.

In the 1950s there was a sort of Islamic resurgence, sparked off by the creation of Israel. This was regarded by the Arabs and also the Muslims everywhere as a dagger in their heart; consequently a strong anti-West feeling was generated, which, in turn, gave an impetus to Islamization. In the flush of newly acquired freedom, many Muslim countries wanted to assert their power. They were not successful on the battle fields but the oil boom helped to strengthen their international clout.

All in all Islam became a dominant factor in their politics. Some of the Arab countries were already fundamentalist in their outlook; others like Egypt, Syria and Iraq in the Arab world and Malaysia and Indonesia as far away as South-East Asia, were also shaken by the Islamic resurgence. Each one of them brought in some measure of Islamization. However, in most of these nations, the Islamization, as it turned out, was more show than substance.

Pakistan alone, under Zia, embarked on the process in right earnest. One of the first steps he took in this direction was the Hudud Ordinance, under which theft was made punishable with the amputation of hands and adultery and slander with flogging and death. Soon after its promulgation the Pakistani courts were inundated with cases alleging all kinds of atrocities against women. A Karachi court sentenced twenty-five-year-old Shahida Praveen and thirty-year-old Muhammad Sarwar to death by stoning them on the charge of adultery; but as the case dragged on, some disturbing facts were brought to light. It transpired that Shahida was legally divorced by her first husband. They had signed the relevant papers in a magistrate's court. After waiting for a ninety-day period, as required by the ordinance, she had married Muhammad Sarwar with a Lahore court confirming her status as an adult person free to marry whosoever she wished. Her first husband, after having failed in his bid to remarry, had decided to have Shahida back. He took the plea that since the divorce papers were not properly registered Shahida continued to be his wife. His plea was accepted by a Karachi court and Shahida and her second husband were convicted of adultery and sentenced to death by stoning. In another instance, twenty-four-year-old Roshan Jan moved the court for divorce, alleging physical torture by her husband. She then left her home (as required by the ordinance) and moved into a neighbour's house. Meanwhile, her husband lodged a complaint with the police, accusing her of committing adultery with the neighbour, who was married. On the basis of the complaint Roshan Jan was arrested.

Commenting on such instances, the influential Pakistani daily. *Muslim* of Islamabad said there were dozens of Muslim women kept in jail without trial and pointed out that unscrupulous men were taking full advantage of the ordinance to indulge in the sexual exploitation of women. It was also disclosed that the police often apprehended close relatives in such cases and punished them with lashes on the ground that they were accomplices. In Karachi alone, it pointed out, there were at least three cases of elderly parents who were in jail. Even the provision for bail had been misused, often by the husband, the *Muslim* reported. The paper mentioned another case, that of eighteen-year-old Parveen, married by her parents to a youth, who after his marriage found a job in the Gulf. He left his wife behind with her parents. During the husband's absence, the parents sold her to a moneylender to settle an outstanding loan. Her husband, on his return, filed a case of zina (adultery) against her and had her arrested. He then bailed her out, lived with her for a while and just as he was leaving for the Gulf again, got her bail cancelled. Parveen went back to jail.[25]

These instances are horrifying and show how the shari'ah laws, however, well-intended, are misused; in the days of the Prophet and 'rightly guided' caliphs no one dared make a false allegation or give false evidence. The standards of morality then were high; but today they have fallen so low that Muslims must, as Iqbal has said, 'reinterpret the foundational legal principles in the light of their own experience and the altered conditions of modern life'.[26]

However, instead of giving a progressive interpretation to the Qur'ānic texts, the fundamentalists insist on adhering to the outmoded views of classical jurists. One such instance is their demand for the banning of interest on investments and deposits; this is being done in Saudi Arabia; and several other Muslim countries are now experimenting with it. The high priest of the Dawoodi Bohras has called upon his followers to withdraw their deposits from banks. The fundamentalists have devised an alternative scheme of investments in trade and business and property transactions with guaranteed profit as against the bank interest, which has been done away with. But it has not produced the expected returns, which is not surprising, as it does not fit into the international monetary arrangement. Can the Muslims cut themselves off from the rest of the world and carry on their commercial and other activities with their own outmoded devices? Allama Abdullah Yusuf Ali, a highly respected commentator of the Qur'an, has opined that the 'usury' of the old times is not the same as the 'interest' of today. The one was exploitative, the other is socially productive. Each generation has to look to its own requirements; as Iqbal explained, 'The teaching of the Qur'an, that life is a process of progressive creation, necessitates that each generation guided, but unhampered, by the work of its predecessors should be permitted to solve its own problems.'[27]

As regards a universal state based on the concept of Islamic brotherhood, it ceased to exist after the fall of the Umayyads; in fact, even during their rule, cracks had begun to develop. During the Abbasid period, as we have noted, dissensions and revolts proliferated, with a new kingdom challenging the authority of the caliph emerging almost every few years. The Saljuqs slowed down the process, but rebels kept cropping up; the Muslims were more involved through all these centuries in fighting Muslims and shedding one another's blood rather than that of the non-Muslims. The Fatimids preferred to make peace with the Christian powers of Europe rather than with the Abbasids. Likewise, the Sunni Ottoman Turks left no stone unturned to destroy the Shi'a Safavids, while the Mughals in India never trusted either of them. Surprisingly, despite this disunity in the Muslim ranks on such a colossal scale, the vitality of their various ruling groups was not sapped; they not only managed to hold their own against external threats but also ruled in a manner which was far more humane and civilized than what prevailed in the rest of the world. It is a fact that Europe owes much to them, as also Asia and Africa. Political unity was, however, never the strength of Islam; it has always been the religious bond, not on the material but the spiritual plane, which has united the faithful under one brotherhood and has injected a unique dynamism in them.

There is, therefore, no basis to the bogey of Muslims ganging up against non-Muslims; it was insidiously floated by the Christians—especially after the outbreak of the Crusades. The so-called division of the world into dar-ul Islam (sphere of Islam) and dar-ul harab (sphere of war) is not mentioned in the Qur'an; nor is it found in the sunna. It is the invention of the classical jurists, which the Christians and the Jews have used to their advantage. Unfortunately, due to the increasing influence of the West on the thinking of the world since the eighteenth century other non-Muslims, particularly the Hindus and the Buddhists, easily succumbed to this view.

Our survey shows how unrealistic this assessment has been. Even today there is no ganging up among the Muslims, though efforts are made every now and again to have a common approach among the Muslim-majority states to their own and other world problems. They have not been belligerent towards the non-Muslims; nor have the Muslims tried to convert dār-ul harab into dār-ul Islam either by force or otherwise. On the contrary, their efforts have been directed solely towards settling disputes among the Muslims, except in respect of their campaign against Israel, which they regard as a dagger in the heart of Islam. There are about forty-five Muslim-majority states, which comprise nearly seventy per cent of the total Muslim population; the other thirty per cent live as minorities in non-Muslim states. There have been wars or guerrilla skirmishes between one Muslim state and another; for instance between Malaysia and Indonesia, Pakistan and Bangladesh, Egypt and Saudi Arabia, South Yemen and North Yemen, Oman and South Yemen, Libya and Chad, Libya and Moroccco, Libya and Algeria, Pakistan and Afghanistan, and the most horrible of these wars, the eight-year war between Iraq and Iran. As compared to these bloody conflicts there have been hardly any disputes, bloody or otherwise, between the Muslim and non-Muslim states, barring the Arab-Israeli and India-Pakistan wars.

Muslims have, no doubt, tried in modern times, much more actively than ever before, to unite under a single—albeit loose—political banner. After the abolition of the Caliphate by Ataturk in 1924, several congresses were organized to revive the institution; one congress followed another—from Mecca to Cairo to Jerusalem and sometimes in such remote places as Geneva, Tokyo and even Moscow.[28] But nothing came out of it; today every Muslim state guards its sovereignty jealously. None of them is prepared to shed a whit of it—the Union between Egypt and Syria was a disaster—and each one is determined to preserve its own identity, however small and economically unviable it may be. Their attitude to Muslim foreigners within their respective states is no better than that towards the non-Muslims; both are subject to the same restrictions in terms of immigration and employment. A

Saudi housing minister once told me that they preferred to employ Hindu Indians and Buddhist Koreans in their construction works to Indian and Pakistan Muslims, who waste too much time going out during working hours pretending to pray. Islam recognizes no territorial barriers between the Muslims of one land and another; all are brethren-in-faith, but Muslim states, whether Pakistan or Saudi Arabia, do not practise it.

To the chagrin of the fundamentalists, secular considerations continue to dominate the affairs of state now, as in the past, whether in the national or international spheres.

In the last two decades, summit conferences of the heads of Muslim states and governments have been held five times under the auspices of the Organization of Islamic Conference: in Rabat in 1969; in Lahore in 1974; in Mecca in 1981; in Casablanca in 1984; and in Kuwait in 1987; but they have 'never taken the form of fanaticism or bigotry'. On the contrary, as the amir of Kuwait, Shaikh Jabir al-Ahmad al-Jabir, emphasized:

> The call for Islamic solidarity has, in fact, originated from the long suffering and oppression of the Muslim peoples, and continued to proceed along with the Arab countries' independence from foreign dominance and imperialism. Even before the Arabs had accepted to proceed gradually towards unity, through the establishment of the Arab League, the Islamic people and countries were struggling to liberate themselves from imperialism in order to formulate a non-fanatic religious bloc representative of such Islamic cohesion, co-operation, tolerance and solidarity as may give humanity an example of how people should observe their duties and obligations.[28]

This is as secular an approach as there can be; it has been applauded by the secretary-general of the United Nations, Perez de Cuellar. True, the appeal for Islamic brotherhood does not fail to strike a chord in the heart of a Muslim—more so now than before. The Western onslaught on his religion, culture and social mores has awakened in him a new spirit of self-preservation and a pride in his historical past. There may be a tinge of fundamentalism in this, but certainly no desire to establish a theocratic order.

Fundamentalists do cause some disturbances here and there; but they have not succeeded, as we have seen, in taking over power and moulding the world in their own image. Even the Khomeini revolution in recent years has produced more frustration than fulfilment among the Shi'a Iranians. In the rest of the Muslim world secularists are on the move, directly or indirectly, openly or surreptitiously; the fundamentalists cannot defeat them. Their thinking is outdated; their outlook is unrealistic. Piety is, no doubt, important in the life of an individual; but on it alone 'collectivity'—a term wisely used by Imam Shafi, to connote a nation—cannot be built.

Prof. Ziauddin Sardar of King Abdul Aziz University of Jeddah has described in a somewhat picturesque manner the negative role of the fundamentalists:

> By emphasizing the precision in the mechanics of prayer and ablution, length of beard and mode of dress, they have lost sight of individual freedom, the dynamic nature of many Islamic injunctions, and the creativity and innovation that Islam fosters within its framework. They have founded intolerant, compulsive and tyrannical orders and have provided political legitimacy to despotic and nepotistic systems of government. They have closed and constricted many enquiring minds by their insistence on unobjective parallels, unending quibbles over semantics. They have divorced themselves from human needs and conditions. No wonder then that the majority of Muslims today pay little attention to them and even foster open hostility towards them.[30]

In their muddled zeal the modern fundamentalists forget that it was not Hasan al-Banna, Maududi, and Sayyid Qutb who freed the Muslims from colonial exploitation and gave them a better and more secure future, but Ataturk, who despite his heresies, saved Turkey from the clutches of European power; Jinnah, a non-practising Muslim, who single-handedly created the most powerful Muslim state in the world; Nasser, who liberated the Arabs from the foreign yoke and gave them new strength and hope; Sukarno, who brought freedom to more Muslims than any other leader and united the Indonesians under one banner; Tenku Abdul Rahman, who breathed new life into the Malaysian Muslims and made them a force in South-East Asia;

Mujibur Rahman, an avowed secularist who founded the second biggest Muslim state (Bangladesh) in the world; Qaddafi, whom the fundamentalists disown, but who challenged the might of America in North Africa; Boumedienne, who fought the imperialists and provided a socialist system to their people. These and many more in the secular mould were the real builders of modern Islam. Without them the Muslims would not have breathed the fresh air of liberty and equality; without them they would not have been able to hold their heads high in the comity of nations; without them they would have continued to be hewers of wood and drawers of water. These leaders might not have been pious and puritancial, orthodox and traditional; some of them might not have offered their prayers regularly; most of them did not fit into the straitjacket of scholastic theology; but they all brought Muslims out of the sloughs of despondency and despair and made them once again a power to reckon with. Like the achievements of their predecessors in the remote past—the Umayyads and the Abbasids, the Ottomans and the Mughals, the Fatimids and the Safavids—the contribution of the present Muslim rulers has also, by and large, been decried by the fundamentalists; but the fact remains that despite their lapses and faults they have taken Islam ahead and by their secular outlook ensured the future of nearly a billion Muslims all over the world.

In the poetic words of Iqbal:

What's a nation? How to lead?
Poor mullá! That's beyond his creed.[31]

Appendices

Appendix I
WHO IS A MUSLIM?

A Muslim is one who declares publicly: 'There is no God but God and Muhammad is His Prophet.' He must also accept that Muhammad is the last of God's prophets on this earth. This is the first pillar of Islam. The other four are that a Muslim must:

1. Pray five times a day, either at home, in a mosque or any other place, in a prescribed manner, at dawn, noon, afternoon, evening and night; the Shi'as reduce it to three times.
2. Fast every day during the whole month of Ramadān from dawn to sunset without drinking or eating.
3. Give zakāt or alms to the poor and the needy out of his earnings and wealth.
4. Perform hajj, or pilgrimage to Mecca to circumambulate the Ka'ba or the House of God, at least once in his lifetime, provided he can afford it.

In case a Muslim fails to fulfil any of these obligations he does not go out of the pale of Islam but becomes a sinner, punishable on the Day of Judgement. A Muslim must also accept the Qur'ān as the word of God, immutable and unalterable; it contains guidelines which a Muslim must follow. Its main emphasis is on the unity of God and 'amalus-saleh' or good deeds; it recognizes other prophets before Muhammad and states that there is no people to whom God has not shown the right path. In Islam there is no priesthood; no one is high or low. (The Shi'as, however, recognize priesthood.) In the eyes of God all are equal, except that those who are pious and who tread the right path are more meritorious. A Muslim is accountable for his deeds or misdeeds only to Allah on the Day of Judgement. If he has performed even a single good deed on this earth Allah may forgive him all his sins, for Allah is Most Beneficent and All Merciful.

Theologians have complicated the definition of a Muslim with various rules on how he should bathe, shave, keep his beard, trim his moustache, clean his nostrils, wash his private parts, dress, talk, walk and sleep; to them Ghazâli, who is universally acknowledged as hujjat-al-Islâm or 'proof of Islam', has replied in his *Faysal al-Tafriqa* thus:

Among the most extreme and extravagant of men are a group of scholastic theologians who dismiss the Muslim common people as unbelievers and claim that whoever does not know scholastic theology in the form they recognize and does not know the prescriptions of the Holy Law according to the proofs which they have adduced is an unbeliever.

These people have constricted the vast mercy of God to His servants and made paradise the preserve of a small clique of theologians. They have disregarded what is handed down by the sunna, for it is clear that in the time of the Prophet, may God bless and save him, and in the time of the Companions of the Prophet, may God be pleased with them, the Islam of whole groups of rude Arabs was recognized, though they were busy worshipping idols. They did not concern themselves with the science of analogical proof and would have understood nothing of it if they had.

Whoever claims that theology, abstract proof, and systematic classifications are the foundation of belief is an innovator. Rather is belief a light which God bestows on the hearts of His creatures as the gift and bounty from Him, sometimes through an explainable conviction from within, sometimes because of a dream in sleep, sometimes by seeing the state of bliss of a pious man and the transmission of his light through association and conversation with him, sometimes through one's own state of bliss.

THE SUNNIS

The Sunnis are Muslims, who (unlike the Shi'as) accept all the four immediate successors of the Prophet as the 'rightly guided' caliphs. They make no distinction between his son-in-law Ali, the fourth caliph and the earlier three caliphs. Nor do they believe that the succession had necessarily to pass to the family of the Prophet. They accept ijmā, or the consensus of the learned of the community, as the test of succession. They also do not believe in the infallibility of the leader, namely the caliph or imam. The leader is liable to err and is as much subject to the law as are his followers.

The Sunnis constitute more than ninety per cent of all Muslims and have no sects. They are broadly divided into four madhhahib or schools which provide guidelines in the performance of obligatory duties and rites. There is no conflict between the schools; they coexist and respect the rules and practices of each other. They came into existence within 200 years of the Prophet's death and exercised a decisive influence in the evolution of Islamic jurisprudence. The works of the founders of these schools form the major corpus of all Sunni laws and regulations. The four schools were founded by the four great imams and are known after their founders.

Hanafis (founded by Abu Hanifa: 699–767)
This school lays emphasis on qiyās (analogy) and istihsān (equity) and is the most popular of the four schools. Adherents are found mostly in India, Pakistan, Bangladesh, Egypt, Syria, Lebanon, Afghanistan, Turkey, Iraq, Jordan, Sudan, Libya and in the Asian Republics of the

USSR. The Chinese Muslims also belong to this school. Their imam is known as 'Imam Aazam', or the greatest imam.

The school was given official recognition by the Abbasids and the Mughals in India. The most important compilation of Hanafi fatwās is 'Fatwā-i-Alamgiriya' prepared during the reign of Aurangazéb.

Mālikis (founded by Mālik-ibn Anas: 715–95)

This school gives equal importance to 'masalahatal mursalah' or public interest, qiyās (analogy) and istihsān (equity). Followers accept local customs and traditions with Islamic tenets and practices. They predominate in North Africa, the Gulf shaikhdoms, and several African states south of the Sahara.

Shāfiis (founded by Muhammad Ibn Idris al-Shāfi'i: 767–820)

This school strikes a balance between reason and authority and consequently promotes a system of jurisprudence which combines dogmatism with practical requirements. The Muslim scholars and jurists revere Shāfi'i for his wisdom and adherence to the rules of the shari'ah. He is regarded as the restorer of the faith. The Shāfi'is are found in Egypt: al-Azhar has been under their influence for centuries. They are also found in parts of India, Pakistan and Bangladesh and in large numbers in Malaysia and Indonesia.

Hanbalis (founded by Ahmad Ibn Hanbal: 780–855)

This school stresses the puritanical aspects of Islam and is uncompromising in its adherence to orthodoxy. Its followers go by the letter of the Qur'ān and assert that theological truths cannot be reached by aql or reasoning; they are the forerunners of Wahhābism, which condemns any kind of innovation in or deviation from scriptural dogmas and Qur'ānic injunctions. They are found mostly in Saudi Arabia and both parts of Yemen.

Appendix III

THE SHĪ'AS

These Muslims believe that Ali, because of his filial link with the Prophet through Fātima, his only surviving child, was the rightful successor appointed by the Prophet himself—a few weeks before his death. They reject the succession of the first three caliphs, Abū Bakr, Umar and Uthmān, whom they regard as usurpers. For them Ali is the real walī or imam endowed with divine powers, which could only be bestowed on the progeny of the Prophet. Ali and his sons and their sons and guardians (who constitute the Imamate) were blessed with divine dispensation and hence were without blemish or capacity to sin. After Ali, the Shī'as believe that the Imamate went to his eldest son, Hasan, and after Hasan to his younger brother Husayn whose martyrdom at Karbalā is the central creed of Shī'ism. After the two brothers, Husayn's direct progeny succeeded to the Imamate and then it split into three schisms. The first took place on the death of Zayn al-Ābidīn, the son of Husayn, when a section which opted for Zayn al-Ābidīn's son, Zaid, broke away and described themselves as Zaidis. They are not very numerous and are largely confined to the Caspian area of Persia, Yemen, Syria and the Lebanon. The second sect arose on the death of Ja'far al-Sādiq when, instead of his eldest son, Ismā'il, Sādiq nominated his second son Musa as successor. A section refused to accept Musā as the imam and gave their allegiance to Ismā'il; they are known as the Sabiyah, i.e., Seveners (Ismā'il being the seventh imam) or Ismā'ilis. The Iṣmā'ili Caliphate of Tunisia (founded in 909) and Fatimid Caliphate of Egypt (founded in 969) belonged to this sect, and declared each of their kings as imams. With the death of al-Mustansir (1094), the eighth Fatimid caliph, the Ismā'ilis became divided. The younger son al-Mustali became the Fatimid caliph in 1095 and the elder son al-Nizar was imprisoned. A group of Ismā'ilis in the Abbasid territory refused to accept the Imamate of al-Mustali and took Nizar's son to one of their mountain fortresses, named Alamut. Thus they became known as 'Nizaris'. When the Mongols destroyed their stronghold, they moved to Persia. In 1817, one of the Qājār Shahs of Persia gave their imam the title 'Agha Khan'. Nizari da'is succeeded in converting a considerable number of Hindus in India to their sect and the imam moved to India in the nineteenth century. They are called 'Khojas'.

The line of Mustali imams ended in 1130 with the death of al-Amir, son of Mustali. The Fatimid caliphs who succeeded to the Imamate, not being in the direct line of succession, were not recognized as imams. After the end of the Fatimid Caliphate in 1171, the leadership of the sect passed to the da'is in Yemen, who converted a number of Hindus in Gujarat and West India. These Muslims are called 'Bohras'.

The overwhelming majority of Shi'as acknowledge Mūsā as the rightful imam. He was succeeded by five more imams, until the last, Abul Qasim Muhammad al-Mahdi (who was persecuted by the Abbasids), disappeared in a well. Muhammad is regarded as the twelfth imam and is believed to be alive and biding his time to reappear. His followers are known as Ithna 'Ashariyah or the Twelvers. They are found mainly in Iran, Pakistan, India, Bangladesh, Iraq, Saudi Arabia, Bahrain, and a part of Central Asia. The two Isma'ili sects are concentrated in parts of Africa, Pakistan, Bangladesh, Afghanistan, and the Tajik republic of the USSR.

The major role in evolving a Shi'a system of jurisprudence was played by Imam Muhammad Baqir (677–733) and Imam Ja'far al-Sādiq (702–65). The tree on the next page shows the hereditary succession of the imams and the divisions among their followers:

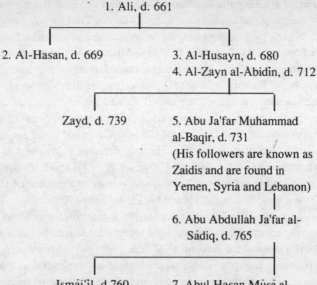

1. Ali, d. 661

2. Al-Hasan, d. 669

3. Al-Husayn, d. 680
4. Al-Zayn al-Abidin, d. 712

Zayd, d. 739

5. Abu Ja'far Muhammad al-Baqir, d. 731
(His followers are known as Zaidis and are found in Yemen, Syria and Lebanon)

6. Abu Abdullah Ja'far al-Sādiq, d. 765

Ismāi'il, d.760
(His followers are called Ismāi'ilis or Seveners. According to them Ismāi'il was the seventh imam, being the eldest son of his father Ja'far al-Sādiq.)

7. Abul Hasan Mūsā al-Kazim, d.799
8. Abul Hasan Ali al-Rida, d. 818
9. Abu Jafar Muhammad al-Taqi, d. 835
10. Abul Hasan Ali al-Naqi (al-Hadi), d. 868
11. Abu Muhammad Hasan al-Askari, d. 874
12. Abul Qasim Muhammad al-Mahdi (Muntazzar), d. 878 (disappeared to reappear on the Day of Judgement.)
(The followers of these twelve imams known as Ithna 'Ashariyah or Twelvers, constitute the overwhelming majority of Shi'as throughout the world.)

BASIS OF THE SHARĪ'AH

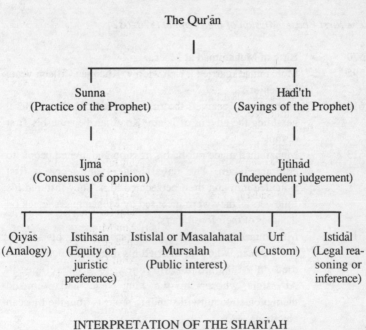

The Qur'ān

Sunna
(Practice of the Prophet)

Hadī'th
(Sayings of the Prophet)

Ijmā
(Consensus of opinion)

Ijtihād
(Independent judgement)

Qiyās
(Analogy)

Istihsān
(Equity or
juristic
preference)

Istislal or Masalahatal
Mursalah
(Public interest)

Urf
(Custom)

Istidāl
(Legal rea-
soning or
inference)

INTERPRETATION OF THE SHARĪ'AH

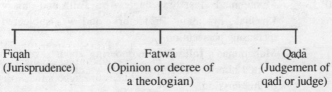

Fiqah
(Jurisprudence)

Fatwā
(Opinion or decree of
a theologian)

Qadā
(Judgement of
qadi or judge)

Appendix V

CHRONOLOGICAL HISTORY

The First Phase: Mission of the Prophet (570–632)

570	Birth of Muhammad at Mecca.
595	Muhammad married a rich widow, Khadijah, fifteen years his senior.
610	Muhammad received the first revelation at Mount Hera, heralding the advent of Islam. Khadijah became his first disciple.
613	Muhammad made public his mission and invited people to embrace Islam. The tribal leaders of Mecca at first ridiculed him and then persecuted him. They tortured his followers as they were incensed by Muhammad's attack on the gods of their forefathers.
615	Muhammad advised his followers, including his son-in-law Uthman, who had married his daughter Ruqaiya (she died in Muhammad's lifetime), to seek refuge in Abyssinia, whose Christian king Negus had promised them protection notwithstanding protests from the Meccan chieftains.
620	Muhammad lost his uncle Abu Talib and his wife Khadijah, his main 'Protectors', and was subjected to increasing persecution.
621	Muhammad's followers, numbering about seventy-two, invited him to Yathrib, latter known as Madina, to carry on his mission.

622   Muhammad, accompanied by his close companion, Abū Bakr, migrated to Madīna and assumed the leadership of the city. This year marks the commencement of the Islamic calendar.

623   The Prophet promulgated a charter which guaranteed to every inhabitant, whether Christian, Jew or pagan, equality of status and treatment, civil liberty and religious freedom. This charter, which later came to be known as the 'Constitution of Madīna', fostered unity among the different religious communities and eliminated general feuding and blood vengeance. This enabled the city to withstand external attack. The charter decreed that in an attack on Muslims alone, the non-Muslim populace of Madīna need not participate but would have to pay a sum known as jaziya towards the cost of the war.

624   Muhammad and his followers were attacked by Meccan tribal leaders; a fierce battle took place at Badr, in which victory reinforced faith in the new religion.

625   The Meccan chieftains defeated Muhammad and his followers in the battle at Uhud, but failed to uproot the Muslims from Madīna. Muhammad expelled a number of Jews and executed others for conspiring with the enemy.

627   The Meccans besieged Madīna in the campaign of al-Khandaq or the Ditch. The sudden onset of a furious storm and driving sand forced the Meccans to retreat, which gave Muhammad much needed respite.

628   The Muslims embarked on a peaceful pilgrimage to Mecca to perform umra, a secondary pilgrimage to hajj. The tribal leaders, however, prevented them from entering the city; subsequent negotiations led to the Treaty of Hudaybiah which permitted Muslims to make the hajj pilgrimage the following year and thereafter. The treaty was to last for ten years.

629   The Meccans breached the treaty and Muhammad attacked Mecca with ten thousand followers. Abu Sufyan, the leader of the Meccans, surrendered and converted to Islam; the rest of the Meccans followed suit. Muhammad entered Mecca and occupied the Ka'ba, the house of God. He

destroyed idols to underpin the Islamic tenet of monotheism.

631   The neighbouring areas of Taif and Yemen pledged their loyalty to Islam.

632   Muhammad's 'farewell' hajj during which he urged his followers to remain united. He died after his return to Madina and was buried in the Masjid al-Nabawi, the first mosque that Muhammad himself had built and which is today the second holiest shrine in Islam, next only to the Ka'ba.

The Second Phase: The Rightly Guided Caliphs (632–61)

632–34   Abū Bakr was elected by the congregation at Saqifa Banù Sā'ida as the successor to the Prophet—the first caliph. Immediately he set about consolidating the hold of Islam. The rebellious Bedouins were ruthlessly suppressed. Syria was conquered by his commander Osama and southern Mesopotamia by his other two commanders Khālid bin Walid and Muthanna. During his short rule, the caliph brought the whole of Arabia under the banner of Islam. Before his death he nominated Umar as his successor.

634–44   The caliphate of Umar is the brightest period in the annals of Islam. During his reign the writ of the caliphate ran to parts of the Fertile Crescent, including Iraq, Syria and the Gulf regions, Palestine, Egypt, the greater part of Iran, Tabristan, Azerbaijan and Armenia. He developed a strong administrative and military base, a sound financial system and a competent buraucracy. Umar organized the majlis as-shura which deliberated on matters of policy and guided him in their implementation. He was the first to assume the title of Amir al-Muminin, or the Commander of the Faithful. He was assassinated by a disgruntled Iranian slave in 644. He left behind a powerful edifice of Muslim solidarity.

644–56   Uthmān became the third caliph. He belonged to the House of Umayya. He continued Islam's march eastward into Iran and westward into Egypt. Success brought much wealth and privileges to the leading Muslims, which in turn created internal squabbles and jealousies. Uthmān was unable to control the mounting discontent and as a result fitna, or civil war broke out. Uthmān was ambushed in his house and murdered. His greatest contribution was to codify the text of the Qur'ān and to make it available in a uniform edition throughout the Caliphate.

656–61 Ali, the Prophet's son-in-law, was the fourth caliph at Madīna. Mu'āwiya, who was then the governor of Syria, dissented and accused Ali of complicity in the murder of his kinsman Uthmān. To suppress the rebellion, Ali abandoned Madīna as the capital and established his headquarters at Kufa in Iraq. Following the Battle of the Camel (656) and the Battle of Siffīn (657), Mu'āwiya sought arbitration on the basis of the Qur'ān. Ali accepted the offer in good faith but some of Ali's followers revolted against his acceptance, calling it a betrayal of the faith. These dissenters came to be known as khawārij and one of them assassinated Ali while he was praying in a mosque. Ali's murder led to the birth of Shī'ism, a section of Muslims who regard him as the rightful successor to the Prophet in view of his filial connections.

The Third Phase: The Umayyads (661–750)

661–80 In the confused aftermath of Ali's rule, Mu'āwiya proclaimed himself the caliph. He shifted the capital to Damascus and persuaded Ali's elder son Hasan to renounce his claim to the Caliphate in his favour. Mu'āwiya embarked on a series of conquests to buttress his position. He organized a powerful fleet in the Mediterranean, the first naval force in Islam and extended the empire to North Africa on one side and eastern Afghanistan on the other. He suppressed internal dissension. Before his death he nominated his son Yazīd as his successor and obtained the approval of the tribal chieftains. Thus began the hereditary rule of his family, Banu Ummaya or the House of Umayya—hence the name Umayyads for the caliphs from this family.

680–83   Yazid ambushed and killed the grandson of the Prophet and the second son of Ali, Husayn, and his family members at Karbalā, sixty-two miles from Baghdad. Husayn's head was severed from his body and sent to Yazid. Husayn's martyrdom deepened the division between the Sunnis, the overwhelming majority of Muslims who accept the legitimacy of the first four caliphs, and the Shi'ites, who regard the first three caliphs as usurpers and only Ali as the legitimate successor to the Prophet.

683–85   Yazid's son and successor Mu'āwiya II, encountered deep hostility from the Companions of the Prophet and the Muslims at large because of the cruelties perpetrated by his father against members of the Prophet's family. Despite his effort at conciliation, he was forced to abdicate after three months. Marwan bin al-Hakam, a court dignitary, became the caliph in 684. Meanwhile, Ibn Zubayr, a rebel leader, captured Madina and Mecca and also proclaimed himself the caliph.

685–705   On Marwan's death his son Abd al-Malik succeeded to the Caliphate at Damascus. Civil war broke out. Mukhtār Thaqfi and his men captured Kufa and declared Ali's son, Muhammad Ibn al-Hanafiya, the caliph. Hence there were three caliphs in Islam at this time. Eventually, however, Abd al-Malik and the Umayyads regained control. To restore his image, Abd al-Malik constructed the famous Dome of the Rock, Masjid al-Aqsa, on the site of the start of the Prophet's nocturnal journey to the heavens. Muslims revere this mosque as the third holiest shrine, after Ka'ba in Mecca and the Mosque of the Prophet, Masjid al-Nabawi, in Madina. Abd al-Malik was the first caliph to introduce Islamic/Arab coinage. He established the official mint in Damascus. The coinage were dinar (gold), dirham (silver) and fils (copper). He made Arabic the official language of the Islamic empire.

705–15   Abd al-Malik was succeeded by his son, Walid, who continued the policy of expansionism. One of his generals
Qutayba conquered Transoxiana and subjugated the whole
of Central Asia. Another general Tāriq landed in Spain
near the mountain, which was to bear his name Jabal al-
Tāriq (hence Gibraltar). He conquered Spain in 711 and
thereafter annexed Portugal. Another general Mūsā crossed
into France but the caliph stopped him from advancing
further and ordered him instead to repulse the Christian
counter-attack in Spain. Another general, Muhammad bin
Qāsim, launched a successful expedition in 710 of six
thousand Syrian horses and an equal number of Iraqi
camels against the rajas of Sind. Muslim rule was now
established from Sind to Multan in Punjab. Sicily was
also invaded during this period. Walid was a good but
despotic administrator. He patronized all forms of arts,
including literature and architecture, and encouraged industrial development.

715–50   On Walid's death, his brother Sulaymān succeeded to the
Caliphate; after him, his cousin Umar bin Abd al-Aziz
became the ruler. The Muslims hail him as the fifth
'rightly guided' caliph because of his piety, goodness and
adherence to the rules of the shari'ah. The ruling elite,
however, resented his pious administration and had him
murdered. His successor and cousin Yazid II lived a life of
ease and comfort and reversed his predecessor's ordinances.
The orthodox were aghast, and rebelled against him. Yazid
II died in 724 and was succeeded by Hisham, who made
court officials responsive to public requirements.

His successor, Walid-II, who ascended the throne in
743, was ease-loving, indolent and lazy; the people led by
Abu Muslim, an ally of Banu Abbas, and the leaders of
disgruntled Iranians, rebelled against him. In a series of
skirmishes the Umayyads were finally routed at Zab and
the last of their line, Marwan II was killed. Thus ended in
750 the dynastic rule of the Umayyads.

756   Al-Saffah, the founder of the next dynasty, which
belonged to Abbās, uncle of the Prophet (hence the

nomenclature Abbasids) took full revenge for the atrocities committed by the Umayyads on the family of the Prophet. The only Umayyads who survived the bloody massacre was Abd al-Rahman, grandson of Hisham, who escaped to North Africa and later laid the foundation of Umayyad rule in Spain.

The Fourth Phase: The Abbasids and other Kingdoms (750–1055)

750–54   The Abbasids came to the throne in the wake of a popular uprising to restore the purity of the faith. On assuming power al-Saffah struck the first blow at the Syrians and gave importance to the Iraqis, who had stood by the family of the Prophet. He also favoured the Iranians, who had supported the rebellion. However, he could not hold the empire together; there were several revolts, most notably in Spain, where an Umayyad challenged the authority of the caliph while West Africa claimed near autonomous status. Undeterred by these developments al-Saffah and his successors concentrated on consolidating their hold over the remaining dominions under their control and providing to the faithful a better administration than that of the Umayyads. As a French historian has observed, 'The reign of the first Abbasids was the era of the greatest splendour of the Eastern Saracens. The age of conquest had passed; that of civilization had commenced.'

754–55   After al-Saffah's death, his brother Abu Ja'far, better known as al-Mansur or Mansur, became the caliph; during his long rule he laid the foundation of the Abbasid power and brought the State and the religion closer to each other. He undertook various measures in the public interest, which the other caliphs continued. He constructed a new capital, and called it Baghdad.

Mansur faced a revolt by Muhammad, popularly known as al-Nafsal Zakiyah, 'the pure soul'—a great-grandson of Hasan, the elder son of Ali—who was proclaimed by both the Sunnis and the Shi'as in Madina as the rightful caliph.

Mansür contested it on the ground that the Prophet's daughter's children were not entitled to his inheritance; it could devolve only on the descendants of his paternal uncle, Abbäs. In a battle between two unequal forces, Muhammad was killed. Mansür wreaked vengeance on the Shi'ites.

Imam Ja'far al-Sädiq, one of the most venerated spiritual leaders of the Shi'as, was threatened with death. Imam Malik was publicly flogged and Imam Abu Hanifa was imprisoned. Mansür also stopped the practice of one brother succeeding another brother to the throne and nominated his son, Muhammad, with the title of al-Mahdi, as his successor.

Imam Ja'far al-Sädiq did not nominate his eldest son Ismä'il and instead appointed his other son, Müsä, surnamed al-Kazim, as his spiritual successor. Some of his followers, however, refused to accept Müsä. They opted for Habib, the son of Ismä'il, as their imam. Thus began the Ismä'ili sect.

Literature and the arts flourished during the reign of Mansür. Imam Malik compiled the *Muwatta*; Ibn Ishäq wrote *Maghazi* and Ibn al-Muqaffa translated the Sanskrit book *Panchatantra* into Arabic under the title, *Kalilah wa Dimhan*.

754–75   During the last and declining phase of the Umayyad dynasty and the ascendant phase of the Abbasids, Spain was ruled by governors who were frequently changed. Abd al-Rahman Mu'äwiya, grandson of Umayyad Caliph Hisham, who had taken refuge in North Africa, contacted his Umayyad kinsmen in Spain, and entered it in August 755. In May 756 he defeated the governor, Yüsuf al-Fahri, who had acted as an independent ruler, paying only nominal allegiance to the Umayyad caliphs. Abd al-Rahman made Cordova the seat of his government and adopted the title 'amir'.

755–86   In the Abbasid capital of Baghdad, Mansür was succeeded by his son al-Mahdi. He suppressed the rebellion in Khurasan, led by Häshim bin Hakim (al-Muqanna), who had posed as 'the veiled prophet'. Mahdi was succeeded by his son Mūsā, with the title al-Hadi. Al-Hadi was ill suited for the task and was replaced by his brother, the famous Harūn al-Rashīd. Harūn became the undisputed caliph in 786.

786–809   Harūn ushered in an era of glory and magnificence unparalleled in the history of Islam. He defeated the Romans and swept over the whole of Asia Minor. (During his regime Idrīs ibn Abdullah, great grandson of Hasan, founded the Idrisid dynasty in North Africa in 788. It was the first Shī'ite dynasty. Its capital was Fez in Morocco.)

Harūn's chief qadi, Abu Yūsuf, a disciple of Imam Abu Hanīfa, systematized the Hanafī school of jurisprudence. This became the standard work for the majority of Sunni Muslims. A number of scientific works from different parts of the world were translated into Arabic. Harūn founded the Bait al-Hikmah or the 'House of Wisdom' and the Dār al-Tarjima or the 'Department of Translation'. His wife Zubayda played a notable part in the affairs of the Caliphate.

In Spain, Abd al-Rahman I, who built the Great Mosque at Cordova, died in September 788 and was succeeded by his second son Hisham (788–96), whose accession provoked a dynastic war. His son al-Hakam (796–822) who succeeded him also had to face a long period of trouble.

809–33   In Baghdad civil war broke out on Harūn's death. The contestants were Harūn's two sons, Ma'mūn and Amīn; ultimately Ma'mūn won and took over the caliphate. Ma'mūn was a munificent patron of the arts and science. He developed the Bait al-Hikmah or the 'House of Wisdom' and brought foreign intellectual treasures to be translated into Arabic. He patronized Ya'qūb al-Kindi, who introduced Aristotelian and neo-Platonic philosophy to the Arabs; likewise he encouraged the study of mathematics and astronomy. During his rule, the telescope was invented by Abu'l Hasan, who calculated the size of the earth. Ma'mūn also established an observatory at Shamsiyah. The works of Euclid and Ptolemy were translated. Impressed by the Mutazillite doctrine about the creation of the Qur'ân, he gave them his full backing and persecuted those who did not adhere to the doctrine. This was the first and only inquisition in Islam. Imam Hanbāl was chained and paraded in the streets of Baghdad for refusing to comply with it. Ma'mūn failed to hold Khūrasan, which became independent under Tāhir ibn al-Husayn, who founded the Tahirid dynasty in 821 with his capital at Nishapur. It lasted till 873.

In Spain the Umayyad ruler al-Hakam I died in 822 and his son Abd al-Rahman II succeeded him (822–52). He restored political calm and peace in the state. His rule is noted for intellectual revival and glory. He reorganized the administrative set-up on the same lines as those of the Abbasids. He encouraged music and art. His patronage was so proverbial that the most noted exponent of music, Ziryab, came from Baghdad to his court.

833–42   After Ma'mūn, his brother Mu'tasim became the caliph. He succeeded in supressing the Jat rebellion. The Jats had come in swarms from India and settled in Basra and Wasit.

842–70   Mu'tasim was succeeded by Wāthiq, who was the last of the great Abbasids; he delegated his powers to a corps of slaves, largely Turks, who came from Transoxiana. They played a predominant part in the Caliphate and grew so powerful that the caliphs became puppets in their hands. They murdered the next caliph, Mutawakkil (847–61) and made and unmade caliphs thereafter. Their intrigues led to the disruption of the Caliphate. Governors of districts and provinces became independent and founded their own dynastic kingdoms. For instance, the Saffarids (867–908) in Seistan, which is a part of Iran today; the Samanids (874–99) in the valley of the Oxus under whom Bukhara and Samarqand became great centres of arts and culture; and the Ghaznavids (962–1186) in parts of Afghanistan and Iran. Likewise in Africa, first the Tulunids (868–905) and then the Fatimids (969–1171) created their own powerful empires: the Fatimids with their capital at Cairo became almost a rival to the Abbasids in every respect— militarily, administratively and culturally.

842–70   In Spain the fourth Umayyad monarch Abd al-Rahman II died in 852 and was succeeded by his son Muhammad I (852–86), under whom there were several uprisings in different parts of the country.

870–932   During the Caliphate of al-Mutamid (870–92) the negro slaves from Zanzibar revolted under the leadership of Ali ibn Muhammad, who claimed to be the mahdi. They could not be easily suppressed. According to Noldeke, it was 'one of the bloodiest and most destructive rebellions which the history of western Asia records'. Taking advantage of the unrest and decline in the Caliphate's power, many petty dynasties began to surface in different parts of the Caliphate.

In 891 the Carmathians with their revolutionary zeal, bordering on some sort of 'communism', founded an independent state on the western shores of the Gulf with al-Asha as the capital. They conducted raids on their neighbours and even sacked the Ka'ba and stole the black stone.

In 929 another dynasty came into existence in north Mesopotamia; it was known as the Hamadanids. They were Shi'ites. The philosopher Farabi and the poet Mutanabbi flourished in their court.

In Spain Muhammad I suppressed the uprisings against the kingdom. He was succeeded by al-Mundhir (886–88) and Abdullah (888–912) but neither of them was able to check the disgruntled elements, who had become troublesome. However, when Abd al-Rahman III (912–61) succeeded to the throne, he brought order out of chaos and put Spain, once again, on the path of progress.

932–46   In Baghdad, after the murder of Muqtadir at the hands of his own soldiers, Qahir (932–4) became the caliph; and he was soon deposed, blinded and made to beg in the streets. He was succeeded by Radi (934–40). His rule was also full of unrest. Taking advantage of the unsettled conditions a Turk, Muhammad Ibn Tughj, founded the Ikshidid dynasty in Egypt in 935; they later subjugated Palestine and took over Mecca and Madina. Their rule lasted till 969. The Abbyssinian slave Kafur was the real power behind the throne. Radi was succeeded by Muttaqi (940–44) and the Abbasid Caliphate continued to languish.

946–1055   Mustakfi (944–6) succeeded Muttaqi. He welcomed the arrival of the Shi'ite general Ahmad Ibn Buwayhia from Iran to Baghdad, made him amir al-umra or commander-in-chief and handed over all powers to him. He and his descendants became the real rulers at Baghdad and established in the heart of Sunnism, the greatest Shi'ite power base. The Abbasids were nominally on the throne but the Buwayhids controlled everything from 1035 to 1194. During this period (1001–24) the Ghaznavid ruler Mahmud (999–1030) raided India several times and annexed Punjab with its capital Lahore to his dominion. He also wrested Iraq from the Buwayhids. His dynasty lasted till 1186; the Arab traveller al-Biruni flourished in his court. In 1037 Tughril founded the Slujug dynasty, which played a most important role in the affairs of the caliphate.

In Spain after the death of Abd al-Rahman III his son al-Hakam II (961–76) succeeded him. He was as enlightened a ruler as his father. However, he was followed by one weak ruler after another. Finally in 1031 the dynasty collapsed and an era of 'Party Kingdom' (Mulk al-Tawaif) began in Spain.

The Fifth Phase: The Seljuqs (1055–1260)

1055–1194   The Seljuqs were Turks who came from Turkistan. They conquered Khurasan, Marv and Naysabur; their general Tughril Beg marched to Baghdad with his Turkoman tribes and was welcomed by the Abbasid caliph Qaim as their deliverer from the Buwayhids. He hailed Tughril Beg as 'the king of the East and the West' and bestowed on him the title of sultan. Tughril Beg (1037–63) was succeeded by Alp Arslan (1063–72) and then by his son Malikshah (1072–92). They extended their conquests in all directions, humbled the turbulent Shī'as and restored the supremacy of the Abbasid Caliphate. Their prime minister, Nizam al-Mulk Ṭūsi, was a distinguished scholar and able administrator. He reorganized the administrative set-up in such a way that while the Seljuqs acted as de facto rulers the Abbasid caliphs were respected as de jure rulers. His death at the hands of an assassin, a disciple of Hasan-i-Sabbāh, the 'Old Man of the Mountain' and founder of organized terrorism in Islam, gave a fatal blow to Seljuq domination which had already begun to weaken due to internal dissension. This was the worst period of the Caliphate, when the Crusaders had brought their armies to their knees in Syria and Palestine.

In Ghazna, after Mahmud's death, the throne was seized by a rival Turkish tribe led by Muhammad of Ghur and his able lieutenant Qutubuddin Aibak. Their forces raided India in 1175, destroyed the Ghaznavid garrison at Peshawar, captured Lahore in 1186 and Delhi in 1193 and founded their own dynastic rule.

The Seljuq power had, meanwhile, collapsed and on its ruins the local Turkish leaders had founded several petty kingdoms: the Zengids in northern Mesopotamia and Syria, the Ortoqids in the mountains and valleys of the upper Euphrates, and Khwarazmshah in north-eastern Iran. Surprisingly, despite the decline in Seljuq power, the other Turkish tribal chiefs continued to retain their respective domains.

Earlier, on an appeal from the pope, many Christian rulers had organized the Crusades to destroy the might of Islam. The first two Crusades lasted from 1095 to 1187 and were fairly successful as neither the Seljuqs nor the other Muslim rulers were able to stop their march, except in a part of Syria by Nuruddin; in the second Crusade Saladin struck a crushing blow to their might and recaptured Jerusalem (1187) which the Crusaders had captured in 1099. He also destroyed the Fatimid state in Egypt, which was reeling under misrule and corruption. Adding many other victories to his achievements, Saladin restored the supremacy of the Abbasids and helped the caliph, Nasir (1180–1225), to regain something of the ancient glory of the Caliphate. But it proved to be the last flicker of a dying flame.

1194–1260 Soon thereafter Halagu with his Mongol hordes, riding fleet horses and armed with strong bows, conquered Transoxiana and Khurasan, destroyed the mosques in Bukhara, butchered the inhabitants of Samarqand and descended like a scourge of God on Baghdad, ransacking the city and killing the caliph. Only the Mamlūks, a dynasty of slaves who had established their own kingdom (1250–1517) in Egypt after routing the Ayyubids on the death of Saladin, were able to turn them back; later they captured Mecca and Madina and became a formidable force.

In India on the assassination of Muhammad Ghori his slave Qutubuddin Aibak proclaimed himself in 1206 as sultan of Delhi and founded another slave dynasty. He was succeeded by his son-in-law Iltutmish (1211–36) who consolidated the Sultanate and persuaded many local Hindu chiefs and petty rajas to accept his suzerainty. On his death his daughter Razia became the sultan. The forty amirs who dominated the affairs of the Sultanate did not relish being ruled by a woman and intrigued against her. After having ruled for less than four years, Razia was killed in a civil war (1240).

All through this period Islam, which in its heartlands was caught between what Hitti has called 'the mounted archers of the wild Mongols in the East and mailed knights of the Crusaders in the West', began to rise again; within less than fifty years after the sack of Baghdad the descendants of the hated Mongols had finally embraced Islam and restored its military glory which their forefathers had so wantonly destroyed.

The Sixth Phase: The Ottomans (The Safavids and the Mughals)
(1260–1807)

1260-1421   Ghazan Khan, the Ilkhanid ruler of Iran and a descendant of
Halagu, was one of the first tribal chiefs to embrace
Islam; his example was followed by other Mongols,
including Uthmán, who founded the Osmanali or Ottoman
dynasty (1288), carved out of the crumbling Seljuq empire. He invaded the Byzantine territories and conquered
Kara Sie valley south of Niceea. He captured Yeninsheshir
near Bursa and proclaimed himself the amir. He then took
over Ak Hisar and reached the Bosporus in 1326. Bursa
was made the capital of the Ottoman kingdom. His
successor Urkhan (1325–59) extended his rule up to
Constantinople, crossing the Bosporus into Europe and
occupying Gallipoli. The next sultan Murád I (1359–89)
conquered Angora (Ankara) and Adianople (Edirne), which
was made the new capital.

In North India one of the forty amirs, the astute Balban,
seized the throne of Delhi and proclaimed himself the sultan (1266). He patronized the Afghans and the Indian-born
Muslims and consolidated his administration. On his
death, however, one of his generals Jalaluddin Firuz Khilji
staged a coup and founded the second slave dynasty in
Delhi (1290). He encouraged the non-Turkish indigenous
people, which caused resentment among his fellow
Turkish tribesmen. In 1296 his nephew Alauddin Khilji
murdered him and took over the reins. During Alauddin's
rule (1296–1316) the Sultanate acquired imperial dimensions and reached the peak of glory. He had a most able
lieutenant, a negroid slave, Málik Káfúr, who conquered
the regions of Deccan and Gujarat and humbled the Rajput
chiefs in the north. Alauddin's sons could not keep the
empire together and were defeated by the forces of
Ghiyasuddin Tughlaq in 1320. Ghiyasuddin was succeeded
in 1325 by his son Muhammad (1325–51). Ibn Baṭṭúta
visited Delhi during his reign and was attached to his court
till 1342.

Another slave, the Turkomán Baybar al-Bunduqdari (1260–77) took over the reins of Mamlūk power in Egypt. He broke the back of the Crusaders. He also crushed the Assassins, who had continued their murderous attacks on Muslim rulers and their advisers. Baybar conquered Nubia and strengthened his hold over Syria.

Baybar inaugurated a new series of Abbasid caliphs, who were nominal rulers with no power. He invited to Cairo the son of the caliph Záhir, who had escaped the Mongol massacre and installed him as the caliph by the name of Mustansir. In turn the caliph gave Baybar the diploma of investiture, authorizing him to rule over Egypt, Syria, Diyar Bakr, Hijaz and the territories around the Euphrates. After Mustansir, Hákim was installed as caliph and then other descendants in succession for almost 250 years; they were, however, puppets in the hands of the Mamlūks.

After Baybar, the other outstanding Mamlūk sultan was Qalawun (1280–90) who first eliminated the Franks in Syria and then improved his relations with the newly converted Mongol Muslims. He improved the administrative apparatus of his kingdom and beautified Cairo and Damascus and introduced many welfare measures for his subjects.

In North Africa, the Almohad dynasty which had replaced the Hammanids was overthrown by the Marinids (1196–1549). They attempted to rebuild their empire in the Maghrib and to reconquer Spain.

On the death of the Ottoman sultan, Murád I, Bayezid (1389–1403) ascended the throne and seized the emirates of Menteshe and Aydin and advanced to the Danube, subduing the emirates of Rostoman, Samsum and Sivas. In Central Asia Timūr Lang or Tamerlane rose like a cyclone and with his Tartar hordes initiated a long series of campaigns, which brought Afghanistan, Persia, Faris and Kurdistán under his heel. In 1393 his forces captured Moscow. Three years later he invaded North India and sacked Delhi (1398). Turning westward he swept over

Syria and entered Damascus in 1401. During the next two years Timūr invaded Asia Minor, inflicted a crushing defeat on the Ottomans and made the Ottoman sultan Bayezid his prisoner. Then he turned his wrath on China and while warring against it died in 1404, thus providing respite to both the Ottomans and Mamlūks, who began regrouping their forces and recovering their lost territories.

After Timūr, his successors in Khurasan and Transoxiana consolidated their kingdom and fostered literature, science and miniature painting. One of their kings, Ulugh Beg, patronized several astronomical investigations. He built the famous observatory at Samarqand.

In Anatolia, Mehmed I (1413–21) reunited the Ottoman empire and his successor Murād II (1421–51) thwarted Hungarian attacks. Mehmed II (1451–81) who succeeded him conquered Constantinople and made it the new capital, turning it into a beehive of learning and culture, taking as much from Byzantine and other sources as from Islamic traditions.

In India Muhammad bin Tughlaq (1325–51) subdued the revolts in the south and established a second capital at Daulatabad. Notwithstanding this, independent Hindu and Muslim kingdoms arose: Vijayanagar was founded by Hindu chiefs, Madurā by Ahsan Shah and Bahmani by Hasan Gangu. Bengal became independent in 1338 and was ruled for almost a century by the Ilyas Shahi dynasty. Muhammad Tughlaq died in a battle fought to curb a rebellion in Sind in 1351. He was succeeded by his cousin Firuz (1351–88), who reorganized the economy, particularly the agricultural sector. After his death, the power of the Sultanate declined; it received a near fatal blow at the hands of Timūr (1398).

1421–51   The Ottoman sultan Murād II (1421–51) won the war against Venice and captured Salonika. He abdicated after making peace with the Crusaders. However, he regained the throne and repulsed the Crusaders at Varna.

1451–1520   His successor Mehmed II (1451–81) captured Constantinople and subdued the Byzantine empire. He entrenched himself astride the Bosporus with one foot in Europe and the other in Asia. Bayezid II (1481–1512) and Selim I (1512–20) carried on the conquests and extended the frontiers of their empire. They also crushed the Mamlūks in Egypt and took over their territories in Syria.

In Iran, Shah Ismāʿil (1502–24) organized his Shīʿite followers and founded the Safavid kingdom. He defied the authority of the Ottomans, persecuted the Sunnis and made Twelver Shīʿism the State religion, forcing the Sunnis to convert. His policy was pursued by his son and successor Tahmāsp (1524–76) who gave encouragement to Iranian arts and letters. Bihzad, the foremost minature painter and Zainuddin al-Amili, the noted Shīʿite theologian, flourished in his court.

After the fall of the Tughlaqs, North India was ruled by the Sayyids (1414–51) and the Lodis (1451–1526). One of the remarkable rulers of those times was Sikandar Lodi (1489–1517), who gave impetus to arts and learning and tried to help syncretize Islam and Hinduism. Kabir, the Muslim weaver (1440–1518), spearheaded the Bhakti movement and Nanak, the founder of Sikhism (1469–1538), propagated Hindu-Muslim unity. Sikandar's son, Ibrahim Lodi (1517–26) was the last of the Delhi sultans. He faced revolts from many sides—Bihar, Punjab and the Hindu confederacy of Rajput princes led by Rana Sanga of Mewar. Finally the forces of Bābur, on horseback and armed with gun powder, defeated his forces on the battlefield of Panipat on 21 April 1526 and founded the great Mughal empire.

In South-East Asia, Muslims had begun to penetrate the islands of Java and Sumatra. Muslim sultans replaced the Hindu rajas one by one. The most outstanding was Sultan Ali Mughayat Shah, who founded his kingdom in Aceh; in other regions also the dominant Hindu Majapahit forces were defeated by the invading Muslims, who Islamized the whole archipelago, barring Bali, which remained Hindu.

1520–60   The Ottomans continued their conquests and became the mightiest power in Asia and Europe. Under Selim's son,

Süleymän I (1520–66), better known as the Magnificent, they brought almost half the known world under their heel. He captured Hungary, occupied Rhodes and besieged Vienna. He also brought most of North Africa under his domain; Tripoli, Tunis, and Algiers bowed before his authority though retaining their autonomy. Aden was annexed in 1547 and Muscat in 1551. Süleymän was also a just ruler; to his subjects he was known as the Qänüni or law giver. He codified the laws and made his code, Multaqa al-Abhur (Confluence of the Seas) the standard work of Ottoman jurisprudence. The magnificent mosque, Sulaymäniyah, is a standing monument to the architectural greatness of his rule.

In Iran the Safavids thwarted the attacks from the Ottomans and turned them out of Azerbaijan and Iraq. They also defeated the Ozbegs and pushed them out of Khurasan. Their greatest ruler, Shah Abbäs (1588–1629), a contemporary of Süleymän the Magnificent and Akbar the Great, was also a man of exceptional qualities. He proclaimed himself the deputy of the hidden imam and assumed dictatorial powers, both in temporal and religious affairs. An astute ruler, he was equally successful at home and on the battlefield. He gave a new vigour and vitality to Shi'ism and made his empire as powerful as that of the Ottomans. He revived the ancient arts and culture of Iran and ushered in the golden period which fused Shi'ism with the ancient traditions of the Sassanians.

In India, Bäbur was succeeded by his son, Humayun (1530), who was driven out of India for a short time by one of his own generals Sher Shah Suri (1540–55). Humayun, however, regained the throne with the help of the Safavid shah Tahmäsp (1555) and on his death a year later was succeeded by his minor son Akbar (1556–1605), who ushered in an era of peace and prosperity. He treated all his subjects, irrespective of their creed, equally, and was, by all accounts, the greatest of the Mughals.

1566–1623   In Istanbul, after the death of Süleymän, the downward trend of the Ottoman power began, albeit slowly. His successors Selim II (1566–74) and Murad III (1574–95) pursued peace rather than war. During their rule, only Cyprus was added to the Ottoman empire (1570); at home a policy of liberalization was followed. However, their four successors were so weak and ineffective that dissension and disruption spread; the janissaries, an elite force of young officers and men specially chosen by the sultan, became increasingly powerful. In India, Akbar (1556–1605) expanded his territories in the south and up to Kashmir in the north and Bengal in the east. He worked relentlessly for inter-religious harmony and broad-based cultural and artistic renaissance.

Muhammad IV (1648–1687)—the Ottoman caliph— asserted his authority over the janissaries, who habitually made and unmade ministers and advisers. They indulged in intrigues and conspiracies. Muhammad IV reorganized the military and made it personally accountable to him, thus weakening the hold of the janissaries, who had made the military so weak that it could not defeat the attacks from Austria and Poland and had to lose Hungary and Belgrade to the Hapsburgs.

1623–1718 In India, Akbar's son and successor Jahangir (1605–27), born of a Hindu mother, a Rajput princess, continued his father's policy of communal harmony. He gave much patronage to arts and letters. He also gave trade facilities to the Europeans, particularly the Portuguese and the British. Jahangir was succeeded by his son, Shahjahan (1628–57), who built the famous Taj Mahal at Agra in memory of his wife, Mumtaz Mahal. He also built many other monuments—forts, mosques, mausoleums and gardens—which recall the grandeur of his rule. He was succeeded by his third son Aurangazeb (1658–1707), who was a pious Muslim devoted to prayers and fasting; he led a simple and orthodox life under the influence of the ulama. Aurangazeb reversed Akbar's policy of inter-religious understanding and imposed the shari'ah on his people. He attempted to subdue the Shi'a kingdoms in the Deccan and Gujarat and had to encounter the rise of Maratha power under Shivaji, who posed the greatest danger to him. On Aurangazēb's death in 1707 the empire began to disintegrate and the era of the great Mughals came to an end.

The Safavid kings lost their prestige and power in Iran and outside; during 1629 to 1694 one king after another came to be dominated by harem politics. In the process, Iraq was retaken by the Ottomans. Husayn (1694–1722), the last Safavid shah, indulged in repressive measures against the people and ruthless elimination of his enemies, which provoked widespread revolt against his rule. His mentor, the noted Shī'ite theologian Baqir al-Majlisi, died soon after his accession, leaving him without much theological support. In 1726 Nādir Khan (Qulī) defeated the Afghans and entered Asfahan (1729), restoring the Safavid dynasty. In 1736 he usurped all authority and crowned himself Nādir Shāh. His kingdom disintegrated with his assassination (1747). Then Karim Khān Zand captured Persia and ruled from 1750–79.

1718–89   The Ottoman sultan Ahmad III (1703–30) ushered in the so-called Tulip age under Western influence and introduced constitutional and legal reforms. One of his advisors, Ibrahim al-Mutaferriqa founded the first printing press (1727) which opened up the West to the Muslims. The ulamā and janissaries resisted this development and, in the face of high taxation and rising prices, revolted against Ahmad III. The revolt was unsuccessful. His successor Mahmud I (1730–54) entered into treaties with Austria and Russia, under which the division of territories among the various European powers was regularized by his successors. Uthmān III (1754–57) and Mustafā III (1757–74) were unable to continue the process of peace. They embarked on a war with Russia, which resulted in the defeat of the Ottoman forces. The Treaty of Kuchrik Kaynardji in 1774 recognized Russian suzerainty over Crimea and acknowledged the czar as the protector of the Orthodox Christians in the Ottoman empire.

In Iran, the Ottomans continued to be at war with the Safavids, who were making increasing inroads into their territories.

1789–1807   Selim III (1789–1807) embarked on a series of reforms in Ottoman administration along the lines of the West and overhauled the whole system.

In Egypt, the Mamlūks were engaged in internecine wars when Napoleon Bonaparte and his French army landed in Alexandria (1798). Napoleon's objective was to checkmate the growth of British influence in the East. In this he did not succeed and had to leave Egypt in 1799. The Ottoman army under the command of Muhammad Ali helped to drive out his army (1801). The sultan elevated Muhammad Ali to the position of the pasha of Egypt in 1805; he then founded his own dynasty, which ruled Egypt until 1948, when King Fārūq was overthrown by Nasser's 'Free Officers' in a coup in 1952.

In Iran, in 1794 Agha Muhammad Khan founded the Qājār dynasty and reunited the country. He put the economy on a sound footing and streamlined the administrative set-up. Teheran was made the capital (1796). The Qājār dynasty ruled until 1924. Agha Muhammad was succeeded by his nephew Fath Ali Shāh (1797–1834), who got involved in the rivalries of Russia, France and Britain. He exploited the strategic position of Iran across the routes to the West, in which both France and Britain were vitally interested and took their help to thwart czarist imperial designs against Iran.

The Seventh Phase: European Penetration and Occupation (1808–1920)

1808-1920   Russia invaded Iran and was forced under the Treaty of Gulistan (1813), to cede Georgia, Qarabagh, Daghestan, etc., in Caucasia. Later in 1825 the Russians took over Erivan and in 1828, Tabriz.

Fath Ali Shah died in 1834 and was succeeded by Muhammad Shah (1834–48) and Nasir al-Din Shah (1848–96).

Meanwhile, in 1857, the British forced Iran to grant independence to Afghanistan and extracted several concessions from Nasir al-Din Shah, specially in regard to rail, road, mining and banking. This was the cause of much rivalry between the British and the Russians as both were interested in the commercial exploitation of Iran.

In 1863 Mirza Husayn Ali Baha-allah declared himself a prophet. His followers came to be known as the Bahais. By 1892 nationalist feelings had been so roused, with the mullas taking the lead, that the shah had to cancel the tobacco concessions granted to the British in 1890. In 1896 Nasir al-Din was assassinated and was succeeded by his son Muzaffar al-Din Shah (1896–1907). Muzaffar was a weak ruler, and was unable to ward off Russian encroachment. In 1906 there was a merchant uprising. Shops were closed and people gathered in a mosque in Teheran, demanding constitutional reforms. The shah conceded them and Iran became a constitutional monarchy.

In 1909, Muhammad Ali Shah succeeded to the throne and abrogated the Constitution, abolished the majlis and imposed martial law. In 1909, the Bakhtiyari tribe rose in support of the nationalist rebels and occupied Teheran. They deposed the shah and declared his eleven-year-old son, Ahmad, as successor. The Constitution was restored. Russia was openly hostile to the new regime and in 1911 the ex-shah Muhammad Ali was brought back from exile by the Russians. He was, however, defeated. Incensed, Russia engineered the overthrow of the Iranian government, and the abolition of the majlis.

During World War I (1914–18) Iran suffered heavily, as it was a battlefield for the Ottoman, Russian and British forces. In 1919 the Anglo-Persian Treaty was signed, which guaranteed Persia an independent status under British supervision.

In Turkey, on his accession Sultan Mahmud II (1808–39) destroyed the power of the janissaries, eliminated the hold of the ulamā and centralized his personal control by effecting modern reforms in the administration and the army. The sultan faced revolts by his Christian subjects in Serbia (1815–16), which he had hardly suppressed when there was a full scale war for independence by Greece, which lasted from 1832–48, resulting ultimately in the formation of an independent state of Greece due to the intervention of Russia and other European powers.

His successor Sultan Abd ül-Mejid (1839–61) had to reconcile to the loss of several Ottoman territories. He had also to face revolts in the Balkans. Meanwhile, czarist Russia instigated the sultan's Christian subjects, which resulted in a bloody war (1854–56) in which his authority in Central Asia was considerably undermined. These setbacks forced the sultan to modernize his governmental setup to face the new challenges. He embarked on radical reforms, which came to be known as tanzimat.

His successor, Sultan Abd al-Aziz (1861–70), followed the same policies. He gave an impetus to tanzimat and borrowed funds heavily from European bankers and merchants to buy arms and equipments from Europe. In the result Ottoman finances came to be controlled by several European governments. This was resented by the Turkish intelligentsia, which formed the Young Ottoman Society under the leadership of three of its leading lights: Nāmiq Kemāl, Ziyā Pasha and Ali Suavi (1865). It created a wave of patriotism among Turks through journalistic writings and literary works. They demanded a constitutional government and reforms of the shari'ah. Rebellion broke out. Sultan Abd al-Aziz was deposed and Murād V (1876) was made the sultan, but soon he was also dethroned in favour of Abd al-Hamid II (1876–1909).

The leader of the rebels, Midhat Pasha, was appointed the prime minister and the first Ottoman Constitution on Western lines was promulgated. However, the sultan betrayed the faith of the people, refused to share power with the elected deputies and suspended the Constitution. The more despotic he became, the more the rebels worked underground; it also led to mounting unrest among the Christian minorities. In 1889 military students in Istanbul founded the first Young Turks Organization under the name of 'Ottoman Committee of Union and Progress'.

The sultan ruthlessly suppressed the Christians in Armenia, which revived anti-Turkish feelings in Europe. There was a revolt in Crete and outbreak of war with Greece (1896–97). The sultan faced problems all around; in 1908 he was forced to restore the Constitution and grant a considerable measure of freedom to his Turkish subjects. Though there was a counter-revolution in 1909 in favour of the sultan, it did not last and was crushed by the Young Turks, who deposed Abd al-Hamid and enthroned Muhammad V (1909–18). The new sultan immediately faced a revolt by his Christian subjects in Albania (1910) and a little later a full-fledged war in the Balkans in which the Turks lost Tripoli to Italy.

Soon after, the Young Turks seized power by a military coup; the triumvirate of Enver, Talat and Jemal Pashas, suspicious of the intention of the Allies, joined Germany on the outbreak of World War I (1914–18) and lost all its territories by its end. Mustafā Kemāl, later known as the Ataturk, emerged as the supreme commander of the reorganized Turkish forces, which turned the tide and saved Turkey from subjugation by the Allies.

In Afghanistan the pro-Russian policies of the Afghan ruler Emir Dost Muhammad led to the First Afghan War in 1839; the British conquered Kabul and captured Dost Muhammad, who agreed to toe the British line. However, in 1878 his successor Emir Shir Ali turned to Russia for aid and refused to submit to the British; this led to the Second Afghan War; in the result the British occupied a large part of the country, ousted Shir Ali, installed Ya'qūb as his successor and concluded the Treaty of Gandamak. In 1880, Ya'qūb abdicated and Abdur Rahman became the ruler. He was followed in 1901 by Habibullah (1901–19).

During World War I (1914–18) Afghanistan remained neutral. In 1919 Habibullah was proclaimed emir, but Habibullah's son Amanullah ousted him and became the ruler. He proclaimed jihād against the British and invaded India; this led to the Third Afghan War, which ended in the Treaty of Rawalpindi under which Afghanistan's independence was guaranteed.

Central Asia, which was a major centre of Muslim power in these times, was under different Khanates; these were often subjected to czarist onslaughts and ultimately came under Russian control one by one. Three of these Khanates were Bukhara, Khiva and Khokand, which recognized Russian suzerainty in 1868, 1873 and 1875 respectively; by the end of the nineteenth century Russia claimed to have under its hold the third largest Muslim population in the world. It was spread over the Volga-Ural region, Siberia, Central Asia (Turkistān), the Crimea and the Caucasus. After the October 1917 Revolution, Lenin started winning over the Muslims and promised them relief from oppression, which they had suffered under the czar. He issued a declaration signed by himself and Stalin as the Commissioner of Nationalities in December 1917, in which their beliefs, customs, ethnic and cultural institutions were declared free and inviolable. This enthused the Muslims to volunteer to fight for the revolution and to enlist in the Red Army, in which they played an important part. They were mainly responsible for the Bolshevik victory of Kalchak. However, the Bolsheviks soon began destroying Muslim religious institutions. Stalin established the Central Commissariat for Muslim Affairs to propagate the atheistic ideology among the Muslims; it set up communist units in Muslim areas. Religious affiliations were frowned upon; they were tolerated under ethnic grouping and given a certain latitude on the basis of nationalities; but religious practices were discouraged. In 1920 Soviet Republics were formed in regions where Muslims formed a majority; their mosques and madrasas were closed down, religious teaching in schools were stopped, the ulamā were persecuted, and the ṣūfi orders banned.

In Arabia, when the Ottomans refused Ibrahim Pasha the governorship of Syria, he invaded it in 1833. In 1861 civil war broke out between Christians, Muslims and Druzes, which resulted in French troops landing in Beirut. A settlement was reached, providing autonomy within the empire for the Christian inhaḅitants. At this time Britain established herself on the southern and eastern shores of the Arabian peninsula where there existed hardly any Ottoman authority. From 1820 Britain concluded a series of treaties with Arab rulers guaranteeing their protection; in 1839 Britain occupied Aden. In 1890 a treaty was signed with the sultan of Oman and Muscat; likewise in 1892 with Bahrain and in 1899 with Kuwait. Under these treaties Britain became their sole protector.

In 1887 the Fertile Crescent was reorganized with the Vilayet of Aleppo in the north, the Vilayet of Beirut in the west, the Vilayet of Syria in the east, the autonomous Sanjak (county) of the Lebanon and the autonomous Sanjak of Jerusalem to the south. Iraq was divided into three vilayets: of Mosul, Baghdad and Basra. Arabia continued to be under Ottoman rule; in 1841 the governor-general of Hejaz shared powers with the Arab grand sharifs, the traditional rulers of Mecca and Madina. In 1871 al-Hasa in eastern Arabia and in 1872 Sanaa, the capital of Yemen, were brought under the control of the Ottoman Caliphate. But large areas of the interior of the peninsula—namely the principalities of Nejd and Shammar, ruled by the families of Ibn Sa'ūd and Ibn Rashīd exercised independent authority. Ibn Sa'ūd took over Riyadh and ousted Ibn Rashid (1904); in 1913 he seized al-Hasa from the Ottomans. In 1914 he signed a treaty with the British, which acknowledged the independence of Nejd.

In 1916 Sharif Hussein revolted against the Ottomans; he captured Mecca and Jedda with the assistance of Capt. T.E. Lawrence, who masterminded the guerrilla warfare.

Another British General, Sir Edmund Allenby, took over Jerusalem and the British forces captured Baghdad and forced the Ottomans to surrender. In 1916 Sharif Hussein was proclaimed king of the Arab countries by his followers; but the French refused to recognize him; in 1917 a compromise was reached between the British and the French and his kingship was acknowledged. On 2 November 1917 the British came out with the Balfour Declaration which favoured the establishment of a 'National Home for the Jewish People in Palestine'. After the end of World War I (1919) Allenby took over Syria and thus put the last nail in the Ottoman coffin in the Arab world.

In Egypt Muhammad Ali ousted the Ayubids and took over control, first as a vassal of the Ottomans, later as a rebel against them founding his own dynastic kingdom, extending his rule up to Syria and Anatolia, though nominally acknowledging the Ottoman caliph. On his death in 1848, Abbās I succeeded him, and ruled till 1854. Due to anti-European feelings the Westernizing reforms introduced by the late founder Muhammad Ali were interrupted and were not resumed until Muhammad Sā'id (1854–63) came to power; he granted concessions in the Suez Canal to the French and the British. Ismā'il (1863–79) became the ruler in 1867; he obtained the title of 'khedive' from the Ottoman caliph, but turned more to the British for help and protection. Moreover, due to the American Civil War and the opening of the Suez Canal in 1869 to international trade and commerce, he benefited from the boom in cotton trade in the West, which bought the commodity from Egypt. However, due to excessive borrowings from the European financiers, the khedive was forced to part with the Suez Canal shares and to depend on the British and the French, with the result that Egypt was thrown wide open to European bankers and traders. This in turn unleashed anti-British feelings in Egypt, openly expressed by newspapers and journals, which had mushroomed due to the import of printing machinery. There was growing opposition to the misrule of the khedive and intensification of the demand for constitutional reforms.

The activities of Jamal al-Din Al-Afghani and Muhammad Abduh, the pioneers of pan-Islamism, added fuel to the fire. As a result Khedive Isma'il was deposed and Tawfiq was installed as the new khedive in 1879. But the change did not stem the tide of popular discontent. The reformists and pan-Islamists under Ahmad Arabi, a native Egyptian, who spearheaded the movement, forced the khedive to accept Arabi as the head of a new government in 1882. Sensing danger to their interests, the British naval squadron bombarded Alexandria. British forces defeated Arabi at Tel el-Kebir and reinforced the hold of the khedive. In 1883 Sir Evelyn Baring (later Lord Cromer) arrived in Cairo as the British consul general and diplomatic agent; in reality he was virtual ruler of Egypt. Though Ottoman suzerainty over Egypt was nominally recognized until 1914 when it was declared a British protectorate, the pro-Ottoman khedive Abbas II was deposed. In 1915 Ottomans attacked the Suez Canal, but they were repulsed by the British. In 1917 Sultan Hussein died and was replaced by his brother Fuad, son of Khedive Isma'il. After World War I Egyptian nationalism found a new voice in Sa'ud Zaghlul, who opposed the British and demanded complete independence. In 1917 he founded the Wafd party; two years later he was deported, but had to be brought back later under popular pressure and made the prime minister.

Northern Sudan, ancient Nubia, the Funj Sultanate of Sennar, and Kordofan were conquered by Muhammad Ali of Egypt in 1820; however, in 1885, a popular revolt led by Muhammad Ahmad, who called himself the 'Mahdi', resulted in the defeat of the British army and the death of General Gordon at Khartoum; they were supporting the khedive of Egypt. Mahdi ruled Sudan for thirteen years, until an Anglo-Egyptian force succeeded in crushing his rule. An Anglo-Egyptian government was established in Sudan (1898), which remained effective for some time.

In North Africa Morocco was ruled by Sultan Mawlay Sulaymān, who died in 1822; he was succeeded by Mawlay Abd al-Rahman (1822–59), who opened his kingdom to European trade. Thereafter several successive rulers tried to preserve the unity of their land; but could not succeed and ultimately the different parts of the country were occupied by different European powers. Between 1907 and 1911 there was increasing anarchy which helped France to negotiate a treaty of protectorateship and finally in March 1912 Morocco became a French protectorate.

Algeria was ruled by the Deys as the regents of the Ottomans. Between 1671 to 1830 twenty-eight Deys came to power; but half of them were assassinated; the economic situation worsened. France, which was the dominant power in that region, sent an expedition against Algeria and occupied it.

Tunisia, ruled by the descendants of Husayn Bey, as the regents of the Ottoman sultans, began to witness increasing financial difficulties which resulted in commercial penetration by the Europeans. Sea trade, which was extensive, was particularly exploited by their local agents.

The French conquest of Algeria intensified Arab resentment against European domination. Then there was the growing economic crisis. Muhammad Bey (1855–59) introduced various reforms. But drought, poverty and the cholera epidemic during 1866–67 brought Tunisia to the verge of bankruptcy; consequently it accepted the tutelage of an International Financial Commission in 1869, which led to a sort of triple protectorate of France, Italy and Britain over the economy of Tunisia. However, in 1881, on the pretext that some mountain tribes had intruded in Algeria, France occupied Tunisia and made it a protectorate (1883). By 1911 popular revolt against France started to grow, led by Young Tunisians with Habib Bourguiba at the head. He crystallized it by founding the Dastur party, with the aim of capturing political power.

India came gradually under the domination of the East India Company, with one region after another falling to

British arms; the final revolt took place in 1857, under the command of the last Mughal emperor Bahadur Shah Zafar; this was easily crushed. Queen Victoria assumed full powers and terminated the rule of the Company. Henceforth India was ruled from London, with a British viceroy and a governor-general exercising authority in the name of the Crown. Queen Victoria was declared the empress of India and her secretary of state for India and the British Parliament were made responsible for the governance of the British colony. Muslims were suspected of disloyalty by the British and had to suffer innumerable hardships. Sir Syed Ahmad Khan took pains to dispel the British suspicion and to instil a sense of loyalty among the Muslims. After his death in 1898 his mission was carried forward by his lieutenants, who formed the All-India Muslim League at Dhaka in 1906 to counter the freedom movement started by some of the foremost Hindu leaders under the name of the Indian National Congress, which was founded at Bombay in 1885.

As a result, educated Hindus and Muslims remained politically apart and the British used their differences to strengthen their rule. However, due to the Balkan wars, in which Turkey was ranged against Greece, with the support of the British, the feelings of the Muslims were once again roused against the British, especially in view of the threat that their anti-Turkish stand posed to the custodianship of the holy places of Mecca and Madina. They organized mass protests against the British under the auspices of the All-India Khilafat Committee. Gandhi mobilized the Hindus in support of the Muslims and the two major communities presented a united front demanding the end of British rule. The first non-cooperation movement, which shook the British, was the result of the unity between the Hindus and the Muslims brought about by Gandhi and the Congress leaders on one side and the Ali brothers (Mohammed and Shaukat) and Azad on the other. Though the whole of India had come under the grip of the British, nationalist forces under the leadership of Gandhi began to challenge its authority, which in turn resulted in more repressive measures by the British such as the Jallianwala Bagh massacre at Amritsar (1919), the repression of the Khilafat movement and the internment of their foremost leaders, the Ali brothers and Azad.

In South-East Asia, the Dutch East India Company had suffered an eclipse, and the British took over Java (1811). However, the Dutch returned to Java and established colonial rule (1816). Hostilities began between them and the Muslim sultans who organized jihād and guerrilla warfare against them, which continued till 1837. The sultans were ultimately' defeated (1855) and Dutch rule was firmly established.

Unlike the Muslims in Java and parts of Sumatra, the Malay states of the peninsula were fully protected by the forces of the British East India Co. In 1824, the sultan of Johore ceded Singapore to the British and in 1867 the latter established the 'Straits Settlements', which made Penang, Malacca and Singapore a crown colony. In 1888, the British declared North Borneo (Sabah), Sarawak and Brunei British protectorates.

Aceh, once the great Sultanate and traditionally the most vigorous Islamic state, came under the Dutch in 1824; its ruler unsuccessfully sought military aid from the Ottomans in 1860 and by 1873 the Dutch were able to launch an armed invasion against Aceh and turn it into a colony.

The Eighth Phase: The Impact of the West (1920–45)

1920–45 After the Ottomans lost their territories one by one (1920), and these were occupied by the victorious allied powers as 'mandated territories', Turkey declared itself a republic (1923). Mustafā Kemāl became the president and his lieutenant Ismet Pasha the premier. They abolished the Caliphate (1924) and vigorously pursued secular policies. Between 1925 and 1926 the civil codes of Switzerland,

Italy and Germany were substituted for the shari'ah. In 1928 Islam ceased to be the religion of the State. The Arabic call to prayers was replaced by Turkish. Arabic surnames were changed into Turkish and those like Pasha and Bey were discarded. Kemäl Pasha became Kemäl Ataturk and Ismet Pasha, Ismet Inounu. In 1938 Ataturk died and Ismet Inounu became the president and Celal Beyar the prime minister.

During World War II (1939–45) Turkey remained neutral. Iran continued to be occupied by Russian and British troops, which resulted in popular revolt and in February 1921, Reza Khan, an officer in the Cossack Brigade and Sayyid Zia al-Din Tabatabai, a radical writer and reformer, staged a military coup against the puppet shah. Reza Khan became first the commander-in-chief of the armed forces and then the prime minister. He exiled Ahmad Shah. In 1925 a bill was passed in the majlis terminating the 125-year-old Qäjär rule; Reza Khan under pressure from Shi'a ulamä agreed to become the king and established the Pahlavi dynasty. He embarked on several measures of Westernization and strengthened its economy. His rule was interrupted by the outbreak of World War II (1939). Reza Shah declared Iran's neutrality which compelled the Allied powers to invade Iran forcing Reza Shah to abdicate in favour of his twenty-year-old son, Muhammad Reza.

Russia and Britain divided Iran into two zones of occupation: Russia obtained control of Azerbaijan, Gilan, Mazanderan, Gorgan and Khorasan, and Britain the rest of the country. In 1942 Iran concluded a 'Tripartite Treaty of Alliance' with the Allies, under which they agreed to withdraw their troops not later than six months after the end of World War II. In 1945 the Soviets engineered revolts in Azerbaijan and the Kurds established their own republic supported by the Red Army. These events were a severe blow to the integrity of Iran, hampering its progress.

In Afghanistan Emir Amanullah leaned heavily on Russia, upsetting the British. In 1921 he concluded a treaty with Russia; but soon the conditions of the Muslims in Bukhara and Central Asia made him realize that the Bolsheviks could not be trusted and so he concluded a treaty with the British. Between 1923 and 1924 he introduced several reforms aimed at the modernization of the country. This provoked a tribal rebellion, which was encouraged by the mullas and the British. As a result Amanullah Khan abdicated in favour of his elder brother Inayatullah but the latter was overthrown by a Tajik highway robber, Bacha-i-Sakao, or Habibullah Ghazi, who stormed the capital and became the king in 1929. But within months of his rule he was brought down by Muhammad Nadir Khan, who in October 1929 was proclaimed the new king. In 1932 he promulgated a new constitution and established a bicameral legislature. In 1933 Nadir Khan was assassinated and his twenty-year-old son Muhammad Zahir Shah succeeded him. During World War II (1939–45) Afghanistan remained neutral.

In Central Asia the Bolsheviks continued with their anti-religious policy, undermining the hold of the mullas, discouraging Islamic practices and banning the sufi orders. They also abolished the Arabic script in 1928 and persecuted religious functionaries. In Central Asia 14,000 mosques were closed; in Volga-Ural 6,000; in Caucasia 4,000 and in Crimea 1,000. Hakim Zade, a communist known for his atheism, was torn to pieces by the mullas; but World War II brought some relief to them. Sensing the dangerous consequences of the German attack in June (1941), religious sentiments were appeased, and ulama were used to whip up the patriotism of Muslim soldiers in the fight against the Germans in the name of Islam.

In Syria, Lebanon and Iraq revolts broke out against Britain and France specially because of their support to the Zionists in Palestine.

The British placated Arab sentiments by proclaiming in March 1920 Faysal as the king of the 'United Kingdom of

Syria' and his brother Abdullah as the king of an independent Iraq. Lebanon was also given freedom. As events
moved fast the Allied Supreme Council met at San Remo
in April 1920, which assigned the mandates for
Mesopotamia and Palestine to Britain and Lebanon to
France. Thus Faysal's rule in Syria was brought to an end.
But soon the mandatory powers changed their policy and
catered to nationalist feelings. In September 1920, France
brought into existence the state of Great Lebanon with
Beirut as its capital. Amir Faysal, who ceased to be the
ruler of Syria, was declared the king of Iraq in 1921. In
1924 a new constitution was enacted which guaranteed full
sovereignty. Syria and Lebanon were given a republican
parliamentary form of government and new constitutions
were enacted for Lebanon and Syria in 1926 and 1930
respectively.

Iraq became formally independent by being admitted to
the League of Nations in 1932. The nationalist Arab leaders opposed the mandate system; they resorted to strikes,
demonstrations and agitations. In Palestine Jewish
immigration between 1933–36 multiplied, leading to
bloodshed and open rebellion by the Arabs against the
Jewish immigrants and the local authorities.

In Iraq General Baqr Sidqi staged a military coup in
1936; but he was overthrown by another General Rashid
Ali al-Gaylani in 1941 with the support of the Iraqi army,
aided by German arms and aircrafts he in turn was defeated
by British troops and once again Iraq came under their
influence. The British put up Nuri al-Sā'id Pasha as the
new prime minister. In 1941 General de Gaulle ended the
mandatory regime in Syria and Lebanon and declared them
independent. But the Allied powers maintained their hold
in the areas under their control. Meanwhile, nationalist
forces went ahead consolidating their rule in Syria,
Lebanon and Iraq.

In Transjordan Britain recognized the Hashemite amir
Abdullah (Faysal's elder brother) as the ruler (1921). In

1928 a formal treaty was signed by which Britain retained its control over finance, foreign affairs and the armed forces and granted autonomy in other spheres to the amir.

In Central Arabia King Hussain abdicated in favour of his son Ali in 1924. Later Ibn Sa'ūd's supporters, the Wahhābis captured Jeddah, Madina and Yanby; Ali was forced into exile. Thus Central Arabia became an independent kingdom under Ibn Sa'ūd. In the coastal regions, where several principalities and shaikhdoms exist, Britain retained its direct hold. Towards 1933 the new oil-fields were discovered in the Arabian peninsula which brought fabulous wealth to Saudi Arabia, Iraq, Kuwait and other gulf territories. This helped them to raise the standard of living and multiplied their resources.

In Egypt there was an outbreak of riots in 1921 against the British whereupon Sā'ad Zaghlul and other leaders were again deported. Finally the British decided to put an end to the protectorate. In 1922 Egypt was formally declared independent under King Fuad, though British control on defence and foreign affairs continued. Sudan was put under the joint rule of Britain and Egypt. In Egypt under the new constitution (1923), the Wafdists gained control of the newly-elected Parliament and formed a government in 1924, but British interference did not cease. In disgust the Wafdists refused to cooperate with the British. In 1927 Sā'ad Zaghlul died and was succeeded by Mustafā Nahas Pasha, whose government was more cooperative with the British. In 1935 King Fuad died; he was succeeded by his son Farouk. After an interregnum of two years a treaty was signed between the Wafdists and the British (1936) granting Egypt more powers but this did not satisfy the extremists. There were widespread revolts and terrorist activities, especially in Cairo.

After the outbreak of World War II (1939–45) Egypt became a centre of Allied warfare. The British once again strengthened their hold on the country. At the end of the war, nationalist feelings were once more roused and the demand for severance of the British connection mounted.

In 1944 King Farouk dismissed Nahas Pasha and called for elections in 1945, which were boycotted by the Wafdists. A coalition of some other parties secured a majority in the National Assembly; but the people alleged that the elections were rigged and widespread rioting took place. Tension mounted and the cry of 'Egypt for Egyptians' was heard everywhere. In Sudan there was a spurt of nationalist revolts which continued for a long time; to crystallize the popular demand for independence two political parties, one under Abd al-Rahman al-Mahdi, called the Umma party and the other called the Ashiqqa with Isma'il al-Azhari as the leader were formed; but they were unable to resolve the constitutional deadlock with Egypt or obtain any major concessions from the British.

In Morocco the Rif revolt took place (1920) led by Berber warrior Abd al-Karim; he established his rule over a large area but by 1926 he surrendered to the French. In 1930 a group of young nationalists formed the Moroccan National party, which forced the sultan to abrogate the treaty with the occupying power and succeeded in gaining independence (1944).

Algeria went through many bloody conflicts. There were constant riots and skirmishes between the nationalists and the French army. In 1945, a number of Europeans were assassinated; in turn several thousand Algerians were massacred. Blood flowed freely in the streets of Algeria.

In Tunisia the failure of the discussions on the demands of the neo-Dastur Party resulted in harsh measures against its leaders and intimidation and isolation of the Bey by the French. Inflation, increase in prices and non-availability of food worsened the conditions. There were strikes and even bloody riots in 1937 and 1938. Bourguiba was put into prison and released by the Germans only when they occupied Tunisia in 1942. But after the defeat of the Axis forces Tunisia, once again, came under the control of France. No sooner was Bourguiba freed than he continued the fight against the French.

In South-East Asia, between 1920–30 the Indonesian nationalists intensified their demand for political independence; they formed the Indonesia Communist party. In 1926–27 there was a full-scale popularist rising, which was suppressed; in the process the leadership passed into the hands of nationalists like Sukarno, Muhammad Hatta and Sultan Sjahrir. In 1934 they were interned and released only when the Japanese took over Indonesia in 1942.

Malaya continued to be under the British. Tenku Abdul Rahman organized the nationalist elements, and demanded transfer of power to popular representatives. As the war had seriously weakened the position of the colonial powers—France, Britain and the Netherlands—in South-East Asia this provided an opportunity to Japan to occupy these lands in February 1942. Japan conquered Malaya and Singapore and stayed put until the war turned in favour of the Allies who recovered these territories after Japan surrendered them in August 1945.

In India Hindu-Muslim relations, which had blossomed during the Khilafat and non-cooperation movements against the British (1919–21), deteriorated further due to the outbreak of communal disturbances in the south. Gandhi was heartbroken; so were the Ali brothers who left the Congress in disgust. The Congress and the League, despite efforts by their leaders to forge a common front, also drifted apart. Various constitutional measures such as the Montford-Chelmsford reforms (1919), the Simon Commission (1929), followed by the holding of the three Round Table Conferences in London (1930–32) and the enforcement of the Government of India Act (1935) did not improve the situation. The elections to the provincial assemblies (1937), in which both Congress and League candidates took part, worsened the situation. The formation of the Congress ministries created a further gap between the two parties. Jinnah emerged as the supreme leader of the Muslims and carried on a relentless campaign against the 'anti-Muslim' policies and activities of the Congress. The League demanded a separate homeland for

Muslims in the north-west and east of India, where they formed the majority after it came under Jinnah's full control; its Lahore Resolution (1940) opted for the partition of the sub-continent on communal lines, striking a near fatal blow to the concept of a united India.

Meanwhile, the British tried to mobilize Indian public opinion against the threat of a Japanese invasion and Churchill sent in 1941 one of his senior ministers, Sir Stafford Cripps, belonging to the Labour party, with an offer of limited participation by representatives of the Congress and the League in the government of India and the promise of dominion status after the end of the war. Both the parties rejected the offer, though for different reasons. The Congress launched the 'Quit India' movement and its leaders were put into prison. In 1945 the constitutional deadlock continued. Churchill replaced Linlithgow with Wavell as viceroy, who released the Congress leaders and embarked on negotiations with them. He convened a conference at Simla (1945) of the Congress and League leaders to break the political deadlock; but failed to arrive at a mutually agreeable constitutional framework for the transfer of power.

The Ninth Phase: Emergence of Muslim Nation-States (1945–88)

1945–88   During this period one Muslim country after another attained independence, with the result that the Organization of Islamic Conference, established in August 1954 with the object of promoting a sense of unity among the Muslim states, acquired a membership of forty-seven states, run by the faithful. Its headquarters are in Jeddah in Saudi Arabia.

India was one of the first countries to be freed at the end of World War II (1939–45), which unleashed new forces of freedom everywhere, including Asia and Africa which had been under the subjugation of one Allied power or another for the past several decades. However, the country was divided by Britain—albeit by mutual agreement between the two major communities, Hindus and Muslims—into two dominions: one called Pakistan, constituting the Muslim-majority regions and the other called India, constituting the rest of the country. The dominions came into existence on 14 and 15 August 1947 respectively. The creation of an exclusively Islamic state with one wing in the north-west and the other in the north-east of India, provided great impetus to the forces of pan-Islamism, but riots broke out between Hindus and Muslims on either side of the border; more than a million people were killed and about five million became refugees. Gandhi was murdered by a fanatic Hindu Nathuram Godse on 30 January 1948 as a result of religious frenzy; in less than a year Jinnah also died.

In the Arab world, Egypt broke ties with Britain. Their puppet King Faruq was deposed by the 'Free Officers' under Colonel Gamal Abd al- Nasser in a successful coup (1952). Iraq, though nominally independent, continued to be under Western influence and in 1955 joined the British-sponsored military pact, known as the Baghdad Pact. It was aimed at curbing the growing influence of Nasser and other leaders of the liberation movement and, therefore, resented by the people of Iraq, who rose in revolt against the prime minister of Iraq, Nurie es-Säʾid and King Faysal. Both were killed (1958) and the rebel leader General Abd al-Karim Kassem took over the reins of the government; in 1963 Colonel Abd al-Salam Arif, in collaboration with the Ba'athist leaders, staged a coup against Kassem and executed him. In 1966 Abd al-Salam Arif was killed in a helicopter crash; he was succeeded by his brother Abd al-Rahman Arif. In 1968 he was overthrown and a revolutionary command council of the Ba'athist party under General Ahmad Hassan al-Bakr came to power. During his ten-year rule Iraq neither enjoyed stability nor competent administration. Hence in 1979 the vice-president Saddam Hussain replaced al-Bakr as the president. In 1980 on the issue of the disputed Shatt al-Arab waterway Iraq went to war with Khomeini's newly freed Iran; the war lasted eight years and ended in August 1988 through the intervention of the United Nations.

Syria became fully independent in 1945, after the French troops withdrew from its soil. During the 1950s political leadership passed gradually from the hands of old-style nationalists to more radical and anti-Western Ba'athists who helped to bring Syria into union with Nasser's Egypt (1958). The Union did not produce the desired results and was abandoned in 1962. In 1965 a split took place in the Ba'athist party and the splinter group of Alawites and Druzes gained the upper hand. However, by 1970 differences arose between the Ba'athist-Alawite regime led by Salah Jedid and its military wing led by the defence minister Hafez Assad; in November 1970 the latter ousted the former and assumed full control. Assad became the president and continues to rule Syria with an iron hand. He played a decisive role in the struggle for Arab Palestine and aided the Muslims in the civil war in Lebanon (1976).

The Hashemite kingdom of Jordan, created as Transjordan by the British in 1921, on the west bank of the river Jordan for the benefit of Amir Abdullah, continued under the rule of his family. The amir was assassinated in 1951 and was succeeded by his son Hussain in 1952, who has been ruling the kingdom through the vicissitudes of all these years in West Asia.

Lebanon became a fully independent republic in 1946, when French forces were withdrawn; it was agreed between the various political groups that its president would be a Maronite Christian, its prime minister a Sunni Muslim and the Speaker of its National Assembly a Shi'a Muslim. Lebanon did not participate in the Arab-Israel wars of 1948, 1956 and 1967. However, because of the presence on its soil of the Palestinian Commando Organization, Lebanon was turned into a state within a state: this resulted in frequent clashes between the Palestinian commandos and the Lebanese army. Also Lebanon suffered from the indiscriminate Israeli raids on its territory; Israel managed to create a rift between Muslims and Christians in Lebanon. As a result sporadic clashes between Christians and Muslims occurred, and still occur, causing havoc to the economy of Lebanon, once one of the most flourishing states in the Arab world.

In Saudi Arabia Abd al-Aziz Ibn Sa'ud, after having defeated his rival Ibn Rashid with the support of the British, consolidated his hold on various tribes and united his kingdom. He died in 1953 and was succeeded by his son, Sa'ud, who lacked his father's dynamism and organizing capacity. Moreover, his anti-Nasser stance alienated him from the militant Arabs; Egypt retaliated by giving military support to anti-Saudi forces in neighbouring Yemen (1062). Its ruler Imam Yahya was deposed. Sa'ud, therefore, abdicated and Crown Prince Faysal became the king. He introduced sweeping changes in the administration and in the aftermath of the 1967 Arab-Israel war a settlement was reached over Yemen between Egypt and Saudi Arabia. Faysal was assassinated on 25 March 1975, at the hands of a deranged nephew and was succeeded by Crown Prince Khalid; but he succumbed to a fatal illness (1982) and was succeeded by Fahd.

Kuwait, a small trading and fishing port, underwent a dramatic change in the 1950s with the export of oil by the Kuwait Oil Company (half British and half American). The shrewd Shaikh Abdullah on becoming the ruler (1950) turned Kuwait into a welfare state with a modicum of democracy. There was resistance to this from many members of the ruling al-Sabah family, divided traditionally between the al-Salem and al-Jabir branches; Shaikh Abdullah persisted in his democratization programme. However, after his death (1965) Shaikh Sabah al-Salem adopted a more cautious attitude to reforms; he died in 1977 and was succeeded by Shaikh Jabir, who modernized the administrative set-up and brought in many economic reforms, but he has been hesitant to revive the Parliament and give popular representation to his subjects.

Bahrain was the first Arab state to explore for oil (1934) but its output has been small. It gained its independence from the British in 1971. It is ruled by the Khalifa family, which is Sunni, though about 60 per cent of its population is Shi'ite. There have been serious Shi'ite disturbances and an attempted coup with alleged Iranian support (1980–82), specially after the advent of Khomeini and the establishment of his rule in Iran.

Qatar is the smallest of the Gulf states; prior to its oil export (1950) it was a desolate, desperately poor peninsula. However, now it has more oil than Bahrain. It was granted independent status by the British in 1971. It is ruled by the al-Thani family. Its ruler Shaikh Ali al-Thani was ousted by his cousin, Shaikh Khalifa, the present ruler, in a bloodless coup. A good administrator, Qatar has developed under him as a flourishing city-state. He has made his kingdom self-sufficient in food production. Like the Saudis, the Qataris are also strict Wahhābis.

The UAE came into existence when the rulers of six of the seven Trucial shaikhdoms agreed to form a federation, after Britain relinquished its hold (1971). It consists of Abu Dhabi, Ajman, Dubai, Fujaira, Sharjah and Umm al-Qaiwain. Ras al-Khaima remained outside for some years, but joined it later in 1972. Shaikh Zaid bin al-Nihan of Abu Dhabi has been the president since its inception. There has been steady economic progress and large-scale modernization. It has nationalized its oil wealth which has given it international clout. The UAE has successfully used this to buttress its economy and strengthen its position in the comity of nations.

Oman is also an oil-rich Sultanate; it became independent in 1971. Oman and Muscat have a long history— once it was one of the most important Arab countries controlling much of the Iranian and Pakistani coasts, and exercising control as far away as Zanzibar. It had been under British domination since 1798. Its ruler Said Ibn Taimur ruled as a despot and ruined the economy and was, therefore, replaced by his son Qābūs in 1973. Qābūs has used its oil resources diligently and modernized and industrialized the country despite the war he has fought in Defour against the rebels.

North Yemen, which became an independent kingdom under Imam Yahya (1918) remained in a sorry state until Yahya was assassinated (1948) and replaced by his son Ahmad. In 1958 Ahmad attached Yemen to the United Arab Republic of Syria and Egypt; but after the dissolution of the Union and his death (1961) his son Imam al-Badr, who succeeded him, was ousted by a coup led by Abdulla al-Sallal, a pro-Nasser officer. He seized Sanaa and declared Yemen a republic. Imam al-Badr with the help of Saudi Arabia and Jordan mobilized his forces; civil war broke out. Colonel Sallal appealed to Nasser for help and a large Egyptian force was sent to help him. Finally after the Arab-Israel war (1967) Nasser came to terms with Saudi Arabia and withdrew his troops from Yemen. Colonel Sallal was replaced but thereafter one president has been replaced by another through military coup and assassination. Major Ali Saleh has been in effective control for some time.

South Yemen, ruled by the British and known as the 'Aden Protectorate', was freed by the Marxists, led by Qahtan al-Shaabi (1967) with the support of the Soviet Union. In 1969 Qahtan was ousted and another Marxist regime took over. More changes occurred, with one president being executed and replaced by another. However, each one remained committed to the communist ideology though of late a show of Islamization is being put up to appease the local inhabitants and to cater to Islamic sentiment abroad.

In Palestine, Jewish underground organizations intensified terrorist activities; the British were unable to stop these and notified the United Nations that they intended to surrender their mandate. In November 1947, the UN

General Assembly passed a resolution dividing Palestine
into Jewish and Arab areas. The British forces left the
mandated territory on 1 May 1948 and the state of Israel
was created. There was renewed fighting between the
Arabs and the Jews, which was brought to an end on 24
February 1949. Egypt, Iraq, Lebanon and Jordan signed
armistice treaties with Israel. The result was that only the
West Bank remained with the Arabs, which was united to
Transjordan, which later became the kingdom of Jordan.
Since then there have been three wars, in 1956, 1967 and
1973 between the Arabs and the Zionists, Israelis and the
Egyptians but these have not affected in any way the
position of Israel. On the contrary, it has gained more
territory, including Jerusalem. The Palestine Liberation
Organization under Yasir Arafat has been continuing its
guerrilla warfare against Israel for achieving a homeland
for its people but has not succeeded in its mission despite
the support of most Arab states and the sympathy of the
Muslim countries all over the world. Its dream of a
Palestine state for the Arabs remains to be fulfilled.

Nasser took the lead in fighting the cause of the
Palestinians; he was emboldened in his resolve when he
successfully nationalized the Suez Canal and warded off
the continued British-French-Israel attack (1956). He
emerged then as the unchallenged leader of the Arabs.
However, his defeat in the subsequent six-day war against
Israel (1967) gave a near fatal blow to his pre-eminent
position. Frustrated he died at the young age of 53 (1970).
His vice president Anwar al-Sadat became the president.
He attacked Israel in October 1973 to avenge the earlier
defeat suffered by Egypt. His strategy and skill restored
Egypt's prestige and Israel was, for the first time, humili-
ated. America helped with the peace process and President
Carter brought the Israeli prime minister Begin and
Egyptian president Sadat together at Camp David (1979);
an accord was signed between them, which was resented
by the rest of the Arab world, including the Palestinians;

as a result Egypt was ostracized by the rest of the Arab world and expelled from the Islamic Summit. In Egypt also the Muslim Brotherhood condemned his accord as anti-Islamic and one of its sympathizers in the army gunned down Sadat. His vice president Hosni Mubarak took over as the president and has been trying to appease the fundamentalists ever since. He has brought Egypt back into the Arab and Islamic brotherhood and made peace with the Muslim Brotherhood.

Sudan became independent in January 1956 and held elections and installed a popular government but the economic situation deteriorated. Thereafter there was unrest and the army chief General Ibrahim Abboud in a bloodless coup declared martial law and took over the administration. In 1964 the military returned to the baracks and handed over power to the civilians; the political parties were, however, unable to cope with the situation. Hence in 1969 another military take-over took place and Colonel Jaffar Nimeiry formed the government. In 1971 pro-communist elements attempted a coup against Nimeiry, but it was ruthlessly suppressed and its leaders executed. In 1982 Sudan and Egypt signed an agreement for the complete harmonization of relations between the two countries and in 1983 President Nimeiry embarked on a programme of Islamization, abolishing the colonial legal system and introducing the shari'ah as the basis of jurisprudence in order to win the support of the local Muslims and the fundamentalists abroad. He was unable to stem the popular resentment against his dictatorial rule and as a result a massive revolt by workers and peasants led by intellectuals and professionals took place, in which he was overthrown and a popular government, headed by Sadiq al-Mahdi, was formed, which continues in power even today, though beset by all kinds of difficulties.

Libya was occupied by Britain and France after World War II (1939–45); it gained independence in 1951 when Sayyid Idris, leader of the Sanusi tribe, which had been spearheading the freedom struggle, liberated it from the colonizers and was proclaimed the king. In 1957 oil was discovered; it transformed the economy. On 1 September 1969, Colonel Muammar Qaddafi and his military junta overthrew the seventy-nine-year-old king and declared Libya a People's Republic; it has been ruled by Qaddafi in his characteristic style since then.

Algeria organized a series of protests, demonstrations and revolts to achieve its liberation from the French whose police and army struck against the agitators. Their leaders formed a provisional government in Cairo to focus world attention on their demand and to intensify the liberation struggle. More than one million Algerians died in clashes with the French police and army. At last after bloodshed President de Gaulle of France conceded Algerians their freedom, evacuated 800,000 French civilians and armed personnel stationed in Algeria, including technicians, teachers and doctors. Algeria emerged victorious from one of the bloodiest struggles (1962–63) that an Afro-Asian country ever faced. One of its leaders Ahmad ben Bella became the president of free Algeria (1964). Soon he was ousted by Colonel Houari Boumedienne, one of his colleagues in charge of the armed forces; Boumedienne constituted a revolutionary council (1965) to run the government and embarked on a massive socialist programme. On his death in 1978 his lieutenant Chadli Benjadid succeeded him; he follows the same policies as Boumedienne, though he is trying to give a more Islamic touch to his socialism.

Tunisia became independent in 1956; Habib Bourguiba, the leader of the freedom movement, took over the government and abolished the monarchy (1957). He established a republic with himself as the life-president. He introduced many secular measures, including reforms in Muslim Personal Law. He pursued a pro-West foreign policy and was, therefore, not liked in the Arab world. His hold on the government and the army remained firm, but in 1987 he was toppled by Prime Minister Ibn Ali—

appointed by Bourguiba himself—and the long rule of the life-president came to an end.

Of the Muslim countries in Africa south of the Sahara, Chad is the largest in terms of area; it was formerly a part of French Equatorial Africa. It became independent in 1960 and was declared a republic. Its war with Libya has done much damage to its economy; recently peace has been established between the two neighbours.

Morocco, which has been a protectorate was subjected to a revolt by tribal chiefs led by Thami al Glawi, who opposed the modernization programme of Sultan Muhammad V; they were supported surprisingly by the French, with the result that the king had to flee. Disturbances followed and the king was brought back (1955) and Morocco was granted independence. On Muhammad V's death (1961), his son Hassan II ascended the throne (1961). The new king promulgated a constitution which guaranteed adult suffrage and the establishment of a two-chamber parliament (1962). A year later fighting broke out between Morocco and Algeria on the issue of undemarcated frontiers. A cease-fire was signed (1964) and peace between the two countries was restored.

Mauritania, situated at the top of the West African bulge, was granted self-rule in 1946 with representation in the French Parliament. In 1958 it became an autonomous republic within the French community and in 1960 attained full independence. A year later it adopted the presidential form of government and declared the ruling Peoples party as the sole political organization.

Mali has a glorious Islamic past, having had successive Negro-Berber empires that brought power and prosperity to the Muslims, at a time when Europe was in darkness. It was the centre of the legendary Timbuktu, a Saharan metropolis of merchants and scholars. A French colony, Mali was granted limited internal autonomy in 1946 and in 1959 Sudan and Senegal joined it to form the Federation of Mali, which, however, did not last due to political and economic differences. In 1968, a coup ended the socialist regime and now it is run by a more popular democratic set-up.

Niger, in the interior of North Africa and in the neighbourhood of Libya, became a republic on attaining its freedom from the French in 1960. It still retains close economic and cultural ties with France. The first president Hamani Diori was ousted in a military coup in 1974. But since then there has been no crisis and the country is running smoothly.

Senegal, the former administrative and commercial centre of the French West African empire, became an autonomous republic within the short-lived French community in 1958; in less than two years it proclaimed itself a republic and is run under a democratic constitution.

Gambia is a finger of land almost surrounded by Senegal; culturally the two are closely linked. It won its independence in 1965 and became a member of the British Commonwealth in 1970. It is one of the few functioning democracies in Africa.

Guinea on the Atlantic coast of West Africa is also a republic. It was under French control in 1849; but in 1958 it obtained independence under Sekou Toure, who set up a militant one-party state. He died in 1984, and since then a military junta has been in control.

Gabon, the smallest Muslim state in Africa, became independent in 1960; it is run by a one-party government backed by the army.

Comoros are three islands between Madagascar and South-East Africa, and were ruled by various sultans until the French took them over in 1841 and established their rule. In 1974 they became independent and are now governed by native tribal leaders.

Djibouti, on the east coast of Africa, separated from the Arabian Peninsula by the strategically vital strait of Bab al-Mandeb, remained under the French until 1977 when it became independent. Though a republic, its economy is controlled by France and sustained by French aid.

Somalia, located at the eastern horn of Africa, is a Sunni Muslim state; it was an Italian protectorate but later was taken over as a trust by Britain under the aegis of the United Nations. It was once again given back to Italy. However in 1960 it was granted independence; in 1969 the army seized power in a bloodless coup and the junta has been in charge ever since.

In Asia, next to Pakistan, the most important Islamic state is Iran, which has gone through various phases of transformation since the end of World War II, in 1945 the Soviet Union in a daring bid deposed the Iranian governor of Tabriz and helped to establish the autonomous republic of Azerbaijan. A year later Soviet troops withdrew from Iran and the British with the help of America managed to stage a comeback. The prime minister Mohammad Mossadiq, with the support of leftish parties, nationalized the oil industry in 1951 and struck a blow at British hegemony. Britain retaliated by imposing an oil blockade on Iran. There was a popular revolt and the king Mohammad Reza Shah, considered a stooge of the West, fled from Iran but within a year returned with the aid of the CIA. He replaced Mossadiq with General Zahedi (1953) as prime minister, launched populist measures, and embarked on modernizing the country. He gradually consolidated his position but in the process resorted to more and more ruthless methods. He spent lavishly on himself and remained cut off from the people. As a result popular resentment mounted against him and he was overthrown by Imam Khomeini, who spearheaded the movement of liberation (1979). The Shah died in exile in Cairo in 1980. Since then Iran has been ruled by a religious Shi'ite oligarchy, which owes absolute allegiance to Khomeini; his word is law unto his people; he vowed to destroy Saddam Hussain, president of Iraq, who launched a war against Iran, but after fighting for eight years, the Imam agreed to a cease-fire with Iraq under UN auspices.

In Afghanistan between 1947 and 1949 the problem of Pakhtunistan came to a head; tension mounted. In 1953

Prime Minister Mahmud Shah Khan resigned and was replaced by General Mohammad Daud Khan, who relied for economic assistance more on Russia than Britain. He organized a military coup in 1973 and converted Afghanistan from a kingdom into a republic. In 1978 a pro-Soviet group of army officers murdered Daud and his colleagues and took over power; one Marxist group replaced another with Soviet support, until in 1981 Najibullah became the president. Troops and tanks were sent by the Soviet Union to help the Marxists but the Islamic Mujahideen, who are backed by Pakistan and America, organized resistance against the Marxist regime. There has recently been an overall settlement between the two superpowers under which Russia is to withdraw its troops in stages and Pakistan is to cooperate in bringing peace and stability in Afghanistan. But the Mujahideen are yet to reconcile to the rule of Najibullah and his Marxist colleagues; they are resolved to oust them from power and usher in an Islamic state in Afghanistan on the lines of Zia's Pakistan. There is, therefore, an unsatisfactory truce.

Turkey, which remained neutral in World War II, joined the Allies at the fag end in 1945. Soon thereafter it liberalized the political process at home; as a result a new opposition party known as the Democratic Party was formed by Celal Bayar, Adnan Menderes, Refik Koraltan and Fuat Koprulu. It came to power defeating the People's Party founded by Ataturk. However, due to political instability and factional fights, it was unable to run the government and a army junta led by General Cemal Gursel staged a coup in 1960. The Democratic party was banned. Menderes and many other leaders were tried and hanged. Several other politicians were sentenced to long terms of imprisonment. In 1961–62 a new democratic constitution was promulgated; it was approved in a referendum. Gursel was elected president and Ismet Inonu became the prime minister. They held elections (1965) in which Suleyman Demirel's pro-Islam Motherland Party obtained majority and formed the government. But with one government replacing another political instability continued; law and order deteriorated; the army once again took over (1971) the government. Meanwhile, Turkey invaded Cyprus by sea and air and occupied Forty per cent of the island, and a Turkish-Cypriot state was formed. Consequently the US-Turkish relations were strained; the US stopped economic aid. Turkey retaliated by suspending use of US military bases on its soil. In 1978 US aid was restored. In 1979 civilian rule once again was restored and Demirel returned to power as the head of a minority government. This was followed by strikes and terrorist activities. There was rising unemployment and uncontrolled inflation. The army again took over the government under General Evran (1980). A new revised constitution was approved by ninety-one per cent of the voters in a referendum (1982). Evran was elected president and Turgut Ozal's Motherland Party came to power (1983). Ozal attempted a compromise between Islam and secularism. He gave more religious freedom and established closer links with the Arab and Muslim countries. He allowed greater political rights to the people. Economically also Turkey was put on a sound footing. All political leaders were released. Ozal called for elections before the expiry of the stipulated period. The released leaders and their supporters contested the election (1987) but Ozal's party won an overwhelming majority in parliament and has continued to head the government, with Evran as the president.

In Central Asia, which was once a major centre of Muslim power and is now a part of the Soviet Union spread over six republics, Uzbekistan, Kazakhistan, Kirghiz, Turkman, Tajikistan and Azerbaijan and ten autonomous republics such as Tartar and Bashkir, there was some softening in the official attitude towards Islam. Relaxation in religious practices was also noticed under Brezhnev, though Gorbachev has reversed the process and has made it clear that communism stands for atheism and is an enemy of religion.

In China and other communist countries which once contained large Muslim populations, the official approach has been more or less the same as that of Russia; in fact it was much harsher under the Cultural Revolution, when many mosques were desecrated and mullās put to hard labour but it has differed in style from the Soviet Union. The new regime under Deng has allowed greater freedom to Muslims to practise their faith. There are also much fewer obstructions in the way of religious functionaries; mosques have been restored and Muslim institutions are given some financial assistance.

In South Asia, during 1948–49 there was undeclared war between the two newly-created dominions, Pakistan and India, over the accession of Jammu and Kashmir; a cease-fire was arranged through the United Nations. Pakistan adopted a new constitution and became an Islamic republic. Meanwhile unrest prevailed due to the assassination of its first prime minister, Liyāqat Ali Khan (1951), leading to political instability. General Iskander Mirza, therefore, took over the reins of government and became the president. Constant turmoil in both wings of Pakistan made the situation worse; General Mohammad Ayub Khan, the army chief, declared martial law and suspended civilian rule. In 1962 he ended military rule and enacted a new constitution with basic democracy as its main feature. In 1965 he was elected president defeating Jinnah's sister, Fātima Jinnah. Soon after war broke out between Pakistan and India over the issue of the Rann of Kutch; it ended with the famous Tashkent Accord (1965). Under Ayub's leadership Pakistan made substantial economic progress, but there was no democratic functioning. In 1969 widespread political unrest took place. Ayub resigned and handed over power to General Yahya Khan, who imposed once again martial law. The Bengali-speaking Pakistanis, exploited by their western counterparts, demanded separation under the leadership of Shaikh Mujibur Rahman. The result was civil war. India intervened militarily and Pakistan surrendered (1971). Thus, Bangladesh was born as an independent state.

In the western wing, General Yahya Khan was replaced by Zulfikar Ali Bhutto, leader of the Pakistan People's party; he reorganized the State apparatus, but was ruthless and autocratic in his functioning. In 1977 Bhutto was overthrown in a military coup led by General Ziaul Haq, who prosecuted him for murder and executed him after a Supreme Court verdict in 1979. Zia embarked on an intensive programme of Islamization, curbed political activities, but allowed limited democracy, which he sus- pended when he found that his position became weak; the influx of Afghan refugees in the wake of the Soviet inva- sion of Afghanistan in 1980 provided Zia with an opportunity to obtain massive economic and military aid from America. However, the situation changed after the two superpowers reached an agreement and peace was sought to be restored in Afghanistan in mid-1988. He was compelled to call for elections to normalize the political atmosphere in Pakistan. He was killed in a plane crash in August 1988 and one of his trusted colleagues, Ghulam Ishaq Khan, chairman of the Senate, took over as acting president. In the elections that followed Benazir Bhutto's Pakistan People's party (PPP) won a significant victory.

Bangladesh was declared a secular republic in 1971, after it separated from Pakistan. Shaikh Mujibur Rahman became prime minister and later president. In 1974 he and his family members were killed by some disgruntled army officers with Pakistan leanings. The army chief Ziaur Rahman then took effective control; but he was also killed in a coup (1981). Finally, General H.M. Ershad assumed all powers (1982). Though he has held several elections since then the opposition parties led by Shaikh Hasina Wajed, daughter of the assassinated founder of the republic, Shaikh Mujib, and Begum Zia, the widow of another assassinated president Ziaur Rahman, have refused to accept the electoral verdict, alleging that the elections were all rigged. The newly elected Parliament, under

Ershad's directive, has declared Bangladesh an Islamic state hoping thereby to gain popular support for Ershad's rule.

The Maldives in the Indian Ocean, towards the south-west of India, is a Sunni Muslim republic; it consists of about 1,087 islands and has been a British protectorate since 1887. It became independent in 1965 and a republic in 1968. Despite three attempted military coups—the latest in November 1988 was foiled by the intervention of an Indian contingent at the request of President Gayoom—it continuous to be a rather uncertain democracy.

In South-East Asia, which gave birth to the independent Malay state, later known as Malaysia, and to free Indonesia, containing the largest Muslim population concentrated in one region, the Japanese took over both the countries during World War II. After their surrender in 1945 the British created the Union of Malaya by uniting Penang and Malacca with the nine states which were ruled by the Muslim sultans. In 1948 the Union was transformed into a Federation and in 1957 Malaya gained independence, with Tenku Abdul Rahman as the first prime minister. Indonesia disapproved of the formation of the Federation in its neighbourhood, considering it a colonial outpost on its borders and encouraged sporadic guerrilla activities. The two Muslim countries were virtually at war, which ended in 1966.

There has always been ethnic tension between the Muslim Malays, who are in the majority and the minority Buddhist Chinese, who control the economy; the ruling Malay party known as United Malay National Organization (UMNO) has so far managed to keep in check ethnic conflicts; it has always collaborated with the Malayan Chinese Association (MCA) and the Malayan-Indian Congress (MIC). Despite the fact that Muslim fundamentalists create trouble every now and again, UMNO has, so far, managed to keep them in check. However, the internal political situation continues to be unstable. Apart from ethnic conflicts, which erupt every now and again, there has recently occurred a serious rift in the ruling party and the present prime minister Dr Mahathir Mohammed is facing crisis after crisis; the latest is his row with the Supreme Court, and his quarrel with the senior leaders of his party.

Indonesia, an archipelago of nearly 13,500 green and fertile islands, strung like a jewel along the Equator, was occupied by the Japanese during World War II. They overthrew the Dutch in 1941 who had colonized these islands since the eighteenth century. On the Japanese surrender in 1945, the Dutch reoccupied them; but the nationalist movement under Sukarno became so powerful that they could not stop the formation of the United States of Indonesia (1950) with Sukarno as the president of the new republic. He opted for a secular state and evolved his famous Panchsheela or five principles: (1) Nationalism, (2) Internationalism, (3) Democracy, (4) Social justice and (5) Belief in one God, as the basis of the new state. Later, in order to assume dictatorial powers he propounded the doctrine of 'guided democracy' and even collaborated with the communists, and with their aid, organized a coup in 1965 to take full control of the government. The army under its chief Suharto foiled the move; more than 300,000 Indonesians, suspected of communist leanings, were massacred and even Sukarno was put under house arrest. He died in 1970. Meanwhile, Suharto having taken over the presidentship managed the affairs of the state adroitly and got himself reelected four times. He formed his own Golkar party, which gives no quarter to fundamentalists, though the latter create trouble every now and again. Suharto has reiterated his faith in Panchsheela and has modified it to make it more secular.

The Sultanate of Brunei, located on the north coast of the island of Borneo, was once a powerful state, especially in the sixteenth century. It ruled the islands of Borneo and Philippines. The Treaty of 1888 placed it under British protection. It became independent in 1983 and is ruled by a sultan, who is said to be the richest man in the world.

Appendix VI

List of countries in the world which are independent and have a Muslim majority or near-majority. They are members of the United Nations and also of the Organization of Islamic Conference.

Most of the information in this Appendix is based on *Islamic Solidarity*, a book compiled by the Information and Research Department of the Kuwait News Agency for the fifth Islamic Summit Conference held in Kuwait in January 1987. Several Yearbooks and Almanacs have also been consulted.

Democratic Republic of Afghanistan

AFGHANISTAN

It is situated in South-West Asia bounded to the north by the USSR, to the north-east by China, to the west by Iran and to the east and south by Pakistan.

Its area is 650,090 sq. km and population, 14,792,000.

Its capital is Kabul (7,50,000); Muslims constitute ninety-nine per cent of the population.

Economy: Dependent on agriculture which contributes over sixty per cent to the national economy; wheat, cotton, fruit and nuts are the main agricultural products. The main industries are rugs, textiles and cotton. Good reserves of natural gas, oil and copper; also has semi-precious stones.

ALBANIA

People's Socialist Republic of Albania

It is situated in South-East Europe, with a coastline on the Adriatic Sea; Yugoslavia is to the north and east and Greece to the south.

Its area is 28,748 sq. km and its population, 3,100,000.

Its capital is Tirana (200,000) and Muslims constitute seventy per cent of the population, though, being under a communist regime, they are not practising Muslims.

Economy: Land used for agriculture; almost half the population is involved in labour; principal agricultural products are: wheat, corn, potato, sugar beet, cotton, tobacco; labour force in industry is about eighteen per cent. Major industrial products are textile, timber, construction material, fuel, semi-processed minerals. Exports: minerals, metals, fuels, foodstuffs, agricultural materials. Imports: machinery equipment and spare parts, construction material, foodstuffs, wheat.

ALGERIA

Democratic and Popular Republic of Algeria

It is a part of North Africa, bounded in the south by Mauritania, Mali and Niger, in the east by Tunisia and Libya, in the west by Morocco and in the north by the Mediterranean Sea.

Its area is 2,381,751 sq. km and population, 22,025,000.

Its capital is Algiers (2,500,000) and Muslims constitute ninety-seven per cent of the population.

Economy: Cultivable land is only ten per cent of the total area. Agriculture, though small, still employs about forty per cent of the total labour force. Crops include grain, grapes, fruit, dates and vegetables; but sixty-five per cent of its food requirements are imported. Rich in oil, natural gas, iron ore and phosphates. Exports of natural gas total forty billion cubic feet.

BAHRAIN

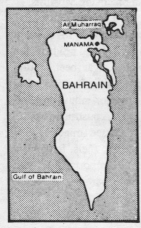

People's State of Bahrain

It is situated in the Gulf in West Asia, comprising thirty-five islands, twenty-four km off the coast of Saudi Arabia and twenty-eight km off the west coast of Qatar. The largest island Bahrain is fifty km long and between thirteen and twenty-five km wide.

Its area is 659 sq. km and population, 400,000.

Its capital is Manama (150,000) and Muslims constitute sixty-five per cent of the population, mostly Shias.

Economy: Oil represents sixty-five per cent of the national economy and its production exceeds 45,000 barrels per day. The agricultural sector is poor; it produces vegetables and fruit; it also has poultry farming; but it has to depend on imports to meet the growing consumer requirements. Offshore banking is the main prop of the economy and is responsible for making the country a beehive of commercial and financial activities in the Gulf.

BANGLADESH

People's Republic of Bangladesh

It is situated in South Asia, on the Bay of Bengal, bounded to thenorth, west and east by India with a short outlet to Burma in the south-east. In the south it is bounded by the Bay of Bengal.

Its area is 143,998 sq. km and population, 107,100,000.

Its capital is Dhaka (3,950,000) and Muslims constitute eighty-five per cent of the population; the rest are mostly Hindus.

Economy: Mainly agricultural; the principal product is jute. Other crops include rice, tea, tobacco, wheat, sugar-cane, spices and oil-seeds. Rich in natural gas and coal reserves. About eighty per cent of the population is engaged in agriculture. Exports: jute products, industrialization is still in its infancy. Floods occur every year and cause much devastation to its economy.

BENIN

People's Republic of Benin

It is situated on the west coast of Africa, forming a coastal strip on the Gulf of Guinea; it is bounded in the east by Nigeria and north by Niger and Burkina Faso; Togo is to its west.

Its area is 112,622 sq. km and population, 4,300,000.

Its capital is Porto-Novo (208,000) and Muslims constitute about fifty per cent of the population.

Economy: Mainly agricultural with about forty per cent of the population engaged in growing palm trees, cotton, cocoa, manioc and maize, fishing is next in importance. Oil-fields located in Seme, ten miles off-shore, produce an average of 2200–4000 barrels per day. Total oil production amounts to more than four million barrels per day.

BRUNEI

It is situated in South-East Asia, bounded to thenorth by the Sea of China, and east, west and south by Sarawak.

Its area is 5,765 sq. km and population, 221,000.

Its capital is Bandar Seri Begawan (70,000) and Muslims constitute seventy-five per cent of the population.

Economy: Oil and natural gas are the main sources of national income. Oil production exceeds 150,000 barrels per day. Natural gas reserves are about 1.5 billion barrels and 150 billion cubic mtrs respectively. Rich in agricultural products such as rubber, rice and pepper; major industrial products are petroleum and natural gas and exports are crude petroleum and liquefied natural gas. Imports include machinery and electric equipment and foodstuffs.

State of Brunei

COMOROS

It is an archipelago of four islands, situated in the Mozambique Strait, between Madagascar and the eastern coast of Africa.

Its area is 1,862 sq. km and population, 469,000.

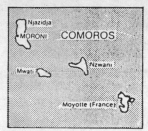

Federal Islamic Republic of the Comoros

Its capital is Moroni (on Grande Comoro), population 20,000 and Muslims constitute about ninety-five per cent of the population.

Economy: Mainly agricultural with about ninety per cent of the total labour force engaged in agriculture. Main crops are manihot, potato, rice, coconut, spices and banana. Livestock number over 170,000 head and fish catch exceeds 5000 tons per year. Major industry is perfume distillation; it exports perfume, vanilla, copra, chemicals, cotton textile and cement.

CHAD

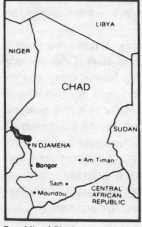

Republic of Chad

It is landlocked in North-Central Africa, bounded to the south by the Central African Republic, to the west by Niger, Nigeria and Cameroon, to the east by Sudan and to the north by Libya.

Its area is 1,284,000 sq. km and population, 4,600,000.

Its capital is N'djamena (511,700) and Muslims constitute eighty per cent of the population.

Economy: Agriculture, animal husbandry and fishing are the main economic activities, employing ninety per cent of the population. Cotton is the major product, which is exported and forms the cornerstone of the economy. Livestock totals about nine million head. The per capita income is one of the lowest in the world. Chad is hopeful of striking oil to the north of Lake Chadand; other mineral deposits are also indicated. Despite having excess production of grain and cereal, its transportation and distribution systems are poor, which often create food shortages in certain parts.

Republic of Cameroon

CAMEROON

It is situated in West Central Africa, bounded by Nigeria in the west, east by Chad and Central African Republic and south by Congo, Gabon and Equatorial Guinea.

Its area is 475,442 sq. km and population, 9,873,000.

Its capital is Yaounde (450,000) and Muslims constitute fifty-five per cent of the population.

Economy: Mainly agricultural, despite increased oil production. Crops include cocoa, coffee, tea, banana, cotton and tobacco; labour involved in agriculture is sixty per cent. Major industrial products include petroleum, natural gas, processed food, uranium and manganese; oil reserves are estimated at 150 million barrels. Imports: machinery and electric equipment, foodstuffs and textile; exports: cocoa, coffee, timber, aluminium and cotton.

DJIBOUTI

It is situated in North-East Africa, with Somalia to its south-east and Ethiopia to the south and west.

Its area is 23,300 sq. km and population, 300,000.

Its capital is Djibouti (200,000) and Mus-

Republic of Djibouti

Arab Republic of Egypt

lims constitute 94 per cent of the population.

Economy: It is dependant on goats, sheep and camels; construction work employs some labour. Port and maritime activities also help. It exports hide and cattle, and imports foodstuffs and transport equipment.

EGYPT

It is situated in North-East Africa, bounded to the west by Libya, south by Sudan, north-east by Palestine and north by the Mediterranean.

Its area is 1,002,000 sq. km and population, 48,305,000.

Its capital is Cairo (12,560,000) and Muslims constitute ninety-three per cent of the population; the rest are Christians, known as Copts.

Economy: Agriculture is the mainstay with millions of hectares of cultivated land. Main crops are cotton, wheat, corn, vegetables, fruit, sugarcane and rice. It also produces timber, balsam, gold, silver, coal, copper, iron, zinc, mercury and sulphur. Industrial products include textile, iron and steel, cement, copper, aluminium and petrochemicals. It is rich in oil and natural gas reserves. Oil production is substantial; tourism is also a major source of foreign exchange, apart from revenue from the Suez Canal. Its main export is cotton, while imports are machinery and electric equipment and fertilizers.

Gabonese Republic

GABON

It is situated on the west coast of Africa, bounded to the north by Cameroon and to the east and south by the Republic of Congo and to the west by the Atlantic Ocean.

Its area is 267,667 sq. km and population, 1,200,000.

Its capital is Libreville (257,000) and Muslims constitute about fifty per cent of the population.

Economy: Agricultural production does not contribute more than ten per cent to the economy. Major crops are bananas, rice, maize, cocoa, coffee, peanuts and sugarcane. Forests cover more than twenty-five million hectares; hence wood is the most important export item. Industries include cement, paints, aluminium, copper and paper. Oil contributes almost fifty per cent to the economy.

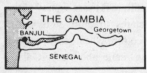

Republic of the Gambia

GAMBIA

It is situated in West Africa, bounded on the west by the Atlantic Ocean and on all other sides by Senegal.

Its area is 10,660 sq. km and population, 800,000.

Its capital is Banjul (48,000) and Muslims constitute eighty-five per cent of the population.

Economy: Principal products are groundnuts, rice, maize, and palm-kernel; also fish. Seventy-five per cent of its population is engaged in agriculture; groundnuts are exported and constitute ninety per cent of its foreign exchange earnings. Imports include textiles, foodstuffs and machinery.

Republic of Guinea

GUINEA

It is situated in West Africa, bounded to the north by Senegal and Guinea-Bissau, north-east by Mali, south-east by the Ivory Coast and south by Liberia and Sierra Leone. It is a coastal state.

Its area is 245,857 sq. km and population, 6,400,000.

Its capital is Conakry (656,000) and Muslims constitute ninety-two per cent of the population.

Economy: Rich in natural resources, mainly uranium, gold, copper, diamonds, iron ore and bauxite. Main agricultural crops are rice, groundnut, banana, palm-oil, pineapple, coffee and citrus fruit. Its industrial products include bauxite, alumina and processed goods.

Republic of Guinea-Bissau

GUINEA-BISSAU

It is situated in West Africa, bounded to the south-east by the Republic of Guinea, and north by Senegal. It borders on the Atlantic in the west and encompasses a number of islands.

Its area is 36,125 sq. km and population, 900,000.

Its capital is Bissau (110,000) and Muslims constitute fifty-two per cent of the population.

Economy: Main crops are groundnut, cotton, rice, palm-oil; light industries: timber and marine products; minerals: bauxite and phosphates. It has considerable animal wealth especially cattle. Ninety per cent of its population is engaged in agriculture. Exports are of groundnut, coconut, fish and wood; while imports include foodstuffs and manufactured goods.

INDONESIA

Republic of Indonesia

It is an archipelago situated in South-East Asia, consisting of 13,677 islands of which about 6000 are inhabited; it lies between Asia in the north, Australia in the south, the Indian Ocean in the west and south and the Pacific ocean in the east. Its main islands are Java, Sumatra, Sulawesi (Celebes), Maluku (Moluccas), Kalimantan (Borneo) and Irian Java (west Irian).

Its area is 1,904,344 sq. km and its population, 174,900,000.

Its capital is Jakarta and Muslims constitute ninety per cent of the population. It is the largest Muslim state.

Economy: Principal crops are rice, durian, citrus fruit, bamboo, coconut, rice, palm-oil, maize, nuts, tobacco, sugar, spices, potato and rubber. Natural resources include oil and natural gas and contribute substantially to the economy. Also rich in fish, sea-weed, shrimp and pearl. Industrialization is concentrated in oil refining and in the production of fertilizer, cement, chemicals, textile, printing paper and light and hand-made artifacts. It exports oil, timber, rubber, and tin and imports include foodstuffs, chemicals and textiles.

Islamic Republic of Iran

IRAN

It is situated to the south of the Caspian Sea and to the north of the Gulf. It is bounded to the north by the USSR, to the south by the Gulf of Omán, to the west by Iraq and Turkey and to the east by Pakistan and Afghanistan.

Its area is 1,648,000 sq. km and its population, 54,400,000.

Its capital is Teheran (6,037,658) and Muslim constitute ninety-eight per cent of the population, mostly Shias.

Economy : Main agricultural products are: wheat, barley, rice, cotton, sugar, dates and raisins. Also sheep and goats. However, industry contributes more to the economy and manufactures products of iron, steel, copper, coal, zinc, petrochemicals, manganese, cement and rugs. Iran's oil reserves exceed sixty million barrels per day; its production is more than 2.5 million barrels per day. Its major industrial products include textiles, cement, food and beverages and fertilizers. Apart from oil, it also exports timber, rubber and tin; its imports include foodstuffs, textiles and chemicals.

IRAQ

It is situated in West Asia, bounded to the north by Turkey, east by Iran, west by Syria, Jordan and Saudi Arabia and south by the Gulf, Kuwait and Saudi Arabia.

Republic of Iraq

Its area is 438,446 sq. km and population, 15,507,000.

Its capital is Baghdad (3,300,000) and Muslims constitute ninety-six per cent of the population, the majority being Shias.

Economy : Main crops are wheat, barley, cotton, fruits and vegetables. Also livestock. Only fifteen per cent of its population is engaged in agriculture though the huge area of fertile cultivable land enables it to produce grain, cotton, vegetables and fruits in large quantities, in addition to a considerable volume of dates. It has a number of advanced industries, e.g., textiles, fertilizers, cement. However its main source of national income is its large oil reserves which produce every day 3.50 million barrels of petroleum. Its exports include petroleum and dates and imports are of foodgrains, machinery and manufactured goods.

JORDAN

The Hashemite Kingdom of Jordan

It is situated in West Asia, bounded to the north by Syria, north-east by Iraq, east and south by Saudi Arabia and west by occupied Palestine.

Its area is 96,599 sq. km and population, 3,700,000.

Its capital is Amman (800,000) and Muslims constitute ninety-three per cent of the population.

Economy : Main crops are wheat, barley, olive, legume, fruit and vegetables. As a result of development of the irrigation and cultivation system, the agricultural sector has considerably increased, though not more than five per cent of its labour population is engaged in agriculture. Working Jordanians abroad contribute substantially to foreign exchange earnings. Industry engages about twenty-five per cent of its labour force. Jordan manufactures phosphate products, refined petroleum and cement; its imports are textiles and capital goods.

KUWAIT

State of Kuwait

It is situated at the north-west extremity of the Gulf; it shares to the north and west a border of 240 kms with Iraq, and to the south and south-west a border of 255 kms with Saudi Arabia. To the east it has a coastline of 290 kms in the Gulf.

Its area is 20,150 sq. kms and its population, 1,900,000.

Its capital is Kuwait (60,525) and Muslims constitute ninety-five per cent of the population.

Economy: Basically dependent on oil production, with average daily production of more than two million barrels. Reserves of oil and natural gas are large. However, its agricultural sector is also developing. Fish and shrimp are largely exported. Major industrial products are crude and refined oil, fertilizers and chemicals. It exports crude and refined petroleum and shrimp and imports foodstuffs, textiles, machinery goods and building material.

Republic of Lebanon

LEBANON

It is situated in West Asia, to the east of the Mediterranean Sea, it is bounded to the north and east by Syria and south by Israel. Its area is 10,400 sq. km and its population, is 2,619,000.

Its capital is Beirut (750,000) and Muslims constitute fifty-five per cent of the population.

Economy: Main agricultural products are grains, olives, fruits, vegetables and tobacco; major industrial products are textiles, cement, chemicals, refined oil and processed food. Tourism was once a flourishing industry; but has suffered heavily due to civil war. It exports fruits, vegetables, textiles and imports foodstuffs and machinery goods.

Socialist People's Libyan Arab Jamahiriya

LIBYA

It is situated in North Africa, bordering the Mediterranean Sea and is bounded to the east by Egypt, to the south-east by Sudan, to the south by Chad and Niger to the west and north-west by Algeria and Tunisia.

Its area is 1,759,998 sq. km and population 3,800,000.

Its capital is Tripoli (5,87,400) and Muslims constitute ninety-eight per cent of the population.

Economy: Principal crops are wheat, barley, olives, dates, citrus fruit and groundnut. However, more of its labour force is employed in industry than agriculture. Oil is the mainstay of the economy (about twenty-five billion barrels); its products are exported. So also with natural gas. It imports foodstuffs.

MALAYSIA

Malaysia

It is situated in South-East Asia and is bounded to the north-west by Thailand, to the south-east by Indonesia and to the south by Singapore.

Its area is 332,370 sq. km and population 16,100,000.

Its capital is Kuala Lumpur (1,000,000) and Muslims constitute more than fifty per cent of the population; the rest are Chinese Buddhists and Hindu Tamils.

Economy : Mainly agricultural. Major crops which are exported are rubber and palm-oil. Also rice, cocoa, pepper and wood; wheat is also exported and provides substantial foreign exchange earnings. It is also a major world exporter of tin. However, oil revenues represent more than twenty-five per cent of its total exports and is the mainstay of its economy. Its other industrial products include processed rubber and timber and palm-oil.

MALDIVES

It is situated in the Indian Ocean, about 671 km south-west of Sri Lanka. It consists of some 1,300 coral islands of which only 200 are inhabited.

Its area is 298 sq. km and population, 200,000.

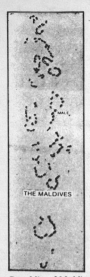

Republic of Maldives

Its capital is Male (46,344) and Muslims constitute 100 per cent of the population.

Economy: Based on fishing industry, its production is exported in fresh and processed form to neighbouring countries, particularly Sri Lanka. About fifty per cent of the labour force is engaged in this industry; agricultural production is mainly coconuts and millets and contributes five per cent of its income. Fish is one main source of foreign exchange. Tourist traffic is developing. It imports foodstuffs, textiles and drugs.

MALI

It is situated in West Africa, bounded to the north by Algeria, to the west by Mauritania and Senegal, to the south by Guinea and the Ivory Coast and the east by Burkina Faso and Niger.

Its area is 1,240,142 sq. km and its population, 8,400,000.

Its capital is Bamako (750,000) and Muslims constitute ninety per cent of the population.

Economy : Main crops are rice, sugar, cotton, groundnuts, millet and livestock. Its natural resources are iron ore, bauxite, manganese phosphate, salt, limestone and gold. Its major industrial products include processed food, canned fish, textiles andcigarettes. It exports meat, fish, textiles and tannery products . Its imports include foodstuffs, petroleum products, textiles, chemicals and drugs.

Republic of Mali

MOROCCO

Kingdom of Morocco

It is situated in the north-west of Africa, bordering the Mediterranean Sea to the west, the Straits of Gibraltar and the Atlantic Ocean to the north. It is bounded by Algeria.

Its area is 458,730 sq. km and population, 24,400,000.

Its capital is Rabat (556,000) and Muslims constitute ninety-six per cent of the population.

Economy: Agriculture and mining are the major economic sectors, employing two-thirds of the labour force. They contribute more than twenty-five per cent of the total exports. Main crops are wheat, barley, maize, vegetables and citrus fruits. Fish products rank third on the list of exports; a substantial part of these products is exported. Manufacture of cigarettes, clothing, carpets and leather products contribute substantially to industrial production. Natural resources include phosphates, iron, manganese and lead; also livestock. Exports are citrus fruits, vegetables and canned fish. It imports foodstuffs, consumer goods, and machines.

MAURITANIA

It is situated in the north-west of Africa, bounded to the north by Algeria, to the east by Mali, to the south by Senegal and to the west by the Atlantic Ocean.

Its area is 1,030,700 sq. km and population, 2,000,000.

Islamic Republic of Mauritania

Its capital is Nouakchott (175,000) and Muslims constitute ninety-nine per cent of the population.

Economy: Around seventy-five per cent of the labour population is engaged in raising cattle and sheep. Agriculture and farming is concentrated in the Senegal Valley, where the main crops are dates, rice, tobacco, wheat millet and maize. Natural resources include copper, iron ore and gypsum. Also livestock. Major industrial products are iron ore and processed fish, which are exported. It imports foodstuffs, petroleum and machinery goods.

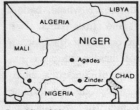

Republic of Niger

NIGER

It is situated in North-Central Africa, bounded to the north by Libya and Algeria, south by Nigeria and Benin, west by Mali and Burkina Faso and east by Chad.

Its area is 1,267,044 sq. km and population, 7,000,000.

Its capital is Niamey (399,100) and Muslims constitute ninety per cent of the population.

Economy: Agriculture and stock-breeding contribute almost fifty per cent of the economy and employ ninety per cent of the labour force. Main crops are cotton and goundnuts. Uranium reserves are estimated at 200 thousand tons and it stands fifth among world uranium exporters, excluding the East European countries. Uranium exports represent seventy-five per cent of the total foreign trade. Other minerals include coal, phosphates, zinc and oil.

It exports, apart from uranium, oil, cocoa, rubber, tin, timber and palm products. Its imports are machinery goods, chemicals and drugs.

NIGERIA

Federal Republic of Nigeria

It is situated in the west coast of Africa, bounded to the west by Benin, north by Niger, north-east by Chad, east and south-east by Cameroon, and south by the Gulf of Guinea.

Its area is 923,853 sq. km and population, 108,600,000.

Its capital is Lagos (1,097,000) and Muslims constitute more than fifty per cent of the population.

Economy: One of the world's leading oil producers, the average per day production is more than 2.5 million barrels. Agriculture is the main occupation of the population and employs around two-thirds of the labour force. Apart from the extensive forest wealth a substantial section of the population make their living from fishing. Rich in deposits of coal, tin, zinc, uranium and iron ore, it has established an extensive iron and steel complex; its exports include, apart from petroleum, palm products, cocoa, rubber, timber and tin. It imports machinery goods, chemicals and drugs.

OMAN

It is situated in South-East Arabia, bounded on the west and north by United

Sultanate of Oman

Arab Emirates, with Saudi Arabia and Yemen Arab Democratic Republic to its south-west.

Its area is 2,71,950 sq. km and population, 1,300,000.

Its capital is Muscat (70,000) and Muslims constitute ninety-nine per cent of the population.

Economy: Agricultural activities are concentrated in the coastal region and in valleys throughout the country. The crops are dates, cereals and also livestock. Oil and gas production is a major source of revenue. It has also a copper moulding and processing complex, and its proceeds amount to about fifty per cent of the foreign exchange earnings; apart from these oil and cement are also produced and exported. Its industries include petroleum drilling, fishing and construction. It imports foodstuffs, machinery goods, tobacco and drugs.

PAKISTAN

It is situated in South Asia, bounded to the east by India, west by Afghanistan and Iran, north by the People's Republic of China and the Arabian Sea on the south.

Its area is 803,936 sq. km and population, 104,600,000.

Its capital is Islamabad (210,000) and Muslims constitute about ninety-seven per cent of the population.

Economy: Mainly agricultural. Over fifty per cent of the labour force is employed in this sector. Main crops are wheat, rice, sugarcane and cotton. Industries include tex-

Islamic Republic of Pakistan

tiles, petrochemicals, steel, iron ore and food canning and about twenty-five per cent of the labour force is engaged in their manufacture and distribution. Major products are textiles, processed food, chemicals, natural gas and tobacco. It exports both raw and manufactured cotton, carpets, leather goods, and rice. Its imports include edible oil, crude oil, machinery goods, vehicles and chemicals.

QATAR

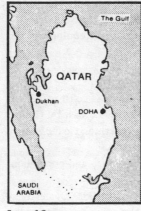

State of Qatar

It is situated on the west coast of the Gulf, bounded to the south by Saudi Arabia and the United Arab Emirates to the south-east. Its area is 11,437 sq. km and population, 300,000.

Its capital is Doha (190,000) and Muslims constitute ninety-nine per cent of the population.

Economy: Dependent on oil which contributes almost eighty-five per cent of the economy. Fertilizer and petrochemicals production is another source of national income. Vegetable and fish production are substantial enough to cover domestic needs, though some of these are imported.

SENEGAL

Republic of Senegal

It is situated on the west coast of Africa; bounded by Mauritania to the north, by Mali to the east and by Guinea and Guinea-Bissau to the south.

Its area is 196,722 sq. km and population, 7,100,000.

Its capital is Dakar (196,000) and Muslims constitute ninety-one per cent of the population.

Economy: Agriculture is the main economic activity, employing seventy per cent of the labour force and contributes half the total export earnings. Groundnuts are the primary cash crop and constitute one-third of the total exports. Besides rice and vegetables, cotton, sorghum, millet are also produced. Apart from fish-canning, petrochemicals are also manufactured; likewise, iron ore, fertilizers, cement and processed food and fish are in production. Surveys also indicate the presence of deposits of uranium, oil, natural gas and gold. Its imports include foodstuffs, consumer goods, machinery and electrical equipment and drugs.

SIERRA LEONE

It is situated on the west coast of Africa; bounded to the north and east by Guinea and south-east by Liberia and to the west by the Atlantic Ocean.

Its area is 72,326 sq. km and population, 3,883,000.

Its capital is Freetown (500,000) and Muslims constitute sixty-five per cent of the population.

Republic of Sierra Leone

Economy: The agricultural sector employs one-third of the labour force and contributes thirty per cent of the earnings from export. Rice is the main crop, but production is not adequate to satisfy domestic needs. Other crops include ginger, cocoa, coffee, palm-oil, groundnut, sugarcane, fruit and vegetables. Forest and fishing industries are being developed. It exports diamond, textile, iron ore, furniture and foodstuffs; it imports petroleum, food-

Somali Democratic Republic

stuffs, chemicals and machinery goods.

SOMALIA

It is situated on the east coast of Africa, bounded to the north-west by Ethiopia and west by Kenya. The Somali coast extends for a long distance along the Indian Ocean. Its area is 637,655 sq. km and population, 7,700,000.

Its capital is Mogadishu (7,00,000) and Muslims constitute ninety-nine per cent of the population.

Economy: Based on agriculture and live-stock-rearing (cattle, goats and camels), about eighty per cent of the labour force is employed in this sector. Sales of livestock amounts to eighty per cent of the proceeds from export earnings. Though eight million hectares of land are cultivable the culti-vated area presently is no more than one million hectares. It grows grain, banana, sugarcane, cotton, peanuts and gum. Deposits of copper, tin, zinc, manganese, uranium and iron ore have been found but not yet extracted. It exports livestock, skin, hides and bananas. Its imports include machinery goods and transport equipment.

SAUDI ARABIA

It is situated in South-West Asia, covering four-fifths of the Arabian peninsula. Bounded to the north by Jordan, Iraq and Kuwait, south by the People's Democratic Republic of Yemen and Arab Republic of Yemen, east by UAE, Qatar and the Arabian Gulf and to the west by the Red Sea. Its area is 2,250,070 sq. km and population,

Kingdom of Saudi Arabia

14,800,000.

Its capital is Riyadh (1,250,000) and Muslims constitute 100 per cent of the population.

Economy: Its oil reserves are estimated to be one quarter of the world's total, while its natural gas reserves are also very high, about 3,200,000 million cubic feet. Eighty-five per cent of its revenue comes from export of petroleum products. Agriculture is also developed now and is producing more goods than required for domestic needs. Its main crops are dates and grain; also livestock. It is also producing large quantities of dairy products, eggs, poultry, and around thirty per cent of the total labour force is employed in this sector. Manufacturing industries also have come up, particularly of iron, steel, fertilizer and petrochemical plants, cement and plastic goods. All these constitute a significant source of revenue. Surveys and data confirm the presence of several mineral deposits, especially gold, copper, zinc, silver and uranium.

SUDAN

It is situated in North-East Africa; bounded to the north by Egypt, east by the Red Sea and Ethiopia, west by central Africa, Chad and Libya, south by Kenya, Uganda and Zaire.

Its area is 2,505,802 sq. km and population, 23,500,000.

Its capital is Khartoum (1,250,000) and Muslims constitute about eighty-five per

Democratic Republic of the Sudan

cent of the population.

Economy: Out of eighty million hectares of cultivable land, only 5.5 million hectares are cultivated, with eighty per cent of the labour force engaged in this sector. Main crops are maize, wheat, rice, coffee, cotton, sugarcane and groundnuts. Industrial products are cement, textiles, pharmaceuticals, leather goods and processed food. Exports include cotton, though extraction of mineral deposits such as iron ore, manganese, gold and chrome still limited. Deposits of gold estimated at 150 thousand million tons and oil-fields discovered in south-west Sudan produce 190,000 barrels per day. Imports include foodstuffs, machinery goods, livestock and transport equipment.

SYRIA

Syrian Arab Republic

It is situated in West Asia, bounded to the north by Turkey, east by Iraq, south by Jordan, south-west by Lebanon and occupied Palestine and west by the Mediterranean Sea.

Its area is 185,180 sq. km and population, 11,300,000.

Its capital is Damascus (1,200,000) and Muslims constitute eighty-seven per cent of the population.

Economy: Agriculture plays a major role, employing more than thirty per cent of the labour force. Cotton is the main crop, and is the major source of foreign trade, representing almost eighty per cent of the export earnings. Sugar production is also substantial; industrial products include textile, cement, glass, petroleum products and processed food and soap. Exports are petroleum, textile, cement, glass and processed food; also fruit and vegetables. It imports machinery goods and metal products.

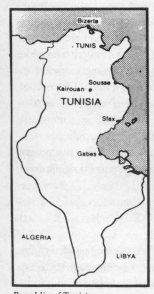

Republic of Tunisia

TUNISIA

It is situated in North Africa, bounded to the west by Algeria, south-east by Libya and north and east by the Mediterranean Sea. Its area is 164,152 sq. km and population, 7,600,000.

Its capital is Tunis (600,000) and Muslims constitute ninety-nine per cent of the population.

Economy: Agriculture and mining are the main sources of national income. Main crops are wheat, barley, olives, vine, citrus fruit, vegetables and dates. More than fifty per cent of the labour force is engaged in agriculture. Revenues from oil and phosphates represent twenty-five per cent of the total earnings from exports. Other products are olives, textile, leather goods, chemicals and fertilizers. Imports are foodstuffs, machinery goods and drugs.

Republic of Turkey

TURKEY

It is situated on the frontiers of South-East Europe and West Asia. Its coast edges the Black Sea in the north, the Mediterranean in the south-west and the Aegean Sea in the west. Bounded to the east by the USSR and Iran, south by Iraq and Syria and west by

Greece and Bulgaria.

Its area is 779,452 sq. km and population 51,400,000.

Its capital is Ankara (3,462,880) and Muslims constitute ninety-eight per cent of the population.

Economy: The agricultural sector employs around sixty per cent of the total labour force, its products constitute about thirty-five per cent of the total exports and about twenty per cent of the national income. Cultivated land is about twenty-five million hectares, i.e., one-third of the total area. Its principal crops are cotton, tobacco, cereals, sugarcane, fruits and nuts. Industrial production surpasses agricultural production, with industrial products representing about sixty-five per cent of the total exports. Turkey also exports chromite, copper, coal and alumina in addition to oil, fruit, nuts and livestock. Oil reserves amount to around 125 million barrels. It imports fertilizers, chemicals, metals, machinery goods, crude oil and transport equipment.

THE UNITED ARAB EMIRATES

It is situated in East Arabia, bounded to the south and west by Saudi Arabia, east by the Sultanate of Oman and north-west by the state of Qatar. Its coast extends 650 sq. km along the Arabian Gulf.

Its area is 82,880 sq. km and population, 1,400,000.

Its capital is Abu Dhabi (225,000) and Muslims constitute ninety-five per cent of the population.

Economy: Mainly dependent on oil, its reserves of both oil and natural gas are estimated at thirty-two billion barrels and 31,205 billion cubic feet respectively. The daily production of oil averages over 1.2 million barrels. Despite climatic difficulties, agricultural production is being developed, specially eggs, fish and white-meat. It imports foodstuffs, consumer goods, machinery and electrical equipment and vehicles.

SOUTH YEMEN

It is situated in the south-west corner of the Arabian peninsula, bounded to the north-west by Yemen Arab Republic, north by Saudi Arabia, east by the Sultanate of Oman and south by the Gulf of Aden.

Its area is 287,490 sq. km and population, 12,400,000.

Its capital is Aden (365,000) and Muslims constitute almost ninety-eight per cent of the population.

Economy: Agriculture and fishing are the mainstay of the economy. Crops include sorghum and wheat in addition to cotton, sesame, coffee and barley. Almost fifty per cent of the labour force is engaged in this sector. Industry employs about fifteen per cent of the labour force and its products include refined oil, salt, canned fish, meat, and textiles. It exports mainly petroleum products, textiles and cotton; imports are foodstuffs and machinery goods.

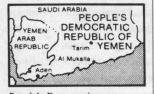

People's Democratic Republic of Yemen

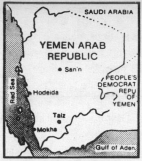

Yemen Arab Republic

NORTH YEMEN

It is situated in the south-western part of the Arabian peninsula, bounded to the north by Saudi Arabia, south by the People's Democratic Republic of Yemen, west by the Red Sea and east by the Rub Al-Khali (Empty Quarter).

Its area is 195,000 sq. km and population, 6,500,000.

Its capital is Saana (427,185) and Muslims constitute ninety-nine per cent of the population.

Economy: The agricultural sector is well-developed; it employs about twenty-five per cent of the labour force. Principal crops are wheat, sorghum, cotton and fruit. Also cattle and sheep. Marib Dam, with a length of 763 kms and a height of thirty-nine meters irrigates 10,000 hectares of land to produce fruits and vegetables and to supply electricity to a number of cities and towns. There is an oil refinery with a capacity of 10,000 barrels per day. Other industrial products include consumer goods and construction materials. Imports are foodstuffs, crude oil and manufactured goods.

Appendix VII

A. List of countries in the world where Muslims form a significant minority, with the percentage of the Muslim population being above 10 per cent of the total in each country.

B. List of countries in the world where Muslims do not form a substantial part of the population being less than 10 per cent of the total in each country.

For both lists the source of information is the *Cultural Atlas of Islam*, New York, 1986.

Muslim Minorities in the World

A. Where the Muslims are more than ten per cent of the total population:

Country	Total Population (in thousands)	Muslim Population (in thousands)	Percentage
Angola	6,870	1,717	25
Armenia SSR	2,618	343	13
Bulgaria	8,898	1,388	16
Burma	35,269	3,529	10
Burundi	4,318	863	20
China	1,052,000	107,525	10.2
Congo	1,583	172	11
Cyprus	652	241	37
Equatorial Guinea	256	86	34

Fiji Islands	642	69	11
Gabon	699	269	40
Georgia SSR	4,781	1,130	24
Ghana	12,329	5,047	45
Guyana	857	131	15
India	6,93,680	79,243	11
Kenya	16,567	4,234	26
Liberia	1,877	572	30
Lesotho	1,370	138	10
Malagasay Republic	8,766	1,552	18
Malawi	6,155	1,928	31
Malta	354	52	15
Mauritius	969	162	17
Mozambique	10,531	2,535	24
Philippines	50,061	5,551	11
Portuguese Timor	672	147	22
Reunion	493	108	22
Singapore	2,250	382	17
Surinam	424	123	29
Thailand	48,087	6,406	13
Trinidad & Tobago	1,207	146	12
Uganda	13,621	4,460	33
Ukrania SSR	48,078	6,505	14
Yugoslavia	22,617	4,821	21
Zambia	5,931	800	13
Zimbabwe	7,544	1,017	13.5

B. Where the Muslims are less than ten per cent of the total population:

Country	Total Population (in thousands)	Muslim Population (in thousands)	Percentage
Argentina	28,571	559	2
Australia	15,128	152	1
Austria	7,656	41	.5
Belgium	10,243	200	2

Bhutan	1,337	63	5
Botswana	802	39	5
Brazil	124,950	242	.01
Byelorussia SSR	9,183	621	7
Canada	24,399	824	3.5
Central America & the Carribean	37,595	120	.03
Chile	11,173	57	.5
Finland	4,812	4	.08
France	54,120	1,360	2.5
Germany (West)	62,528	1,012	1.6
Greece	9,595	310	3
Hong Kong	4,243	48	1
Hungary	10,817	120	1
Italy	57,446	631	1
Japan	118,777	255	.02
Kampuchea	7,500	805	1
Laos	3,643	37	1
Moldavia SSR	3,643	123	3
Namibia	703	39	5.5
Nepal	15,338	553	3.6
New Zealand	3,169	33	1
Panama	1,969	58	2.9
Poland	35,931	382	1
Rumania	22,498	216	1
Russian SFSR	132,600	8,976	6.7
South Africa	29,189	545	1.9
South Korea	39,928	86	.02
Sri Lanka	15,031	1,374	1
Swaziland	562	52	9
Taiwan	17,980	155	.08
United Kingdom	57,019	2,800	5
United States	224,113	4,344	1.9
Vietnam	54,212	245	.5
Zaire	29,494	2,742	1

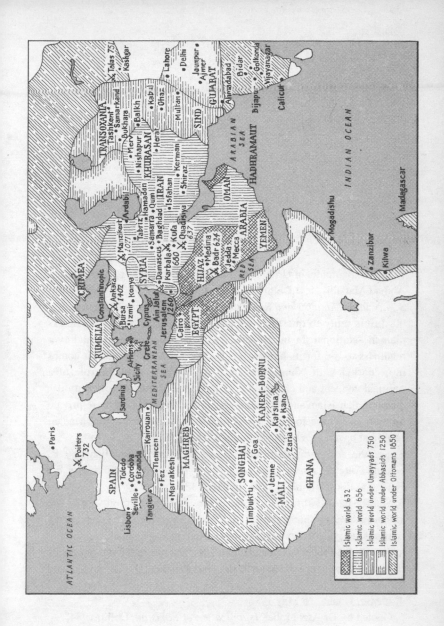

Notes to the Chapters

INTRODUCTION

1. See the pamphlet in Urdu, *Muttahida Qaumiyat aur Islam* by Husain Ahmad Madani, New Delhi. Also see Iqbal's views on nationalism in S.A. Vahid, *Thoughts and Reflections of Iqbal*, Lahore, 1964, pp. 256–90. In his reply to questions raised by Jawaharlal Nehru, Iqbal explained, 'Nationalism in the sense of love of one's country and ever readiness to die for its honour is a part of the Muslim faith; it comes into conflict with Islam only when it begins to play the role of a political concept and claims to be a principle of human solidarity demanding that Islam should recede to the background of a mere private opinion and cease to be a living factor in the national life.' Madani could not have agreed more with this viewpoint.

2. See the article entitled 'Ideology of Muslim Nationalism' by R. Gordon Polonskya in the book *Iqbal: Poet–Philosopher of Pakistan*, ed. Hafeez Malik, Columbia, 1971, pp. 108–135.

3. See Rashad Khalifa, *Quran, Hadith and Islam*, Tucson, 1982. The author observes in his preface: 'The continued research then unveiled a startling fact; that the extremely popular hadith and sunna have nothing to do with the Prophet Muhammad and that adherence thereto represents flagrant disobedience of God and His final Prophet (Qur'ân, 6: 112 and 25: 31)'.

4. *Ittefaq*, Dhaka, 25 May 1986.

5. Quoted by Dr Afzal Iqbal, *Islamization of Pakistan*, Delhi, 1984, p. 25.

6. See Altaf Gauhar's article, 'Islam and Secularism' in *The Challenge of Islam*, ed. by Altaf Gauhar, London, 1978, pp. 298–311.

7. Quoted in Emmanuel Siwan, *Radical Islam*, Yale, 1985, p. 43.

8. Muhammad Munir, *From Jinnah to Zia*, Lahore, 1980, p. 65.

9. Abd al-Salam Faraj, *The Absent Precept (al-Fardia al-Ghaiba)* in the Arabic newspaper *Al-Ahram*, Cairo, 14 December 1981.

CHAPTER 1

1. See H.A.R. Gibb, *Modern Trends in Islam*, Chicago, 1947, p. 117. 'So long as the secular governments did not interfere with the social institutions of Islam and formally recognised the shari'ah, the conscience of the believers was not outraged and the task of building up a state and universal Muslim society could go on.'

2. R.M. Maclever, *The Modern State*, Oxford, 1966, p. 169.

3. Sidney Z. Ehler and John E. Morrall, *Church and State through the Centuries*, A Collection of Historic Documents with Commentaries, Westminster, Maryland, 1954, p. 11.

4. See John Locke's *Letter Concerning Toleration*, in which he categorically states that religion must be kept out of affairs of state. Also see Donald Eugene Smith, *India as a Secular State*, Princeton, 1963, p. 14.

5. Quoted by M. Searle Bates, *Religious Liberty: An Enquiry*, New York, 1945, pp. 193–194.

6. Altaf Gauhar, *Translations from The Quran*, Lahore, 1975, pp. 16–30.

7. Laurence Urdang and Stuart Berg Flexner (ed.), *The Random House Dictionary of the English Language*, New York, 1969, p. 1190.

8. Donald Eugene Smith, *India as a Secular State*, op. cit., p. 4.

9. *The Shorter Oxford English Dictionary on Historical Principles*, Oxford, 1973, Vol. II, p. 1926.

10. H.A.R. Gibb and J.H.Kramers (ed.), *Shorter Encyclopaedia of Islam*, New York, 1965, states that 'the imam who was guilty of moral sins did not cease to be a Muslim and must be obeyed'. This is the Shi'ite version. According to the Sunnis, 'It is obligatory on a Muslim that he should listen to the ruler and obey him whether he likes it or not, except when he is ordered to do a sinful thing. If he is ordered to

do a sinful act, a Muslim should neither listen to him nor should he obey his orders.' Also see Abdul Hamid Siddiqui, *Sahih Muslim* (English translation), Vol. III, Lahore, 1973, p. 412.

11. Murji'ites or Murjiya (which literally means 'procrastinators') are an early sect of Islam; they believe that 'the judgement of every true believer, who hath bear guilty of a grievous sin will be deferred till the Resurrection; for which reason they pass no sentence on him in this world, either of absolution or condemnation.' See Thomas Patrick Hughes, *A Dictionary of Islam*, 1973, p. 421.

12. Bernard Lewis, *The Arabs in History*, London, 1958, p. 177.

CHAPTER 2

1. See Muhammad Munir, *From Jinnah to Zia*, op. cit., p. 65, wherein the following dialogue between the Commission and Maududi is quoted: '*Q*. If we have this form of government in Pakistan (treating non–Muslims as Zimmis), will you permit Hindus to have their constitution on the basis of their religion? *A*. Certainly. I should have no objection even if the Muslims of India are treated in that form of government as shudras and malishes and Manu's laws are applied to them depriving them of all share in the government and the rights of a citizen.'

2. See for the text of the Constitution of Madina, W. Montgomery Watt, *Muhammad at Madina*, Oxford, 1956, pp. 221–28.

3. See for an analysis of the developments of the 'two nations' theory and the demand for Pakistan, C.H. Philips and Mary Doreen Wainwright (ed.), *The Partition of India : Policies and Perspectives 1935–1947*, London, 1970. Also see Jamilud–din Ahmad (ed.), *Some Recent Speeches and Writings*, Lahore, 1942.

4. Quoted from *Kitab Futuh al–Buldan* in the English translation of it by Philip K. Hitti, *The Origins of the Islamic State*, New York, 1916, Vol.1, pp. 100–01.

5. H.G.Wells, *The Outline of History*, London, 1956, pp. 613–14.

6. W. Montgomery Watt, *Muhammad at Madina*, op. cit., p. 237.

7. Maxime Rodinson, *Mohammed* (translated from the French into English by Anne Carter), London, 1971, p. 155.

8. A more systematic compilation of the Qur'ānic verses, which relate to the obligations of a state, has been made by Tahir Mahmud in his draft code, as presented by him in *Islamic and Comparative Law Quarterly*, the journal of the Department of Islamic and Comparative Law, Indian Institute of Islamic Studies, New Delhi, March 1987, Vol. VII, No. 1, pp. 3–32.

9. Bernard Lewis, *Jews of Islam*, Princeton, 1984, p. 14.

10. Quoted in Abdul Rahman i–Doi, *Shariah: The Islamic Law*, London, 1984, pp. 244–46.

11. Abdulla Yusuf Ali, *The Holy Qur'ān*, Beirut, 1968, p. III.

12. Fazlur Rahman, *Islam and Modernity*, op. cit., p. 19.

CHAPTER 3

1. See for full details of the conflict between Umar and the supporters of Ali, S.H.M. Jaferi, *The Origins and Early Development of Shi'a Islam*, London, 1979, pp. 27–35.

2. Quoted in Shibli Numani, *Umar The Great* (translated into the English by Zafar Ali Khan), Lahore, 1947, Vol. I, p. 92. Some Shi'a historians have alleged that Umar tried to put his threat into practice by allowing his followers to collect firewood to set fire to the house in which Fātima lived; they quote Fātima remonstrating them thus: 'O people. It is only yesterday that my father, the holy Prophet, departed from you and today you have the audacity to attack his house, in which his daughter is mourning for him and which he did not enter without saluting its inmates.' The noted Sunni scholar, Shibli Numani in his work, *al–Faruq* has said that in view of Umar's excitable nature, such an eventuality could be considered 'probable'. See S.V. Mir Ahmad Ali, *Husayn – the King of Martyrs*, Karachi, n.d., p. 73.

3. Sayyid Muhammad Husayn Tabatabai, *Shi'ite Islam* (translated from the Persian and edited with an Introduction and Notes by Sayyid Hossein Nasr), London, 1975, p. 42. Also see for a scholastic Shi'ite exposition of the question of succession Moojan Momen, *An Introduction to Shi'ite Islam*, Oxford, 1985, pp. 11–22.

4. See W. Montgomery Watt, *Islamic Political Thought* (in the series 'Islamic Survey'), Edinburgh, 1980, pp. 26–28. Also see for a detailed

404 *The Struggle within Islam*

analysis of the origin of the title Khalifa or Caliph, Patricia Crone and Martin Hinds, *God's Caliph*, Cambridge, 1986, pp. 4–24.

5. Sir William Muir, *The Caliphate*, London, 1984, p. 86.

6. Quoted in H.G.Wells, *Outline of History*, London, 1956, p. 608.

7. Quoted from Ibn Hisham's *as-Sira* in Syed Amir Ali, *A Short History of the Saracens*, New Delhi, 1981, pp. 21–22.

8. Quoted in Syed Amir Ali, ibid., p. 23.

9. Quoted in Irfan Mahmud Raana's, *Economic System under the Great Umar*, Lahore, 1970, pp. 1–2. 'Everywhere he governed the subject races on one and the same principle; everywhere he sought to keep the Arabs apart from the native population and to maintain as a military caste, and everywhere he forbade them from making a settlement or acquiring landed property.' S. Khuda Baksh, *Politics in Islam* (based on Von Kremer's *Staatsidee des Islams*, and researches of Wellhausan, Goldziher and other orientalists), Delhi, 1975, pp. 25–26.

10. Quoted from Abu Yusuf's *Kitab al–Kharāj*, ibid., p. 17. Also see William Muir, *The Caliphate, Its Rise, Decline and Fall*, London, 1984, pp. 159–60, wherein the celebrated author observes: 'The State had by this time an income swollen by tribute of conquered cities, poll tax of subjugated peoples, land assessments, spoils of war and tithes. The first charge was for the revenue and civil administration; the next for military requirements, which soon assumed a sustained and permanet form; the surplus was for the support of the nation.'

11. Umar himself was conscious of this deterioration in the character of the Arabs. He wrote to Amar bin al–As, the commander–in–chief of the Arab forces in Egypt, when the seige lasted long: 'Perchance the luxuries of Egypt have tended to make you indolent and luxury-loving like the Christians, else victory would not have been so long delayed.' Quoted in Shibli Numani, *Umar the Great;* op. cit.,Vol. I, p. 92.

12. Quoted in S.H.M. Jaferi, *The Origin and Early Development of Shi'a Islam*, op. cit., p. 88.

13. A.S. Tritton, *The Caliphs and their Non–Muslim Subjects*, London, 1970, pp. 5–17. Tritton remarks : 'Suspicion arises that the covenant is not the work of Umar. It presupposes closer intercourses between Christians and Muslims than was possible in the early days of the conquest. We cannot save it by arguing that it was legislation for the future.' (p.10) Sir William Muir also says that 'it would be a libel

on that tolerant ruler' to attribute it to Umar. See his *The Caliphate*, op. cit., p. 147.

14. The general impression about Uthmān having been a weak caliph is refuted by P.M. Holt, Anna K.S. Lambton and Bernard Lewis (ed.), *The Cambridge History of Islam*, Cambridge, 1970, Vol.1, p. 68. 'The historians attribute the intensification of unrest partly to the fact that Uthmān was a weak man, but some of his actions, for example his firm opposition to abdicate, and his dignified behaviour in the face of death, seem to contradict this assumption.'

15. Quoted in S.H.M. Jaferi, *The Origins and Early Development of Shi'a Islam*, op. cit., p. 88.

16. Syed Amir Ali, *A Short History of the Saracens*, op. cit., p. 52.

17. See S.A.Q. Husaini, *Arab Administration*, Lahore, 1970, p. 73.

CHAPTER 4

1. Quoted from *Maqatil* in S.H.M. Jaferi, *The Origins and Early Development of Shi'a Islam*, London, 1979, pp. 135–36.

2. Qouted from ibid., p. 136.

3. Quoted from Ibn al-Ibri, p. 188 in Philip K. Hitti, *History of the Arabs*, London, 1973, p. 197.

4. See Syed Muhammad Zulquarnain Zaidi Alhuma, *Hazrat Amir Muawiya Tarikh ke Aieene main* (Urdu text), Rawalpindi, 1969, pp. 7–8.

5. Quoted in S.H.M. Jaferi, *The Origins and Early Development of Shi'a Islam*, op. cit., p. 175.

6. See G.E. von Grunebaum, *Classical Islam: A History 600–1258* (translated by Katherine Watson), London, 1970, in which the author describes the significance of the martyrdom of Husayn thus: 'Within a few years this had provided the Shi'as with a human hero of metaphysical significance, around whose martyrdom the emotional life of the movement crystallized until our own time.' (p. 71)

7. Syed Amir Ali, *A Short History of the Saracens*, New Delhi, 1981, p. 88.

CHAPTER 5

1. See H.M. Balyuzi, *Muhammad and the Course of Islam*, 1976, Oxford, p. 212. The author writes: 'As the first century of the Hijrah drew to its close, expectations ran high that with the passage of a hundred years the hand of Providence would bring down those who wielded power not rightly theirs, and that the legitimacy of power would be restored.'

2. See W. Montgomery Watt, *The Majesty that was Islam*, London, 1974, p. 99. Also see Patricia Crone and Martin Hinds, *God's Caliph*, op. cit., pp. 80–96.

3. However, it would not be quite correct to say that Baghdad was the centre of only power and wealth; it was equally famous for 'intellect and creativity'. See Philip K. Hitti, *Capital Cities of Arab Islam*, Minnesota, 1973, p. 94.

4. Historians are divided on the real reason for the ouster of Barmakids; according to one legend it was because of the incest by Harūn's prime minister Jafar with the latter's own sister Abbasa; but Ibn Khaldūn repudiates it. See H.M. Balyuzi, *Muhammad and the Course of Islam*, op. cit., p. 241.

5. Despite the ulamās' protest, poetry and music flourished in Islamic countries. According to O. Wright, this was 'connected with the emergence of the Mukhannathun, a class of effeminates who indulged in various immoral as well as artistic activities. The violent disapproval they provoked among the pious may have contributed significantly to the strong anti-music bias of the four orthodox law–schools which, if it could not hinder the efflorescene of court music, at least prevented the acceptance of music as a respectable activity in society at large.' See Joseph Schacht and C.E. Bosworth (ed.), *The Legacy of Islam*, Oxford, 1974, p. 496.

6. 'At the start, Ma'mūn made no attempt to impose the Mutazillite doctrines. . . .Indeed, his favourite saying was that he liked a position to be gained and superiority established by argument and sound proof, and not by the use of force. . . .But towards the end of his reign, the controversy over the nature of the Qur'ān had reached such a high pitch that Ma'mūn was swayed into promulgating the Mutazillite belief by compulsion.' See H.M. Balyuzi, *Muhammad and the Course of Islam*, op. cit., p. 249.

CHAPTER 6

1. Quoted from *Siyását-Namah*, p. 200 in Haroon Khan Sherwani, *Early Muslim Political Thought and Administration*, Delhi, 1976, pp. 178–79.
2. Ibid., p. 181.
3. Ibid., p. 183.
4. Quoted from Tabari, ibid., p. 217.
5. Stanley Lane–Poole, *Moors of Spain*, quoted by Syed Amir Ali, *A Short History of the Saracens*, op. cit., p. 564.
6. Abul Hassan Ali b. Muhammad b. Habib al–Mawardi, *Ahkamus Sultaniyah* (Arabic), Chapter II. Also See Haroon Khan Sherwani, *Early Muslim Political Thought*, op. cit., p. 154.
7. Despite his deep orthodoxy, Mawardi, one of the greatest jurists of Islam, was pragmatic enough to accept the realities of a situation. As G.E. von Grunebaum observes in his book, *Islam*, London, 1955, p. 68: 'Never once did he stop to bring his postulates in accordance with the world in which he was living. . . .He recognized and deplored the shortcomings of his period, but he took note of them for his system.'
8. Quoted from Ghazāli's *Kimiya–i–Saadat*, p. 7. in Haroon Khan Sherwani, *Early Muslim Political Thought*, op. cit., pp. 212–13.

CHAPTER 7

1. T.W. Arnold, *The Preaching of Islam*, London, 1973, p. 3.
2. Ibid., p. 5.
3. G.E. von Grunebaum, *Modern Islam : The Search for Cultural at Identity*, New York, 1962, p. 17.
4. Quoted from al–Kalabadhi, *Kitab al–Ta'arruf*, Cairo, 1934, p. 10 in P.M. Holt, Anna K.S. Lambton and Bernard Lewis (ed.), *The Cambridge History of India*, op. cit., Vol. 2, p. 605.
5. H.A.R. Gibb, *Mohammedanism*, London, 1964, p. 156.
6. See for a critical analysis of the influence of Buddhism and Hinduism on Ṣūfism, Reynold A. Nicholson, *The Mystics of Islam*, New York, 1975, pp. 16–19, wherein the author says, '. . .I think we may conclude that the Ṣūfi theory of fana was influenced to some extent by Buddhism as well as by Perso–Indian pantheism.'

7. E.H. Whindfield (translated and abridged), *Masnavi–i–Ma'navi: The Spiritual Couplets of Maulānā Jalal ud–Dīn Muhammad Rumi*, London, 1898, p. 139.

8. J. Spencer Trimingham, *The Sufi Orders in Islam*, Oxford, 1973, pp. 254–55.

CHAPTER 8

1. From the moment he became the ruler, Mehmed II behaved as the protector of both Muslims and non–Muslims. He was cosmopolitan. Though Islam was supreme, the Christian church enjoyed freedom of worship in respect of its observances and customs. Religious minorities were given special status; they were recognized as millets or nations, with their own head and laws and usages. He gave the same respect to the Greek Orthodox Patriarch, the Armenian Patriarch, and the Jewish Chief Rabbi. See Lord Kinross, *The Ottoman Centuries*, New York, 1979, pp. 112–13.

2. After Selīm I's victory over the Mamlūks, the titular caliph Mutawakkil transferred to Selīm I and his heirs all rights to the Caliphate at a ceremony in the mosque of Aya Safya, Istanbul; there is, however, no contemporary record of this; thereafter the Ottoman sultans called themselves caliphs and were accepted as such by the Muslims generally. See P.M. Holt, Anna K.S. Lambton and Bernard Lewis (ed), *The Cambridge History of Islam*, op. cit., Vol. I, pp. 320–23.

3. Sūleymān the Magnificent, the tenth Ottoman sultan, was 'in Muslim eyes the living incarnation of the blessed number ten—the number of man's fingers and toes, and the ten senses, the ten parts of the Qur'ān and its variants, the ten commandments of the pentateuch, the ten disciples of the Prophet, the ten skies of the Islamic heavens and the ten guardian spirits presiding within them.' See Lord Kinross Morrow Quill, *The Ottoman Centuries*, op. cit., p. 173.

4. Quoted from the Annual Report of the Board of Useful Affairs of 1838 in ibid., p. 464.

5. Ibid., p. 514.

6. A critical analysis of the Committee of Union and Progress of the Young Turks and why it failed to achieve its objective is given by the noted Turkish intellectual, Halide Edib in her lectures to Jamia Millia

Islamia, Delhi, published under the title, *Conflict of East and in Turkey*, Lahore, 1963, pp. 89–90.

CHAPTER 9

1. The ulamā were against at the move of Alauddin Khilji, and though he had considerably curtailed their power, their influence on the course of political development was too deep–rooted to be challenged. As Khiliq Ahmad Nizami points out, they acted more 'as politicans who had aligned themselves with one or the other of the political groups and dabbled in politics regardless of their dignity and position as religious leaders.' See his *Some Aspects of Religion and Politics in India during the Thirteenth Century*, op. cit., p. 171.

2. Though many of the Delhi sultans were not militarily powerful, they had succeeded in warding off outside invasions. Many of their regimes were short–lived. In a period of 300 years, five dynasties sat on the throne of Delhi; 'but it was the richest of all the Islamic states during the period.' See D.P. Singhal, *A History of the Indian People*, London, 1983.

3. E.V. Sachan, *Al-Biruni's India*, London, 1914, Vol. I, p. 137. Also see S.M. Ikram, *Muslim Civilization in India* (ed.) Ainslie T. Embree, New York, 1969, pp. 26–28.

4. Quoted from S.A. Rashid's article in *Medieval Indian Quarterly*, Vol. I, Nos. 3 and 4, pp. 104–5, in S.M. Ikram, *Muslim Civilization in India*, op. cit., p. 48.

5. See H.M. Elliot and John Dowson, *A History of India as Told by its own Historians*, Vol. III, London, 1867, p. 100. Balban is reported to have once remarked, 'All that I can do is to crush the cruelties of the cruel and to see that all persons are equal before the law.' Also see Balban's *Wasays*, testament to his son and heir–apparent, in which while advising on the functions and duties of kingship, Balban says, 'How can we the slaves be competent to rule in the manner in which Umar b. Khatab and Umar b. Abd al-Aziz ruled?' Quoted from *Tarikh–i–Firozshai* in K.A. Nizami, *Some Aspects of Religion and Politics during the Thirteenth Century*, op. cit., p. 98.

6. Quoted in R.C. Majumdar, H.C. Raychaudhuri and Kalinkar Datta, *An Advanced History of India*, Madras, 1985, pp. 298–99.

7. According to the available sources of the times, 'the early Turkish sultans of Delhi gave full religious liberty to their non–Muslim subjects. Even in the imperial city of Delhi they bowed before their idols, blowed their conches, bathed in the river Jumna and took out their religious processions without let or hindrance.' Ibid., p. 320.

8. Quoted in ibid., p. 406.

9. Khushwant Singh, *Hymns of Guru Nanak* (translated into English), New Delhi, 1969, p. 98.

10. Ibid., p. 99.

11. Quoted from al-Biruni's India in S.M. Ikram, *Muslim Civilization in India*, op. cit., p. 131.

12. Quoted in Mahdi Husain, *The Rihla of Ibn Battuta*, Baroda, 1953, p. 182.

13. Quoted in Sri Ram Sharma, *The Religious Policy of the Mughal Emperors*, Bombay, 1962, p. 44. The ulamā's advice to Akbar was couched in convincing terms: 'Religion and law and creeds ought never to be made subjects of discussion by Your Majesty, for these are concerns of prophets, not the business of kings. Religion and law spring from heavenly revelation; they are never established by the plans and designs of man. From the days of Adam till now they have been the mission of prophets and apostles as rule and government have been the duty of kings.' Quoted in V.A. Smith, *Akbar, the Great Moghul*, London, 1917, p. 210.

14. Quoted in Sri Ram Sharma, *The Religious Policy of the Mughal Emperors*, op. cit., pp. 31–32.

15. The charge has no basis; it is based on the statement of a contemporary chronicler Mullā Ahmad, who mentions it in his *Muktubat*, Vol. II, No. 7, p. 93. Badayuni, no doubt, refers to Akbar turning mosques into stables and handing them over to Hindus and Vincent Smith in his *Akbar the Great Moghul*, op. it., exploits it fully, but the Jesuit Fathers did not find mosques in Delhi turned into stables or chowkis. See Du Jarric's *Akbar and the Jesuits* and Sir Edward Maclagan's *The Jesuits and the Great Moghul*, London, 1917.

16. Jahāngir's chain of justice had sixty bells and could be used by anyone desirous of obtaining justice. It became the most popular instrument of ventilating a grievance. The emperor inflicted the severest punishments even on his suporters, making no distinction between a prince, a commoner, a Muslim and a non-Muslim. See *Tuzuk–i–*

Jahāngìr, Memoirs of Jehangir (translated by Alexander Regers and H. Beveridge), London, 1909. Also see Elliot and Dowson, *A History of India as Told by its Own Historians*, op. cit., Vol. VI, p. 300.

17. Quoted from the introduction of Dārā Shikōh's *Majma–ul–Bahrain* in S.M. Ikram, *Muslim Civilization in India*, op. cit., pp. 187–88.

18. Despite Aurangazēb's devotion to Islam as he perceived it and his dedication to the strengthening of the empire, he struck, by his policies, a fatal blow to its future. As he lay dying he realized that he had failed to achieve his objective. In his letter to his second son, he wrote: 'My fever has left me, leaving but the skin and the husks behind it. All the soldiers are helpless, bewildered and perturbed like me. . . .I know not what punishement will befall me. Though I have a firm hope in God's grace, yet for my deeds anxiety ever remains with me.' Quoted in J. Allan, S.T. Wolselley Haig and H.H. Dodwell, *The Cambridge Shorter History of India*, New Delhi, 1969, p. 450.

CHAPTER 10

1. See Moojan Momen, *An Introduction to Shī'i Islam*, Oxford, 1985, pp. 11–22. Also see the article by Juan R. Cole in Nikki R. Keddie (ed.), *Religion and Politics in Iran*, New Haven, 1983, p. 36, in which Cole explains the difference thus:

> That Shī'is have used terms like ijmā' (consensus) and ijtihād in a radically different sense from the one intended by these words among Sunnis has given rise to much confusion. It is often stated, for instance, that the door of ijtihad was never closed for Shī'is. The closing of the door of ijtihād refers to the belief held by many Sunnis that absolute ijtihad was no longer possible after the death of as-Shafi'i. But since Shī'is at first rejected personal opinion, ijtihad, and the validity of considered opinion (as opposed to a decisive jugment) their jurisprudents were theoretically far more constricted than those of the Sunnis.

Also for a concise and lucid account of the growth and development of Shī'ism, see Bernard Lewis' article, 'The Shī'a', in *New York Review of Books*, 15 August 1985.

2. For a fuller analysis of the origin of the Fatimid state, see P.J. Vatikiotis, *The Fatimid Theory of State*, Lahore, 1981, pp. 1–22.

412   *The Struggle within Islam*

3. See Nikki R. Keddie (ed.), *Religion and Politics in Iran*, op. cit., p. 171, in which Gregory Rose in his contribution writes:

> The anomaly of a Shī'i Buyid government governing a predominantly Sunni population in the name of a Sunni Abbasid caliph led Shī'i jurisprudents to discuss the degree to which Shī'i fiqh permitted the faithful to participate in an illegitimate (mubtil), oppressive government. There could be no question in the Shī'i mind that the rightful (muhiqq) ruler was the twelfth imam, then in occultation, not the Abbasid caliph. Indeed, no matter how fervently Shī'i the Buyids might be in their faith, doctrine held that any government—no matter how necessary or just—was oppressive and illegitimate if it was not that of the imam. This dicussion led to a theory of deputation of believers by the imams to participate in government activities: in the case at hand, to serve as administrators and sharī'ah court judges.

4. For an understanding of Allama Hilli's contribution to the development of a Shī'ite state see Moojan Momen, *Shī'i Islam*, op. cit., pp. 184–86. According to *The Encyclopaedia of Islam*, Leiden, 1971, Vol. III, p. 390, it was due to his efforts that Twelver Shī'ism became the State religion in Persia; his books are even today taught as fundamental texts to the Shī'a Twelvers.

5. The Akhbāris, who contested the clerical prerogative of ijtihād, were definitively defeated by the Usūlis, who supported clerical ijtihād. The Usūli victory had important political consequences. During the decades of persecution the Akhbāris gained a following based on the fear of clerical, social and political involvement that the power of ijtihād implied. Had they continued to be the dominant current within Shī'ism, the legitimacy of the clergy's political role would have been drastically reduced. Their defeat, on the other hand, encouraged a revival of clerical, social and political leadership,

writes Azhar Tabari in his contribution in Nikki R. Keddie, *Religion and Politics in Iran*, op. cit., p. 48.

6. At first the Qājār rulers carried on smoothly with the Shī'a ulamā but after 1850, when they began to modernize the State apparatus, there was tension and conflict. Likewise, the ulamā forced Reza Shah Pahlāvi to turn Persia into a kingdom, though he was for establishing a republic. They associated a republic with Ataturk, whom they condemned as

a heretic, though Reza Shah applauded his reforms. See Nikki R. Keddie, *Religion and Politics in Iran*, op. cit., p. 10.

7. See Arnold J. Toynbee, *A Study of History* (abridgement by D.C. Somervell), Oxford, 1960, p. 786.

CHAPTER 11

1. Quoted in Al-Jabarti's *Ajaib al-Athor fi al-Tarajin wa-al-Akhbar*, Vol. 1, pp. 422 and 353 and translated into English in *Copies of the Original Letters from the Army of General Bonaparte in Egypt*, intercepted by the Fleet under the Command of Admiral Ford Nelson, London, 1978, Vol. 1, pp. 235–7.

2. As a Western observer had succinctly put it:

> Such was the strength of the Mahdi's legitimacy and political-military acumen that he was able to dislodge the Egyptians, humiliate the British through the extermination of the Hicks and Gordon expeditions, and through his successor, hold the Anglo-Egyptian forces at bay for fourteen years. Although the Mahdi died only a few months after his capture of Khartoum in 1885, he passed along to his successor, the Khalifa Abd Allahi, the rediments of a coherent polity; and the Khalifa succeeded in maintaining it under increasingly unfavourable conditions.

Michael C. Hudson, *Arab Politics*, Yale, 1977, p. 330. For a fuller picture see P.M. Holt, *The Mahdist State in the Sudan, 1881–1898*, Oxford, 1958.

3. See Khushwant Singh, *A History of the Sikhs*, Princeton, 1963, pp. 273–74. Also see for a fuller account of the role of Sayyid Ahmad Shahid and his lieutenants and followers, Sayyid Athar Abbas Rizvi, *Shah Abd al–Aziz*, Lucknow, 1982, pp. 471–541.

4. See M. Rafiq Khan, *Islam in China*, Delhi, 1963, pp. 25–26. Also the article, 'The Hui (Muslim) Minority in China: A Historical Overview' in *The Journal Institute of Muslim Minority Affairs*, Vol. VIII, No. 1, London, January 1987, pp. 62–78.

5. Francis Robinson, *Atlas of the Islamic World since 1500*, Oxford, 1982, p. 129.

6. By his piety, bravery and other qualities of leadership Abd al-Qadir had acquired such legendary reputation that the English poet Thackeray wrote of him:

It was not in fight they bore him down: he never cried amen,
He never sank his sword before the prince of Franghistan.
But with traitors all around him, his star upon the wane,
He heard the voice of Allah, and would not strive in vain.

Norman Daniel in his classic *Islam, Europe and Empire*, Edinburgh, 1966, pp. 534–535 comments: 'This pious hero of Islam ended his days honoured throughout Europe; he was the noble enemy; but the cause of the nationalist Muslim peoples which he had led was nowhere honoured.' Also see Michael K. Clark, *Algeria in Turmoil*, London, 1960, p. 14. Clark puts the place of Abd al-Qadir in the freeing of Algeria thus: 'The Emir Abd-el-Kader symbolized, more nobly perhaps than any of his successors, Algerian resistance to French domination.'

7. See Maxime Rodinson's article, 'The Western Image and Western Studies of Islam', in Joseph Schacht and C.E. Bosworth (ed.), *The Legacy of Islam*, Oxford, 1974, p. 52.

CHAPTER 12

1. Nikki R. Keddie in his *An Islamic Response to Imperialism*, Berkeley, 1968, pp. 34–35, has summed up Afghani's role thus: 'For all his faults and lack of religion, Afghani surely contributed something of positive value to the modern Muslim. After a century of denigration by the West, he helped present those parts of Muslim tradition that might be worthy of pride, and suggested that reform could and should take part within the boundaries of Islam.'

2. Afghani mounted a frontal attack on Sir Syed Ahmad Khan for 'co-operation with the British'. In an article in his journal *al-Urwa al-Wuthqa*, Afghani wrote that Sir Syed and his companions 'became an army for the English government in India. They drew their swords to cut the throats of the Muslims, while weeping for them and crying: We kill you only out of compassion and pity for you and seeking to improve you and make your lives comfortable. The English saw that this was the most likely means to attain their goal: the weakness of Islam

and the Muslims.' Quoted in Nikki R. Keddie, *An Islamic Response to Imperialism*, op. cit., p. 71.

3. Despite being Afghani's disciple, there was a difference in the approach of Abduh and Afghani. 'The latter was a revolutionary who aimed at a forcible upheaval; Muhammad Abduh, on the other hand, held that no political revolution could take the place of a gradual transformation of mentality. See *Shorter Encyclopaedia of Islam*, (ed. H.A.R. Gibb and S.K. Kramers), New York, 1965, p. 406.

4. Rashid Rida (1865–1935) did not go in for the reformism of his mentor in later years. He wrote in his *al-Manar* exegesis that those Muslim rulers who abolished such penalties as cutting off the hands of thieves or stoning adulterers and prostitutes were 'infidels'. Quoted in Emmanuel Siwan, *Radical Islam*, op. cit., p. 101. Rida was firmly of opinion that Islam provides 'the only adequate solution for modern social, political and religious problems'. See G.E. von Grunebaum, *Islam*, 1969, p. 190.

5. The more the Ottoman sultan Abd al-Hamid played upon pan-Islamism as a counter against the West, the more Britain, France and Russia worked against Turkey and instigated the Arabs to demand liberation from the Ottoman yoke. To quote Halide Edib,

Among the Arabs, with or without Western encouragement, national self-consciousness was bound to come, for they are fifteen millions, as large a unit as the Turks. The point at which the West aimed was to create nationalist sentiment at a stage when the Turks, Arabs and the Muslim peoples were not politically advanced enough to find a modus vivendi which would keep the foreigner out.

Conflict of East and West in Turkey, op. cit., p. 59.

6. The poem is by Muhammad Bahjat al-Athari as quoted in Abd al-Razaq al-Hasani, *Tarikh al-Iraq al-Siyasi al-Hadith* (Modern Political History of Iraq), Beirut, 1948, p. 269. Also see Muhammad A. Tarbush, *The Role of the Military in Politics*, London, 1982, pp. 60–62.

7. Sarekat Islam or Partai Serikat Islam Indonesia was the first political experiment on a national level, founded in 1911. It developed gradually and became the largest organization of the Muslims in Indonesia. *Muhammadiyah* was primarily religious, with its emphasis on social welfare. It was inspired by the teachings of Muhammad Abduh of

416   *The Struggle within Islam*

pEgypt and was founded by one of his disciples, Kiyahi Haji Ahmad Dahlan of Jogjakarta in 1912. See C.A.O. Van Nieuwenhuijze, *Aspects of Islam in Post-Colonial Indonesia*, The Hague, 1958, p. 45.

CHAPTER 13

1. As David Holden and Richard Johns have put it:

Peninsular Arabia especially was once more sunk in the sort of corruption, idolatry and lawlessness that Muhammad himself had encountered. Instead of worshipping God alone, men were offering prayers to a multitude of saints. Stones, trees and statues were. . .sacred, the once simple mosques had become elaborate temples and the laws of the Qur'ān were treated with contempt. . .Abd al-Wahhāb was a true zealot, come to cleanse the stinking stables of Arabia once more with the word of God. But the word alone proved insufficient for the task. Like the Prophet, Abd al-Wahhāb needed a sword as well and to his eternal joy he found one in Muhammad bin Saud and his family.

See their book *The House of Saud*, London, 1981 pp. 20–21.

2. A picturesque description of the growing rift between Ikhwān and Ibn Sa'ūd is given by David Holden and Richard Johns in ibid., pp. 86–95.

3. As Daniel Pipes remarks: 'From 1745 to 1934, virtually every battle the Wahhābis fought was against Muslim enemies; they justified their expansion by refusing to recognize the Islamic credentials of non-Wahhābi Muslims. Unlike most other examples of Muslims weeding their opponents out of Islam—an obvious tactic almost never effective—the Wahhābis genuinely considered other Muslims untrue to the faith and therefore proper objects of jihād. Religious differences motivated these wars and were not merely a cover for other reasons.' See his book, *In the Path of God*, New York, 1940, p. 231.

4. See Michael Curtis (ed.), *Religion and Politics in The Middle East*, Boulder, 1981, p. 282.

5. Ibid., p. 283.

6. Ibid., p. 284.

7. The growing power of populist Islam in the Persian Gulf region is not monolithic in character. There are Sunni as well as Shī'i dimensions and the important Sunni movement is itself divided.

> Populist Sunni Islam is a potent force in the Gulf countries, representing a particularly stony challenge to the social and political status quo. . . .To meet this growing challenge, ruling elites in the region are taking unprecedented action to demonstrate their own fidelity to Islam.

See article by James A. Bill entitled 'Resurgent Islam in the Persian Gulf' *in Foreign Affairs*, Fall 1984, New York, pp. 108–27.

8. In his fight against the communist guerrillas in Dhufar, King Qābus used Islam as a weapon. See the leaflet dropped by SOAF planes over western Dhufar, as quoted in Fred Halliday, *Arabia Without Sultans*, London, 1974, pp. 304–5. However, it was not his Arab co-rulers in the Gulf or the Sunni Saudi Arabia, who helped Qābus but the Shi'ite Shah of Iran, 'who quickly despatched both weapons and men to the beleaguered Omanis'. See Lawrence Ziring, *Iran, Turkey and Afghanistan*, New York, 1981, p. 139.

CHAPTER 14

1. For a critique of the Muslim Brotherhood in Egypt and their conflict with Nasser, see Gilles Kepel, *The Prophet and Pharaoh: Muslim Extremism in Egypt*, London, 1985, pp. 16–102. Also see for the rise and development of the movement Ishaq Musa Husainin, *The Moslem Brethren*, Beirut, 1956.

2. Nasser's *Philosophy of the Revolution*, a leaflet issued one year after the revolution (1953), dealt with Egypt's role in three circles: Arab, Muslim and African, and according to Robert Stephens was a 'little different in character and motive from Winston Churchill's description of Britain's position at the intersection of the three spheres of Europe, the Commonwealth and the Anglo-American Aliiance'. See Robert Stephen, *Nasser: A Political Biography*, London, 1971, p. 142.

3. At this meeting, which was largely attended, a member of the Muslim Brotherhood, Mahmud Abdul Latif, a carpenter by profession, fired six shorts at Nasser, but hit two men standing near Nasser. The crowd began to panic; it was then that Nasser, keeping his cool, made his famous statement: 'Remember that if anything should happen to me, the revolution will go on, for each one of you is Gamal Abdul Nasser.' Also see for the growth and development of the Muslim

Brotherhood's conflict with Nasser; Gilles Kepel, *The Prophet and Pharaoh*, op. cit., pp. 36–69. Also see Kenneth Cragg, *The Pen and the Faith*, London, 1985, pp. 53-71.

4. Quoted from Sayyid Qutb's *Signposts* (*Maalim fil Tariq*) Cairo, 1964, in Gilles Kepel, *The Prophet and Pharaoh*, op. cit., pp. 51–52. Also see Muhammad Qutb, *Islam--the Misunderstood Religion*, Delhi, 1968, particularly the chapter on modern systems which explains that 'it is not a spent force but a living dynamic force'.

5. See Gilles Kepel, *The Prophet and Pharaoh*, op. cit., pp. 60–61.

6. Quoted from Hasan al-Hudaybi's *Duiah la Qudah* (*Preachers, Not Judges*), in Gilles Kepel, *The Prophet and Pharaoh*, op. cit., pp. 61–63.

7. See the proceedings of the criminal trial of the Muslim Brotherhood, in which Shukri was the principal accused; the trial was held in-camera by the Military Court of the State Security in Cairo on 6, 7, 8 November 1977; Shukri gave a free and frank exposition of his views.

8. For an account of the al-Jihād organization, founded secretly in 1978, as a result of its members' involvement in anti-Copt riots, and its subsequent role in the assassination of Sadat, see R. Hrair Dekmejian, *Islam in Revolution*, New York, 1985, pp. 97–101.

9. Quoted in Gilles Kepel, *The Prophet and Pharaoh*, op. cit., pp. 150–51.

10. Quoted in ibid., pp. 150–51.

11. Quoted in ibid., pp. 152–53.

12. See Metin Heper and Raphael Israeli (ed.), *Islam and Politics in the Modern Middle East*, London, 1984, pp. 64–78.

13. Quoted in Gilles Kepel, *The Prophet and Pharaoh*, op. cit., p. 183.

14. As quoted in *The Guardian* (overseas edition), 25 May 1986.

15. Dr Nawal Sadawi, *International Herald Tribune*, 27 July 1985.

16. *New York Magazine*, 9 June 1985.

17. See the article, 'Will the Brotherhood come into the family?' in *The Guardian*, London, 18 September 1987.

CHAPTER 15

1. Quoted in Michael Curtis (ed.), *Religion and Politics in the Middle East*, Boulder, 1981, pp. 310–11.

2. Sudan has, indeed, been caught on a political tightrope. Andrew Buckocke, the Khartoum correspondent of *The Times*, reported:

Despite Mr al-Mahdi's often-declared intention of repeating or modifying the shar'iah, the leaders of his New National Umma party, based on the Muslim Ansar sect of which he is the hereditary head, as well as those of Mr el-Mirghani's Democratic Unionist party, are constantly looking over their shoulders at Dr Hassan Turabi and the National Islamic Front. No northern politician is ready to be associated with actions that could be construed as anti-Muslim. But many northern Muslims are far from strict observers of the faith—alcohol is widely consumed at private parties—and the amputations and floggings prescribed by the shar'iah have not been inflicted since President Nimeiry was deposed in 1985.

See *The Times*, London, 19 January 1988.

3. See Introduction by I.M. Lewis to the Studies edited by him titled *Islam in Tropical Africa,* Oxford, 1969, pp. 4–91.

4. Ibid., p.60.

5. See James Kritzeck and William H. Lewis (ed.), *Islam in Africa*, New York, p. 7, in which the editors write:

In its spread through Tropical Africa, Islam has been plastic, little concerned with the preservation of broad standards. As a result Islam has become a folk religion, adjusting itself to local tribal and clan situations, blending with the pantheon of indigenous religious beliefs and prevailing social patterns. In the process Islam has lost its universalistic qualities and assumed the characteristics of a particularistic cult, expressing itself in a melange of localized animistic ritual and Islamic practice which would shock the sensibilities of even the least pious orthodox savant.

6. Quoted by I.M. Lewis in his Introduction to the Studies edited by him under the title *Islam in Tropical Africa*, op. cit., p. 215.

7. See H.A. Gailey, *A History of Gambia*, London, 1964, p. 201.

8. See P.M. Holt, Anna K.S. Lambton and Bernard Lewis (ed.), *The Cambridge History of Islam*, op. cit. , Vol. 2, p. 401.

CHAPTER 16

1. The declaration was easy to be made but it was difficult to implement. As one of his biographers write: 'Mustafā Kemāl decided for the West. . . The nations of the West still hesitated to accept this new and

bold candidate for admission to their circle; still they could not bring themselves to accept him as a European.' Hanns Troembgen, *Kemâl Ataturk* (translated from the German by Kenneth Kirkness), London, pp. 230–31.

2. See Edward Mortimer, *Faith and Power*, London, 1982, p. 134.

3. Quoted from the Turkish newspaper *Tanin*, 11 November 1923.

4. There was an uproar for the retention of the Caliphate in many parts of the Muslim world; two Muslim leaders from India, the Agha Khan and Syed Amir Ali urged 'the imminent necessity for maintaining the religious and moral solidarity of Islam by placing the Caliphate on a basis which would command the confidence and esteem of the Muslim nations. . . .' Kemâl chastized them, said they had fought against the Caliphate in World War I and accused them of being British agents. See extracts of Ataturk's speech on this question in William H. Mcneill and Marilyn Robinson Waldman, *The Islamic World*, Oxford, 1973, pp. 438–42.

Ataturk gave cogent reasons for abolishing the Caliphate; he said,

> The Arabs founded a Caliphate in Baghdad, but they also established another one in Cordova. Neither the Persians, nor the Afghans, nor the Muslims of Africa ever recognized the Caliph of Constantinople. The notion of a single caliph, exercising supreme religious authority over all the Muslim people, is one which has come out of books, not reality. The caliph has never exercised over the Muslims a power similar to that held by the pope over the Catholics. Our religion has neither the same requirements, nor the same discipline as Christianity. The criticisms provoked by our recent reform (separating the Caliphate from the Sultanate) are inspired by an abstract, unreal idea: the idea of pan-Islamism. Such an idea has never been translated into reality. We have held the Caliphate in high esteem acording to an ancient and venerable tradition. We honour the Caliph. We attend to his needs, and those of his family. I add that in the whole of the Muslim world, the Turks are the only nation which effectively ensures the Caliph's livelihood. Those who advocate a universal caliph have so far refused to make any contribution. They would be expecting too much of us.

Quoted in Hamid Enayat, *Modern Islamic Political Thought*, Austin, 1982, p. 54.

5. Quoted in Bernard Lewis, *The Emergence of Modern Turkey*, London, 1961, p. 258. Also see the statement: 'Mustafā Kemāl's reform programme aimed at altering social behaviour as much as it sought the elimination and replacement of old institutions', in Lawrence Ziring, *Iran, Turkey and Afghanistan: A Political Chronology*, op. cit. , p. 74.

6. 'We want to construct a Turkish Islam which will be ours, relevant to and integrated with our society just as Anglicanism is Christainity in a thoroughly English fashion.' Extract from Ataturk's speech quoted in Wilfred Cantwell Smith, *Islam in Modern History*, Princeton, 1957, p. 193.

7. See Ataturk's speech on 25 Nov. 1925, as reported in *The Islamic World*, op. cit., p. 446.

8. Quoted in Bernard Lewis, *The Emergence of Modern Turkey*, op. cit., p. 270. Also see Ataturk's statement, wherein he put his case bluntly, 'A civilized, international dress is worthy and appropriate for our nation and we will wear it. Boots or shoes on our feet, trousers on our legs, shirt and tie, jacket and waistcoat--and of course, to complete these, a cover with a brim on our head.' Quoted in *Ibid*, p. 269. For further light on the subject see Edward Mortimer, *Faith and Power*, op. cit., pp. 142–47.

9. Quoted in Afkar, *Inquiry*, London, Vol. 3, No. 2, p. 36. This view is more fully elaborated by Ozel in his books *Three Problems-- Technology, Civilisation and Alienation* and *Stone Eating is Banned*.

10. See for Ali Bulae's quotation, *Afkar: Inquiry*, Vol. 3, No. 2, London, February 1986, p. 37. His book *Intellectual Problems of the Islamic World* is a thought-provoking essay on contemporary problems facing the world of Islam.

CHAPTER 17

1. See for differences between Nasserism and Ba'athism, Maxime Rodinson, *Marxism and the Muslim World*, London, 1979, p. 118.

2. See Michael C. Hudson, *Arab Politics: The Struggle for Legitimacy*, Yale, 1977, pp. 262–67.

3. In February, 1955 Iraq and Turkey entered a military alliance at the initiative of Britain, which the latter joined a few months later;

Pakistan and Iran followed suit. This alliance came to be known as Baghdad Pact and was directed to contain Soviet activities in West Asia. Abdel Moghny Said observes: 'The Baghdad Pact was an anti-communist device. Nassser opposed it. So Washington and London concluded Nasser was pro-communist, a misapprehension which supporters of Israel have often been happy to sustain. In fact Nasser's hostility to the Baghdad Pact was nothing to do with his attitude to communism, but sprang from the antipathy he and the growing middle class leadership of the Arab world felt towards pacts and bases with their "strings" and veiled control over the junior partners' governments.' See his book *Arab Socialism*, London, 1972, p. 5.

4. For an analysis of the failure of the Union between Syria and Egypt see Edouard Sab, *La Syrie ou la revolution dons la rancoeur*, Paris, 1968, p. 92; and Robert Stephens, *Nasser*, London, 1971, pp. 321–43.

5. Saddam Hussain was so incensed with Khomeini's activities in Iraq that he sent his half-brother, Barzan Takriti, to the Shah to say that the Iraqi president was prepared to help him in every way to finish the Ayatollah. The Shah asked for Khomeini's expulsion, which Saddam promptly carried out. See Amir Taheri, *The Spirit of Allah*, Bethesda, 1986, pp. 225–27.

6. Khomeini considered both Shah Muhammad Reza Pahlávi and Saddam Husain as stooges of America; hence as soon as the Ayatollah's men captured power in Iran they showed hostility towards Iraq. They repudiated the Algiers Agreement of 1975 on the Shat al-Arab waters and the demarcation of boundaries. As Sepehr Zabih explains, 'Of all Iran's Moslem neighbours, Iraq was the land where the most holy Shi'a shrines, namely Najaf and Karbala, were located. When in December 1979 the Islamic constitution was approved, the principle of pan-Islamism became the official doctrine of Khomeini's Iran. Consequently, Iraq became convinced that given the opportunity Khomeini would not hesitate in the least to take active measures for exporting his brand of Shi'a fundamentalism into Iraq.' See his book *Iran since the Revolution*, Baltimore, 1982, pp. 176–77.

7. Baqir al-Sadr came very close to Khomeini and until his death in 1980 remained in constant touch with the Ayatollah. On 1 February 1979 al-Sadr sent Khomeini six studies on Islamic theory and practice of administration. It was meant to help the Iranian leader in the framing

of a constitution for Iran; it provided a most valuable aid to Khomeini for clarifying his role as the supreme juris-consult.

8. Apart from his political thesis, al-Sadr propounded economic theories, which greatly influenced Khomeini's Iran. See Nikki R. Keddie, *Religion and Politics in Iran,* op. cit., pp. 145–65.

9. See Jean-Claude Vatin's article 'Revival in the Maghreb: Islam as an alternative political language', in *Islamic Resurgence in the Arab World*, New York, 1982, pp. 232–38.

10. Boumedienne and the leaders of Algeria, though socialist, do not accept entirely the Marxist approach; they tried to mix the two ideologies. But they were clear in their mind that 'the Qur'ān constitutes a more authoritative and comprehensive scheme for the regulation of human society than does the *Communist Manifesto* or *Das Kapital*'. See Abdel Moghny Said, *Arab Socialism*, op. cit., p. 78.

11. Quoted from Khalid Muhyi al-Din's book, *Religion and Socialism* as cited in Fouad Ajami's article 'In the Pharaoh's Shadow: Religion and Authority in Egypt', in James P. Piscatori (ed.), *Islam in the Political Process*, Cambridge, 1983, pp. 19–22.

12. Qaddafi's views have been succinctly summarized from his two Green Books and his various speeches by Ramond n. Habiby in his contributions to the book Michael Curtis (ed.), *Religion and Politics in the Middle East*, op. cit., pp. 247–73.

13. Ibid., p. 269.

CHAPTER 18

1. Quoted in Muhammad Munir, *From Jinnah to Zia*, op. cit. , p. 30.

2. Ibid.

3. Quoted in Javid Iqbal, *Ideology of Pakistan*, Lahore, 1971, p. 4.

4. Quoted in Dr Azal Iqbal, *Islamization of Pakistan*, Delhi, 1984, p. 25.

5 For an objective and succinct analysis of the Quadiani movement and the claims of its founder see Freeland Abbott, *Islam and Pakistan*, New York, 1968, pp. 148–63.

6. See *Report of the Court of Inquiry to enquire into the Punjab Disturbances of 1953*, Lahore, 1954.

7. For an account of the wranglings in the Constituent Assembly of Pakistan on the Objectives Resolution, see Leonard Binder, *Religion and Politics in Pakistan*, Berkeley, 1963, pp. 137–54.

8. Quoted from *Pakistan Observer*, 25 January 1960, in Freeland Abbott, *Islam and Pakistan*, op. cit., p. 197.

9. Chaudhary Muhammad Ali was a deeply religious man, though trained in the steel frame of Indian Civil Service. He played a prominent part in shaping the early phase of Pakistan. In his Iqbal Day Address, delivered in Karachi on 21 April 1952, he expounded his views on 'The Task Ahead'. See Freeland Abbott, *Islam and Pakistan*, op. cit., pp. 194–95.

10. There was much confusion among the ulamā on the question of Miss Jinnah's candidature. A representative gathering of the ulamā, in fact, issued a fatwa , declaring that Islam did not allow a woman to be a head of state. Maududi was in a quandary. He got out of it by pronouncing that she could be, but it was not desirable. See Herbert Feldman, *From Crisis to Crisis*, Oxford, 1972, p. 73.

11. Muhammad Munir, *From Jinnah to Zia*, op. cit., p. 18.

12. See for an objective assessment of the fall of Bhutto, Lawrence Ziring, *Pakistan: The Enigma of Political Development*, Kent, 1980, pp. 121–33.

13. For an account of Zia's efforts towards Islamization of Pakistan see Dr Afzal Iqbal, *Islamisation of Pakistan*, op. cit., pp. 107–21. Also Farūq Hassan, *The Concept of State and Law in Islam*, London, 1979, p. 144.

14. As regards the imposition of shar'iah taxes by Zia, there was a lot of theological controversies among both the Sunni and Shi'a ulamā; the Shi'as protested by taking out public demonstrations and succeeded in getting themselves exempted. See the article 'Pakistan Bows to Shi'ites in Islamic Law Dispute' in *The Washington Post*, 8 July 1985.

15. *The Times*, London, 3 March 1985.

16. Farūq Hassan, *The Concept of State and Law in Islam*, op. cit., p. 145. Hassan also explains that though this party was best organized and its founder Maududi had a great intellectual impact, 'the people of Pakistan had never, as a political commitment, embraced the party which professed to further Islam. In all elections which had been held, the parties which had been able to gain any form of strength in the as-

semblies were those which had put forth before the electorate an egalitarian philosophy.'

17. Quoted in Syed Ziaullah and Samuel Baid, *Pakistan: An End Without Beginning*, op. cit., pp. 68–69 and 164–66.

18. See *Far Eastern Economic Review*, Hong Kong, 5 February 1987 for the controversies on the process of Islamization in Pakistan.

19. Benazir Bhutto has been debunking Zia's 'Islamization' programme ever since her return from exile in London in 1986 in practically every press interview; she has been doing the same in her speeches throughout Pakistan for the poll held on 16 November 1988. In her latest interview to Javed Anand for the *Sunday Observer*, Bombay, dated 26 August to 3 September 1988, she has been almost devastating:

> What is Zia's Islamization all about? It boils down to two issues-- the amputation of hands and the stoning of people in certain cases. Yet Zia himself knew that there was no consensus for this. And therefore, despite these laws having been passed, there have been very few instances either of amputation or of stoning. What Zia did was not so much in substance.

> Apart from enacting these and some laws which are discriminatory and must be removed, what he actually did was to create a climate of hysteria within the country which made it very difficult for working women and minorities and even those sects which did not concur with the official interpretation of Islamic laws.

> [She turns around to one of her lieutenants to ask a question: 'Zaid, can you tell me what else he did because I have been racking my brains and I can't see what there was apart from a lot of rhetoric.' 'It was all propaganda,' says Zaid.] Benazir added:

> Because he couldn't justify military repression, he tried to cloak it in the name of religion and the consequence was the brutalisation of our society.

20. Quoted from Benazir Bhutto's interview to Karan Thapar, reproduced in *Indian Express*, Bombay, dated 21 August 1988.

CHAPTER 19

1. See Philip M. Stoddard, David C. Cuthell, Margaret W. Sullivan (ed.), *Change and the Muslim World*, New York, 1981, p. 76.

2. Ibid., p. 76.

3: Ibid, p. 78.

4. See the editorial in *The Times*, London, 18 March 1988, which commented, 'Bangladesh, however, is not Pakistan and President Ershad's scheme goes against the grain of his country's history and character. . .What President Ershad's plan will not bring . .is the one thing he most desires: the popular mandate that would make his rule legitimate.' Also see Aaba Dixit's article, 'Islamization of Bangladesh' in *Mainstream*, Delhi, 10 September 1988.

5. See G. Mean's article entitled 'The Role of Islam in the Political Development of Malaysia', in *Comparative Politics*, January 1964, as quoted in John L. Esposito (ed.) *Islam and Development*, New York, 1980, p. 167.

6. See Fred P. von Der Mehden's article entitled 'Malaysia: Islam and Multi-Ethnic Politics', in John L. Esposito (ed.) *Islam in Asia*, op. cit., p. 190. The author writes:

> Also disturbing to other religions are efforts to propagate Islam, arguably the faith of only a bare manority of Malaysians, by way of the media, public forums, official pronouncements, subsidies to Islamic institutions, attempts to make Muslim holy days national celebrations, support of dakwah (missionary) organizations in their work to convert non-Muslims, news programmes rejoicing at such conversions, and so on. Programmes to raise the religious consciousness of Muslims is one thing, but perceptions that there is increasing pressure for the Islamization of the population as a whole have obviously created uneasiness among non-Muslims. These fears were heightened when Islamic courts called for the punishment of non-believers caught in khalwat with Muslims, when state governments demanded a ban on non-halal meat in all hotels and restaurants (later rescinded), or when a deputy within the prime minister's office discussed a morals law with leaders of other faiths, even though he said it would be based on all religions and the government later backed down.

7. For trouble within UMNO, see the article 'The Gathering Storm', in *Far Eastern Economic Review*, Hong Kong, 13 October 1988.

8. Lately there has been a better understanding of the rights of non-Muslims in Malaysia; Anwar Ibrahim, who had led the Malaysian Youth Islamic Movement, and is now a minister, had to concede that

Islamic leadership 'should not be chauvinistic and should not try to belie the importance of the aid and support of other groups and minorities'. As quoted in John L. Esposito, *Islam and Development*, op. cit., p. 174.

9. See Sachacht Joseph and C.E. Bosworth (ed.), *The Legacy of Islam*, London, 1974, p. 155, wherein C.A.O. van Nieuwenhuijze has rightly observed:

> In the process of unification of the Indonesian nation and polity, Islam has been the second factor in order of importance, colonial rule with the response elicited by it being the first. In respect of the cohesion of present-day Indonesian society it is one of several factors, one of which is a keen national awareness. When and where their simultaneous occurrence appears a struggle for predominance, the outcome is uncertain. There is no saying in advance that Islam must be every round. Yet its persistence appears as a basic datum.

10. For a full account of Islam's thrust in Indonesia see G.A.O. van Njeuwenhijize, *Aspects of Islam in Post-Colonial Indonesia*, The Hague and Bandung, 1958, and B.J. Boland, *The Struggle of Islam in Modern Indeonesia*, The Hague, 1982. Also see Dilip Mukherjee's acticle, 'Indonesia's Islamic Equation' in *The Times of India*, Bombay, 10 February 1988.

11. For an account of how Indonesia has tried to contain the fundamentalist pressure and retain the secular character of the republic see the article 'Indonesia, Islam and Cultural Pluralism' by Anthony M. Johns in John L. Esposito (ed.),*Islam in Asia*, op. cit., pp. 223–28.

Also see the article 'Paradise Preserved' in *Time*, New York, 5 October 1987, wherein the weekly has pointed out,

> Suharto's moves effectively destroyed a powerful movement of Muslim fundamentalists, who during the 1970s were calling for the imposition of a Muslim state, and who had gained considerable strength in western Sumatra. According to the panchasila principles, anyone calling for a theocratic state, like Khomeini's Iran, was beyond the legal pale. If the person did not desist, he could end up behind bars. As a result, the PPP's vote fell from the 27.2% it had received in 1982 to 16% and Golkar even managed to win in the west Sumatran city of Aceh, Indonesia's traditional Muslim stronghold. The government now feels that the fundamentalists are

finished. 'We've been successful in introducing a national outlook to national politics,' says Sarwano Kusumaatumadja, Secretary-General of Golkar, 'as opposed to the sectarian politics which plagued us in the past.'

CHAPTER 20

1. Quoted by Sir Rafiuddin Ahmed in his article entitled 'A Muslim view of Abdul Hamid and the Powers' in the *Nineteenth Century*, London, July 1985, p. 162.

2. Quoted in *Islamic Quarterly*, London, Vol. XIX, Nos. 3 and 4, 1975, pp. 157–63.

3. For an account of the Khilafat Movement in India, see Gail Missault, *The Khilafat Movement*, Delhi, 1982.

4. Quoted in Rafiq Zakaria (ed.), *Hundred Glorious Years*, (a centenary publication of the Indian National Congress), Bombay, 1985, p. 144.

5. For an account of the fight that the leaders of Jam'iyyat al-Ulama-i-Hind put up in defence of composite nationalism see Tara Chand, *History of the Freedom Movement in India*, Vol. III, 1972, pp. 254–66.

6. For an account of Khudai Khitmatgar and Khan Abdul Ghaffar Khan's role in cementing Hindu-Muslim relations see D.G. Tendulkar, *Abdul Gaffar Khan*, Bombay, 1967. The author quotes the Khan on Hindu-Muslim unity thus:

Abdul Gaffar preached Hindu-Muslim unity. 'Oh, what a vain attempt', exclaimed a Muslim divine. 'Hindus are idol-worshippers. How can we have any dealings with them?' Abdul Gaffar Khan remonstrated: 'If they are idol worshippers, what are we? What is this worship of tombs? How are they any the less devotees of God when I know they believe in one God. And why do you despair of Hindu-Muslim unity? No true effort goes in vain. Look at the fields over there. The grain sown therein has to remain in the earth for a certain time, then it sprouts, and in due time yields hundreds of its kind. The same is the case about every effort in a good cause.'

7. There is hardly any report or book dealing with the economic plight of Indian Muslims; a study was made by the High-Powered Panel for

Minorities appointed by the Government of India of which Dr Gopal Singh was the Chairman and Dr Rafiq Zakaria, the Member-Secretary. It has not yet seen the light of the day, though the journal *Muslim India*, New Delhi managed to publish some extracts from it. Frequent references to their plight are found in various newspaper and magazine articles. Indian Muslims are much worse off economically than ever before. See S. Abdul Hasan Ali Nadwi, *Muslims in India*, Lucknow, pp. 137–40.

8. For the controversy on the Shah Bano case, including the judgement of the Supreme Court of India and the subsequent development resulting in the enactment of the legislation for the maintenance of Muslim divorced women, see issue Nos. 29 to 40 of *Muslim India*, New Delhi and for the reaction of the reformist section see *Freedom First*, Bombay, April 1986. Also see a perceptive article on the Hindu backlash, in the wake of the Muslim agitation, by the late Romesh Thapar, reproduced in *Delhi Recorder*, New Delhi, 30 September 1987.

9. M.J. Akbar, *Riot After Riot*, New Delhi, 1988, p. 128. Also see for a historical analysis of the location of the Ramjanambhoomi temple at Ayodhya, Sushil Srivastava's article, 'Whither Indian Muslims', reproduced in *Muslim India*, No. 50, February 1987.

10. Iqbal has denounced such inactivity in many verses, as he was a champion of change. He wrote:

They have no claim to the sorrows and delights of tomorrow
Who today do not bestir themselves and whose hearts do not burn.
A nation which is nothing today
Cannot expect a fulsome tomorrow.

Quoted in Hafeez Malik (ed.), *Iqbal: Poet-Philosopher of Pakistan*, New York, 1971, p. 168.

CHAPTER 21

1. The full text is reproduced in C.J. Huzewitz, *Diplomacy in the Near and Middle East*, Princeton, 1956, Vol. II, pp. 27–28. Also for an account of the early Soviet attitude towards the Muslims in Central Asia and the Caucasus, see Michael Rywkin's contribution in Yaacov Ro (ed.), *The USSR and the Muslim World*, London, 1984, pp. 3–14. Also the contribution by Dov B. Yaroshevski, ibid, pp. 16–35.

2. Quoted by Bohdan R. Bociurkiw in his article 'Changing Soviet Image of Islam: The Domestic Scene', in *The Journal Institute of Minority Affairs*, London, Vol. II, No. 2 and Vol. III, No. 1, Winter 1980 and Summer 1981, pp. 11–12.

3. See Fazlur Rahman's article, 'Evolution of Soviet Policy Toward Muslims in Russia: 1917–1965', in *The Journal Institute of Minority Affairs*, London, Vol. I, No. 2, and Vol. II, No. 1 (combined issue), Winter 1979 and Summer 1980, pp. 35–36.

4. Quoted in Bohdan R. Bociurkiw's article 'Changing Soviet Image of Islam: The Domestic Scene', op. cit., p. 15.

5. Ibid.

6. For an account of the Soviet attitude to Muslims since the end of World War II, see S. Enders Wimbush's article, 'Soviet Muslims in the 1980s', in *The Journal Institute of Muslim Minority Affairs*, London, Vol. VI, No. 1, January 1985, pp. 152–66.

7. Quoted in Alexandre Bennigsen's contribution entitled 'Modernization and Conservatism in Soviet Islam' in Dennis J. Dunn (ed.), *Religion and Modernization in the Soviet Union*, Boulder, 1977, p. 236.

8. For the varying attitude of Soviet authorities towards revival of Islam in Central Asia, see Alexandre Bennigsen, S. Enders Wimbush, *Muslims of the Soviet Empire*, London, 1985. Prof. Hans Braker, in his foreword to this book observes, 'Most observers have simply failed to see that the Soviet Muslim lands never lost whatever it is that Soviet social engineering is supposed to have destroyed. Certainly Islamic belief and Muslim politics have taken new and frequently imaginative forms, but Islamic culture never disappeared. The bedrock for intense belief and provocative political activity remains as solid as ever.'

9. For a recent account of how Islamic practices are continuing among the Muslims in Central Asian Republics of the USSR, see the article, 'In Central Asia, Age-old Islam Meets Soviet Rule' in *New York Times*, 8 July 1985. Also see the article by David Remnick, 'Despite Pressure to Assimilate, Soviet Muslims Keep Identity', in *International Herald Tribune*, Singapore, 1 November 1988.

10. For an account of the communist Chinese attitude towards Muslims and the latter's activities and institutions, see Ibrahim Ma Zhao-chun's article, 'Islam in China—The Internal Dimension', in *The*

Journal Institute of Muslim Minority Affairs, London, Vol. VII, No. 2, 2 July, 1986, pp. 372–83. Also see Francoise Aubin's contribution entitled 'Islam and the State in the People's Republic of China', in Olivier Cazze, *Islam and the State in the World Today*, New Delhi, 1987, pp. 159–78. Also see R.G. Gidadhubli (ed.) *Socio-Economic Transformation of Soviet Central Asia*, New Delhi, 1987, pp. 41–42.

11. See Yaacov Ro'i (ed.), *The USSR and the Muslim World*, London, 1984, pp. 169–70. Also see John O.Voll's article, 'Muslim Minority Alternatives: Implications of Muslim Experiences in China and the Soviet Union', in *The Journal Institute of Muslim Minority Affairs*, Vol. VI, No. 2, July 1983, pp. 332–52.

12. For a fuller account of the activities of the Muslims in East European countries see Suhail Balic's article in *The Journal Institute of Muslim Minority Affairs*, Jeddah, Vol. I, No. 2 and Vol. II, No. 1, Winter 1979 and Summer 1980.

13. For a detailed account of the conflict between communism and Islam in Afghanistan and the role of the Soviet Union on the one side and of America and Pakistan on the other, see Olivier Roy, *Islam and Resistance in Afghanistan*, Cambridge, 1986. Also see the interview given by Dr Najibullah, the president of Afghanistan, to the *Sunday Observer*, Bombay, 1 May 1988, in which he frankly admits,

> Our people are Muslims and our country is Muslim. Our society is still very feudal and under-developed. It was our mistake that we did not recognize this fact earlier. . . .Some people in our party even seemed to believe that they were bringing communism in Afghanistan sooner than in the Soviet Union and thereby committed extremist mistakes. Lenin has rightly said that a true revolutionary party remains only one step ahead of the masses and leads them as they get prepared for further changes. But in the case of our party we chose to remain in aasmaan (sky), leaving the masses down below on zameen (ground).

Najibullah has, therefore, enforced the shari'ah and kept eating places closed in Ramadán during day-time.

According to *New Statesman*, London, 26 February 1988, the communist regime 'prides itself on the number of mosques it has repaired and new mosques it has built. It gives favourable treatment to clerical and financial support to Islamic education in schools and universities.' Also see *Newsweek*, 12 October 1987.

14. *Newsweek*, New York, 12 October 1987.

15. For an account of the conflict between Islam and communism in South Yemen see Norman Cigar's article, 'State and Society in South Yemen', in the journal *Problems of Communism*, Washington, May–June 1985, pp. 41–58.

CHAPTER 22

1. See the *Encyclopaedia of Islam*, Bernard Lewis, V.L. Menage, Ch. Pellat and J.Schacht (ed.), Lieden, 1971, Vol. III, pp. 1061–62, wherein it explains ikhtilāf thus:

> The ancient schools of Law, on the one hand, accepted geographical differeences of doctrines as natural; on the other hand, they voiced strong objections to disagreement within each school, an opinion which was mitigated by their acceptance as legitimate of different opinions, if based on ijtihād. . . .The recording of these differences of opinion has produced a considerable literature since the beginnings of the study of fikh.

2. See Iqbal's reply to the questions raised by Jawaharlal Nehru in his three articles in *Modern Review* of Calcutta, on the attitude of Indian Muslims towards the Ahmadis or Qadianis, in Syed Abdul Vahid (ed.), *Thoughts and Reflections of Iqbal*, Lahore, 1964, p. 28.

3. See *Report of the Court of Inquiry constituted under Punjab Act II of 1954 to enquire into the Punjab Disturbances of 1953*, Lahore, pp. 214–18. Also see Javid Iqbal, *Ideology of Pakistan*, Lahore, 1971, pp. 107–8, wherein the author, who is the son of the great poet and himself an eminent jurist, criticises the *Report* on this account and the reply to him by the chairman of the court, the then chief justice of Pakistan, Mr Justice Muhammad Munir in his book, *From Jinnah to Zia*, op. cit., pp. 69–73.

4. Quoted in *Ibn Taimiyya on Public and Private Laws in Islam,* (translated into the English by Dr Omar A. Farrukh), Beirut, 1966, p. 73.

5. For an understanding of his theory of asabiya see Ibn Khaldūn, *The Muqaddimah* (translated, edited and abridged by N.J. Dawood), Princeton, 1970. In his introduction Dawood explains that Ibn Khaldūn defined asabiya as ' "soldiarity", "group feeling", "group conscious-

ness", which knit people together' (xi). It is, as the noted scholar Najib Ullah elaborates, 'the positive and active expression of men's attachment to one another in a family, in a tribe, in a clan and in a nation—the expression that can be translated into patriotism and nationalism.' See *Islamic Literature*, New York, 1963, p. 103. Arnold Toynbee has described Ibn Khaldūn's doctrine of asabiya as 'the basic protoplasm out of which all bodies politic and bodies social are built up.' See his *A Study of History*, Oxford, 1934, Vol. III, p. 474.

6. Dr Sayed Riaz Ahmed, *Maulana Maududi and the Islamic State*, Lahore, 1976, p. 116. The author explains Maududi's stand succinctly thus:

> Maulana Maududi believes that the amir and the legislator could be elected or selected by an agreed method by the umma. Direct or indirect election or appointment followed by the oath of allegiance, or any variations of these methods, could also be adopted by the constitution-making body. He is of the opinion that none of these methods are un-Islamic as long as the spirit of Islam is embodied in the constitution and the electing body is fully conscious of the principles involved. To support this view he draws upon the various methods by which the first four khalifas of Islam came to hold their office.

7. Muhammad Iqbal, *Reconstruction of Religious Thought in Islam*, op. cit., p. 157.

8. On 20 September 1977 Begum Nusrat Bhutto, wife of the deposed prime minister, filed a petition in the Supreme Court of Pakistan, challenging the validity of the imposition of martial law; however, Ziaul Haq, the martial law administrator, circumvented it by demanding that all judges should be sworn in again, declaring their allegiance to the new regime. The chief justice, Mr Justice Yaqb Ali refused and was promptly replaced by Mr. Justice Anwarul Haq. He constituted the constitutional bench, which decreed that the martial law, as during the past in similar circumstances, stood validated under the time-honoured 'doctrine of necessity'. See Victoria Schofield, *Bhutto: Trial and Execution*, London, 1979, p. 24.

9. Quoted in Syed Amir Ali, *A Short History of the Saracens*, New Delhi, 1981, pp. 17–18.

10. Maududi has elaborated his ideas in a compilation of his writings, edited and translated into English by Khurshid Ahmad under the title, *The Islamic Law and Constitution*, Delhi, 1986, pp. 123–273.

11. Quoted from *The Necklace* (an encyclopaedic anthology) by Ibn Abd Rabbihi (d. 940), in John Alden Williams (ed.), *Themes of Islamic Civilization*, Berkeley, 1982, p. 70.

12. Kawakibi (1849–1902) was influenced in this respect more by his love for Arabism than any religious consideration. He was one of the first among the Arab ulamā to come out openly against the Turks; and as Sylvia G. Haim points out in *Arab Nationalism: An Anthology*, Berkeley, 1962, p. 27, 'For all his preoccupation with the state of Islam, al-Kawakibi, once he introduced the idea of a spiritual caliph, was led to consider politics as an autonomous activity divorced from divine presumption and fully subject to the will of men.'

13. This statement is from the Prophet's farewell address. For an authentic account of it, which he delivered at the time of his last hajj, see Muhammad Ibn Ishaq's *Seerat Rasul Allah* (translated into English with introduction by A. Guillaume), Oxford, 1955, pp. 650–52.

14. Quoted in Najib Ullah (ed.), *Islamic Literature*, New York, 1963, pp. 385–86.

15. The statement is from the note of dissent that Maulānā Ihstisham-ul Haq, who was the only representative of the ulamā appointed in 1955 by President Ayub Khan of Pakistan on the seven-member Commission on Marriage and Family Laws; six of them recommended reforms in inheritance, marriage and divorce, which were later in 1961 incorporated in the Muslim Family Laws Ordinance, one of the most progressive measures Pakistan ever enacted. The Maulānā dissented. See the *Gazette of Pakistan*, 30 August 1956, as quoted in John J. Donohue and John L. Esposito, *Islam in Trasition*, Oxford, 1982, p. 206.

16. Translated from the Urdu poem of Iqbal by V.G. Kiernan, *Poems from Iqbal*, Bombay, 1947, pp. 73–74.

17. See Khurshid Ahmad (ed.), *Islamic Law and Constitution*, op. cit., p. 90.

18. Ali Abdal Raziq's position in this regard was clear. He wrote:

> The truth is that Islam is innocent of the institution of Caliphate as it is commonly understood by Muslims. It is innocent of all the apparel of seduction and intimidation, and the pomp of force

and power with which they surrounded the institution of the Caliphate. This institution has nothing in common with religious functions, no more than the judiciary and the other essential functions and machinery of power and state. Religion neither admits nor denies them. It neither orders nor forbids them. It simply leaves them to our free choice so that we will have recourse to rational judgement in this reegard and base our judgement on the experience of the notions and the rules of politics.

See extract from his book *Islam and the Bases of Power*, in John J. Donohue and Esposito (ed.), *Islam in Transition*, Oxford, 1982, pp. 29–37.

19. Quoted from Ibn Jama'ah's book, *Kitab Tahrir-ul Ahkam*, in Khuda Baksh, *Politics in Islam*, Delhi, 1975, p. 119.

20. See K.G. Saiyidain, *Islam—The Religion of Peace*, New Delhi, 1976, pp. 21–71, and Syed Abdul Latif, *Bases of Islamic Culture*, Hyderabad, 1959, pp. 13–23 and 179–85. Also see M.M. Pickthall, *The Cultural Side of Islam*, Lahore, 1969, p. 104, and Kenneth W. Morgan (ed.), *Islam—The Straight Path*, Delhi, 1958, p. 128.

21. See Kenneth W. Morgan (ed.), *Islam—The Straight Path*, op. cit., p.128.

22. See A.S. Tritton, *The Caliphs and Their Non-Muslim Subjects*, op. cit., p. 24.

23. Quoted from his poem by Husn-ul Nuhadara from his book *Suyuti*, in ibid., p. 25.

24. Azad has given a lucid exposition of the rationale behind the imposition of jaziya. While the Muslims were required to do 'compulsory military service', the non-Muslims were exempt. As he explains, 'It was not considered proper for any state pursuing Islamic ideology in administration to compel its non-Muslim population to undergo so serious a sacrifice.' They were, therefore, asked 'to share in some manner the military expenditure'. However, 'there were certain taxes specially levied on the Muslims, taxes such as zakāt and sadaqat, which were not levied on the non-Muslims'. Abdul Kalam Azad, *Tarjuman al-Qur'ān* (edited and rendered into English by Dr Syed Abdul Latif), Hyderabad, 1978, Vol. III, pp. 87–8.

This has also been collaborated by T.W. Arnold, who writes: '. . .the jaziyah was levied on the able-bodied males in lieu of the military service they would have been called upon to perform had they been

Muslims; and it is very noticeable that when any Christian people served in the Muslim army, they were exempted from the payment of this tax.' See his *The Preaching of Islam*, op. cit., p. 63.

Prof. Watt has said that except the pagans in Arabia, who were given the choice of 'Islam or the sword', as they were the inveterate enemies of the Prophet, the rest were regarded as 'protected minorities'. In this connection, Watt points that 'a very liberal interpretation was given to the conception of a monotheistic religion with written scriptures', with the result that apart from Christians and Jews, Zoroastrians, and later Hindus and Buddhists became protected minorities. See W.M. Watt, *Islamic Political Thought*, in the series *Islamic Survey*, 6, Edinburgh, 1968, p. 51. Imam Abu Hanifa also included the Hindus among 'peoples of the book'.

25. Quoted from *Muslim* of Islamabad in *Indian Express*, 12 December 1987.
26. Muhammad Iqbal, *The Reconstruction of Religious Thought in Islam*, op. cit., p. 168.
27. Ibid.
28. For a historical record of the various Muslim Congresses held from time to time, see Martin Kramer, *Islam Assembled*, New York, 1986.
29. See the book *Islamic Solidarity*, prepared on the occasion of the Fifth Islamic Summit Conference held in January 1987 in Kuwait by Kuwait News Agency, p. 10.
30. Ziauddin Sardar, *The Future of Muslim Civilization*, London, 1979, p. 58.
31. This verse is from Iqbal's book of poems, *Zarbe Kaleem*. The English translation is by Rafiq Zakaria.

Bibliography

For the various Quranic verses and their interpretations, the following works have been consulted:

Ali, Abdullah Yusuf. *The Holy Quran*. Beirut, 1968.

Arberry, A.J. *The Quran. Interpreted*. 2 vols. London, 1955.

Ayoub, Mahmud M. *Qur'an and its Interpreters*, vol. 1. New York, 1984.

Bell, Richard. *Introduction to the Quran*. Edinburgh, 1953.

Cragg, Kenneth. *The Event of the Quran*. London, 1971.

Mahmud, Y. Zayid. *The Quran* (English translation). Beirut, 1980.

Mauudi, Syed Abu A'la. *The Meaning of the Quran* (translated into the English). 4 vols. Delhi, 1970.

Syed, Abdul Latif. *The Tarjuman al-Quran* (edited and rendered into English, the commentary by Abul Kalam Azad). 3 vols. Vols. 1 & 2, Bombay 1967. Vol. 3, Hyderabad, 1978.

————. *Al-Quran*, Hyderabad, 1969.

Watt, Montgomery W. *Companion to the Quran*. London, 1967.

For the relevant hadith (or Traditions of the Prophet) I have referred to the following:

Ali, Muhammad. *Sahih al-Bukhari* (translated into the English). 9 vols. Madina, 1974.

Khan, Muhammad Muhsin. *A Manual of Hadith*. Lahore.

Siddiqi, Abdul Hamid. *Sahih Muslim* (rendered into the English). 4 vols. Lahore, 1973.

Rahimuddin, Muhammad. *Muatta Imam Malik* (translated into the English with exhaustive notes). New Delhi, 1981.

Robson, James. *Mishkat al-Masabin* (translated into the English with explanatory notes). 4 vols. 1973.

Shabbir, Mohd. *The Authority and Authenticity of Hadith*. New Delhi, 1982.

I have found useful the various editions and volumes of the *Encyclopaedia of Islam*, Leiden, *The Islamic Survey*, Edinburgh, and the *Cambridge History of Islam*, London. Also Ibn Ishaq, *Sirat Rosul Allah* (translated into the English with introduction and notes by A. Guillaume), London, 1955, *A Dictionary of Islam* by Thomas Patrick Hughes, *Islamic Encyclopaedia* (Urdu) edited by Qasim Mahmud, Karachi, 1984 and *The World of Islam*, edited by Bernard Lewis, London, 1976. I have also used the following atlases, H.W. Hazard, *Atlas of Islamic History*, Princeton,

1954; Roolvink R., *Historical Atlas of the Muslim Peoples*, Amsterdam, 1957; Francis Robinson *Atlas of the Islamic World since 1500*, Oxford, 1982, and Ismail, R. and al-Faruqi Lois Lamayad, *Cultural Atlas of Islam*, New York, 1986. Likewise, I have gathered much information from such journals as *Journal Institute of Muslim Minority Affairs*, published first from Jeddah and now London; *Afkar Inquiry*, London; *Arabia*, London (now defunct); *Islamic Culture*, Hyderabad; *Risalat al-Jihad* (English), Rome; *The Muslim World*, Leiden; *Islamic Studies*, Islamabad; *al-Tawhid* (English), Tehran, *Muslim India*, New Delhi.

Abbott, Freeland. *Islam and Pakistan*. New York, 1968.

Agwani, M.S. *Politics in the Gulf.* Delhi, 1978.

———. *Islamic Fundamentalism in India*. Chandigarh, 1986.

Ahmad, Ilyas. *The Social Contract and Islamic State..* New Delhi, 1981.

Ahmad, Khurshid (ed.). *First International Conference on Islamic Economics*. Delhi, 1984.

Ahmad, Mohiuddin. *Saiyid Ahmad Shahid.* Lucknow, 1975.

Ahmad, Sayed Riyaz. *Maulana Maudidi and the Islamic State*. Lahore, . 1976.

Ahmad, Ziauddin Iqbal, and Munawwar Khan, M.F. *Money and Banking in Islam*. Islamabad, 1983.

Ahmed, Akbar. *Pakistan Society*. New York, 1986.

Ahmed, Aziz. *Islamic Modernization in India and Pakistan*. London, 1967.

———. *Studies in Islamic Culture in the Indian Environment*. London, 1966.

Ahmed, J.M. *The Intellectual Origins of Egyptian Nationalism*. London, 1987.

Ahmad, Khurshid and Zafar Ishaq Ansari. *Islamic Perspectives*. Leicester, 1980.

Akbar, M.J. *Riot after Riot*. New Delhi, 1988.

Allworth E. (ed.). *Central Asia: A Century of Russian Rule*. New York, 1967.

Ali, Iqbal. *Islamic Sufism*. Delhi, 1979.

Andasheve, Khabibulla and Shukurov Shaukat. *Soviet Muslims*. Moscow, 1984.

Anderson J.N.D. *Islamic Law in the Modern World*. London, 1964.

Antonius G. *The Arab Awakening*. London, 1938.

Ali, Imam. *Peak of Eloquence.* Bombay, 1979.

Ali, Tariq. *Can Pakistan Survive.* Harmondsworth, 1983.

Andrae, Tor. *Mohammed* (translated into the English). London, 1956.

Arberry, A.J. *Sufism*. London, 1950.

————. *Aspects of Islamic Civilization*. Michigan, 1964.

————. *Tales from the Masnavi*. London, 1968.

————. *Religion in the Middle East*. 2 vols. London. 1969.

———— . *Discourses of Rumi*. New York, 1961.

Arnold, Thomas and Alfred Guillaume (ed.). *The Legancy of Islam*. New York, 1931.

Arnold, Thomas W. *The Caliphate*. London, 1924.

————. *The Preaching of Islam*. London, 1913.

Aslam, Muhammad. *Muslim Conduct of State*. Lahore, 1974.

Arsalam, Amir Sbakib. *Our Decline and its Causes*. Lahore, 1944.

As-Sufi, Abdal Qadir. *Jihad-A Ground Plan*. London, 1978.

Asad, Muhammad. *The Road To Mecca*. New York, 1954.

Askari, Hasan. *Society and State in Islam--an Introduction*. Delhi, 1978.

Ather, Saiyid & Rizvi, Abbas. *A History of Sufism in India*. 2 vols. New Delhi, 1983.

Atiyah E. *The Arabs*. London, 1955.

Atta, Mohi ud-Din. *Abu Bakr*. Delhi, 1968.

Azad, Abul Kalam. *India Wins Freedom*. New York, 1988.

Baker, Raymond William. *Egypt's Uncertain Revolution under Nasser and Sadat*. London, 1978.

Balyuzi, H.M. *Muhammad and the Course of Islam*, London, 1976.

Baijon, D.D. Jr. *The Reforms and Religious Ideas of Sir Sayed Ahmad Khan*. Lahore, 1958.

Banani, A. *The Modernization of Iran 1921–1941*. Standard, 1961.

Bell, R. *The Origins of Islam in its Christian Environment*. London, 1926.

Bennigsen A and Quelquejay C.L. *Islam in the Soviet Union*. London, 1967.

————. *The Evolution of the Muslim Nationalities of the U.S.S.R and their Linguistic Problems*. London, 1961.

————. and Wimbush S. Enders. *Muslims of the Soviet Empire—a Guide*. London, 1985.

————. *Muslim National Communism in the Soviet Union*. Chicago, 1979.

Berger, Morro. *Islam in Egypt Today*. London, 1970.

Bianco, Mirella. *Gaddafi—Voice from the Desert*. London, 1975.

Berkes, N. *The Development of Secularism in Turkey*. Montreal, 1964.

Bhutto, Benazir. *Daughter of the East*. London, 1988.

Binder, L. *The Ideological Revolution in the Middle East*. New York, 1964.

―――. *Iran: Political Development in a Changing Society.*
    Berkeley, 1962.
Religion and Politics in Pakistan. London, 1963.
Blandford. Linda. *Oil Sheikhs.* London, 1976.
Boer, T.J. De. *The History of Philosophy in Islam.* New York, 1967.
Blyden, Edward W. *Christianity, Islam and the Negro Race.* Edinburgh,
    1967.
Boland, B.J. *The Struggle of Islam in Modern Indonesia.* The Hague,
    1971.
Bolle, Kees W. *The Study of Religion: A Historical Approach.* The
    Hague, 1961.
Bradsher, Henry S. *Afghanistan and the Soviet Union.* Drham, 1983.
Birge, J.K. *The Bektashi Order of Dervishes.* London, 1937.
Brohi, A.K. *Islam in the Modern World.* Lahore, n.d.
Brockelmann, Carl. *History of the Islamic Peoples.* New York, 1973.
Brown, L. Carl. *International Politics and the Middle East.* Princeton,
    1984.
Browne, E.G. *The Persian Revolution of 1905–1909.* Cambridge, 1918.
Burknanov, Shaukat Gusarov Vladilen. *Soviet Power and Islam.* Moscow,
    1984.
Burney, S.M.H. *Iqbal―Poet Patriot of India.* New Delhi, 1987.
Carre, Oliver (ed.). *Islam and the State in the World Today.* New Delhi,
    1987.
Chand, Tara. *History of the Freedom Movement in India.* 4 vols. New
    Delhi, 1972.
Chopra, Pran. *The Challenge of Bangladesh.* Bombay, 1971.
Clark, Micheal J. *Algeria in Turmoil.* London, 1960.
Cottam, R.W. *Nationalism in Iran.* Cambridge, 1964.
Cragg, Kenneth. *Counsels in Contemporary Islam.* Edinburgh, 1965.
―――. *The Pen and the Faith.* London, 1965.
Crone, Patricia and Hinds Martin. *God's Caliph: Religious Authority in
    the First Centuries of Islam.* London, 1986.
Cudsi, Alexander S. and Alie Dessouki E.H. *Islam and Power.* London,
    1981.
Daniel, Norman. *Islam, Europe and Empire.* Edinburgh, 1966.
Davison, R.H. *Reform in the Ottoman Empire. 1856–1876.* Princeton,
    1963.
Dekmejian, R. Hrair. *Islam in Revolution.* New York, 1985.
Dessouki, Ali E. Hilal. *Islamic Resurgence in the Arab World.* New York,
    1982.
Devereux, R. *The First Ottoman Constitutional Period.* Baltimore, 1963.

Dodge, B. Al-Ashar. *Religious and Political Trends in Modern Egypt.*
    Washington, 1950.
Dodwell, H. *The Founder of Egypt.* Cambridge, 1923.
Edib, Halide. *Conflict of East and West Turkey.* Lahore, 1935.
El-Sadat, Anwar. *In Search Of Identity.* Dehradun, 1984.
Embree, Ainslie T. *Islam—In India's Transition
    to Modernity.* New Delhi, 1968.
Emin, Leon. *Muslims in the USSR.* Moscow, 1984.
Enayat, Hamid. *Modern Islamic Political Thought.* Austin, 1982.
Engineer, Asghar Ali. *The Islamic State.* New Delhi, 1980.
Espisito, John L. (ed.). *Voices of Resurgent Islam.* New York, 1983.
———. (ed) *Islam in Asia.* London, 1987.
———. (ed) *Islam and Development.* New York, 1980.
———. *Islam and Politics.* New York, 1984.
Farah, Ceasar E. Islam.*Beliefs and Observances.* New York, 1968.
Farrukh, Omar A. *Ibn Taimiyya on Public and Private Law in Islam.*
    Beirut. 1966.
Faridi, F.R. and Siddiqi M.N. *Muslim Personal Law.* Bombay, 1973.
Faruqi, Nisar A. *Early Muslim Historiography.* Delhi, 1979.
Faruqui, Isma'il. *On Arabism, Urubah and Religion.* Amsterdam, 1962.
Faruqui, N.A. *Ahmadiyat in the Service of Islam.* Lahore, 1983.
Fayzee, Asaf A.A. *A Modern Approach to Islam.* Bombay, 1963.
———. *Outlines of Muhammadan Law.* London, 1964.
Feldman, Herbert. *From Crisis to Crisis.* London, 1972.
Fernau, F.W. *Moslems on The March.* London, 1955.
Frye, R.N. (ed.). *Islam and the West.* The Hague, 1957.
Gabriell, F. *Muhammad and the Conquests of Islam.* London, 1968.
Gamal, Abd el-Nasser. *The Philosophy of the Revolution.* Cairo, 1951.
Gajendragadkar, P.B. *Secularism and the Constitution of India.* Bombay,
    1971.
Gauhar, Altaf. *Translations from the Quran.* Lahore, 1975.
———. (ed.) *The Challenge of Islam.* London, 1978.
Ghazali, Abdul Hamid. *Book of Knowledge* (translated into the English).
    New Delhi, 1963
Gellner, Ernest. *Muslim Society.* 2 vols. Cambridge, 1981.
Gibb H.A.R and Bowem H. (ed.). *Islamic Society and the West.* London,
    1950.
Gibb H.A.R. *Modern Trends in Islam.* Chicago, 1947.
———. *Mohammedanism: A Historical Survey.* London, 1964.
———. *Studies on the Civilization of Islam.* Princeton, 1982.

442   *The Struggle within Islam*

Gilani, Riyaz-ul-Hasan. *The Reconstruction of Legal Thought in Islam.* Delhi, 1982.

Globb, John. *A Short History of the Arab Peoples.* New York, 1939.

Goitein, S. *Jews and Arabs.* New York, 1955.

Goldziher, Ignaz. *Introduction to Islamic Theology and Law.* Princeton, 1981.

Gokalp, Z. *Turkish Nationalism and Western Civilization* (ed. and translated by Niyazi Berkes). New York, 1959.

Golwash, Ahmed A. *The Religion of Islam.* Cairo, 1957.

Grewal, J.S. *Muslim Rule in India.* Calcutta, 1970.

Griffith, Tom. *Sound the Alarm.* Washington, 1981.

Grunebaum G.E., Von. *Modern Islam: The Search for Cultural Identity.* Berkeley, 1962.

———. *Medieval Islam.* New York, 1964.

———. *Islam.* London, 1955.

Guillaume, A. *Islam.* 1954.

———. *The Life of Muhammad.* London, 1955.

Habidullah, A.B.M. *The Foundation of Muslim Rule in India.* Allahabad, 1961.

Haddad, Yvonne Yazbeck. *Contemporary Islam and the Challenge of History.* Albany, 1982.

Haim, S. *Arab Nationalism: an Anuthology.* Berkely, California, 1962.

Hakim, Khalifa Abdul. *Islamic Ideology.* Lahore, 1951.

Halliday, Fred. *Arabia without Sultans.* Maryland, 1974.

Halpern, M. *The Politics of Social Change in the Middle East.* Leiden, 1964.

Hameed, Abdul. *Muslim Separatism in India.* London, 1971.

Hamidullah, M. *The Muslim Conduct of State.* Lahore, 1945.

Hamzavi, A.H. *Persia and the Powers.* London, 1946.

Hanna, Sami A. and George H. Gardner. *Arab Socialism.* Salt Lake City, 1969.

Haq, Mushirul. *Muslim Politics in Modern India.* Meerut, 1970.

Islam in Secular India. Simla, 1972.

Hasan, Mushirul. *Communual and Pan-Islamic Trends in Colonial India.* New Delhi, 1981.

Hashmi, Anwar. *An Introduction to Islamic Ideology.* Karachi, 1967.

Hasluck, F.W. *Christianity and Islam under the Sultans.* 2 vols. Oxford, 1929.

Hasan, Farooq. *The Concept of State and Law in Islam.* London, 1979.

Hawley, Donald. *The Trucial States.* London, 1970.

Hayes, Louis D. *Politics in Pakistan.* London, 1984.

Heikal, Muhammed. *The Return of the Ayatollah*. London, 1983.
——. *Iran—The Untold Story*. New York, 1982.
——. and Nasser. *The Cairo Documents*. London, 1973.
Hayes, John R. *The Genesis of Arab Civilization*. New York, 1983.
Haykal, M. *The Life of Muhammad* (translated from the English). Washington, 1976.
Herbert, Feldman. *The End and The Beginning: Pakistan 1969-1971*. London, 1975.
Hitt, Philip K. *History of the Arabs*. London, 1974.
——. *Capital Cities of Arab Islam*. London, 1973.
——. *Islam—A Way of Life*. London, 1970.
——. *Makers of Arab History*. New York, 1971.
Heper, Martin. and Raphael Israeli (ed.). *Islam and Politics in the Modern Middle East*. Sydney, 1984.
Hirst, David and Irene Beeson. *Sadat*. London, 1981.
Hodgson, M.G.S. *The Order of Assassins*. The Hague, 1955.
Holden, David and Richard Johns. *The House of Saud*. London, 1981.
Holt, P.M. *Political and Social Change in Modern Egypt*. London, 1968.
Hottinger, Arnold. *The Arabs*. London, 1963.
Hourani, A.H. *Syria and Lebanon*. London, 1946.
——. *Arabic Thought in the Liberal Age 1798-1938*. London, 1962.
——. *Minorities in the Arab World*. London, 1947.
——. *Europe and the Middle East*. London, 1980.
Hudson, Michael C. *Arab Politics*. London, 1982.
Hurstfield, Joel. *The Arabs in History*. London, 1950.
Hussain, S. Abid. *The Destiny of Indian Muslims*. Bombay, 1965.
Husaini, S.A.G. *Arab Administration*. Lahore, 1970.
Hussain, Arif. *Pakistan: Its Ideology and Foreign Policy*. London, 1986.
Hussain, Mahmud and others (eds.). *A History of the Freedom Movement*. Karachi, 1957.
Hussaini, Ishak Musa. *The Moslem Brethren*. Beirut, 1956.
Doi, I. Abdur Rahman. *Shariah—The Islamic Law*. London, 1984.
Ikram, S.M. *Muslim Civilization in India*. New York, 1964.
Iqbal, Afzal. *Islamization of Pakistan*. Delhi, 1984.
Iqbal, Javid. *Ideology of Pakistan*. Lahore. 1971.
Iqbal, Mohammed. *The Reconstruction of Religious Thought in Islam*. Lahore, 1971.
Ismael, Tareq Y. *The Arab Left*. New York, 1976.
Ismael, Tareq Y. and Jacqueline Ismael. *Government and Politics in Islam*. London. 1985.
Israeli, Raphael. *The Crescent in the East*. London, 1982.

Johns, Anthony H. (ed.). *Islam in Asia*. New York, 1984.

Jafri, S.H.M. *Origins and Early Development of Shia Islam*. New York, 1979.

James, Kritzeck. *Modern Islamic Literature from 1800 to the Present*. New York, 1970.

————. *Anthology of Islamic Literature*. New York, 1964.

Jansen, G.H. *Militant Islam*. London, 1979.

Jalbani, S.N. *Teachings of Shah Waliyullah*. Lahore, 1967.

John, J. Donohue and John L. Esposito. *Islam in Transition*. New York, 1985.

Jones, L. Bevan. *The People of The Mosque*. Calcutta, 1939.

Kabir, M. *The Buwaybid Dynasty of Baghdad*. Calcutta, 1964.

Kadri, Anwar Ahmad. *Islamic Jurisprudence in the Modern World*. Lahore 1963.

Keddie, N.R. *An Islamic Response to Imperialism*. Los Angeles, 1968.

————. *Religion and Politics in Iran*. London, 1983.

Kedourie, E. *The Middle East and the West*. London, 1964.

————. *Afghani and Abduh*. London, 1966.

————. *Islam in The Modern World*. New York, 1980.

Kepel, Gilles. *The Prophet and Pharaoh*. London, 1985.

Khadduri, M. *Independant Iraq 1932-1958*. London, 1960.

Khaldun, S. Al-Hasry. *Three Reformers*. Beirut, 1966.

Khan, M. Asghar. *Pakistan at the Crossroads*. Lahore, 1969.

Khan, Ziauddin Ibn Ishan, Babakhan. *Islam and Muslims in the Land of Soviets*. Tashkent, 1980.

Khuda Baksh, S. and D.S Margoliouth. *The Renaissance of Islam*. New Delhi 1937.

Khuda, Baksh S. *Politics in Islam*. New Delhi, 1975.

Kiernan, Thomas. *The Arabs*. London, 1978.

Kiernan, V.G. *Poems From Iqbal*. London, 1955.

Kinross Lord. *The Rebirth of a Nation*. London, 1964.

————. *The Ottoman Centuries: The Rise and Fall of The Turkish Empire*. New York, 1977.

Kolarz, W. *Religion in the Soviet Union*. London, 1962.

Kritzeck, James and William H. Lewis (ed.). *Modern Islamic Literature*. New York, 1970.

————. *Islam in Africa*. Chicago, 1969.

Kulkarni, V.B. *India and Pakistan*. Bombay, 1973.

Kurtis, Michael (ed.). *Religion and Politics in the Middle East*. New York, 1981.

Lacey, Robert. *The Kingdom—Arabia and The House of Saud*. New York, 1981.

Lal, Bahadur. *Struggle for Pakistan*. New Delhi, 1988.

Lambton, A.K.S. *Islamic Society in Persia*. London, 1954.

Latif, Syed Abdul. *Bases of Islamic Culture*. Hyderabad, 1959.

————. *An Outline of the Cultural History of India*. Hyderabad, 1958.

Lavan, Spencer. *The Ahmadiyyah Movement*. Delhi, 1974.

Levy, Reuben. *The Social Structure of Islam*. Cambridge. 1971

Legge, J.D. *Sukarno*. London, 1973.

Lewis, Bernard. *The Muslim Discovery of Europe*. New York, 1982.

————. *The Arabs in History*. London, 1958.

————. *The Origins of Isma'ilism*. Cambridge, 1940.

————. *The Middle East and the West*. London, 1964.

————. *The Emergence of Modern Turkey* . London, 1968.

————. *Islam in History*. London, 1973.

————. *Iraq—1900 to 1905*. London, 1953.

————. *The Jews of Islam*. New Jersey, 1984.

————. *The Political Language of Islam*. Chicago, 1988.

————. *Islam—From the Prophet to the Capture of Constantinople*. 2 vol. New York, 1974.

Lewis, Bernard and Holt P.M. *Historians of the Middle East*. London, 1964.

Lewis, I.M. *Islam in Tropical Africa*. London, 1969.

Lings, Martin. *Islam and the Future*. Kuwait, 1987.

————. *Muhammad*, New Delhi 1983.

————. *What is Islam*. London, 1975.

Lokhandwala S.T. (ed.). *India and Contemporary Islam*. Simla, 1971.

Lutsky, V. *Modern History of the Arab Countries*. Moscow, 1969.

Lybyer, A.H. *The Government of Ottoman Empire in the Time of Suleiman the Magnificent*. Cambridge, 1913.

Maclever, R.M. *The Modern State*. London, 1926.

Mathur, Y.B. *Muslims and Changing India*. New Delhi 1972.

Mcneill, William H. and Marilyn Robinson Waldman. *The Islamic World*. London, 1973.

Madan T.N. (ed.). *Muslim Communities of South Asia*. New Delhi, 1976.

Macdonald, Duncan B. *Development of Muslim Theology*.

————. *Jurisprudence and Constitutional Theory*. New Delhi, 1903.

————. *The Religions Attitude and Life Islam*. Beirut, 1965.

Mahmood, Tahir. *Personal Law in Islamic Countries*. New Delhi, 1987.

Malik, Hafeez. *Iqbal*. New York, 1971.

Mansfield, Peter. *The Ottoman Empire and its Successors*. London, 1973.

――――. *The Arabs*. London, 1976.

Mardin, S. *The Genesis of Young Ottoman Thought*. Princeton, 1962.

Margoliouth, D.S. *Lectures on Arabic Historians*. Delhi, 1930.

Mehta, J.L. *Advanced Study in the History of Medieval India—Vol. III*. New Delhi, 1985.

Momen, Moojan. *An Introduction to Shii Islam*. New York, 1985.

Minault, Gali. *The Khilafat Movement*. New Delhi, 1972.

Minault, Gali and Troll C.D. *Abu'l Kalam Azad*. Delhi, 1988.

Moghnysaid, Abdel. *Arab Socialism*. Blandford, 1972.

Mortimer, Edward. *Faith and Power*. London, 1981.

Mottahedeh, Roy. *The Mantle of Prophet*. London, 1985.

――――. *Loyalty and Leadership in an Early Islamic Society*. 1980.

Muhajeri, Masih. *Islamic Revolution—Future Path of the Nations*. Tehran, 1982.

Mir Ahmed, Ali S.V. *Husain--The King of Martyrs*. Karachi, 1964.

Maududi, Syed Abula' la. *The Islamic Law and Constitution*. Bombay, 1986.

――――. *Fundamentals of Islam*. Bombay, 1978.

Muhammad, Ali. *The Religion of Islam*. Lahore, 1950.

Muir W. *The Caliphate, its Rise and Fall*. London, 1984.

――――. *The Life of Muhammed*. Ediinburgh, 1923.

Mujtabai F. *Hindu–Muslim Cultural Relations*. New Delhi. 1983.

Mujeeb M. *The Indian Muslims*. London, 1967.

Mutahbari M. *Social and Historical Change* (translated into the English). Bombay 1986.

Munir, Muhammed. *From Jinnah to Zia*. Lahore, 1979.

Muslehuddin M. *Philosophy of Islamic Law and the Orientalists*. New Delhi 1986.

Nadwi, Abul Hasan Ali. *Saviours of Islamic Spirit*. Lucknow, 1955.

――――. *Muslims in India*, Lucknow, 1960.

Nasr, S.H. *Science and Civilization in Islam*, New York. 1970.

――――. *Ideals and Realities of Islam*. London, 1966.

――――. *Islamic Life and Thought*. London, 1981.

――――. *Three Muslim Sages--Avicenna, Suhrawardi, Ibn Arabi*, Cambridge, 1964.

――――. *The Traditional Islam in the Modern World*. London, 1987.

Nicholson, R.A. *Studies in Islamic Mysticism*. Cambridge, 1921.

Nima, Ramy. *The Wrath of Allah*. London 1983.

Nieuwenluijze, G.A.O. van. *Aspects of Islam in Post Colonial Indonesia*. The Hague, 1958.

Nizami, Khaliq Ahmed. *Some Aspects of Religion and Politics in India during the 13th Century*, Aligarh, 1961.

Nu'mani, Shibli. *Sirat-un-Nabi*, vol. I (translated into the English). Delhi, 1979.

————. *Umar The Great* (translated into the English). Lahore, 1939.

Nuseibeh, N.Z. *The Ideas of Arab Nationalism*. Cornell, 1956.

O'Leary, De Lacy. *A Short History of the Fatimid Khalifate*. 1923.

Peretz, Don-Moench R.U. and Mohsen S.K. *Islam—Legacy of the Past, Challenge of the Future*. 1984.

Peters, F.E. *Children of Abraham*. New Jersey, 1982.

————. *Allah's Commonwealth*. New York, 1973.

Philby, H.St. J. *Saudi Arabia*. London, 1955.

Philips, C.H. and Wainwright, M.D. (ed.). *The Partition of India*. London, 1970.

Phillip, H.S., David C.C. and Margaret W.S. *Islam and Power*. London, 1981.

Pickthall, M. *Cultural Side of Islam*. Lahore, 1961.

Pipes, Deniel. *In the Path of God*. New York, 1980.

Pirenne, Henri. *Muhammad and Charlemagne*. London, 1986.

Piscatori, James P. *Islam in the Political Process*. London, 1983.

Qadri, Anwar A. *Justice in Historical Islam*. New Delhi, 1982.

————. *Islamic Jurisprudence in the Modern World*. Lahore, 1981.

Qureshi, Anwar Iqbal. *Fiscal System of Islam*. Lahore 1978.

————. *Islam and the Theory of Interest*. Delhi, 1979.

Qureshi, Ishatiaq Hussain. *The Muslim Community of the Indo-Pakistan Subcontinent*. The Hague, 1962.

Rahman, Fazlur. *Islam And Modernity*. London, 1982.

————. *Islam*. London, 1966.

Rajaee, Farhang. *Islamic Values and World View*. London, 1983.

Ramsaur, F.E. *The Young Turks*. Princeton, 1957.

Rastogi, T.C. *Islamic Mysticism, Sufism*. New Delhi, 1982.

Raunaq, Jahan. *Pakistan: Failure in National Integration*. New York, 1972.

Ranna, Irfan Mahmud. *Economic System under Umar the Great*. Lahore, 1977.

Ray, Jayanta Kumar. *Democracy and Nationalism on Trial*. Simla, 1968.

Rida, Muhammad Rashid. *The Revolution of Muhammad*. Bombay, 1960.

Robert, Roberts. *The Social Laws of the Quran*. London, 1971.

Robinson, Francis. *Separatism Among Indian Muslims*. Delhi, 1975.

Rodinson, Maxime. *Marxism and the Muslim World* (translated into the English by Michael Pallis). New Delhi, 1980.

————. *Muhammad* (translated into the English by Anne Carter). London, 1971.

————. *Islam and Capitalism* (translated into the English by Brian Pearce). Studia Semitica, 2 vols. Cambridge, 1971.

Ronald, M.Green. *Religious Reason*. New York, 1978.

Ronald Robertson (ed.). *Sociology of Religion*. Baltimore, 1972.

Rose, H.A. *Religious History of Islam*. Delhi, 1984.

Rosenthal, Erwin I.J. *Islam in the Modern National State*. Cambridge, 1965.

————. *Political Thought in Medieval Islam*. London, 1958.

Roy R. Anderson, Robert F.S. and John G.W. *Politics and Change in the Middle East*. London, 1982.

Rumi, Jalal-al Din. *Discourses of Rumi* (translated by A.J. Arbery). London, 1961.

Runciman, S. *A History of the Crusades*. Cambridge, 1951.

Ruthven, Malise. *Islam in the World*. New York, 1984.

Rywkin, Michael. *Moscow's Muslim Challenge*. London, 1982.

Schimmel, Annemarie. *And Muhammad is His Messenger*. London, 1985.

Sharma, Sri Ram. *The Religious Policy of the Mughal Emperors*. Bombay, 1962.

Shelat, *J.M. Akbar*. 2 vols. Bombay, 1959.

Schofield, Victoria. *Bhutto—Trial and Execution*. London, 1979.

Said, Abdel Moghny. *Arab Socialism*. London, 1972.

Siddiqi, S.A. *Public Finance in Islam*. Delhi, 1982.

Sivan, Emmanuel. *Radical Islam*. London, 1985.

Smith, E.D. Turkey. *Origins of the Kemalist Movement and Govternment of the Grand National Assembly 191*. Washington, 1959.

Smith, W.C. *Islam in Modern History*. Princeton, 1960.

————. *Modern Islam in India*. London, 1946.

Stepanyants, M.T. *Pakistan Philosophy and Sociology*. Lahore, 1972.

Stephens, Robert. *Nasser*. London, 1971.

Sufi, Abdal-Qatar. *Jihad—The Groundplan*. London, 1978.

Syed, Amir Ali. *A Short History of the Saracens*. Delhi, 1981.

————. *Spirit of Islam*. Delhi, 1968.

Syed, Ziaullah & Samuel, Baid. *Pakistan—an End Without a Beginning*. New Delhi, 1985.

Sykes, P.M. *A History of Persia*. London, 1930.

Tabatabai, S.M. Husayn. *Shiite Islam*. London, 1975.

Taheri, Amir. *The Spirit of Allah*. Maryland, 1986.

Talaqani, Sayyid Mahmood. *Islam and Ownership*. Lexington, 1983.

Tarbush, Mohd. A. *The Role of the Military in Politics—the Case Study of Iraq to 1941*. London, 1985.

Tendular, D.G. *Abdul Ghaffar Khan*. New Delhi, 1987.

Toynbee, Arnold J. *A Historian's Approach to Religion*. London, 1957.

——. *A Study of History* (abridgement by D.C. Somervell). London, 1960.

Trimingham, J.S. *Islam in West Africa*. Oxford, 1959.

Troll Christian W. *Islam in India*. 2 vols. New Delhi, 1985.

——. *The Influence of Islam upon Africa*. London, 1968.

Tritton, A.S. *The Caliphs and their Non-Muslim Subjects*. Oxford, 1930.

Turner, Bryan S. *Weber and Islam*. London, 1974.

Upton, J.M. *The History of Modern Iran*. Cambridge, 1960.

Vatikiotis, P.J. *The Fatimid Theory of State*. Lahore, 1957.

Said, Edward W. *Orientalism* London, 1978.

——. *Converting Islam*. London, 1981.

Saikal, Amin. *The Rise and Fall of Shah*. New Jersey, 1980.

Sardar, Ziauddin. *The Future of Muslim Civilization*. London, 1979.

Saunders, J.J. A. *History of Medieval Islam*. London, 1965.

Sayed, Riza Ahmad. *Maulana Maududi and The Islamic State*. Lahore, 1976.

Sayyid, Qutb. *This Religion of Islam*. Gary, n.d..

——. *Islam—The Misunderstood Religion*. Delhi, 1968.

——. *Milestone*. Kuwait (n.d.)

Schacht, Joseph. *The Origins of Muhammadan Jurisprudence*. London, 1975.

Schacht, Joseph Bosworth C.E. (ed.). *The Legacy Of Islam*. London, 1974.

Serjeant, R.B. *The Islamic City*. Paris, 1980.

Setalvad, M.C. *Secularism*. Delhi, 1967.

Shaban, M.A. *Islamic History*. London, 1971.

Shakir, Moin. *Muslims and Indian National Congress*. Delhi, 1987.

Shan, Muhammad. *Sir Syed Ahmed Khan*. Meerut, 1969.

Sharma, S.R. *Mughal Empire in India*—Part I. Bombay.

——. *Mughal Empire in India*—Part II and III. Bombay.

——. *The Religious Policy of the Mughal Emperors*. London, 1962.

Sherwani, Haroon Khan. *Studies in Muslim Political Thought and Administration*. Lahore, 1942.

Siddiqi, M.N. *Muslim Economic Thinking*. Leicester, n.d..

Siddiqi, S.A. *Public Finance in Islam*. Delhi.

Singh, Khushwant. *A History of The Sikhs*, vols. 1 & 2. Princeton, 1963.

Sinha, V.K. *Secularism in India*, Bombay, 1968.

Vahid, S.A. Iqbal: *His Art and Thought*. Lahore, 1944.

Vorys, Karl Von. *Political Developments in Pakistan*. 1965.

Vries, Jan De. *The Study of Religion--A Historical Approach*. New York, 1961.

Wasswerstein, David. *The Rise and the Fall of the Party-Kings*. Princeton, 1985.

Wahid, Syed Abdul. *Thought and Reflections of Iqbal*. Lahore, 1964.

Waliullah, Mir. *Muslim Jurisprudence and the Quranic Law of Crimes*. Bombay, 1986.

Walter, H.A. *The Ahmadiya Movement*. Oxford, 1918.

Wavell, Viscount. *Allenby in Egypt*. London, 1943.

Weiss, Anita M. *Islamic Reassertion in Pakistan*. New York, 1986.

Wells, H.G. *The Outline of History*. London, 1920.

Wensinck, A.J. *The Islamic Creed*. London, 1932.

Wilber, D.N. *Contemporary Iran*. London, 1963.

Watt, Montgomery W. *The Majesty that was Islam*. London, 1974.

———. *The Faith and Practice of Al-Ghazali*. Lahore, 1963.

———. *Islamic Political Thought*. Edinburgh, 1968.

———. *Islam and the Inegration of Society*. London, 1961.

———. Muhammad at Mecca. Oxford, 1953.

———. Muhammad at Madina. Oxford, 1956.

Williams, John Alden. *Themes of Islamic Civilization*. London, 1971.

Wilson, A.T. *The Persian Gulf*. London, 1928.

Wimbush, S. Enders and Bennigsen, A.A. *Muslim National Communism in the Soviet Union*. 1979.

Winfield, E.H. *Masnavi-i-Ma'navi* (translated into the English). London, 1898.

Yaccov, Ro'I. *The USSR and the Muslim World*. London, 1984.

Ye'or, Bat. *The Dhimmi*. Paris, 1980.

Yves, Lacoste. *Ibn Khaldun*. London, 1984.

Zakaria, Rafiq (ed.). *100 Glorious Years*. Bombay, 1985.

———. *Rise of Muslims in Indian Politics*. Bombay, 1987.

Zabih Sepehr. *Iran Since the Revolution*. Baltimore, 1982.

Zeine, Z.N. *The Struggle for Arab Independence*. Beirut, 1960.

———. *The Emergence of Arab Nationalism*. Beirut, 1966.

Ziring, Lawrence. Pakistan—*The Enigma of Political Development*. London, 1980.

———. *The Ayubkhan Era: Politics in Pakistan (1958-1969)*. London, 1971.

———. *Iran, Turkey and Afghanistan*. New York, 1989.

Index

FOR THE BEST IN PAPERBACKS, LOOK FOR THE 🐧

In every corner of the world, on every subject under the sun, Penguin represents quality and variety – the very best in publishing today.

For complete information about books available from Penguin – including Pelicans, Puffins, Peregrines and Penguin Classics – and how to order them, write to us at the appropriate address below. Please note that for copyright reasons the selection of books varies from country to country.

In the United Kingdom: Please write to *Dept E.P., Penguin Books Ltd, Harmondsworth, Middlesex, UB7 0DA*

If you have any difficulty in obtaining a title, please send your order with the correct money, plus ten per cent for postage and packaging, to *PO Box No 11, West Drayton, Middlesex*

In the United States: Please write to *Dept BA, Penguin, 299 Murray Hill Parkway, East Rutherford, New Jersey 07073*

In Canada: Please write to *Penguin Books Canada Ltd, 2801 John Street, Markham, Ontario L3R 1B4*

In Australia: Please write to the *Marketing Department, Penguin Books Australia Ltd, P.O. Box 257, Ringwood, Victoria 3134*

In New Zealand: Please write to the *Marketing Department, Penguin Books (NZ) Ltd, Private Bag, Takapuna, Auckland 9*

In India: Please write to *Penguin Overseas Ltd, 706 Eros Apartments, 56 Nehru Place, New Delhi, 110019*

In Holland: Please write to *Penguin Books Nederland B.V., Postbus 195, NL–1380AD Weesp, Netherlands*

In Germany: Please write to *Penguin Books Ltd, Friedrichstrasse 10–12, D–6000 Frankfurt Main 1, Federal Republic of Germany*

In Spain: Please write to *Longman Penguin España, Calle San Nicolas 15, E–28013 Madrid, Spain*

In France: Please write to *Penguin Books Ltd, 39 Rue de Montmorency, F-75003, Paris, France*

In Japan: Please write to *Longman Penguin Japan Co Ltd, Yamaguchi Building, 2–12–9 Kanda Jimbocho, Chiyoda-Ku, Tokyo 101, Japan*

FOR THE BEST IN PAPERBACKS, LOOK FOR THE

A CHOICE OF PENGUINS

Beyond the Blue Horizon Alexander Frater

The romance and excitement of the legendary Imperial Airways East-bound Empire service – the world's longest and most adventurous scheduled air route – relived fifty years later in one of the most original travel books of the decade. 'The find of the year' – *Today*

Voyage through the Antarctic Richard Adams and Ronald Lockley

Here is the true, authentic Antarctic of today, brought vividly to life by Richard Adams, author of *Watership Down*, and Ronald Lockley, the world-famous naturalist. 'A good adventure story, with a lot of information and a deal of enthusiasm for Antarctica and its animals' – *Nature*

Getting to Know the General Graham Greene

'In August 1981 my bag was packed for my fifth visit to Panama when the news came to me over the telephone of the death of General Omar Torrijos Herrera, my friend and host . . .' 'Vigorous, deeply felt, at times funny, and for Greene surprisingly frank' – *Sunday Times*

The Search for the Virus Steve Connor and Sharon Kingman

In this gripping book, two leading *New Scientist* journalists tell the remarkable story of how researchers discovered the AIDS virus and examine the links between AIDS and lifestyles. They also look at the progress being made in isolating the virus and finding a cure.

Arabian Sands Wilfred Thesiger

'In the tradition of Burton, Doughty, Lawrence, Philby and Thomas, it is, very likely, the book about Arabia to end all books about Arabia' – *Daily Telegraph*

When the Wind Blows Raymond Briggs

'A visual parable against nuclear war: all the more chilling for being in the form of a strip cartoon' – *Sunday Times* 'The most eloquent anti-Bomb statement you are likely to read' – *Daily Mail*

A CHOICE OF PENGUINS

The Diary of Virginia Woolf
Five volumes edited by Quentin Bell and Anne Olivier Bell

'As an account of intellectual and cultural life of our century, Virginia Woolf's diaries are invaluable; as the record of one bruised and unquiet mind, they are unique' – Peter Ackroyd in the *Sunday Times*

Voices of the Old Sea   Norman Lewis

'I will wager that *Voices of the Old Sea* will be a classic in the literature about Spain' – *Mail on Sunday* 'Limpidly and lovingly Norman Lewis has caught the helpless, unwitting, often foolish, but always hopeful village in its dying summers, and saved the tragedy with sublime comedy' – *Observer*

The First World War   A J P Taylor

In this superb illustrated history, A J P Taylor 'manages to say almost everything that is important for an understanding and, indeed, intellectual digestion of that vast event . . . A special text . . . a remarkable collection of photographs' – *Observer*

Ninety-Two Days   Evelyn Waugh

With characteristic honesty Evelyn Waugh here debunks the romantic notions attached to rough travelling; his journey in Guiana and Brazil is difficult, dangerous and extremely uncomfortable, and his account of it is witty and unquestionably compelling.

When the Mind Hears   Harlan Lane
A History of the Deaf

'Reads like a suspense novel . . . what emerges is evidence of a great wrong done to a minority group, the deaf' – *The New York Times Book Review* 'Impassioned, polemical, at times even virulent . . . (he shows) immense scholarship, powers of historical reconstruction, and deep empathy for the world of the deaf' – Oliver Sacks in *The New York Review of Books*

FOR THE BEST IN PAPERBACKS, LOOK FOR THE

A CHOICE OF PENGUINS

The Literature of the United States   Marcus Cunliffe

The fourth edition of a masterly one-volume survey, described by D. W. Brogan in the *Guardian* as 'a very good book indeed'.

The Sceptical Feminist   Janet Radcliffe Richards

A rigorously argued but sympathetic consideration of feminist claims. 'A triumph' – *Sunday Times*

The Enlightenment   Norman Hampson

A classic survey of the age of Diderot and Voltaire, Goethe and Hume, which forms part of the Pelican History of European Thought.

Defoe to the Victorians   David Skilton

'Learned and stimulating' (*The Times Educational Supplement*). A fascinating survey of two centuries of the English novel.

Reformation to Industrial Revolution   Christopher Hill

This 'formidable little book' (Peter Laslett in the *Guardian*) by one of our leading historians is Volume 2 of the Pelican Economic History of Britain.

The New Pelican Guide to English Literature   Boris Ford (ed.)
Volume 8: The Present

This book brings a major series up to date with important essays on Ted Hughes and Nadine Gordimer, Philip Larkin and V. S. Naipaul, and all the other leading writers of today.

Adieux Simone de Beauvoir

This 'farewell to Sartre' by his life-long companion is a 'true labour of love' (the *Listener*) and 'an extraordinary achievement' (*New Statesman*).

British Society 1914–45 John Stevenson

A major contribution to the Pelican Social History of Britain, which 'will undoubtedly be the standard work for students of modern Britain for many years to come' – *The Times Educational Supplement*

The Pelican History of Greek Literature Peter Levi

A remarkable survey covering all the major writers from Homer to Plutarch, with brilliant translations by the author, one of the leading poets of today.

Art and Literature Sigmund Freud

Volume 14 of the Pelican Freud Library contains Freud's major essays on Leonardo, Michelangelo and Dostoyevsky, plus shorter pieces on Shakespeare, the nature of creativity and much more.

A History of the Crusades Sir Steven Runciman

This three-volume history of the events which transferred world power to Western Europe – and founded Modern History – has been universally acclaimed as a masterpiece.

A Night to Remember Walter Lord

The classic account of the sinking of the *Titanic*. 'A stunning book, incomparably the best on its subject and one of the most exciting books of this or any year' – *The New York Times*

FOR THE BEST IN PAPERBACKS, LOOK FOR THE

A CHOICE OF PENGUINS

The Second World War (6 volumes)   Winston S. Churchill

The definitive history of the cataclysm which swept the world for the second time in thirty years.

1917: The Russian Revolutions and the Origins of Present-Day Communism
Leonard Schapiro

A superb narrative history of one of the greatest episodes in modern history by one of our greatest historians.

Imperial Spain 1496–1716   J. H. Elliot

A brilliant modern study of the sudden rise of a barren and isolated country to be the greatest power on earth, and of its equally sudden decline. 'Outstandingly good' – *Daily Telegraph*

Joan of Arc: The Image of Female Heroism   Marina Warner

'A profound book, about human history in general and the place of women in it' – Christopher Hill

Man and the Natural World: Changing Attitudes in England 1500–1800
Keith Thomas

'A delight to read and a pleasure to own' – Auberon Waugh in the *Sunday Telegraph*

The Making of the English Working Class   E. P. Thompson

Probably the most imaginative – and the most famous – post-war work of English social history.

A CHOICE OF PENGUINS

The French Revolution   Christopher Hibbert

'One of the best accounts of the Revolution that I know . . . Mr Hibbert is outstanding' – J. H. Plumb in the *Sunday Telegraph*

The Germans   Gordon A. Craig

An intimate study of a complex and fascinating nation by 'one of the ablest and most distinguished American historians of modern Germany' – Hugh Trevor-Roper

Ireland: A Positive Proposal   Kevin Boyle and Tom Hadden

A timely and realistic book on Northern Ireland which explains the historical context – and offers a practical and coherent set of proposals which could actually work.

A History of Venice   John Julius Norwich

'Lord Norwich has loved and understood Venice as well as any other Englishman has ever done' – Peter Levi in the *Sunday Times*

Montaillou: Cathars and Catholics in a French Village 1294–1324
Emmanuel Le Roy Ladurie

'A classic adventure in eavesdropping across time' – Michael Ratcliffe in *The Times*

The Defeat of the Spanish Armada   Garrett Mattingly

Published to coincide with the 400th anniversary of the Armada. 'A faultless book; and one which most historians would have given half their working lives to have written' – J. H. Plumb